Regime Interaction and Climate Change

The regulation of greenhouse gas emissions from international aviation and maritime transport has proved to be a difficult task for international climate negotiations such as the Paris Agreement in 2015. Almost two decades prior, Article 2.2 of the Kyoto Protocol excluded emissions from international aviation and maritime transport from its targets, delegating the negotiation of sector-specific regulations to the International Civil Aviation Organization (ICAO) and the International Maritime Organization (IMO), respectively. However, progress at these venues has also been limited.

Regime Interaction and Climate Change maps out the legal frameworks in the climate, ICAO and IMO regimes, and explores the law-making process for the regulation of international aviation and maritime transport through the lenses of fragmentation of international law and regime interaction. The book sheds light on how interaction between these three regimes occurs, what the consequences of such interaction are and how they can be managed to resolve conflicts and promote synergies.

This book will be of great interest to scholars of international environmental law and governance, climate change policy and climate change law.

Beatriz Martinez Romera is Assistant Professor of Environmental and Climate Change Law, Faculty of Law, University of Copenhagen, Denmark. Her research focuses on climate change and international transport.

Routledge Research in Global Environmental Governance

Series Editors:

Philipp Pattberg, *VU University Amsterdam and the Amsterdam Global Change Institute (AGCI), the Netherlands.*

Agni Kalfagianni, *Utrecht University, the Netherlands.*

https://www.routledge.com/Routledge-Research-in-Global-Environmental-Governance/book-series/RRGEG

Global environmental governance has been a prime concern of policy-makers since the United Nations Conference on the Human Environment in 1972. Yet, despite more than nine hundred multi-lateral environmental treaties coming into force over the past forty years and numerous public-private and private initiatives to mitigate global change, human-induced environmental degradation is reaching alarming levels. Scientists see compelling evidence that the entire earth system now operates well outside safe boundaries and at rates that accelerate. The urgent challenge from a social science perspective is how to organize the co-evolution of societies and their surrounding environment; in other words, how to develop effective and equitable governance solutions for today's global problems.

Against this background, the *Routledge Research in Global Environmental Governance* series delivers cutting-edge research on the most vibrant and relevant themes within the academic field of global environmental governance.

Rethinking Authority in Global Climate Governance
How Transnational Climate Initiatives Relate to the International Climate Regime
Thomas Hickmann

Environmental Politics and Governance in the Anthropocene
Institutions and legitimacy in a complex world
Edited by Philipp Pattberg and Fariborz Zelli

Grassroots Environmental Governance
Community engagements with industry
Edited by Leah S. Horowitz & Michael J. Watts

Traditions and Trends in Global Environmental Politics
International Relations and the Earth
Edited by Olaf Corry and Hayley Stevenson

Regime Interaction and Climate Change
The Case of International Aviation and Maritime Transport
Beatriz Martinez Romera

Regime Interaction and Climate Change
The Case of International Aviation and Maritime Transport

Beatriz Martinez Romera

LONDON AND NEW YORK

from Routledge

First published 2018 by Routledge

2 Park Square, Milton Park, Abingdon, Oxfordshire OX14 4RN

52 Vanderbilt Avenue, New York, NY 10017

Routledge is an imprint of the Taylor & Francis Group, an informa business

First issued in paperback 2019

British Library Cataloguing-in-Publication Data
A catalogue record for this book is available from the British Library

Library of Congress Cataloging-in-Publication Data
Names: Martinez Romera, Beatriz.
Title: Regime interaction and climate change : the case of international
    aviation and maritime transport / Beatriz Martinez Romera.
Description: Abingdon, Oxon ; New York, NY : Routledge, 2017. |
    Series: Routledge research in global environmental governance |
    Based on author's thesis (doctoral – Det Juridiske Fakultet, Københavns
    Universitet, 2015), issued under title: Regime interaction in the
    regulation of greenhouse gas emissions from international aviation
    and maritime transport.
Identifiers: LCCN 2017006852 | ISBN 9781138211902 (hb) |
    ISBN 9781315451817 (ebook)
Subjects: LCSH: Climatic changes—Law and legislation. | International
    regimes. | Aeronautics, Commercial—Law and legislation. | Merchant
    marine—Law and legislation. | Aircraft exhaust emissions—Law and
    legislation. | Marine engines—Exhaust gas—Law and legislation. |
    Aeronautics, Commercial—Environmental aspects. | Merchant
    marine—Environmental aspects.
Classification: LCC K3585.5 .M37 2017 | DDC 344.04/633—dc23
LC record available at https://lccn.loc.gov/2017006852

ISBN: 978-1-138-21190-2 (hbk)
ISBN: 978-0-367-34016-2 (pbk)

Typeset in Goudy
by Apex CoVantage, LLC

Contents

Acknowledgements

This book builds largely upon my PhD thesis, entitled *Regime Interaction in the Regulation of Greenhouse Gas Emissions from International Aviation and Maritime Transport*, which was submitted for the Degree of Doctor of Philosophy to Faculty of Law of the University of Copenhagen and successfully defended in January 2015. The book would not have been possible without the following 'enabling framework'. At the level of finance, I am grateful to the Faculty of Law of the University of Copenhagen and the Danish Agency for Science, Technology and Innovation, the Danish Legal Research Education Programme and the Nordic Environmental Law, Governance and Science Network. For academic and administrative support, I would like to thank the Faculty of Law the PhD programme, the Centre for Public Regulation and Administration (CORA) and the Center for Enterprise Liability (CEVIA). In particular, I would like to thank my thesis supervisor, Prof. Peter Pagh, and Prof. Vibe Ulfbeck for supporting and encouraging this book. I also thank Prof. Henrik Palmer Olsen and Prof. Mikael Rask Madsen for their inputs in the project. Outside of Denmark I owe a debt of gratitude to Dr. Harro van Asselt, whose work I draw upon extensively in my thesis, and whom I was fortunate enough to drag into my evaluation seminar, thus benefiting from his invaluable knowledge and feedback. I should also like to acknowledge the welcome and support provided by the Guarini Center at New York University School of Law, the Instituto de Ciencias Ambientales de la Universidad Complutense de Madrid and the Maritime Knowledge Centre at the International Maritime Organization, where I was a visiting scholar. At the IMO, I was helped by the Danish Maritime Authority to assist the negotiations as part of their delegation. Finally, I am indebted to the nurturing sustenance received from colleagues and friends, and from my family, the cornerstone upon which life is built. This project has been fuelled by Eugenia, and the thrill and delight of *getting to know amazing people's amazingness*.

SEEMP	Ship Energy Efficiency Management Plan
SOLAS	Safety of Life at Sea Convention
T&E	Transport and Environment
UNDP	United Nations Development Programme
UNCLOS	United Nations Convention on the Law of the Sea
UNEP	United Nations Environment Programme
UNFCCC	United Nations Framework Convention on Climate Change
VCLT	Vienna Convention on the Law of Treaties
WG	Working Group
WMO	World Meteorological Organization
WSC	World Shipping Council
WTO	World Trade Organization
WWF	World Wildlife Fund

1 Introduction and context

This chapter provides a general overview of the book, including the research questions and the way in which they are answered. The first section defines the subject and focus of this study, explaining the research *problématique* and delimiting its boundaries, followed by two subsections establishing the aims and questions and summarizing the book's structure. Section two provides some context for the research by mapping the field of international aviation and maritime transport, with regard to climate change. This includes their current and projected GHG emissions, the legal circumstances surrounding these sectors, and their role in the global emissions reduction conundrum. The second section is also used to introduce the main scientific and technical concepts and issues that will be referred to throughout the book. The analytical and legal framework, however, will be fully developed in Chapters 2 and 3, respectively.

Introduction

Problem definition

Climate change[1] is a global challenge that cuts across all aspects of our society; it involves diverse social, economic, political and legal issues and defies the main axioms of the way we live.[2] Perhaps for that reason, and unlike other international environmental challenges, the battle against climate change has, so far, been slow and drawn-out, and has resulted in minimal progress.[3]

Even after the adoption of the Paris Agreement (PA),[4] deliberations over how much, who and in what way GHG emissions should be cut are still at the core of the international climate negotiations for making the agreement effective. The issues of how to allocate emissions and the choice of policy and legal instruments have proven to be controversial. The political will to commit to strong emissions reductions is, when existent, weak, and faces the opposition of major political and industrial players. In the middle of this conflictive landscape, the GHGs emissions from international aviation and international maritime transport – so-called international bunker fuels (IBF)[5] – two bursting sectors of the global economy, have remained highly undefined and are awaiting action.[6]

Greenhouse gas emissions from international aviation and international maritime transport account for around 5% of the global total GHG emissions but they are growing faster than any other sectors and it is expected that they will continue to increase exponentially.[7]

Scope

The challenge of climate change is global and complex. Its causes and effects, which cover a diversity of categories, are interconnected and affect all economic sectors, countries and populations. The answer to such a complex and 'super wicked'[8] environmental problem is likely to require an equally complex set of solutions, including a range of norms, backed up by significant financing and technological innovation, in order to be both feasible and effective.[9]

In the quest for solutions, an international legal regime to curb global warming has been put in place. This regime comprises namely the United Nations Framework Convention on Climate Change (UNFCCC), its Kyoto Protocol (KP), and the Paris Agreement (PA). However, the climate change reality touches upon different areas of the law which results in an overlapping of the climate regime with other regimes.[10] The complexity of the climate change problem and the resource distributional challenges related to it has also led to difficulties for the institutions and processes established to that end in providing fast and easy outcomes. A patchwork of different initiatives and fora operating in a more or less disconnected way has emerged over the last decade, driving the climate regime towards decentralization, and in a sense expanding its reach.

In line with the overarching process of fragmentation of international law,[11] the climate arena has undergone the same fate,[12] and norms related to climate change have come from a range of existing treaties, institutions and procedures.[13] The degree of this fragmentation and whether the fragmentation is regarded as positive or negative is the object of multiple debates[14] and will ultimately depend on many variables, including the coordination that the different instruments and institutions are able or willing to provide in order to 'enhance coherence between the different elements of global climate governance'.[15]

The regulation of emissions from international aviation and maritime transport is neither unconnected nor unrelated to this reality; while the work to improve data and the reporting of national inventories has been subsumed under the UNFCCC umbrella,[16] the search for regulation to achieve emissions reductions is divided between two specialized agencies,[17] namely the International Civil Aviation Organization (ICAO) and the International Maritime Organization (IMO). Both institutions have very different, if not contradictory, objectives and principles guiding their actions. Somehow, a third issue, the allocation of emissions, has shifted from the shelter of the Convention to the ICAO and IMO, but hasn't been defined to date. Here, allocation means 'how the remainder of the resources can best be divided among people and countries',[18] in concrete terms: how the risks, burdens and responsibilities for causing environmental problems, in this case climate change induced by international aviation and international maritime transport, are distributed. The problem is not particular or exclusive to these sectors, and it has been pointed out that '*some of the crunch issues in the negotiations – i.e. by how much should we reduce emissions, and who should do what? – remain unresolved.*'[19]

Allocating and regulating emissions from international aviation and maritime transport comprises a law-making process, where different participants, processes and instruments[20] from different regimes interact. However uncertain the outcomes of this law-making processes can be, the question remains linked to what legal principles and norms will inform the allocation and regulation of those emissions. The answer to that question can be understood from the point of view of the interaction established among regimes, its consequences and possibilities for management.

Limitations

There are two main limitations to the scope of this study, which require some explanation and justification. First, this book focuses exclusively on horizontal interactions at the international level. It does not aim to deal with the regional or domestic level and vertical interaction, and only addresses overlapping issues at the global level. As such, this research concerns the interaction of the climate regime with the regimes of ICAO and IMO. However, given the significance of the inclusion of aviation in the European Union Emissions Trading System (EU ETS), and how this has influenced the international level, EU regulation is explored throughout the book as an essential factor prompting developments and shaping the law-making processes and outcomes. Second, at the global level, there is potential for an interaction between the World Trade Organization (WTO) regime and the previously named regimes. Although such interaction could be established, it is not the focus of this research.[21] The reasons for this exclusion are established below.

The objective of the WTO system is to ensure a level playing field, at the international level, of trade activities though rules in different areas, including services, ensuring fair competition. Despite its remit to promote trade liberalization through the principles of Most Favourable Nation and National Treatment, WTO law generally permits exceptions and limitations based on environmental grounds.[22] In that connection, interactions between climate change and trade measures have been established.[23] Transportation is considered a service area[24] and it is comprised in the WTO General Agreement on Trade in Services (GATS)[25] and regulated under the same principles. The regulation of IBF, at the global level, would in principle be compatible with WTO law provided that there is no discrimination between vessels or aircrafts delivering goods or passengers from jurisdiction A to jurisdiction B; that is, that the national treatment in jurisdiction B does not discriminate for international or national ships or aircraft. If, for example, a market-based measure (MBM) is created in the field of international aviation or maritime transport through a convention or any other instrument administered by ICAO and IMO this would greatly reduce the scope for disputes to be settled by the WTO. This is because neither ICAO nor the IMO are members of the WTO and only countries can bring disputes against other members in front of WTO tribunals.[26]

The situation is different in the case of national or regionally enacted legislation, and the inclusion of aviation in the EU ETS could be regarded as a challenge to the GATS. Here, the main question to address legal consistency would be whether or not the measure falls within the GATS Annex on Air Transport Services, which excludes 'traffic rights'. Such definition is affected by the Chicago Convention and other multilateral and bilateral air services agreements. In 2012 the European Court of Justice ruled that EU aviation legislation does not fall under the scope of traffic rights as defined in the GATS.[27]

The decision to exclude an analysis of the tensions and relationship between the WTO regimes and the climate, ICAO and IMO regimes is based, primarily, on the fact that this would imply a length of work beyond the reasonable scope of this monograph. Second, the WTO is not a standard-setting body as such, and the functions of the organization are more focused on dispute resolution. In that connection, the implications of WTO law seem to be more relevant to the EU measures of including aviation in the EU ETS, and not in the eventual regulation of these sectors, at the global level. Third, the scope of the book is also highly defined by article 2.2 of the KP as the main clause triggering interaction and the designation of ICAO and IMO as the competent fora to take action. By pursuing this perspective the book maintains the line of logic regarding the allocation and regulation of IBF, especially in connection to the principle of 'common but differentiated responsibilities and respective capabilities' (CBDRRC)[28] entering other regimes from the climate realm.

Other remarks related to the scope and limitations of this study come from three essential characteristics of the subject; first, the research deals with a moving and evolving subject, at the genesis of the law state which is, at the time of writing, underway; second, the law-making is intertwined with political issues at the level of global negotiations which are relevant for the *problématique*; and third, it encompasses a high degree of technical complexity. Consequently, three boundaries need to be clarified at this point. First, this book considers developments only up until the 31st of December 2016; second, the political elements drenching the legal issues are sometimes used to shed light over the developments. Without this broad perspective of the law, the framework for this study would result in a poor theorizing and a narrow set of conclusions.[29] Third, a certain degree of literature review from different disciplines, such as science or economics is needed as a starting point to understand the context of the issue area we are dealing with.

Research aims and questions

While most of the legal attention around the regulation of emissions from IBF, from an environmental perspective, has focused on the legal challenges and consequences of the inclusion of aviation into the EU ETS for international law,[30] little has been said about the interaction between the climate, ICAO and IMO regimes. Some authors, like Daniel Bodansky, have contributed to the literature by focusing on the role of ICAO and IMO in terms of the potential positive outcome of sectoral approaches to the climate objective.[31] Additionally, the work on emissions from IBF in the climate regime, ICAO and IMO and the legal challenges of the eventual adoption of mechanisms has also been assessed.[32] However, there are few studies embracing the interactions between these regimes,[33] most notably Sebastian Oberthür,[34] who analyzed the interactions between the climate regime and ICAO and IMO in 2003[35] and 2006.[36] However, since then, there have been important developments both in the field of climate change and in the academic literature related to regime interaction that justify and enable this monograph's research focus.

This book aims to contribute to:

- The literature on legal aspects of regulating GHG emissions from international aviation and maritime transport, including a systematic account of the legal and institutional conditions under which climate regulation can emerge, develop and operate through the ICAO and the IMO;
- The literature on fragmentation and regime interaction in international climate change law and governance as a tool and a framework for analysis, specifically in connection to the case of the allocation and regulation of emissions from IBF; and
- The debate on the role and future of the CBDRRC principle in climate change governance, as it relates to the issue of IBF.

This study focuses on the challenges faced in the allocation and regulation of emissions from international aviation and international maritime transport in view of the limited progress made by the international community so far. Specifically, it aims to understand the core of these difficulties, which relates to the tension between the different regimes at play. And, furthermore, to explore synergies between regimes. Beyond the quagmire of technical and political problems around the allocation and regulation of IBF, there is a fundamental legal question that needs to be addressed:

> How can the interaction between different regimes overlapping and competing in the regulation of international aviation and maritime transport be managed in order to avoid and solve conflicts and enhance synergies?

The analysis to answer the above question will be done through the lens of fragmentation of international law related to climate change and the interaction established among different regimes at the law-making stage. Specifically, this book aims to find answers to the following research questions:

1 *Why have IBF emissions remained largely unregulated?*

This includes answering basic sub-questions such as:

- How does the existing legal framework work?
- What are the tools available to address them?
- What have been the developments towards tackling the problem?
- What are the tensions impeding progress?

In order to address these questions, Chapter 3 looks into the state of affairs and the law-making setup of the three regimes. This includes a descriptive and normative analysis along different variables including: actors, processes and instruments.[37] It pays attention to the specificities of international organizations as law-makers.[38] Chapter 3 concludes by summarizing the opportunities and challenges encountered under the respective fora and underlines the differences in objectives, values and principles between regimes. Chapter 3 also highlights that there are tensions within and between regimes slowing down progress.

2   *How does interaction among the selected regimes occur?*

This question can be broken down into the following issues:

- How do the regimes overlap?
- What are the channels of interaction between these regimes, both formal and informal?
- What does the interaction entail and what type of interaction has taken place?
- What are the tensions embedded in the interaction?

The interaction is identified and analyzed in terms of regulatory and administrative interaction, operational interaction and conceptual interactions.[39] This will comprise the content of Chapter 4.

3   *What are the consequences of the interaction for the allocation and regulation of international aviation and international maritime transport?*

This question subsumes a few sub-questions:

- What conflicts and synergies are found in the regulation of IBF emissions among the climate and the ICAO and IMO regimes?
- How do diverging objectives and purposes of the regimes affect the pursuance of meaningful regulation?
- How can the burden of mitigation be distributed given the existence of divergent principles between regimes?
- What are the consequences of the CBDRRC principle entering systems based on equal and non-discriminatory treatment?
- How do conflicts and synergies between the climate, ICAO and IMO regimes affect the choice of regulatory instrument?

4   *How can the tensions be overcome?*

Once the conflicts caused by the interaction have been identified, the book will look into possible conflict solutions: from traditional legal formulas[40] to other approaches based on institutional coordination, as well as other resources to manage regime interaction.[41]

Specifically:

- How can diverging objectives and principles of the climate, ICAO and IMO regimes converge?
- If and how can the CBDRRC principle be applied in regimes that work on an equal and non-discriminatory basis? How can it be reconciled with the objectives and principles of ICAO and IMO?
- How can specific regulatory instruments for IBF benefit from coordination between regimes?
- What techniques can be applied for the avoidance and solution of conflicts and the enhancement of synergistic outcomes in the future?

The ultimate aim is to propose legal solutions, analyze their implications and suggest some policy recommendations to move the regulation of IBF out of a stalemate situation.

Book outline

Following this introductory chapter, the book is organized in the following way. The Chapter 2 ('Analytical framework, key concepts and methodology') provides the theoretical and methodological basis for approaching the object of study. Chapter 3 ('Law-making at the climate, ICAO and IMO regimes') maps the field of the legal framework for the regulation of IBF in the three selected regimes and gives an account of the state of affairs, to date. In doing so, it paints and analyzes the landscape of the current and future regulatory framework. Chapter 4 ('Bunker fuels at the intersection of international legal regimes') focuses on identifying and analyzing the ways in which the interaction occurs, especially in terms of regulatory and administrative interaction, operational interaction and conceptual interactions.[42] Chapter 5 ('The consequences of regime interaction') analyzes the outcomes of interaction, expanding upon the specific conflicts and synergies encountered. Chapter 6 ('Managing interaction') applies the options and tools available to resolve the specific tensions and to enhance synergies in this given issue area. Finally Chapter 7 ('Conclusions and prospects') summarizes the main findings, elaborates on the future regulation of IBF, and concludes by suggesting some ways forward for policy-making.

Context

The contribution of international aviation and international maritime transport to climate change

As a consequence of the globalization process, the international transport of both freight and passengers has grown rapidly over the last 50 years,[43] which has provided some commercial, economic, social and cultural benefits but also some negative environmental externalities.[44] These include noise, air pollution, impacts on the landscape[45] and a contribution to climate change, due mainly to the emission of greenhouse gases into the atmosphere from the combustion of fossil fuels.

In 2004, the global transport sector accounted for 13% of all greenhouse gas emissions.[46] Of this total, global aviation and maritime transport account for around 3.2% and 2.1% respectively, that is, 40% of all transport-related emissions. Of these global figures, international maritime transport emissions accounts for 83% of all shipping emissions, whereas 62% of all aviation emissions are from international flights.[47]

Remarkably, emissions growth rates since 1990 for both sectors have increased above the global average,[48] and they are projected to grow exponentially in the 21st century due to increasing demand.[49] Options to curb emissions in the aviation and maritime sectors differ.[50] Forecasted marginal fuel efficiency improvements and the opportunities for reductions through technical and operational measures for aviation are limited.[51] Maritime transport, by contrast, shows a greater potential to curtail emissions through operational and technical options.[52]

Aviation-induced climate change

Within the transport sector, aviation has grown faster than any other mode of transport and is forecast to grow 5% a year,[53] requiring a steep rise in jet fuel consumption and concomitant GHG emissions.

The main emissions from aircraft include carbon dioxide CO_2, nitrogen oxides (NOx), water vapour,[54] sulphur (SOx) and soot particles, but aviation also causes the formation of condensation trails, or 'contrails', and the enhancement of cirrus clouds. Although the CO_2 emitted by aircraft engines is the biggest known contributor to aviation's impact on climate change, accounting for 2–3% of the total anthropogenic CO_2, estimates on non-CO_2 emissions, excluding the formation of cirrus clouds, over which there remains scientific uncertainties, suggest that they can be responsible for at least a doubling of the climate change impact of aviation. The Intergovernmental Panel on Climate Change (IPCC) in its Special Report on Aviation and the Global Atmosphere,[55] released in 1999, found that the aviation was responsible for around 2% of anthropogenic carbon emissions, while its share of global warming in terms of radiative forcing[56] has been established as higher, accounting for 3.5% of the global total, excluding changes in cirrus clouds, in 2005.[57] Other studies have even suggested a total contribution of 4.9% in terms of radiative forcing in 2005[58] and predict that it could be as much as 7% by 2050.[59] The predictions for CO_2 emissions alone stand to increase by a factor of 2–3.6[60] or even 3–6[61] by 2050.

The 4th Assessment Report of the International Panel on Climate Change (AR4),[62] while updating the figure on the contribution of aviation, stresses two outstanding characteristics of the sector, namely: that its emissions are projected to grow strongly[63] and that the overall contribution of aviation to climate change is between two to four times greater than the estimated for CO_2 alone, that is, including non-CO_2 emissions and excluding the potential impact of cirrus cloud enhancement.[64] The report concludes that:

In the absence of additional measures, projected annual improvements in aircraft fuel efficiency of the order of 1–2% will be largely surpassed by traffic growth of around 5% each year, leading to a projected increase in emissions of 3–4% per year.[65]

Indeed, the Special Report on Aviation and the Global Atmosphere[66] also showed how, in all future growth scenarios, the improvements in fuel efficiency would be undermined by high levels of sustained energy demand in the sector.[67] Since 1970, aircraft fuel efficiency has increased by 70%, running at an annual average rate of 4.5%, although these efficiency gains had dropped to 1.2% per year by the beginning of the 21st century. In addition to this drop-off in efficiency improvements, high demand growth means that absolute levels of energy consumption in the global aviation industry are on the increase. The ICAO's Environmental Report 2007[68] states that almost 4000 billion passenger-kilometres were registered in 2006 and that international passenger traffic is due to increase by an annual rate of 5.3% for the period 2005–2025. With emerging economies joining the Western economic model and consumer lifestyle[69] and the boost of trade activities[70] between Asia, the United States and Europe, energy demand from the aviation sector is due to continue. Other measures, such as the development of aviation biofuels and the optimization of aircraft operations, would not be sufficient to outweigh the growth in air travel. Even under a favourable optimization scenario, CO_2 emissions will be almost twice as high in 2030, compared to 2002.[71]

In the light of the scientific literature, two things can be concluded: first, that the contribution of aviation to climate change is far larger that the impact accounted for by its CO_2 emissions alone, and that these impacts will continue to grow in the 21st century due to increasing demand.[72] Second, the forecasted marginal fuel efficiency improvements, through technical and operational measures and the potential to use biofuels, are unlikely to offset the sector's expanding contribution to climate change.[73] Consequently, it can be argued, there is a pressing need for the regulation of the sector's emissions, that is, mitigation measures in line with the internalization of the climate-related environmental externalities. Traditional regulatory policies,[74] MBMs[75] and voluntary approaches could be part of the solution, bearing in mind that reduction options for aviation most likely will have to include the offsetting of emissions, the lowering of demand[76] and the uptake of sustainable aviation fuels.

Shipping-induced climate change

With regard to the maritime sector, the Fourth Assessment Report of the IPCC, as well as other posterior studies commissioned by the IMO in 2009 and 2014 to a consortium of scientific experts,[77] show that international maritime transport emissions accounted for around 2.7% of the global total in 2007, equivalent to an estimated 870 million tonnes of CO_2. Combined with domestic shipping and fishing, global maritime emissions accounted for 3.3% of total emissions.[78]

Although the maritime sector also has an impact on the climate through other non-CO_2 emissions, this is far less than in the case of aviation. These non-CO_2 emissions include water vapour, nitrogen oxides (NOx),[79] sulphur oxides (SOx), black carbon and other volatile organic compounds, though some of these gases and particles, while causing local and atmospheric pollution, do not contribute much to global warming.

Maritime transport growth is linked mostly to the international trade in a few commodities, mainly agricultural products, fuels and minerals, and manufactured goods, which is expected to increase in the future.[80] Ultimately the demand for international transport is derived from economic growth and is determined by various factors, including the location of factories, the consumption of raw materials, trade patterns, and sea routes. Such demand and the nature of the freight market will not only shape the size of the sector, but also the type of vessels required to meet the demand, and therefore the emissions.[81] The sector is highly dependent on fossil fuels, which was evidenced by the decrease in demand for shipping during the oil crises of the 1970s, where it took 17 years for seaborne trade to return to its 1973 level.[82]

Although maritime transport is one of the least energy-intensive modes of transport,[83] emissions of CO_2 are expected to grow by a factor of 2 or 3, that is, 50–250% by 2050, under a business-as-usual scenario.[84] Despite its low energy intensity, there is still some potential to increase energy efficiency[85] by adopting technical and operational measures, such as fleet and routing optimization and speed reduction. Such opportunities for emissions reduction could yield as much as 40% in the short term while the long-term reduction potential, assuming the implementation of technical or operational measures, would be less than half of that and it would not be sufficient to compensate for the effects of projected fleet growth. Although speed decrease offers the greatest potential for emissions reduction, followed by the implementation of new and improved technologies, '*speed reduction is probably only economically feasible if policy incentives, such as* CO_2 *trading or emissions charges are introduced.*'[86]

Regulating GHG emissions from international aviation and international maritime transport

The climate regime

The growth of scientific evidence in the 1980s put pressure on the international community to pursue an agreement to mitigation and adaptation issues[87] related to climate change. This agreement, the United Nations Framework Convention on Climate Change (UNFCCC),[88] was adopted in 1992 and aimed to stabilize GHG concentrations in the atmosphere at a level that would prevent further interference with the climate system.

As with other environmental treaties dealing with global concerns and common resources, the UNFCCC included, among others, differential treatment between countries as a guiding principle for further developments. This principle, expressed as CBDRRC in the Convention, allowed the agreement to take on board developing countries.

Emissions resulting from fuel combusted by global aviation and shipping activities are also considered by the Convention.[89] Emissions from *domestic* aviation and maritime transport are reported by country parties in their inventories under national totals and are subject to national commitments. However, emissions from *international* aviation and maritime transport fall outside the national scope and are reported separately. To enable these emissions to be reported, it was agreed that IBF would be calculated on the basis of the country where the fuel is sold. However, crucially, this reporting does not equate to responsibility for the associated emissions. The problem of allocation has proven to be contentious since '*international transport by definition raises international competitiveness issues and some countries are reluctant to count emissions from fuels sold for international aviation or maritime transportation towards their national totals, particularly given the dramatic increase in these emissions since 1990.*'[90]

Despite being one of the older agenda items in the climate regime,[91] agreements over allocating and regulating emissions from IBF under the UNFCCC umbrella have been unmanageable, leading to their exclusion from the KP[92] targets in 1997. The reasons for this exclusion are to be found, among others, in the difficulties of allocating responsibility for mobile (IPCC, 2006) emissions on a country basis.[93] This complexity is exacerbated by the web of nations and industries involved in the normal activity of both sectors, where the country of the operator, registration, origin and destination of the vessel or aircraft are often different.[94]

However, discussions about how to improve inventories have taken place in a scientific subsidiary body of the Climate Convention, and negotiations over the options to take action have continued under the long-term dialogues of the UNFCCC process. Despite high expectations, the Conference of the Parties (COP) held in Copenhagen in December 2009 did not address uncertainties surrounding the treatment of emissions from IBF. Since then the topic has lost momentum in the climate regime, and only recovered a certain visibility with the suggestion that IBF could be a source of financing for the Green Climate Fund.[95]

There is a number of reasons why the regulation of IBF emissions would have helped the 2015 climate agreement process:

> Decisions to agree regulation of post 2020 emissions from international aviation and shipping by 2015 would facilitate the 2015 agreement in several ways. First, it would resolve a problematic issue that has beset the climate regime for decades. Second, it would facilitate the reduction of global greenhouse gas emissions by regulating large, rapidly-growing sources of emissions. Third, if all parties have emissions limitation commitments post 2020, regulation of international aviation and shipping emissions would improve equity since they would otherwise be the only unregulated emissions. Finally,

revenue from regulation of international aviation and shipping emissions, if any, could help Parties to implement the financial commitments embodied in a 2015 agreement.[96]

However, in December 2015, the Paris Agreement[97] was adopted without a reference to international aviation and maritime transport emissions leaving unresolved the issue. Nevertheless, the agreement is not without consequences for the regulation of these sectors.[98]

The International Civil Aviation Organization and the International
Maritime Organization

Another reason to exclude IBF from the KP targets was the existence of two specialized agencies in the UN system that deal specifically with international civil aviation and international maritime affairs. These organizations, which were set up in the 1940s, were regarded as the natural fora to address IBF emissions, given their technical expertise on the functioning of their respective sectors and their previous experience in regulating other environmental matters. In 1997, Article 2.2 of the KP placed the IMO[99] and ICAO[100] as responsible for negotiating sector-specific reductions of GHG emissions. However, both organizations have failed to put in place meaningful measures, including MBMs.[101]

However, the adoption of the KP stimulated the ICAO and the IMO to assume a more cooperative role with the climate institutions in terms of improving the data available on emissions from IBF and regularly reporting on their work on potential policy options. ICAO and the IMO have commissioned studies looking into a range of possibilities[102] to address the emissions from their respective sectors and have set up working groups and committees to inform discussions in their governing bodies.

Nevertheless, the regulation of IBF has also proved to be a complicated issue for the ICAO and IMO regimes. Part of this challenge can be attributed to the way in which the climate regime has requested both treaty bodies to regulate emissions from IBF by using a wording that involves the adoption of measures under differentiated premises in regimes where equal treatment is the normal rule. Factors such as divergent basic objectives, principles or processes add an extra-layer of complexity to the already intractable task of curbing their emissions. Due to these issues, ICAO and the IMO now suffer from political quandaries and tensions over how to design and allocate emissions reductions between countries,[103] and minimal progress has been made in their respective arenas towards the regulation of IBF, as has been the case under the climate regime.

If the international community wants to achieve the goal agreed in 2009[104] and further adopted in the Paris Agreement – that is, to avoid a 2°C increase in global temperature above the pre-industrial level – all sectors of the economy are to be taken into account in order to stabilize emissions. While it presents unique challenges to law-makers, there are no technical reasons to exempt IBF from their share of emissions reductions.[105] It has been pointed out that pursuing sectoral agreements to tackle *'discrete dimensions of climate change in other forums'*, can bridge the gap towards the overall objective.[106] This would include the IMO and ICAO.

*The inclusion of international aviation under the European Union
Emissions Trading System (EU ETS)*

As time drew on and the slowness and inaction at the ICAO became more and more apparent, the EU passed legislation and unilaterally included international aviation emissions,[107] or part of them, into the existing EU ETS.[108] From January 2012 all flights departing from, or arriving to, an aerodrome within the EU territory were due to surrender allowances for the emissions occurred during the whole flight, although some exceptions were allowed on a *de minimum* basis and for third countries taking equivalent measures. Otherwise, the allocation of emissions in the EU ETS was done on an equal basis although a certain redistribution of revenues was considered. This regional measure, which has international consequences, contributes to the fragmented landscape, and features prominently in the development of the field since 2008, shaping the discussion in other realms.[109]

The inclusion of aviation in the EU ETS has pushed the envelope of international law, politics and diplomacy. It has resulted in various commercial[110] and political[111] threats, a high-profile court case,[112] and has even provoked the US Congress to pass a bill forbidding their airlines to comply with the EU ETS.[113] Similarly, a few months later, China drafted a climate law envisioning retaliatory responses against the EU aviation action.[114] Under pressure, the European Commission deferred the enforcement of the aviation Directive (the so-called 'stop-the-clock' decision) for non-European countries in 2012,[115] aiming to create more favourable negotiating conditions for ICAO's 38th Assembly, which agreed to decide on a global scheme by 2016 with a view to developing it by 2020. However, uncertainties regarding the type and design of the MBM that would be adopted in 2016 have put the EU in a difficult position in the interim.[116]

In view of the outcomes of the ICAO's 38th Assembly, the Commission proposed in October 2013 to amend the legislation and reduce the scope of application to the emissions over EU territory only, while maintaining international flights in the scheme.[117] In addition, it was stated that in the absence of a global measure for 2020, a report after the 2016 ICAO Assembly would be issued by the Commission, considering '*the appropriate scope for coverage of emissions from activity to and from countries outside the EEA from 2020 onwards in the continued absence of such a global measure.*'[118] However, the proposal didn't succeed and a new temporary derogation for the monitoring, reporting and surrendering of allowances from flights to and from countries outside the EEA from 1 January 2013 to 31 December 2016 was adopted in April 2014.[119] Nonetheless, the EU still reserves the right to initiate changes in reaction to developments at ICAO regarding '*the appropriate scope for coverage of emissions from activity to and from aerodromes located in countries outside the EEA from 1 January 2017 onwards.*'[120]

After the adoption of CORSIA in October 2016,[121] the EU has remained silent about the temporary derogation, which ended on the 31st of December

2016. Potentially, since CORSIA will only start applying in 2021, it is possible that international aviation will remain included in EU ETS for that period. In this connection, a proposal is expected in early 2017. Also, the EU might consider that the ICAO mechanism is not ambitious enough, in which case, the EU might pursue regional measures to ensure that the contribution of aviation to the climate problem is in line with the Paris Agreement goals.

EU steps towards the regulation of GHG emissions from international maritime transport

As with aviation, the lack of progress in the IMO pushed the EU to consider including the maritime transport sector in the EU's emission reduction policies at a later date:

> In the event that no international agreement which includes international maritime emissions in its reduction targets through the International Maritime Organisation has been approved by the Member States or no such agreement through the UNFCCC has been approved by the Community by 31 December 2011, the Commission should make a proposal to include international maritime emissions in the Community reduction commitment with the aim of the proposed act entering into force by 2013.[122]

Whether it was progress made at the IMO that satisfied the EU, or whether it was the complications that arose from the EU's aviation legislation that diminished the willingness to regulate the maritime sector, the fact is that the EU took no effective measures in that announced time frame. However, in 2013, a proposal was put forward by the Commission to establish a Monitoring, Reporting and Verification (MRV) system for maritime emissions.[123] The MRV system is envisioned as a first step or prerequisite for the inclusion of maritime GHG emissions in the EU's reduction commitments. This would be a '*gradual approach*', consisting of three steps: implementing a system for MRV of emissions, defining the reduction targets for the sector and applying an MBM.[124] In April 2015, the EU adopted the MRV mechanism for the shipping sector,[125] which can be seen as ways for the EU to not only fulfil its climate obligations, but also as a way to steer the IMO towards adopting its own data collection measures.[126] Indeed, the regulation contains a provision to review the EU MRV in the event of future international developments, particularly if the IMO agrees upon a global data collection mechanism.

In December 2016 by the European Parliament's Environment Committee has agreed to call for the inclusion of maritime transport emissions into the EU ETS from 2023, in the event of no global measure adopted at the international level by 2021.[127] The EU Parliament plenary will vote on this in 2017 and, if successful, a proposal for the amendment of the EU ETS so as to include shipping will be put forward.

Notes

1 The term 'climate change' is used throughout this book as referring to anthropogenic global warming – that is, changes in the climate system attributable to human activities linked mainly with the emission of greenhouse gases and changes in land use. To quote the United Nations Framework Convention on Climate Change (UNFCCC) definition: '*a change of climate which is attributed directly or indirectly to human activity that alters the composition of the global atmosphere and which is in addition to natural climate variability observed over comparable time periods*'.

The greenhouse effect – the energy flow that allows the earth's surface to cool down from the sun's radiation and maintain the carbon cycle in balance – has been disrupted by an increased presence of gases and substances in the atmosphere. These atmospheric gases, which absorb earth's outgoing radiation and reemit it back to earth causing global warming, include water vapour (H_2O), carbon dioxide (CO_2), methane (CH_4), nitrous oxide (NOx) and an array of chlorofluorocarbons (CFCs). Since the industrial revolution, the concentration of CO_2 in the atmosphere has increased from 280 ppm in 1850 to 360 ppm in 1990, with fossil fuel combustion being the main driver.

In 1988 the World Meteorological Organization (WMO) and the United Nations Environment Program (UNEP) established a scientific panel, the Intergovernmental Panel on Climate Change (IPCC), to assess the problem of climate change and provide policy advice. In its 4th Assessment Report (AR4), published in 2007, the IPCC stated that global warming is unequivocal, it is highly likely human induced, it poses a threat to mankind and substantial and immediate actions are needed in order to stabilize the level of GHGs in the atmosphere at 400–470ppm in order to keep the global temperature of the planet under what is considered a safe level. See (IPCC, *Climate Change 2007: Synthesis Report: Contribution of Working Groups I, II and III to the Fourth Assessment Report of the Intergovernmental Panel on Climate Change* [Cambridge University Press, 2007]). Furthermore, the evidence of human influence has grown since the AR4. The 5th Report goes further and states that '*[t]his evidence for human influence has grown since AR4. It is extremely likely that human influence has been the dominant cause of the observed warming since the mid-20th century.*' Extremely likely in the language of the IPCC means 95–100% probable. See, the more recent IPCC 2013, 'Summary for Policymakers', in *Climate Change 2013: The Physical Science Basis: Contribution of Working Group I to the Fifth Assessment Report of the Intergovernmental Panel on Climate Change* (T.F. Stocker et al. eds., 2013). 15.

2 In the words of the Chairman of the 3rd IPCC Panel, Dr. Robert Watson: '*Climate change is not just an environmental issue, but is part of the larger challenge of sustainable development.*' IPCC, Statement on behalf of the Chairman of IPCC, Dr. Robert Watson, delivered by Dr. Bert Metz Co-chair. Seventh Conference of Parties to the United Nations Framework Convention on Climate Change, Marrakech, Morocco, November 7 (2001).

3 UNEP, *The Emissions Gap Report 2012* (UNEP, 2012). 11, states that '*The assessment clearly shows that country pledges, if fully implemented, will help reduce emissions to below the business-as-usual level in 2020, but not to a level consistent with the agreed upon 2°C target, and therefore will lead to a considerable "emissions gap".*' The report estimates the 2020 emissions gap to be 8–13 gig tonnes of equivalent CO_2, larger than previously estimated, because of higher than expected overall economic growth. The Emissions Gap Report 2013 found similar figures '*and showed an increase in projected business-as-usual emissions in 2020 compared to the 2012 report*'. See, UNEP, *The Emissions Gap Report 2013* (UNEP, 2013). 33. In the same vein, UNEP, *The Emissions Gap Report 2014* (UNEP, 2014) and UNEP, *The Emissions Gap Report 2015* (UNEP, 2015). Although the recently adopted Paris Agreement might now change the landscape,

as of today, country reduction pledges on the table are inconsistent with the 2°C (let alone the 1.5°C) pathway, agreed to in Paris.

4 UNFCCC, Paris Agreement (Paris, 12 December 2015, in force 4 November 2016) FCCC/CP/2015/L.9, (2015).

5 The term 'International Bunker Fuels' (hereinafter IBF) is used in the climate context when referring to the fuel used for international aviation and international maritime transport. Although it hasn't been defined by the UNFCCC, the terminology is taken from the IPCC GHG inventory guidelines, which were adopted by the COP, while the IPCC guidelines use the term 'International Bunkers'. The term IBF is used throughout the book to differentiate the international fraction of the global aviation and marine 'bunker fuels' and also to differentiate from the domestic ones. See, for example Daniel Blobel et al., *United Nations Framework Convention on Climate Change: Handbook* (Intergovernmental and Legal Affairs, Climate Change Secretariat, 2006). 186.

6 The EU included aviation in its European emissions trading system, which regulates for part of the international aviation emissions, but at the time of writing there is a moratorium to delay enforcement on non-EU flights. Also, in October 2016, ICAO agreed on a global offsetting mechanism for international aviation, however the measure needs to be detailed and converted into regulation and will only start to be mandatory by 2027. Therefore emissions from international aviation are, *de facto*, still unregulated.

7 IEA, CO_2 *Emissions from Fuel Combustion: Highlights* (IEA, 2012). 11. Emissions from fuel used for aviation and maritime transport were 6.7% and 7% higher in 2010, compared to 2009, respectively.

8 The scholarship has defined climate change as a '*super wicked problem*'. A super wicked problem not only lacks '*simplistic or straightforward planning responses*' but is also characterized by four aspects: '*time is running out; the central authority needed to address them is weak or non-existent; those who cause the problem also seek to create a solution; and hyperbolic discounting occurs that pushes responses into the future when immediate actions are required to set in train longer-term policy solutions.*' The term is introduced in: Kelly Levin et al., 'Playing It Forward: Path Dependency, Progressive Incrementalism, and the "Super Wicked" Problem of Global Climate Change', International Studies Association 48th Annual Convention, February 28, (2007). 3.

9 Nicholas Stern, *The Economics of Climate Change: The Stern Review: Executive Summary* (Cambridge, 2007). 1. The Executive Summary states: '*Climate change is global in its causes and consequences, and international collective action will be critical in driving an effective, efficient and equitable response on the scale required. This response will require deeper international co-operation in many areas – most notably in creating price signals and markets for carbon, spurring technology research, development and deployment, and promoting adaptation, particularly for developing countries.*' In a similar vein, see IPCC 2014, 'Summary for Policymakers', in *Climate Change 2014, Mitigation of Climate Change: Contribution of Working Group III to the Fifth Assessment Report of the Intergovernmental Panel on Climate Change* (O. Edenhofer et al. eds., 2014).

10 For an analysis of regime interaction related to climate change see Margaret A. Young, 'Climate Change Law and Regime Interaction', *Climate Change Law Review*, 2, (2011). 147. Young provides here an overview of interactions of the climate regime with three legal regimes, namely: international trade, heritage protection and the law of the sea.

11 Margaret A. Young, *Regime Interaction in International Law: Facing Fragmentation* (Cambridge University Press, 2012); ILC, *Fragmentation of International Law: Difficulties Arising from the Diversification and Expansion of International Law. Report of the Study Group of the International Law Commission.* UN Doc. A/CN.4/L.682, (2006).

12 See, for instance, Harro van Asselt et al., 'Global Climate Change and the Fragmentation of International Law', *Law and Policy*, 30(4), (2008). 423–449; Harro van

Asselt and Fariborz Zelli, 'Connect the Dots: Managing the Fragmentation of Global Climate Governance Earth System', Governance Working Paper No. 25. Lund and Amsterdam: Earth System Governance Project, (2012); M.A. Young, (2011).
13 M.A. Young, (2011).
14 See for instance, Mario Prost and Paul Kingsley Clark, 'Unity, Diversity and the Fragmentation of International Law: How Much Does the Multiplication of International Organizations Really Matter?', *Chinese Journal of International Law*, 5(2), (2006). 341–348; Pierre-Marie Dupuy, 'The Danger of Fragmentation or Unification of the International Legal System and the International Court of Justice', *New York University Journal of International Law and Politics.*, 31, (1999). 791.
15 H.V. Asselt and F. Zelli, (2012). 5.
16 For a detailed description see Farhana Yamin and Joanna Depledge, *The International Climate Change Regime: A Guide to Rules, Institutions and Procedures* (Cambridge University Press, 2004). 82–87.
17 Kyoto Protocol, Article 2.2 triggered interaction with the regimes that regulate international aviation and maritime transport by requesting the ICAO and the IMO respectively to address the regulation of IBF.
18 Joyeeta Gupta and Louis Lebel, 'Access and Allocation in Earth System Governance: Water and Climate Change Compared', *International Environmental Agreements: Politics, Law and Economics*, 10(4), (2010). 381–386.
19 H.V. Asselt and F. Zelli, (2012). 7. In 2016, the statement remains valid.
20 See Alan E. Boyle and Christine M. Chinkin, *The Making of International Law* (Oxford University Press, 2007).
21 Duncan Brack et al., *International Trade and Climate Change Policies* (Earthscan, 2000). 99–115, on the relations of an eventual taxation on international bunker fuels with the trade regime. For a general overview in links between the climate regime and the WTO see, Kati Kulovesi, 'Climate Change and Trade: At the Intersection of Two International Legal Regimes', in *Climate Change and the Law* (Erkki J. Hollo et al. eds., 2013).
22 M.J. Trebilcock and Robert Howse, *The Regulation of International Trade* (Routledge 3rd ed., 2005). 507–556.
23 D. Brack et al., *International Trade and Climate Change Policies*. (2000).
24 For an overview see Christopher Findlay, 'Transport Services', in Aaditya Mattoo et al., *A Handbook of International Trade in Services* (Oxford University Press, 2008).
25 In 1995 the WTO adopted The General Agreement on Trade in Services (GATS), in order to pursue the elimination of barriers to services trade in a similar fashion as the General Agreement on Tariffs and Trade (GATT) does with the trade in goods. It relies upon the principle of non-discrimination that is translated into two more specific principles: most favourable nation and national treatment, as for products. The usual WTO dispute settlement applies to GATS.
26 A similar explanation was provided in regards to maritime transport at the 62nd MEPC of the IMO in a presentation from a WTO official. Report of the third Intersessional Meeting of the working group on greenhouse gas emissions from ships. Note by the Secretariat. MEPC 62/5/1 (8 April 2011). 19–20. It was contested by the Indian delegation in the Annex of the same document. 4–5.
27 Case C-366/10, (Court of Justice of the European Union). Case C-366/10 Air Transport Association of America and Others v Secretary of State for Energy and Climate Change, EU:C:2011:864.
28 CBDR was formulated in the climate regime with an extra element 'Respective Capabilities' (hereinafter CBDRRC).
29 See chapter two.
30 These include: Kati Kulovesi, 'Make Your Own Special Song, Even If Nobody Else Sings Along: International Aviation Emissions and the EU Emissions Trading Scheme', *University of Eastern Finland Legal Studies Research Paper No. 1*, (2011); B.

Mueller, 'From Confrontation to Collaboration? CBDR and the EU ETS Aviation Dispute with Developing Countries', *Environmental Liability*, 19(6), (2012). Joanne Scott and Lavanya Rajamani, 'EU Climate Change', *European Journal of International Law*, 23(2) (2012). 469–494; Christina Voigt, 'Up in the Air: Aviation, the EU Emissions Trading Scheme and the Question of Jurisdiction', *Cambridge Yearbook of European Legal Studies*, 14(1), (2011). 475–506; Jacques Hartmann, 'A Battle for the Skies: Applying the European Emissions Trading System to International Aviation', *Nordic Journal of International Law*, 82(2), (2013). 187; Steven Truxal, 'At the Sidelines of Implementing the EU ETS: Objections to "Validity"', *International Trade Law and Regulation*, 16(4), (2010). 28–36; Sanja Bogojević, 'Legalising Environmental Leadership: A Comment on the CJEU'S Ruling in C-366/10 on the Inclusion of Aviation in the EU Emissions Trading Scheme', *Journal of Environmental Law*, 24(2), (2012). 345–356; Antto Vihma and Harro van Asselt, 'The Conflict over Aviation Emissions: A Case of Retreating EU Leadership?', *FIIA Briefing Paper 150*, (2014); Joanne Scott, 'The New EU "Extraterritoriality"', *Common Market Law Review*, 51, (2014). 1343–1380; Joanne Scott, 'Extraterritoriality and Territorial Extension in EU Law', *American Journal of Comparative Law*, 62(1), (2014). 87–126. The list is long regarding aviation, but there are also some studies on the potential inclusion of the maritime sector in the EU ETS, see Henrik Ringbom, 'An EU Emission Trading Scheme for Shipping? International Law Challenges', in *Environmental Liabilities in Ports and Coastal Areas: Focus on Public Authorities and Other Actors* (Henrik Rak and Peter Wetterstein eds., 2011). Daniel Perez Rodriguez, 'The Inclusion of Shipping in the EU Emissions Trading Scheme: A Legal Analysis in the Light of Public International Law', *Revista Catalana de Dret Ambiental*, 3(2), (2012). 1.

31 Daniel Bodansky, 'Multilateral Climate Efforts beyond the UNFCCC' (Centre for Climate and Energy Solutions, 2011). ICAO and IMO are considered as multilateral regimes, but the he focuses on complementing sectoral approaches to the UNFCCC. Also, Kati Kulovesi and Katja Keinänen, 'Long-Term Climate Policy: International Legal Aspects of Sector-Based Approaches', *Climate Policy*, 6(3), (2006). 313–325; Harro van Asselt, 'Alongside the UNFCCC: Complementary Venues for Climate Action' (Centre for Climate and Energy Solutions, 2014); Remi Moncel and Harro van Asselt, 'All Hands on Deck! Mobilizing Climate Change Action beyond the UNFCCC', *Review of European Community & International Environmental Law: RECIEL*, 21(3), (2012). 163–176.

32 Among others: Ruwantissa Abeyratne, *Aviation and the Carbon Trade* (Nova Science Publishers, 2011); WMO, *Aviation and the Global Amospheric Environment* (World Meteorological Organization, 2004); Christian Pisani, 'Fair at Sea: The Design of a Future Legal Instrument on Marine Bunker Fules Emissions within the Climate Change Regime', *Ocean Development and Internaional Law*, 33, (2002). 57–76; Aydin Okur, 'The Challenge of Regulating Greenhouse Gas Emissions from Internaional Shipping and the Complicated Principle of "Common But Differentiated Responsibilities", *Dokuz Eylül Üniversitesi Hukuk Fakültesi Dergisi*, 13(1), (2012). 27–49.

33 Bernd Hackmann, 'Analysis of the Governance Architecture to Regulate GHG Emissions from International Shipping', *International Environmental Agreements*, 12, (2012). 85–103.

34 See also, Fariborz Zelli, 'The Fragmentation of the Global Climate Governance Architecture', *Wiley Interdisciplinary Reviews: Climate Change*, 2(2), (2011). 261–262.

35 Sebastian Oberthür, 'Institutional Interaction to Address Greenhouse Gas Emissions from International Transport: ICAO, IMO and the Kyoto Protocol', *Climate Policy*, 3(3), (2003). 191–205. Sebastian Oberthür, 'Institutional Interaction to Address Greenhouse Gas Emissions from Enternational Transport: ICAO, IMO and the EU Burden-Sharing Agreement', *Project Deliverable No. D 3, Final Draft. Ecologic: Institute for International and European Policy*, (2003).

36 Sebastian Oberthür, 'Interactions of the Climate Change Regime with ICAO, IMO and the EU Burden-Sharing Agreement', in *Institutional Interaction in Global Environmental Governance: Synergy and Conflict among International and EU Policies*, (Sebastian Oberthür and Thomas Gehring eds., 2006).

37 A.E. Boyle and C.M. Chinkin, *The Making of International Law*. (2007). Their work offers a structure to be used in order to analyze law-making processes in international law. See, chapter two on analytical framework.

38 José E. Alvarez, *International Organizations as Law-Makers* (Oxford University Press, 2005).

39 The scheme is proposed in Jeffrey Dunoff, 'A New Approach to Regime Interaction', in *Regime Interaction in International Law: Facing Fragmentation* (Margaret A. Young ed., 2012). See further chapter two on the analytical framework.

40 ILC Report (2006).

41 The book builds up here mainly on the work of Prof. Harro van Asselt. See, Harro van Asselt, *The Fragmentation of Global Climate Governance: Consequences and Management of Regime Interactions* (Edward Elgar, 2014); Harro van Asselt, 'Dealing with the Fragmentation of Global Climate Governance: Legal and Political Approaches in Interplay Management', Global Governance Working Paper No. 30, (2007); Harro van Asselt, 'Legal and Political Approaches in Interplay Management: Dealing with the Fragmentation of Global Climate Governance', in *Managing Institutional Complexity: Regime Interplay and Global Environmental Change. Institutional Dimensions of Global Environmental Change* (Sebastian Oberthür and Olav Schram Stokke eds., 2011); H.v. Asselt and F. Zelli, (2012). Harro van Asselt, 'Managing the Fragmentation of International Climate Law', in *Climate Change and the Law* (Erkki J. Hollo et al. eds., 2013). Harro van Asselt, *The Fragmentation of Global Climate Governance: Consequences and Management of Regime Interactions*. (Vrije Universiteit, 2013). See further chapter two.

42 The scheme is proposed in Jeffrey Dunoff, 'A New Approach to Regime Interaction'. (2012).

43 OECD, *Globalization, Transport and the Environment* (OECD, 2010). 14. The development of transportation and the industrialization in the 19th Century, together with advances in communications, enabled our 'globalized' world. Since WWII, this process has involved a strong growth in international shipping activity and air transport, which has also, in itself, fostered globalization. Many structural changes have also taken place as a result of globalization; in the aviation sector, air markets have been liberalized, the networks that airline companies operate have changed, the low cost phenomena has emerged and many airlines have merged. In the maritime sector, the industry has become delocalized and the flow and volume of trade has increased significantly.

44 According to the *Glossary of Environment Statistics*, Studies in Methods, Series F, No. 67 (United Nations, 1997). Environmental externalities are '*uncompensated environmental effects of production and consumption that affect consumer utility and enterprise cost outside the market mechanism*'. Climate change can be classified as 'an example of market failure involving externalities and public goods' See, N. Stern, *The Economics of Climate Change: The Stern Review: Executive Summary*. (2007). 27.

45 For example, the construction of airports and shipping harbours.

46 IPCC, *Climate Change 2007: Synthesis Report: Contribution of Working Groups I, II and III to the Fourth Assessment Report of the Intergovernmental Panel on Climate Change*. (2007). 25.

47 David S. Lee et al., 'Shipping and Aviation Emissions in the Context of a 2°C Emission Pathway' (Manchester Metropolitan University, 2013).

48 T. Barker et al., 'Technical Summary', in *Climate Change 2007: Mitigation of Climate Change: Contribution of Working Group III to the Fourth Assessment Report of the Intergovernmental Panel on Climate Change* (B. Metz et al. eds., 2007). 25; see also S. Kahn Ribeiro et al., 'Transport and Its Infrastructure', in *Climate Change 2007: Mitigation:*

Contribution of Working Group III to the Fourth Assessment Report of the Intergovern-mental Panel on Climate Change (B. Metz et al. eds., 2007). 323; and R. Sims et al., 'Transport', in *Climate Change 2014: Mitigation of Climate Change: Contribution of Working Group III to the Fifth Assessment Report of the Intergovernmental Panel on Climate Change* (O. Edenhofer et al. eds., 2014); R. Sims et al., 'Transport'. (2014). 599; Alice Bows-Larkin, 'All Adrift: Aviation, Shipping, and Climate Change Policy', *Climate Policy*, 15(6), (2015). 681.

49 IEA, CO_2 *Emissions from Fuel Combustion. Highlights.* (2012). 11.

50 Martin Cames et al., *Emission Reduction Targets for International Aviation and Shipping* (European Parliament Committee on Environment, Public Health and Food Safety, 2015).

51 See, D.S. Lee et al., (2013).

52 See A. Bows-Larkin, (2015).

53 S.K. Ribeiro et al., 'Transport and Its Infrastructure'. (2007).

54 Cruise altitudes for subsonic aircraft are between 8–13km, which means that most of the emissions are released in the upper troposphere and lower stratosphere. When water vapour is released in lower parts of the atmosphere it has a non-lasting effect, since it vanishes through precipitation. However, the release of water vapour from aviation at higher altitudes has a bigger impact.

55 The ICAO requested the IPCC to prepare the report with the collaboration of the Scientific Assessment Panel to the Montreal Protocol on Substances that Deplete the Ozone Layer. The report aimed '*to provide accurate, unbiased, policy-relevant information to serve the aviation industry, the expert and policy-making communities*'. Joyce E. Penner et al., *Aviation and the Global Atmosphere: A Special Report of IPCC Working Groups I and III in Collaboration with the Scientific Assessment Panel to the Montreal Protocol on Substances That Deplete the Ozone Layer* (Cambridge University Press, 1999).

56 The Radiative Forcing Index is better suited to aviation since it is able to measure some of the non-CO_2 impacts, whereas the politically accepted index of Global Warming Potential takes a time horizon of 100 years where short-life impacts cannot be reflected properly.

57 David S. Lee et al., 'Aviation and Global Climate Change in the 21st Century', *Atmospheric Environment*, 43(22–23), (2009). 3520–3537; also David S. Lee et al., 'Transport Impacts on Atmosphere and Climate: Aviation', *Atmospheric Environment*, 44(37), (2010). 4678–4734.

58 Bethan Owen et al., 'Flying into the Future: Aviation Emissions Scenarios to 2050', *Environmental Science & Technology*, 44(7), (2010). 2255–2260. A good overview is provided in David W. Fahey and David S. Lee, 'Aviation and the Impacts of Climate Change · Aviation and Climate Change: A Scientific Perspective', *Carbon & Climate Law Review*, 10(2), (2016). 97–104.

59 J.E. Penner et al., *Aviation and the Global Atmosphere: A Special Report of IPCC Working Groups I and III in Collaboration with the Scientific Assessment Panel to the Montreal Protocol on Substances That Deplete the Ozone Layer*. (1999). 185. For a more recent estimates see: D.S. Lee et al., (2009). And also: D.S. Lee et al., (2009). According to this study, the radiative forcing from aviation in 2005 including cirrus cloud enhancement represents 4.9% of the total forcing.

60 B. Owen et al., (2010). Projections are for the period between 2000 and 2050.

61 Xander Olsthoorn, 'Carbon Dioxide Emissions from International Aviation: 1950–2050', *Journal of Air Transport Management*, 7(2), (2001). 87–93. Projections are for the period between 1995 and 2050.

62 T. Barker et al., 'Technical Summary'. (2007). And also: S.K. Ribeiro et al., 'Transport and Its Infrastructure'. (2007).

63 From 1990 to 2000 aviation emissions rose from 330 $MtCO_2$/yr to 480 $MtCO_2$/yr; the report shows that this trend will continue. T. Barker et al., 'Technical Summary'. (2007). 46.

64 'As well as emitting CO_2, aircraft contribute to climate change through the emission of nitrogen oxides (NOx), which are particularly effective in forming the GHG ozone when emitted at cruise altitudes. Aircraft also trigger the formation of condensation trails, or contrails, which are suspected of enhancing the formation of cirrus clouds, which add to the overall global warming effect.' S. Kahn Ribeiro et al., 'Transport and Its Infrastructure'. (2007).

65 Ibid.

66 The ICAO requested the IPCC to prepare the report with the collaboration of the Scientific Assessment Panel to the Montreal Protocol on Substances that Deplete the Ozone Layer. The report aims 'to provide accurate, unbiased, policy-relevant information to serve the aviation industry, the expert and policy-making communities',

67 With an annual average increase of 3% between 1990 and 2015.

68 ICAO, *ICAO Environmental Report 2007* (ICAO, 2007). 103–184.

69 For example, demand for aviation in China has grown an average rate of 14.8% per year since the 1990s.

70 According to OECD, *Globalization, Transport and the Environment*. (2010). 40% of world trade by value now moves by air.

71 Ibid. at. 186–188. The report supports the idea that technological developments are not enough to compensate for the increased demand, so additional measures are necessary.

72 D.S. Lee et al., (2009).

73 Ibid.

74 It refers to traditional 'command-and-control' instruments that do not use economic incentives to achieve environmental objectives. This approach relies on the setting of specification, performance and environmental quality standards and sanctions. They can also be applied at the international level. An example is the Montreal Protocol on Substances that Deplete the Ozone Layer. See Daniel Bodansky, *The Art and Craft of International Environmental Law* (Harvard University Press, 2010). 75–80.

75 In environmental policy, market-based measures, such as tradable permits or taxes, are mechanisms that intend to reduce environmental externalities by providing incentives through the inclusion of the environmental costs. The establishment of a market for permits or allowances offers more flexibility than a taxation option since externalities can allegedly be reduced in a more cost-efficient way. See Barry C. Field and Martha K. Field, *Environmental Economics: An Introduction* (McGraw-Hill/Irwin 3rd ed., 2002), Chapters 4, 12 and 13, and D. Bodansky, *The Art and Craft of International Environmental Law*. (2010). 80–84. Bodansky offers a classification of market-based approaches in two types: price-based instruments such as pollution taxes and charges, subsidies and liability rules, and quantity-based instruments such as cap-and-trade or tradable allowances. See further in Chapter 5.

76 Andrew Macintosh and Lailey Wallace, 'International Aviation Emissions to 2025: Can Emissions Be Stabilised without Restricting Demand?', *Energy Policy*, 37(1), (2009). 264–273; Peter J. McManners, *Fly and Be Damned: What Now for Aviation and Climate Change?* (Zed Books, 2012). He proposed that action should be guided to both reduce demand for conventional aviation and support a movement away from fossil fuels. He challenges the Chicago Convention's premises and stated that such objectives can be better achieved with a tax on aviation fuel.

77 Ø. Buhaug et al., *Second IMO Greenhouse Gas Study 2009: Executive Summary* (IMO, 2009). The study was approved at MEPC59 meeting. It updates a *Study of Greenhouse Gas Emissions from Ships* done in 2000. IMO, *Study of Greenhouse Gas Emissions from Ships* (IMO, 2000). A 2014 update showed slightly lower numbers for the period 2007–2012. Tristan W. Smith et al., *Third IMO Greenhouse Gas Study 2014: Executive Summary and Final Report* (IMO, 2014).

78 However, other data suggests that shipping emissions are about 4.5% of total emissions (i.e. 1.12 billion tonnes of CO_2) compared with the 650 of aviation. See,

David D. Caron, 'Climate Change and the Oceans', in *Regions, Institutions, and Law of the Sea Regions, Institutions, and Law of the Sea: Studies in Ocean Governance* (Harry N. Scheiber and Jin-Hyun Paik eds., 2013). 516–519.

79 NOx emissions can have a cooling effect since they remove methane (CH4) from the atmosphere.

80 Ø. Buhaug et al., *Second IMO Greenhouse Gas Study 2009*. (2009). Around 90% of the volume of trade is transported by sea.

81 Ibid.

82 N. Wijnolst et al., *Shipping Innovation* (IOS Press, 2009). 8 and 46. The IPCC also noted that around 90% of global merchandise is transported by sea. S.K. Ribeiro et al., 'Transport and Its Infrastructure'. (2007).

83 As compared with other sectors, the transport of goods by shipping vessels is by far the least energy-intensive mode. In this regard, measures that aim to create a higher price for seaborne products compared with other transport modes would influence a switch to more energy-intensive transports, jeopardizing the overall objective of reducing emissions.

84 See, Ø. Buhaug et al., *Second IMO Greenhouse Gas Study 2009*. (2009); Gregory Gould et al., 'Greenhouse Gas Emissions from Aviation and Marine Transportation: Mitigation Potential and Policies', *Pew Center on Global Climate Change*, (2009). 10. A table of projections is offered, elaborated from data of the International Energy Agency, the US Federal Aviation Administration and the IMO. See, also, T.W. Smith et al., *Third IMO Greenhouse Gas Study 2014: Executive Summary and Final Report*. (2014). 127–146. Depending on future economic and energy developments, in a business-as-usual scenario, the study projects an increase by 50% to 250% in the period to 2050.

85 Andrew G. Spyrou, *Global Climate Change and the Shipping Industry* (iuniverse, 2010). 221–225. The energy efficiency of new vessels is guarantee by the shipbuilder upon delivery, based on the ship's main engine power output and the speed in calm seas. With rough sea conditions there is more need for speed and therefore fuel consumption.

86 S.K. Ribeiro et al., 'Transport and Its Infrastructure'. (2007). 328–356.

87 While both mitigation and adaptation are part of the climate regime, the focus on adaptation started later, around the IPCC Third Assessment Report 2001, gaining increased attention not only for developing countries but also for developed countries. See, Tim Rayner and Andrew Jordan, 'Adapting to a Changing Climate: An Emerging European Union Policy', in *Climate Change Policy in the European Union: Confronting the Dilemmas of Mitigation and Adaptation?* (Andrew Jordan et al. eds., 2010). 145–149. Similarly, D. Osberghaus et al., 'Individual Adaptation to Climate Change: The Role of Information and Perceived Risk', *Centre for European Economic Research*, MPRA Paper No. 26569, (2010). 1–3.

88 United Nations Framework Convention on Climate Change. New York, 9 May 1992, in force 21 March 1994, 31 International Legal Materials (1992), 849 (1992). (Hereinafter UNFCCC or Climate Convention.) It was adopted on the 9th of May 1992 and opened for signature a month later in Rio de Janeiro during and as part of the UNCED, it remained open for signature at the United Nations Headquarters in New York until June 1993. It entered into force on the 21st of March 1994, in accordance with its article 23, that is, on the ninetieth day after the date of deposit of the fiftieth instrument of ratification, acceptance, approval or accession. Available at: http://unfccc.int/essential_background/convention/items/2627.php

89 UNFCCC, Article 4.1(c) states that all the parties shall '*Promote and cooperate in the development, application and diffusion, including transfer, of technologies, practices and processes that control, reduce or prevent anthropogenic emissions of greenhouse gases not controlled by the Montreal Protocol in all relevant sectors, including the energy, transport, industry, agriculture, forestry and waste management sectors*'.

90 F. Yamin and J. Depledge, *The International Climate Change Regime: A Guide to Rules, Institutions and Procedures.* (2004). 83.

91 INC-UNFCCC, Intergovernmental Negotiating Committee for a Framework Convention on Climate Change, Matters Relating to Commitments. Methodologies for Calculations/Inventories of Emissions and Removals of Greenhouse Gases. Note by the Secretariat (UN Doc. A/AC.237/34, 15 July 1993) (1993).

92 Kyoto Protocol to the United Nations Framework Convention on Climate Change, Kyoto, 10 December 1997, in force 16 February 2005, 37 International Legal Materials (1998). 2303 UNTS 148. (1997).

93 F. Yamin and J. Depledge, *The International Climate Change Regime: A Guide to Rules, Institutions and Procedures.* (2004). 85–89.

94 This will be explained in Chapter 3 in relation of the ICAO regime and the IMO regime.

95 UN, Report of the Secretary-General's High-level Advisory Group on Climate Change Financing. Work Stream 2: Paper on Potential Revenues from International Maritime and Aviation Sector Policy Measures, (2010). Support from the World Bank and The International Monetary Fund followed, Michael Keen et al., 'Market-Based Instruments for International Aviation and Shipping as a Source of Climate Finance. Policy Research Working Paper 5950', *The World Bank & International Monetary Fund*, (2012).

96 E. Haites et al., 'Possible Elements of a 2015 Legal Agreement on Climate Change', Working Paper No. 16/13, IDDRI, (2013).

97 Paris Agreement.

98 See chapter 3 and 7.

99 The IMO is a specialized agency of the United Nations, created in 1948 to promote the safety and security of shipping and the prevention of marine pollution by ships. See Chapter 3.

100 ICAO is a specialized agency of the United Nations created in 1944 to promote the safe and orderly development of international civil aviation throughout the world. See further Chapter 3.

101 Only recently, in October 2016, ICAO has agreed on a global MBM: the Carbon Offsetting and Reduction Scheme for International Aviation (CORSIA). However the pilot phase of the mechanism starts in 2021 and the scheme will only be mandatory from 2027. So, to date, no 'meaningful measure' is in place.

102 These usually involve operational and technologic measures, shifting to lower CO_2 fuels and MBMs.

103 The usual division of countries' preferences within these organization's policy settings haven't necessarily obeyed the divisions created with regard to climate change issues, where the principle of CBDR is invoked to play a major role.

104 Decision 2/CP.15, The Copenhagen Accord, UN Doc. FCCC/CP/2009/7/Add.1, 30 March 2010, (2009). The political agreement stated was '*to reduce global emissions so as to hold the increase in global temperature below 2 degrees Celsius*'. For a summary on the development of the 2°C target, see Samuel Randalls, 'History of the 2°C Climate Target', *Wiley Interdisciplinary Reviews: Climate Change*, 1(4), (2010). 598–605.

105 See D.S. Lee et al., (2013). The United Nations Environment Programme (UNEP) has produced three reports charting progress on pledged emissions reductions by nations and whether there is an 'emissions gap' between the pledges and the shorter-term emission pathway in terms of what is required to reduce the CO_2 emissions (UNEP, 2010; 2011; 2012). The UNEP reports have identified a projected 'emissions gap' of 8 to 13 Gtonnes CO_2-e1 between that required and that projected in 2020, and that this gap is increasing (UNEP, 2012).

106 D. Bodansky, 'Multilateral Climate Efforts beyond the UNFCCC'. (2011). For a general insight on sectoral agreements see Daniel Bodansky, 'International Sectoral Agreements in a Post-2012 Climate Framework', Working Paper Prepared for the Pew Center on Global Climate Change, (2007).

107 Directive 2008/101/EC amending Directive 2003/87/EC so as to include aviation activities in the scheme for greenhouse gas emission allowance trading within the Community.

108 Directive 2003/87/EC establishing a scheme for greenhouse gas emission allowance trading within the community and amending Council Directive 96/61/EC.

109 J. Scott and L. Rajamani, (2012). Benito Müller, 'From Confrontation to Collaboration? CBDR and the EU ETS Aviation Dispute with Developing Countries', *Oxford Energy and Environmental Brief*, (2012).

110 'China Halts 10 More Airbus Orders in EU Row: Sources', Reuters (15 March 2012). Available at: www.reuters.com/article/2012/03/15/us-china-europe-ets-idUSBRE82E0P820120315

111 194th ICAO Council Session. Subject No. 50: Questions related to the environment: Inclusion of the international Civil Aviation in the EU ETS and its impacts. Appendix: Joint Declaration. C-WP/13790 (2011).

112 Case C-366/10.

113 European Union Emissions Trading Scheme Prohibition Act of 2011, S. 1956, 112th Cong. §§ 2–4 (2012). Available at: www.gpo.gov/fdsys/pkg/BILLS-112s1956enr/pdf/BILLS-112s1956enr.pdf

114 See, Jing Men, 'Climate Change and EU-China Partnership: Realist Disguise or Institutionalist Blessing?', *Asia Europe Journal*, 12(1–2), (2014). 56–59.

115 Decision 377/2013/EU of 24 April 2013 derogating temporarily from Directive 2003/87/EC establishing a scheme for greenhouse gas emission allowance trading within the Community. OJ L 113 25.4.2013. The moratorium on the application of the aviation directive for non-European countries until 1st January 2014 shifted the attention towards the international level.

116 See, A. Vihma and H.v. Asselt, (2014).

117 COM(2013) 722. Proposal for a Directive of the European Parliament and of the Council Amending Directive 2003/87/EC Establishing a Scheme for Greenhouse Gas Emission Allowance Trading within the Community.

118 Ibid. at. Art. 28a (7).

119 Regulation No 421/2014 of the European Parliament and of the Council of 16 April 2014 amending Directive 2003/87/EC establishing a scheme for greenhouse gas emission allowance trading within the Community, in view of the implementation by 2020 of an international agreement applying a single global market-based measure to international aviation emissions, (2014).

120 Ibid. at. New art. 28a (8).

121 ICAO, Assembly Resolution A39–3: Consolidated statement of continuing ICAO policies and practices related to environmental protection – Global Market-based Measure (MBM) scheme (2016).

122 Decision No. 406/2009/EC of the European Parliament and of the Council of 23 April 2009 on the effort of member States to Reduce their Greenhouse Gas Emissions to Meet the Community's Greenhouse Gas Emission Reduction Commitments up to 2020, (2009). Recital 2. A very similar text is found in Directive 2009/29/EC amending Directive 2003/87/EC so as to improve and extend the greenhouse gas emission allowance trading scheme of the Community, (2009). Recital 3.

123 COM(2013) 480 final. Proposal for a Regulation of the European Parliament and of the Council on the Monitoring, Reporting and Verification of Carbon Dioxide Emissions from Maritime Transport and Amending Regulation (EU) No. 525/2013 (2013). The proposal aims to establish a legal framework for collecting and publishing verified annual data on CO_2 emissions from 5000 gross tonnes that visit EU ports, irrespective of where the ships are registered. It is expected that by putting the system in place, CO_2 emissions from the journeys covered will be cut by up to 2% compared with a business-as-usual scenario and lead owners to save up to €1.2 billion per year in 2030. See, http://ec.europa.eu/clima/policies/transport/shipping/index_en.htm

124 COM(2013) 479 final. Communication from the Commission to the European Parliament, the Council and the European Economic and Social Committee and the Committee of the Regions. Integrating Maritime Transport Emissions in the EU's Greenhouse Gas Reduction Policies, (2013).
125 Regulation 2015/757/EU of 29 April 2015 on the Monitoring, Reporting and Verification of Carbon Dioxide Emissions from Maritime Transport, and Amending Directive 2009/16/EC, [2015] L123/55.
126 IMO, 'Organization Agrees Mandatory System for Collecting Ships' Fuel Consumption Data', IMO Briefing (22 April 2016). Available at: www.imo.org/en/MediaCentre/PressBriefings/Pages/11-data-collection-.aspx
127 'EU Environment Committee Makes Waves with Call to Include Shipping into Emissions Trading Scheme', *World Maritime News* 2016. Available at: http://world-maritimenews.com/archives/208708/eu-environment-committee-makes-waves-with-call-to-include-shipping-into-emissions-trading-scheme/

Bibliography

Abeyratne, Ruwantissa (2011). *Aviation and the Carbon Trade*, New York, Nova Science Publishers.

Alvarez, José E. (2005). *International Organizations as Law-Makers*, Oxford, UK; New York, Oxford University Press.

Asselt, Harro van (2007). 'Dealing with the Fragmentation of Global Climate Governance: Legal and Political Approaches in Interplay Management', Global Governance Working Paper No. 30.

Asselt, Harro van (2011). 'Legal and Political Approaches in Interplay Management: Dealling with the Fragmentation of Global Climate Governance', in, Sebastian Oberthür and Olav Schram Stokke (eds.), *Managing Institutional Complexity: Regime Interplay and Global Environmental Change: Institutional Dimensions of Global Environmental Change*, Cambridge, MA, MIT Press.

Asselt, Harro van (2013). 'Managing the Fragmentation of International Climate Law', in, Erkki J. Hollo, Kati Kulovesi and Michael Mehling (eds.), Ius Gentium: Comparative Perspective on Law and Justice v. 21 *Climate Change and the Law*, Dordrecht; New York, Springer.

Asselt, Harro van (2014). 'Alongside the UNFCCC: Complementary Venues for Climate Action', Centre for Climate and Energy Solutions.

Asselt, Harro van (2014). *The Fragmentation of Global Climate Governance: Consequences and Management of Regime Interactions*, Cheltenham, UK, Edward Elgar.

Asselt, Harro van, Sindico, Francesco and Mehling, Michael A. (2008). 'Global Climate Change and the Fragmentation of International Law', *Law and Policy*, 30(4), 423–449.

Asselt, Harro van and Zelli, Fariborz (2012). 'Connect the Dots: Managing the Fragmentation of Global Climate Governance Earth System', Governance Working Paper No. 25. Lund and Amsterdam: Earth System Governance Project.

Assembly Resolution A39–3: Consolidated Statement of Continuing ICAO Policies and Practices Related to Environmental Protection: Global Market-Based Measure (MBM) Scheme.

Barker, T., Bashmakov, I., Bernstein, L., Bogner, J.E., Bosch, P.R., Dave, R., Davidson, O.R., Fisher, B.S., Gupta, S., Halsnæs, K., Heij, G.J., Kahn Ribeiro, S., Kobayashi, S., Levine, M.D., Martino, D.L., Masera, O., Metz, B., Meyer, L.A., Nabuurs, G.-J., Najam, A., Nakicenovic, N., Rogner, H.-H., Roy, J., Sathaye, J., Schock, R., Shukla, P., Sims, R.E.H., Smith, P., Tirpak, D.A., Urge-Vorsatz, D., Zhou, D. and Intergovernmental

Panel on Climate Change, Working Group III (2007). 'Technical Summary', in, O.R. Davidson, B. Metz, P.R. Bosch, R. Dave and L.A. Meyer (eds.), *Climate Change 2007: Mitigation of Climate Change: Contribution of Working Group III to the Fourth Assessment Report of the Intergovernmental Panel on Climate Change*, Cambridge, England, UK; New York, Cambridge University Press.

Blobel, Daniel, Meyer-Ohlendorf, Nils, Schlosser-Allera, Carmen and Steel, Penny (2006). *United Nations Framework Convention on Climate Change: Handbook*, Bonn., Germany, Intergovernmental and Legal Affairs, Climate Change Secretariat.

Bodansky, Daniel (2007). 'International Sectoral Agreements in a Post-2012 Climate Framework', Working Paper Prepared for the Pew Center on Global Climate Change.

Bodansky, Daniel (2010). *The Art and Craft of International Environmental Law*, Cambridge, MA, Harvard University Press.

Bodansky, Daniel (2011). 'Multilateral Climate Efforts beyond the UNFCCC', Centre for Climate and Energy Solutions.

Bogojević, Sanja (2012). 'Legalising Environmental Leadership: A Comment on the CJEU'S Ruling in C-366/10 on the Inclusion of Aviation in the EU Emissions Trading Scheme', *Journal of Environmental Law*, 24(2), 345–356.

Bows-Larkin, Alice (2015). 'All Adrift: Aviation, Shipping, and Climate Change Policy', *Climate Policy*, 15(6), 681–702.

Boyle, Alan E. and Chinkin, Christine M. (2007). *The Making of International Law*, Oxford; New York, Oxford University Press.

Brack, Duncan, Grubb, Michael and Windram, Craig (2000). *International Trade and Climate Change Policies*, London, Earthscan.

Buhaug, Øyvind, Corbett, James J., Eyring, Veronika Endresen, Øyvind, Faber, Jasper, Hanayama, Shinichi, Lee, David S., Lee, Donchool, Lindstad, Håkon, Markowska, Agnieszka Z. Mjelde, Alvar, Nelissen, Dagmar, Nilsen, Jørgen, Pålsson, Christopher, Wanquing, Wu, Winebrake, James J., and Yoshida, Koichi. (2009). *Second IMO Greenhouse Gas Study 2009: Executive Summary*, London, UK, IMO.

Cames, Martin, Graichen, Jakob, Siemons, Anne and Cook, Vanessa (2015). *Emission Reduction Targets for International Aviation and Shipping*; Brussels, Belgium, European Parliament Committee on Environment, Public Health and Food Safety. Available at http://www.europarl.europa.eu/studies

Caron, David D. (2013). 'Climate Change and the Oceans', in, Harry N. Scheiber and Jin-Hyun Paik (eds.), *Regions, Institutions, and Law of the Sea Regions, Institutions*, and *Law of the Sea: Studies in Ocean Governance*; Leiden, The Netherlands, Martinus Nijhoff Publishers.

COM (2013) 479 final. Communication from the Commission to the European Parliament, the Council and the European Economic and Social Committee and the Committee of the Regions. Integrating Maritime Transport Emissions in the EU's Greenhouse Gas Reduction Policies.

COM (2013) 480 final. Proposal for a Regulation of the European Parliament and of the Council on the Monitoring, Reporting and Verification of Carbon Dioxide Emissions from Maritime Transport and Amending Regulation (EU) No. 525/2013.

COM (2013) 722. Proposal for a Directive of the European Parliament and of the Council Amending Directive 2003/87/EC Establishing a Scheme for Greenhouse Gas Emission Allowance Trading within the Community.

Decision 2/CP.15, The Copenhagen Accord, UN Doc. FCCC/CP/2009/7/Add.1, 30 March 2010.

Decision No. 406/2009/EC of the European Parliament and of the Council of 23 April 2009 on the effort of Member States to Reduce their Greenhouse Gas Emissions to

Meet the Community's Greenhouse Gas Emission Reduction Commitments up to 2020.

Directive 2009/29/EC Amending Directive 2003/87/EC So as to Improve and Extend the Greenhouse Gas Emission Allowance Trading Scheme of the Community.

Dupuy, Pierre-Marie (1999). 'The Danger of Fragmentation or Unification of the International Legal System and the International Court of Justice', New York University Journal of International Law and Politics., 31, 791.

Fahey, David W. and Lee, David S. (2016). 'Aviation and the Impacts of Climate Change Aviation and Climate Change: A Scientific Perspective', *Carbon & Climate Law Review*, 10(2), 97–104.

Field, Barry C. and Field, Martha K. (2002). *Environmental Economics: An Introduction*, 3rd ed., New York, McGraw-Hill; Irwin.

Glossary of Environment Statistics (1997). Studies in Methods, Series F, No. 67, New York, United Nations.

Gupta, Joyeeta and Lebel, Louis (2010). 'Access and Allocation in Earth System Governance: Water and Climate Change Compared', *International Environmental Agreements: Politics, Law and Economics*, 10(4), 377–395.

Hackmann, Bernd (2012). 'Analysis of the Governance Architecture to Regulate GHG Emissions from International Shipping', *International Environmental Agreements*, 12, 85–103.

Haites, E., Yamin, F. and Höhne, N. (2013). 'Possible Elements of a 2015 Legal Agreement on Climate Change', Working Paper No. 16/13, IDDRI.

Hartmann, Jacques (2013). 'A Battle for the Skies: Applying the European Emissions Trading System to International Aviation', *Nordic Journal of International Law*, 82(2), 187.

ICAO (2007). *ICAO Environmental Report 2007*, Montreal, ICAO.

IEA (2012). CO_2 *Emissions from Fuel Combustion: Highlights*, Luxembourg, IEA.

ILC (2006). *Fragmentation of International Law: Difficulties Arising from the Diversification and Expansion of International Law. Report of the Study Group of the International Law Commission.* UN Doc. A/CN.4/L.682.

IMO (2000). *Study of Greenhouse Gas Emissions from Ships*, London, UK, IMO.

IMO. 'Organization Agrees Mandatory System for Collecting Ships' Fuel Consumption Data', IMO Briefing (22 April 2016).

Intergovernmental Negotiating Committee for a Framework Convention on Climate Change, Matters Relating to Commitments. Methodologies for Calculations/Inventories of Emissions and Removals of Greenhouse Gases. Note by the Secretariat (UN Doc. A/AC.237/34, 15 July 1993).

IPCC (2006). *2006 IPCC Guidelines for National Greenhouse Gas Inventories*, Prepared by the National Greenhouse Gas Inventories Programme, Eggleston, H.S., Buendia, L., Miwa, K., Ngara, T. and Tanabe, K. (eds), Japan, IGES.

IPCC (2007). *Climate Change 2007: Synthesis Report: Contribution of Working Groups I, II and III to the Fourth Assessment Report of the Intergovernmental Panel on Climate Change*, Cambridge, Cambridge University Press.

IPCC 2013 (2013). 'Summary for Policymakers', in, T.F. Stocker, D. Qin, G.-K. Plattner, M. Tignor, S.K. Allen, J. Boschung, A. Nauels, Y. Xia, V. Bex and P.M. Midgley (eds.), *Climate Change 2013: The Physical Science Basis: Contribution of Working Group I to the Fifth Assessment Report of the Intergovernmental Panel on Climate Change*, Cambridge, UK; New York, Cambridge University Press.

IPCC 2014 (2014). 'Summary for Policymakers', in, O. Edenhofer, R. Pichs-Madruga, Y. Sokona, E. Farahani, S. Kadner, K. Seyboth, A. Adler, I. Baum, S. Brunner, P. Eickemeier, B. Kriemann, J. Savolainen, S. Schlömer, C. von Stechow, T. Zwickel and J.C.

Minx (eds.), *Climate Change 2014, Mitigation of Climate Change: Contribution of Working Group III to the Fifth Assessment Report of the Intergovernmental Panel on Climate Change*, Cambridge, UK; New York, Cambridge University Press.

Kahn Ribeiro, S., Kobayashi, S., Beuthe, M., Gasca, J., Greene, D., Lee, D.S., Muromachi, Y., Newton, P.J., Plotkin, S., Sperling, D., Wit, R. and Zhou, P.J. (2007). 'Transport and Its Infrastructure', in, O.R. Davidson, B. Metz, P.R. Bosch, R. Dave, L.A. Meyer (eds), *Climate Change 2007: Mitigation: Contribution of Working Group III to the Fourth Assessment Report of the Intergovernmental Panel on Climate Change*, Cambridge, UK; New York, Cambridge University Press.

Keen, Michael, Parry, Ian and Strand, Jon (2012). 'Market-Based Instruments for International Aviation and Shipping as a Source of Climate Finance', Policy Research Working Paper 5950, The World Bank & International Monetary Fund.

Kulovesi, Kati (2011). '"Make Your Own Special Song, Even If Nobody Else Sings Along": International Aviation Emissions and the EU Emissions Trading Scheme', *University of Eastern Finland Legal Studies Research Paper No. 1*.

Kulovesi, Kati (2013). 'Climate Change and Trade: At the Intersection of Two International Legal Regimes', in, Erkki J. Hollo, Kati Kulovesi and Michael Mehling (eds.), Ius Gentium: Comparative Perspective on Law and Justice v. 21 *Climate Change and the Law*, Dordrecht; New York, Springer.

Kulovesi, Kati and Keinänen, Katja (2006). 'Long-Term Climate Policy: International Legal Aspects of Sector-Based Approaches', *Climate Policy*, 6(3), 313–325.

Lee, David S., Fahey, David W., Forster, Piers M., Newton, Peter J., Wit, Ron C.N., Lim, Ling L., Owen, Bethan and Sausen, Robert (2009). 'Aviation and Global Climate Change in the 21st Century', *Atmospheric Environment*, 43(22–23), 3520–3537.

Lee, David S., Lim, Ling and Owen, Bethan (2013). 'Shipping and Aviation Emissions in the Context of a 2°C Emission Pathway', Manchester Metropolitan University.

Lee, D.S., Pitari, G., Grewe, V., Gierens, K., Penner, J.E., Petzold, A., Prather, M.J., Schumann, U., Bais, A., Berntsen, T., Iachetti, D., Lim, L.L. and Sausen, R. (2010). 'Transport Impacts on Atmosphere and Climate: Aviation', *Atmospheric Environment*, 44(37), 4678–4734.

Levin, Kelly, Cashore, Benjamin, Bernstein, Steven and Auld, Graeme (2007). 'Playing It Forward: Path Dependency, Progressive Incrementalism, and the "Super Wicked" Problem of Global Climate Change'. International Studies Association 48th Annual Convention, February 28.

McCollum, David, Gould, Gregory and Greene, David (2009). 'Greenhouse Gas Emissions from Aviation and Marine Transportation: Mitigation Potential and Policies', *Pew Center on Global Climate Change*.

Macintosh, Andrew and Wallace, Lailey (2009). 'International Aviation Emissions to 2025: Can Emissions Be Stabilised without Restricting Demand?', *Energy Policy*, 37(1), 264–273.

McManners, Peter J. (2012). *Fly and Be Damned: What Now for Aviation and Climate Change?*, London; New York, Zed Books.

Mattoo, Aaditya, Stern, Robert M. and Zanini, Gianni (2008). *A Handbook of International Trade in Services*, Oxford; New York, Oxford University Press.

Men, Jing (2014). 'Climate Change and EU-China Partnership: Realist Disguise or Institutionalist Blessing?', *Asia Europe Journal*, 12(1–2), 49–62.

Moncel, Remi and Asselt, Harro van (2012). 'All Hands on Deck! Mobilizing Climate Change Action beyond the UNFCCC', *Review of European Community & International Environmental Law: RECIEL*, 21(3), 163–176.

Mueller, B. (2012). 'From Confrontation to Collaboration?: CBDR and the EU ETS Aviation Dispute with Developing Countries', *Environmental Liability*, 19(6), 199–214.

Müller, Benito (2012). 'From Confrontation to Collaboration?: CBDR and the EU ETS Aviation Dispute with Developing Countries', *Oxford Energy and Environmental Brief*.

Oberthür, Sebastian (2003). 'Institutional Interaction to Address Greenhouse Gas Emissions from International Transport: ICAO, IMO and the EU Burden-Sharing Agreement', *Project Deliverable No. D 3, Final Draft. Ecologic: Institute for International and European Policy*.

Oberthür, Sebastian (2003). 'Institutional Interaction to Address Greenhouse Gas Emissions from International Transport: ICAO, IMO and the Kyoto Protocol', *Climate Policy*, 3(3), 191–205.

Oberthür, Sebastian (2006). 'Interactions of the Climate Change Regime with ICAO, IMO and the EU Burden-Sharing Agreement', in, Sebastian Oberthür and Thomas Gehring (eds.), *Institutional Interaction in Global Environmental Governance: Synergy and Conflict among International and EU Policies*, 2006 ed., Cambridge, MIT Press.

OECD (2010). *Globalization, Transport and the Environment*, Paris, OECD Publishing.

Okur, Aydin (2012). 'The Challenge of Regulating Greenhouse Gas Emissions from Internaional Shipping and the Complicated Principle of 'Common But Differentiated Responsibilities' ', *Dokuz Eylül Üniversitesi Hukuk Fakültesi Dergisi*, 13(1), 27–49.

Olsthoorn, Xander (2001). 'Carbon Dioxide Emissions from International Aviation: 1950–2050', *Journal of Air Transport Management*, 7(2), 87–93.

Osberghaus, D., Finkel, E. and Pohl, M. (2010). 'Individual Adaptation to Climate Change: The Role of Information and Perceived Risk', *Centre for European Economic Research*, MPRA Paper No. 26569.

Owen, Bethan, Lee, David S. and Lim, Ling (2010). 'Flying into the Future: Aviation Emissions Scenarios to 2050', *Environmental Science & Technology*, 44(7), 2255–2260.

Paris Agreement (Paris, 12 December 2015, in force 4 November 2016) FCCC/CP/2015/L.9.

Penner, Joyce E., Intergovernmental Panel on Climate Change, Working Group I. and Intergovernmental Panel on Climate Change, Working Group III. (1999). *Aviation and the Global Atmosphere: A Special Report of IPCC Working Groups I and III in Collaboration with the Scientific Assessment Panel to the Montreal Protocol on Substances That Deplete the Ozone Layer*, Cambridge, Cambridge University Press.

Perez Rodriguez, Daniel (2012). 'The Inclusion of Shipping in the EU Emissions Trading Scheme: A Legal Analysis in the Light of Public International Law', *Revista Catalana de Dret Ambiental*, 3(2), 1.

Pisani, Christian (2002). 'Fair at Sea: The Design of a Future Legal Instrument on Marine Bunker Fules Emissions within the Climate Change Regime', *Ocean Development and Internaional Law*, 33, 57–76.

Prost, Mario and Clark, Paul Kingsley (2006). 'Unity, Diversity and the Fragmentation of International Law: How Much Does the Multiplication of International Organizations Really Matter?', *Chinese Journal of International Law*, 5(2), 341–370.

Randalls, Samuel (2010). 'History of the 2°C Climate Target', *Wiley Interdisciplinary Reviews: Climate Change*, 1(4), 598–605.

Rayner, Tim and Jordan, Andrew (2010). 'Adapting to a Changing Climate: An Emerging European Union Policy', in, Andrew Jordan, Dave Huitema, Harro van Asselt, Tim Rayner and Frans Berkhout (eds.), *Climate Change Policy in the European Union: Confronting the Dilemmas of Mitigation and Adaptation?*, Cambridge, Cambridge University Press.

Regulation 2015/757/EU of 29 April 2015 on the Monitoring, Reporting and Verification of Carbon Dioxide Emissions from Maritime Transport, and Amending Directive 2009/16/EC, [2015] L123/55.

Regulation No. 421/2014 of the European Parliament and of the Council of 16 April 2014 Amending Directive 2003/87/EC Establishing a Scheme for Greenhouse Gas Emission Allowance Trading within the Community, in View of the Implementation by 2020 of an International Agreement Applying a Single Global Market-Based Measure to International Aviation Emissions.

Report of the Third Intersessional Meeting of the Working Group on Greenhouse Gas Emissions from Ships. Note by the Secretariat. MEPC 62/5/1 (8 April 2011).

Ringbom, Henrik (2011). 'An EU Emission Trading Scheme for Shipping? International Law Challenges', in, Henrik Rak and Peter Wetterstein (ed.), *Environmental Liabilities in Ports and Coastal Areas: Focus on Public Authorities and Other Actors*, Papers from a Seminar, 11–14 August 2010, Korpoström, Finland, Åbo Akademi University.

Scott, Joanne (2014). 'Extraterritoriality and Territorial Extension in EU Law', *American Journal of Comparative Law*, 62(1), 87–126.

Scott, Joanne (2014). 'The New EU "Extraterritoriality"', *Common Market Law Review*, 51(5), 1343–1380.

Scott, Joanne and Rajamani, Lavanya (2012). 'EU Climate Change Unilateralism', *European Journal of International Law*, 23(2), 2012, 469–494.

Sims R., Schaeffer, R., Creutzig, F., Cruz-Núñez, X., D'Agosto, M., Dimitriu, D., Figueroa Meza, M. J., Fulton, L., Kobayashi, S., Lah, O., McKinnon, A., Newman, P., Ouyang, M., Schauer, J. J., Sperling, D., and Tiwari, G. (2014). 'Transport', in, O. Edenhofer, R. Pichs-Madruga, Y. Sokona, E. Farahani, S. Kadner, K. Seyboth, A. Adler, I. Baum, S. Brunner, P. Eickemeier, B. Kriemann, J. Savolainen, S. Schlömer, C. von Stechow, T. Zwickel and J.C. Minx (eds.)., *Climate Change 2014: Mitigation of Climate Change: Contribution of Working Group III to the Fifth Assessment Report of the Intergovernmental Panel on Climate Change*, Cambridge, United Kingdom and New York, Cambridge University Press.

Smith, T.W.P., Jalkanen, J. P., Anderson, B. A., Corbett, J. J., Faber, J., Hanayama, S., O'Keeffe, E., Parker, S., Johansson, L., Aldous, L., Raucci, C., Traut, M., Ettinger, S., Nelissen, D., Lee, D. S., Ng, S., Agrawal, A., Winebrake, J. J., Hoen, M.; Chesworth, S. and Pandey, A. (2014). *Third IMO Greenhouse Gas Study 2014: Executive Summary and Final Report*, London, International Maritime Organization.

Spyrou, Andrew G. (2010). *Global Climate Change and the Shipping Industry*, Bloomington, Iuniverse.

Statement on behalf of the Chairman of IPCC, Dr. Robert Watson, delivered by Dr. Bert Metz Co-chair. Seventh Conference of Parties to the United Nations Framework Convention on Climate Change, Marrakech, Morocco, November 7.

Stern, Nicholas (2007). *The Economics of Climate Change: The Stern Review: Executive Summary*, Cambridge, UK.

Trebilcock, M.J. and Howse, Robert (2005). *The Regulation of International Trade*, 3rd ed., London; New York, Routledge.

Truxal, Steven (2010). 'At the Sidelines of Implementing the EU ETS: Objections to "Validity"', *International Trade Law and Regulation*, 16(4), 28–36.

UN (2010). Report of the Secretary-General's High-Level Advisory Group on Climate Change Financing. Work Stream 2: Paper on Potential Revenues from International Maritime and Aviation Sector Policy Measures.

UNEP (2012). *The Emissions Gap Report 2012*, Nairobi, UNEP.

UNEP (2013). *The Emissions Gap Report 2013*, Nairobi, UNEP.

UNEP (2014). *The Emissions Gap Report 2014*, Nairobi, UNEP.

UNEP (2015). *The Emissions Gap Report 2015*, Nairobi, UNEP.

Vihma, Antto and Asselt, Harro van (2014). 'The Conflict over Aviation Emissions: A Case of Retreating EU Leadership?', *FIIA Briefing Paper 150*.

Voigt, Christina (2011). 'Up in the Air: Aviation, the EU Emissions Trading Scheme and the Question of Jurisdiction', *Cambridge Yearbook of European Legal Studies*, 14(1), 475–506.

Wijnolst, N., Wergeland, Tor and Levander, Kai (2009). *Shipping Innovation*, Amsterdam, IOS Press.

World Meteorological Organization & United Nations Environment Programme (2004). *Aviation and the Global Amospheric Environment*, Geneva, WMO and UNEP.

Yamin, Farhana and Depledge, Joanna (2004). *The International Climate Change Regime: A Guide to Rules, Institutions and Procedures*, Cambridge, UK; New York, Cambridge University Press.

Young, Margaret A. (2011). 'Climate Change Law and Regime Interaction', *Climate Change Law Review*, 2, 147–157.

Young, Margaret A. (2012). *Regime Interaction in International Law: Facing Fragmentation*, Cambridge; New York, Cambridge University Press.

Zelli, Fariborz (2011). 'The Fragmentation of the Global Climate Governance Architecture', *Wiley Interdisciplinary Reviews: Climate Change*, 2(2), 255.

2 Analytical framework, key concepts and methodology

> The fragmentation of the international social world has attained legal significance especially as it has been accompanied by the emergence of specialized and (relatively) autonomous rules or rule-complexes, legal institutions and spheres of legal practice. What once appeared to be governed by 'general international law' has become the field of operation for such specialist systems [. . .] each of them possessing their own principles and institutions. The problem, as lawyers have seen it, is that specialised law-making and institution building tends to take place with relative ignorance of legislative and institutional activities in the adjoining fields and of the general principles and practices of international law.[1]

This chapter sets out the analytical framework that will be applied in subsequent chapters, as well as the research methodology. It includes the definition of several basic concepts that inform the analytical framework, such as what international law and its sources are, and on the main elements of law-making processes. This comprises section one. Sections two and three focus on the theory of fragmentation and regime interaction in international law, the main features of which are briefly explained here and developed in subsequent chapters.

Law, sources of law and law-making in international law

While not wishing to pursue a detailed discussion on the 'essences of law',[2] this chapter shall, at least, start by briefly defining some conceptual issues, specifically with regard to what law and international law-making processes are considered to be for this study. International law can be defined as '*the framework within which international cooperation takes place*'.[3] However, as Daniel Bodansky has noted, the general weakness of enforcement mechanisms in international law can make it difficult to distinguish international law from international politics (and even morality). This issue is especially acute in international environmental law,[4] since environmental problems, such as climate change, are also prone to soft regulatory approaches.[5]

A traditional method to define international law is to delimit its sources.[6] In this connection, a norm would qualify as law '*if (and only if) it was created through a recognized law making process*'.[7] Legal scholars turn to the competence of the

International Court of Justice (ICJ), stated in its Statute[8] to establish the sources of international law. In particular, article 38(1) contains the list of sources available for the court to apply when settling disputes. Such sources are: international treaties,[9] international customs,[10] the general principles of law recognized by civilized nations[11] and, subsidiary to this, judicial decisions[12] and the teachings of the most highly qualified publicists of the various nations.[13] Also, the second part of article 38 confers the ICJ with the power, if the parties so agree, to decide a case *ex aequo et bono*, that is, what is right, fair or equitable regardless of the law.[14] Two main lacunae of article 38 have been highlighted in the literature,[15] namely, lack of any mention to secondary law, and unilateral declarations committing states.[16] This list of sources for Article 38 has been increased by the International Law Commission (ILC) by adding two more sources to it, namely: binding decisions of international organizations and the judgements of international courts and tribunals.[17]

With regards to international institutional law, the binding norms emerging from international organizations can be fitted in the traditional sources of article 38, but not most of the work produced by them. This is the case of hortatory recommendations, even when they produce legal effects, because '*the limited conception of what constitutes international law tends to obscure them.*'[18]

It has been argued that the recourse to article 38(1) is used almost like a 'mantra'[19] that allows international lawyers to sidestep or postpone complex debates and discussions on the function, legitimacies, claims of justice and the politics of the sources of international law: '*The formal nature of article 38(1) obscures the fact that international law is generated by a multi-layered process of interactions, instruments, pressures and principles.*'[20] Despite that, this study takes Article 38 as a starting point, considering that it provides a necessary basis to build upon. However, the increasing relevance of 'soft law'[21] in international law in general, and in the environmental field in particular,[22] has become a strand of the traditional sources listed above,[23] and therefore this book will also fully consider them. As it has been argued, '*law consists on those things that states – or others – actually live up to*'.[24]

Under the term soft law, it is possible to include an assortment of instruments '*that have legal implications but which do not have the imagined "hardness" of binding international obligation*'.[25] However, '*a substantial part of "soft" law today, in an impressionistic way, describes part of the "hard" law of tomorrow.*'[26] Still, 'soft law' not only has a role as part of the multilateral treaty-making process, but is also an alternative to law-making by treaty.[27] Resolutions, declarations, statements, voluntary codes of conduct and other legal documents that don't have the required legal character to be 'hard law' are included in the category of soft law considered in this study.[28]

Binding force, as a differentiator between categories of norms, has its *raison d'être* in the principle of state consent, as a necessary requirement for the States to be obliged by the law. However, on the one hand, States may be obliged by norms they haven't agreed to either through 'tacit consent' or customary law, and on the other hand, State consent is not the only criteria in international law, when thinking about the function of law. In this regard, other values act as an increasingly important counterweight[29] to state consent, because of the expanding role of international organizations in the law-making processes. Additionally, in the specific case of technocratic institutions, '*the distinction between non-binding and binding is not so clear*'.[30] The presence of 'soft law' in international law-making presents a challenge for traditional means '*to describe and explain both the creation and the legal authority of international norms*'.[31] Whether comprised by 'hard' or 'soft' law, a body of international law has emerged without a central legislative authority, which has led to fragmented law-making functions.[32]

Although international law-making processes takes place through binding treaties and norms, there is also an increasing relevance of development of the law through soft-law and other non-binding instruments. However, the problem of such soft-law and non-binding instruments rests on determining whether conflicts among them can fall under the scope of international law.[33] A broad understanding of international law-making refers not only to the specific normative activities of the international community, aimed at establishing legally binding rules of conduct, but also to the operation of various social, economic and political processes and factors that ultimately determine the content of the law.[34]

To explore the making of international law in the IMO, ICAO and Climate regimes, which is the content of Chapter 3, the book follows the framework proposed by Boyle and Chinkin,[35] which provides an understanding of how international law is made.[36] The main elements of the framework (actors, instruments and processes) are explained below.

Actors

International law is the product of State-driven actions and agreements and of abstract values shared by the international community.[37] However it is States that have traditionally had the greatest role in international law-making. In the exercise of their sovereignty,[38] States can consent to enter into international agreements that restrict their actions, for multiple reasons. The power to conclude treaties is inherent to certain positions such as heads of State and foreign ministers,[39] but State consent may require domestic processes of ratification. In their relations with others, States must conduct themselves according to the principle of cooperation among States, which is the basis and essence of international law.[40] However, the concept of legitimacy in international law has evolved and the relevance of State consent in law-making has lost ground, giving space to other participants in the law-making process.[41]

International organizations form a second group of actors in international law-making that is taking an expanding role in the development of international law.[42] There are three elements that define the existence of international organizations, namely: an international agreement that established them, a capability to act independently from its member States and their subjection to international law.[43] Under the rubric of international organizations, different types of units can be found from global institutions (i.e. UN-based bodies and organizations, including specialized agencies); regional organizations such as the Organisation for Economic Co-operation and Development (OECD); bilateral organizations; and international financial institutions, such as the World Bank or the Global Environmental Facility (GEF).[44]

Once created by States, through international agreements to address different concerns, usually to enhance cooperation on a given issue area, international organizations enjoy legal personality and the freedom to act independently within their mandate and conferred powers.[45] However, with a few exceptions,[46] membership of those organizations is the exclusive domain of States. Also, the weight and position of States differs between organizations and is often linked to their economic or political power in the given issue area of the organization. International organizations usually share the same three-body structure, namely: a plenary body that meets infrequently to debate policy lines, a more permanent organ of reduced membership with some executive powers and a secretariat made of international civil servants.[47] These organizations are also likely to create sub-organs, such as subsidiary bodies, committees or expert groups.[48] Indeed the composition of these groups influence the outcomes, in other words, '*there are several ways in which the relationship between organizations and their members colours the law of international organizations.*'[49] Another crucial issue when approaching the law-making process at international organizations is the voting system: from unanimity to majority or weighted voting. Changing trends have been observed in connection to voting at international organizations, for example, the departure from unanimity when casting votes and the move towards operating by consensus.[50]

The increasing role of individuals, corporations and other organizations not only as subjects and beneficiaries, but also as actors, has been acknowledged as a trend in international law that emerged during the 20th century.[51] Such recognisance implies that a mélange of various non-state-based participants occupies a seat at various law-making processes, with an important meaning in terms of legitimacy, since their participation is regarded as the participation of civil society in the process of law creation.[52] These non-state participants include the private sector and public interest organizations (including industry and businesses), knowledge-based networks or epistemic communities and NGOs. These actors have different roles and functions, including informing public debate, observing, participating in and influencing the law-creation process, monitoring implementation and ensuring the enforcement of legal obligations. The role of each actor depends upon its legal personality and the rights and obligations granted by international law; sometimes they enjoy a consultative status within UN institutions.[53]

Processes

In international law, processes refer to the way in which the law is created. Although law can also emerge from judicial decisions, this book mostly focuses on the stage of law-making. Multilateral law-making processes are characterized by diplomatic practices, normally taking place in a UN body, a specialized agency, and international conferences or can be facilitated by treaty bodies within a regime, where there are ongoing matters under negotiation.[54] In these processes, state actors are deemed to be the main players; that is, they act through the institutions. However, States have agreed certain self-imposed limits to their roles by giving international organizations and institutional bodies' powers to decide on specific aspects. This power is both limited to and guarded in their mandates. The law-making powers of international organizations have been expanded and institutions are also involved in '*continuous forms of regulation through the production of formally binding regulations or standards and ostensibly hortatory advisory guides, codes and recommendations*'.[55] This issue raises questions over legitimacy, since sometimes they are permitted to expand their missions beyond what it was originally envisioned in their founding charters. Furthermore, once the ICAO's and IMO's recommendations or standards (for example) are incorporated to parties' domestic legal systems, they acquire legal force.[56]

Law-making processes in a given issue include initiatives, drafting of the text, proposals and the discussion of proposals, voting and consensus decision-making practices, where on many occasions more than one international organization can be involved.[57] In this regard, the term 'informal international law-making'[58] has emerged in the recent literature and is used in opposition to traditional international law-making. These informal law-making processes are characterized not only by leaving aside formalities in traditional processes, but also by widening the range of participants and outcomes.[59]

Instruments

Regarding the nature of the outcomes from international law processes, an account of the nature of 'hard law' and 'soft law' as instruments of international law has been provided earlier in this chapter. It has been acknowledged that although 'international legislation' '*only binds parties who have duly signed the law-making treaty and, where necessary, as it usually is, have ratified it*',[60] most international law comes in softer forms, which can also act as law-making instruments and can interact with other treaties and 'soft law' instruments from different regimes.[61]

The fragmentation of international law

In the words of Margaret Young: '*international law is made up of fragments of normative and institutional activity*.'[62] Although the phenomenon of fragmentation and of conflicts between treaty regimes has already been noted,[63] it was only in 2000 that the ILC[64] included the issue of fragmentation in its work programme, establishing a study group and releasing a report in 2006 under the title: '*Fragmentation of international law: Difficulties arising from the diversification and expansion of international law.*'[65] The study acknowledges that fragmentation of international law derives from two facts, namely: the lack of an international legislative supreme body and the consequent development of the law in separate regimes. Despite the lack of connection between some of the special regimes, no regime exits in isolation from general international law.[66] The increase in the volume of multilateral agreements, and their specialization in the last decades, has motivated research into the study of this phenomenon. Indeed, the specialization of international law emerged from the need to respond to new situations and concerns, where technical and functional expertise is required. These technical, special or self-contained regimes,[67] with either geographical or functional limits, could challenge the coherence of international law. One of the main issues regarding fragmentation is the proliferation of international institutions, a phenomenon that responds, ultimately, to an increasing social complexity.[68]

Fragmentation is not a term exclusive to international law; it also has a tradition in international relations.[69] Although it can refer to different specific issues,[70] this study builds upon the definition of fragmentation as '*the increased specialization and diversification in international institutions, including the overlap of substantive rules and jurisdictions*'.[71] Fragmentation is therefore understood as the situation or state of co-existence of diverse regimes intersecting in a given issue area.[72] This definition implies the demarcation of the term 'regime' and the term 'issue area', which is of particular relevance to this book. A full account of the term 'regime' is provided later.[73] 'Issue area' is understood here as the thematic object, subject or activity of legal and political relevance over which different legal instruments, rules, and jurisdictions converge. In the case of this study the issue area concerns GHG emissions from international aviation and maritime transport. In this space, where different regimes meet, their different objectives, modus operandi, norms, principles and idiosyncrasies lead to tensions. Such tensions are arguably likely to become increasingly frequent in the fragmented landscape of international law.

This book assumes that the nucleus of the international climate regime is the UNFCCC and its KP, as well as other related instruments and outcomes produced by their institutions. It also recognizes that the regulation of climate change happens outside this sphere.[74] It has been pointed out that the laws affecting the regulation of climate change involve other regimes within the environmental realm such as the Montréal Protocol on Substances that Deplete the Ozone Layer or the Convention on Biological Diversity or the Convention to Combat Desertification, but also outside it, such as WTO Law, heritage protection or law of the sea.[75]

With regards to climate change research, Kati Kulovesi has identified two main trends with regards to climate change law and scholarship, namely, '*the realisation*' that climate change happens at different instances and level and the need for analysis of overlaps and influences and the intrinsic '*deformation*' of climate change law through the extensive use of soft law initiatives and the pre-eminence of non-state actors.[76]

Regime interaction

Defining regimes

Although there is a need to understand how varying norms and institutions overlap on issues of global concern, the task of analyzing regime interaction is a risky one for international lawyers.[77] The first conceptual problem comes in defining 'regime' in a legal monograph, since it is not a legal term as such and is used in different disciplines.[78] In proposing a definition, Young has identified[79] four sets of assumptions embedded in the definition of regime offered by the ILC report[80] and other sources of legal literature,[81] which can help to establish the boundaries of the concept. These assumptions relate to four questions: who, what, when and why – that is, of the actors, institutions, states of legal development and emergent practices within the regimes. The concept of regimes is key to determining the analytical scope of this monograph.

First, regarding the actors, who are mostly (though not exclusively) States, but also other participants such as private entities, epistemic communities or communities of professional knowledge. Here, questions regarding state consent and participation are crucial to profiling actors in the regimes. On the second issue, the inclusion of institutions in the concept of regimes, it seems that all concepts of regimes include a certain degree of institutional presence.[82] One of the drawbacks of the ILC study on fragmentation was that the study's mandate did not incorporate the institutional perspective into its analysis of fragmentation. However, when studying regime interaction in climate change governance, an awareness of both institutional and normative interplay can be beneficial.[83] The third issue concerns the stages of legal development and the application of the law. In respect of this, the term 'regime' embraced by this book assumes a broader understanding, including law-creation, implementation and enforcement, as proposed by some authors.[84] The emphasis is placed on the fact that regimes are constituted not only of principles and norms, but are also shaped by decision-making procedures. However, this approach reflects a new analytical trend, since most literature on fragmentation focuses on the post-negotiating stages, especially with regard to the avoidance and resolution of conflicts in pursuit of legal certainty.[85] Jeffrey Dunoff also advocates a new methodology, which embraces the ongoing normative and institutional relations between international regimes in a variety of settings, namely: operational, regulatory and conceptual, not just in connection to litigation.[86] The fourth assumption concerns the question of whether there are system-based or emergent practices, in other words, that certain bodies of norms are emphasized at the expense of disconnecting them from the general international law system.[87]

In summary, and as derived from the above, this study subscribes to the definition of 'regimes' as '*sets of norms, decision-making procedures and organizations coalescing around functional issue-areas and dominated by particular modes of behaviour, assumptions and biases*'.[88] Therefore, the terms 'climate regime', 'ICAO regime' and 'IMO regime' are used throughout the book to allude to both the law (norms) and the institution (organizations and decision-making procedures) level that comprise those entities.[89] These terminologies become useful when considering regime interaction, both regarding how norms influence or clash, and the institutional aspects relevant to interaction.[90] In turn, this definition of regimes can be divided into three categories or levels to facilitate their analysis and systemization, namely: processes, principles and actors.[91]

Defining regime interaction

Regime interaction can be defined as the connections between overlapping regimes where one regime may influence another.[92] *'Regimes are overlapping when their policy goals and regulations prescribed for problem solving intersect within the same issue area.'*[93] The creation of connections between the overlapping regimes occurs in various times and ways, through different objects (both hard law and soft law) and exchanges. As Margaret A. Young expresses it, interaction *'occurs at different stages of a regime's development and application'*.[94] With regards to IBF, although there is potential for interface in the implementation and judicial stage, interactions so far occur mostly in the law-making phase, where existing institutions intermingle in *'the law's formulation and future application'*.[95]

One of the issues of concern around regime interaction is its consequences for sovereignty, as *'whenever and wherever regime interaction occurs, it potentially affects the rights and duties of states.'*[96] Here, issues of asymmetrical membership arise. Some scholars have called for finding a legal basis for interaction, whether in parallel membership, mutual agreement or enclosing in treaties and formal and informal arrangement between and within international organizations, aside from the State, in the development of their functions.[97] In addition, an overall issue takes place: *'regimes are purposeful actors in their own right with independent interest and capabilities'*,[98] which, when applied to Koskenniemi's idea of *'hegemonic regimes'*, are naturally in search of perpetuating themselves by imposing their own vision of the world on others.[99] It is necessary, therefore, to pay attention to these connections, exchanges and influences, which need to be identified and analyzed in the light of this political struggle.

As Gehring and Oberthür point out on various occasions,[100] the disaggregation of regime interaction in cases become especially relevant in situations where *'influence runs back and forth'*.[101] This is often the juncture, when the interaction occurs simultaneously in different ways and directions or involves more than two institutions, but also if regimes are involved in a process of co-evolution. Relations between the climate regime, ICAO and IMO have followed some of these patterns of complex interaction. Therefore this monograph explores the interaction between these regimes by breaking them into more manageable components.[102]

According to the framework proposed by Oberthür and Gehring, each case of interaction allows for the identification of a source regime, a target regime and a 'unidirectional causal pathway' connecting the two regimes, that is, the *'causal pathway that a case of interaction follows'*.[103] While establishing the source and target does not present a significant challenge, elucidating how causal influence takes place is more challenging.[104] The identification of causal pathways and examination of the structures of the interaction requires conceptual categories that permit systematic analysis of the empirical cases. There are however intrinsic difficulties in demonstrating causality by proving that the effects that occurred in the target regime wouldn't have occurred in the absence of action in the source regime. However, one has to bear in mind that the action of the source regime can lead to three different situations: producing effects in the target regime, producing effects in the issue area of interest or not having any influence at all. Climate change is a source and a target of interaction in regards to ICAO and IMO, and both synergistic and disruptive effects are possible.[105]

The value of conceptualizing the causal mechanisms of institutional interaction, as conducted by Oberthür and Gehring, has been acknowledged in the legal scholarship.[106] When researchers face the task of identifying interaction, or cases of interaction, some predetermined ideas of types and forms of the units of analysis are needed.[107] Here a pre-established typology is needed.

Transactional versus relational interactions

Some scholars have supported the idea of a framework for regime interaction which does not focus exclusively on courts,[108] that is, only in the moment after the law has been negotiated or become custom. Margaret A. Young advocates a model of interaction that incorporates the different stages of legal development and application.[109] Young has stressed that interactions can occur during different stages of the law's life, such as during law-making, implementation and dispute settlement. She claims that more critical attention is needed to the law-making phase, since it also has a role in the dispute-settlement stage.

However, the dominant model for legal analysis[110] of regime interaction has focused exclusively in what Dunoff has called '*transactional*' interactions. Such interactions involve a conceptualization of the phenomenon of interaction in '*discrete terms of transactions or disputes*'.[111] Judicial decision-making is at the centre of this methodology, which examines norms from different regimes that collide, and disagreements in courts and tribunals over the law and the application of law to particular cases.[112] While being predominant, this model has been challenged in the academic literature. A sole focus on transactional interaction has been criticized on the basis that regime interaction is an ongoing process of mutual influence, and not just something that happens at a specific moment in time. In this sense, an analysis of regime interaction that only takes on board the case law as an object of study turns out to be both '*partial and misleading*'.[113] It is partial because it does not take into account the fact that regimes interact in '*ongoing, continuous relationships*' and it is misleading because it regards '*discrete transactions*' as the most important part of the interaction between regimes. Dunoff acknowledges that the vast majority of interactions between regimes take place outside the judicial arena, in the ongoing relationships among actors and institutions, in what he calls '*relational interactions*'.[114]

In contraposition to the common approach of transactional interactions, a model that embraces relational interactions allows for reflecting the continuous, active and more diverse physiognomies of relationships between regimes. Where transactional interactions limit interactions to a specific time and space (i.e. the exact case law), relational interactions reveal the ongoing interfaces. Relational interactions are characterized by a more dynamic appeal that allows for the inclusion of a wider array of issues and fora, and considers other actors in addition to states, which is typically the case in international litigation. Their lack of retrospective spirit means that relational interactions tend to be law-creating, since they are mostly focused on the articulation of new norms towards governing relations in the specific area of overlap.[115]

In responding to the regulation of IBF, the challenges are present at the stage of law-making, that is, how existing regimes interact in the creation of the law. Here, the features of regimes – such as aspects of membership, time of development of relevant laws, implementation by different institutions with different powers and the fact that the regimes aim to satisfy a particular set of preferences within the international legal system influence their interaction.[116]

On the basis of these '*relational interactions*' Dunoff proposes a new model for regime interaction based on a threefold typology that comprises the forms of (1) regulatory and administrative interactions, (2) operational interactions and (3) conceptual interactions.[117] These forms will be examined in Chapter 4 with regards to the climate, ICAO and the IMO regimes. Dunoff's framework permits an analytical classification, exposition and immersion in the regime interactions that this study is concerned with, which takes on board the specifics of the law-making stage of IBF regulation.[118] Furthermore, the division proposed by Dunoff intends '*to shed light over the causal mechanisms throughout which regimes impact upon and influence each other.*'[119] This typology allows for seeing interaction from a different perspective.

Because Dunoff's scheme builds upon the work of others[120] and because not all the nuances of interaction between regimes may be inferred from Dunoff's scheme, this book also embraces the classification of regime interaction offered by Sebastian Oberthür,[121] whose is particularly relevant since he examined regime interaction between ICAO, the IMO and the climate regime.[122] His study on the climate regime, ICAO and IMO, throughout this approach of causal pathways, has provided '*an in-depth analysis of this case, shedding light on the restricted cognitive interaction or learning processes among the affected institutions*'.[123]

Oberthür's division comes from the international relations discipline and also serves the purpose of identifying the drivers of interaction. It consists of four categories: (1) cognitive interaction, (2) interaction through commitment, (3) behavioural interaction and (4) impact-level interaction. *Cognitive interaction* refers to the fact that information, knowledge or ideas coming from the source regime can change the perception and deliberations of actors in the target regime. For example, reporting arrangements, scientific or technical information, norms or regulations produced in one regime may feed in another regime through some of its members, NGOs or bureaucracies, influencing the processes in another regime. The second type of interaction referred to as '*interaction through commitment*' alludes to the fact that the commitments made by some actors in the source regime may affect the preferences of actors in the target regime. These situations can lead to incompatible obligations and the use of cooperative arrangements. When interaction affects the target regime at the outcome level – that is, when it produces behavioural effects in one issue area that affects implementation in another institution – we face '*behavioural interaction*'. Although actors are central 'spreaders of influence' between regimes, their role and position in two different regimes can differ. Specifically, the behaviour and reaction of key States to a decision adopted in one regime may affect an area of interest in another regime, undermining it.

Regulatory and administrative, operational and conceptual interaction

The first type of interaction established by Dunoff is referred to as 'regulatory and administrative' and acknowledges the fact that '*regimes engage in ongoing collaborative interactions in the context of regulatory and administrative law-making.*' He gives examples of what is a productive and often underappreciated regime interaction and encourages scholars to look at it.[124] He builds upon the fact that international law develops not only through treaties and agreements, but through an array of '*decision-making processes that regulate and manage vast areas of international relations*'.[125] These are regulatory and administrative decisions, rules involving subsidiary bodies and implementing regimes across systems, and that treaties can provide for them, such is the case of the standards developed by ICAO and the IMO.[126] For example, they can include the creation of an organization or consortium for the participation of various regimes, iterative exchanges that are expressly provide for in a treaty, or come from an invitation to experts from one regime to collaborate with other.

Regulatory and administrative interactions commonly involve frequent and repetitious collaborations and formal and informal exchanges among participants of the different regimes influencing the negotiating texts. In the case of fisheries studied by Margaret A. Young[127] and the case of interactions between ICAO and telecommunications studied by Dunoff,[128] the final outcomes '*bear an imprint of regime interactions*' and incorporate other regimes' views and preferences. This is done, among other means, through technical and scientific studies sparking interaction and dialogue among experts, and ongoing exchanges between civil servants.[129]

Operational interactions are the second group in Dunoff's typology. Here, regimes are also settings for international actors' operational activities; the operational interactions cover this reality, that is, '*the way that actors from different regimes interact in the course of performing their operational activities*'.[130] These include overlapping in operational programmes raising concerns over duplicative efforts and a lack of coordination, but also opportunities to scale synergies with new ventures, joint programmes and funding mechanisms, which improve a regimes' efficiency. In Dunoff's words:

> these interactive, sustained and dynamic operational interactions can be understood as an adaptive strategy that arises in response to the fragmented nature of the international legal order, and that permits the international community to address particular problems, such as the HIV/AIDS crisis, in a comprehensive and holistic fashion.[131]

As such, they do not attract the same level of academic attention compared to jurisprudential interactions; however they are far more common and produce substantive outcomes in ways that litigation cannot. However, a critical eye in these processes is needed since, as Margaret A. Young has highlighted, '*seemingly innocuous arrangements [. . .] can become key tools for entrenching regime hierarchy.*'[132]

The final set of interactions involves conceptual exchanges, influences and creation; collectively termed '*conceptual interactions*' by Dunoff. There is more to regime interaction in law-making than the production of norms and their operationalization, because regimes also *create* knowledge. Following from the definition of regimes embraced by this research – that is, '*sets of norms, decision-making procedures and organizations coalescing around functional issue-areas and dominated by particular modes of behaviour, assumptions and biases*' – it can be inferred that regimes produce more than rules and standards: they are '*part of the processes by which we collectively come to know, describe and imagine the world*',[133] that is, they also create a vision of the world. Such processes occur within regimes and also among them, namely: regimes participating in law-making processes share their visions, through the shaping of concepts and the creation of knowledge.[134] However, this is rarely a separate and independent process, which reveals that '*when international actors embedded within an international regime create rules or engage in operational activities, they at the same time engage in the process of creating social knowledge.*'[135] Therefore, regime interaction also provides a space where different '*conceptual frameworks for understanding parts of our social world*'[136] exert influence over each other.

The consequences of interaction

Regimes are developed to address particular issue areas; however, in a world characterized by complex relations, especially in regard to common (global) environmental problems, the overlapping of regimes in a given area is not infrequent.[137] Such situations can lead to different consequences, and one regime may influence another (e.g. ICAO's objectives are directed at international civil aviation, rather than at aviation emissions), so the recent decisions on adopting emissions regulation[138] can be seen as an example of interaction with the climate regime. The same can be said about the IMO, apropos of maritime transportation and maritime emissions.

The traditional view on fragmentation focuses on conflicts and ignores the potential for positive interactions that '*may lead to a more responsive and effective international legal system than the sum of the constituent regimes*'.[139] However, Martti Koskeniemi's concept of 'hegemonic regimes'[140] offers some scepticism regarding the idea of productive outcomes in regime interaction. He suggests that regimes behave in pursuit of their own interests and act in such a way as to universalize[141] themselves since, '*[l]ike states, functional regimes operate as clusters of interest and knowledge, and like states they act in solipsistic and imperial ways- they are coded so as to perceive only themselves and their own preferences and to translate those mechanically into preferences for everyone.*'[142] In this context, outcomes can range from war or alienation to integration or assimilation, and any middle ground refers to co-existence or the pursuit of joint interests – that is, cooperation between regimes or the creation of hybrid concepts such as sustainable development.

While warning about the difficulties of establishing in practice a clear-cut line between the different consequences of regime interaction,[143] the literature in both international law and international relations suggests that the consequences of interactions first can take two basic forms, namely, conflictive and synergistic outcomes,[144] depending on whether the effects of interaction are adverse or beneficial;[145] and second, these consequences can be actual or potential.[146]

The notion of conflict and synergy

A definition of conflict should be articulated for the purposes of this monograph. The legal scholarship is divided on the concept of conflict,[147] ranging from strict conceptions, where '*direct incompatibility arises only where a party to the two treaties cannot simultaneously comply with its obligations under both treaties*',[148] to broader views, where incompatibilities can also arise from permissions.[149] This is particularly relevant for the climate regime, which relies vastly on permissive norms.[150] However, even the latter conception can be deemed as inadequate to deal with the wide range of tensions that regime interactions can embed.[151]

The ILC report also provides two perspectives on the notion of conflict.[152] The first perspective, based exclusively on the subject matter of the relevant rules and the legal subjects bound by it, is dismissed in their study as being too reductionist for the purposes of determining the existence of a conflict. The second perspective states that a particular norm of a regime may '*frustrate the goals of another treaty without there being any strict incompatibility between their provisions. Two treaties or sets of rules may possess different background justifications or emerge from different legislative policies or aim at divergent ends.*' By extension, this view acknowledges that such 'policy conflicts'[153] may be also relevant for fragmentation.[154] Ultimately, the ILC report adopts the broader definition of conflict as '*a situation where two rules or principles suggest different ways of dealing with a problem*'.[155] However, some scholars have added to the definition that the ' *"different ways" shall lead to contradictory behaviour*'.[156] This study subscribes to this concept due to its capacity of including more divergences and tensions affecting the interaction between the selected regimes at the law-making stage, but also because it allows for '*incompatibilities between regimes which need not be resolved through establishing a hierarchy between them (i.e., one of the norms necessarily prevails)*'.[157] In identifying the existence of these conflicts, the scholarship has pointed towards different indicators such as incompatible norms, diverging or incompatible objectives, use of different or incompatible principles and concepts, opposing economic incentives for behaviour or implementation, impediments in diffusion and learning.[158]

To the extent that there can be tensions between regimes, there is also room for positive and constructive outcomes in regime interaction.[159] The term synergy is used along the book to refer to such situations, where the overlap of regimes has an aggregate positive effect or positive outcome. In a sense, these outcomes benefit from the '*working together*' of the regimes, producing better results than they would have been able to produce on their own.[160] Synergistic outcomes include any situation that has benefited from the interaction such as knowledge or expertise exchange, cooperation in implementation, sharing of mechanisms, joint programmes, etc. Some indicators of synergies identified in the literature include: shared principles or concepts, common economic incentives, stream-lined monitoring and reporting obligations, shared supporting measures, 'positive' diffusion and learning.[161]

When it comes to synergies, they will greatly depend on the type of interaction established. In this connection, Margaret Young explains that the presence of certain elements promotes regime interaction: besides policy coordination at the national level, the promotion of regime interaction emerges from learning and the sharing of information at the international level, through collaboration between secretariats and the participation of non-state actors, where the allo-cation of resources is vital. Conversely, the presence of indicators such as the exclusivity of forum, the lack of transparency and openness and lack of parallel membership pose impediments to regime interaction.[162]

Managing interaction

In order to overcome tensions and enhance the coherence, effectiveness and likelihood of regulating emissions from IBF, this study assumes that the theory and practice of 'managing regime interaction' is possible, necessary and desirable in order to avoid or resolve conflicts and to boost synergies between regimes.[163] Interaction management has been defined as '*deliberate efforts by any relevant actor, group of actors, in whatever form or forum to address and improve institutional interaction and its effects*'.[164] Here, it is important to clarify that the type of inter-action being studied indicates the best way to manage the consequences of these interactions, at the law-making level. There are two related types of solutions that can be of help in managing interaction, namely, legal techniques and insti-tutional cooperation.[165]

Approaches in the ILC study

The Vienna Convention of the Law of Treaties (VCLT)[166] provides a set of legal techniques that can be applied in cases of conflicts between treaties.[167] These legal solutions, as presented in the ILC study on the challenges faced by fragmenta-tion of international law,[168] focus on the avoidance and resolution of conflicts at the substantive level through: treaty interpretation[169] (such as good faith, ordinary meaning, object and purpose, context of the text, subsequent agreements and prac-tices and systemic integration[170]) and question of which rule shall prevail (*lex pos-terior derogate lege priori*,[171] *lex specialis derogat lege generali*[172] and *lex superior derogat lex inferiori*[173]). The value of other legal practices, such as the insertion of conflict clauses in the treaties, where the parties shed light on the relationship between treaties, have also an important role in managing interaction.[174] Other legal techniques include the amendment, modification or suspension of one of the treaties in conflict.

However, it has been pointed out that these techniques are not free from flaws,[175] including their limited practical value, especially in the case of the climate regime.[176] For example, while the ILC study emphasized the promising value of the principle of systemic integration,[177] the literature casts doubt on the principle being '*a universal panacea*',[178] also with regard to its suitability to deal with climate change fragmentation.[179] These techniques also have limited value in situations where the conflict includes hard-law and soft-law clauses, since they do not occupy the same hierarchical structure.

From the above it can be inferred that, in the quest for legal certainty, the role of international law in dealing with fragmentation and regime interaction has been mostly confined to the avoidance and resolution of conflicts. Furthermore, the principle focus is on establishing which treaty would prevail in the case of conflict, using diverse techniques.[180] Conversely, as already mentioned, interactions between regimes can also result in synergies. The absence of conflict does not mean of the creation of synergies; neutral outcomes are also possible.

Approaches beyond the ILC study

Aside from the so-called 'tool box' for international lawyers described above, the second set of possibilities to deal with the consequences of interaction refers to the institutional cooperation[181] among regimes at the decision-making bodies and bureaucracies, such as secretariats and other administration bodies to the regimes. However, this group was not address by the ILC Report, which did not include institutional fragmentation it its work. Elsewhere, the literature proclaims the difficulty of maintaining a clear-cut classification between legal techniques and institutional coordination. For example, in the case of COP decisions they can be regarded as a form of treaty interpretation while treaty changes can be seen as institutional coordination in the negotiation process.[182] However, institutional cooperation suffers from certain limitations, which include unclear mandates for institutions.[183]

It is also possible that individual States and non-state actors can influence the interaction. This is called 'autonomous management'[184] in contrast with collective management. '*State, organizations and individuals are often well aware that action under one institution can affect the evolution or consequences of actions under another, and therefore seek to influence those impacts.*'[185] Furthermore, they may take action to manage the interaction, '*not to pursue, maximize or reconcile the collective agreed upon objectives of interacting institutions*'.[186] For example, the inclusion of aviation in the EU ETS or the threat of including maritime emissions at a later date can be seen as a way to manage interaction between the climate and the international transport regimes.[187] These approaches will be revisit in Chapter 6, when dealing with the specifics of the case study of this book.

Methodology and method

The term 'method' refers to the way in which the research is pursued in connection to the choice of data and the way to examine it: for example, literature review, analysis of documents, observation and case studies.[188] The term 'methodology' covers methods and also includes further theoretical connotations and is linked to more profound concepts and approaches, including how the law is conceptualized.[189] As such, this section explains how the author will answer the research questions with a suitable methodology and method.

In identifying the reasons why environmental law scholarship is often perceived as an immature discipline, E. Fisher et al. pick up on the methodological challenges that environmental law faces given the speed and scale of change in the law, the interdisciplinary and the multi-jurisdictional nature of the subject and the fact that a diverse range of governance arrangements rely on it.[190] In particular, the examination of interactions between environmental and non-environmental regimes is among the most challenging issues to deal with. It confronts the usual parameters and methodological approaches to international environmental law and '*as in relation to governance, there needs to be an acute awareness that there are different ways to characterize these relationships and interfaces.*'[191]

As in other fast-expanding areas of law, climate change research has focused mainly on substantive issues but engaging with theoretical discussions such as fragmentation has been encouraged.[192] Overall, while other frameworks are possible,[193] this study has identified an analytical framework based on fragmentation of international law as the most suitable methodology to answer the main research question, that is, *How can the interaction between different regimes overlapping and competing in the regulation of international aviation and maritime transport be managed?* The lenses of regime interaction allow for an inclusive and deep analysis of the overlap and interfaces between international environmental law and other areas of international law in the regulation of IBF.

In particular, to respond to the first research question, *why have IBF emissions remained largely unregulated?*, the research chooses to delve into the existing legal framework and explore the developments to date by using the division in actors, instruments and processes proposed by Boyle and Chinkin as a way to systematize information and facilitate understanding on law-making in the regimes.

Once the analysis of international law-making in the three selected regimes is examined, the research focuses on understanding of how the regimes overlap in regulating IBF. Since the book focuses exclusively on the regulation phase, regime interaction is seen through the lenses of relational interaction, in Dunoff's sense. However, the research builds mostly on Young's work, which argues that regime interaction occurs at different stages of law, including the law-making. To answer research question two, *How does interaction among the selected regimes occur?*, the book determines and defines interaction, the objects (hard law and soft law) and its drivers, using a typology that focuses on relational interactions, which is better suited for analyzing the case of this study and allows for multiple nuances.

From this point the monograph advances to inspect the outcomes of interaction to answer the research question, *What are the consequences of the interaction for the allocation and regulation of international aviation and international maritime transport?* For this purpose a basic appreciation of what are considered to be the consequences (i.e. the conflicts and synergies) and the main indicators of their presence. Such delimitation guides us through the possibilities of managing interaction to find a solution to the final research question: *How can the tensions be overcome?* At this point, the research builds upon the work of the ILC Report and other scholars.[194]

There is no shortage of legal literature positing the advantages of pursuing interdisciplinary methods to address environmental problems.[195] Given that the focus of this study covers tensions characterized by both legal and political facets, it seems artificial and inadequate to cast aside approaches that could better embody a full understanding of the problem, and offer a broader set of solutions. Therefore, this monograph examines the politics of regime interaction, and in this sense, is not purely an international law study, assuming a broader perspective of law and international relations.[196] This allows for a more satisfactory account of reality, enabling the researcher to go further, using some perspectives from international relations theory, where a pure legal approach cannot provide an appropriate route.[197] In this connection, as concluded in Harro van Asselt's study, the discipline of international law and international relations address related questions, provide complementary insights.[198] He posits the value of the former in '*determining the existence of a normative conflict; examining the possibilities for addressing such conflicts through the law of treaties; and identifying the scope for legal techniques to address conflicts and enhance synergies between international agreements*'. At the same time he acknowledges the usefulness of the latter in '*shedding light on the driving forces behind regime interactions; identifying causal mechanisms for interactions; and assessing the impacts of interaction management on regime effectiveness*'.[199]

Critical academic studies from the discipline of international relations maintain that complex regime interactions can be disaggregated into a number of cases (i.e. units of analysis) for the purposes of conducting empirical studies. A similar case-study approach has been followed by legal scholars for different purposes, such as Margaret A. Young with regards to regime interaction in the area of fisheries.[200]

The method and the data selected for analysis in this monograph relates to two main groups of legal research sources, namely: primary research sources, which include all types of law and case law; and secondary research sources, which include an array of academic texts such as legal monographs and reviews, journal articles or legal encyclopaedias. More concretely this monograph analyzes, in accordance with the framework set out in this chapter, the following data: treaties, international agreements, the outcomes from treaty bodies in the climate change, ICAO, IMO regimes, the EU institutions and relevant case law. Other sources of legitimate data include academic literature in public international law and international relations related to law-making, fragmentation and regime interaction in international law. Non-academic literature, such as reliable press news and various reports, will be only used in those cases where academic literature hasn't yet been produced. This research is also informed by the researcher's ongoing exchanges of information with legal experts and through participation in conferences, seminars, workshops and research stays, and while assisting as an observer to ICAO (2010) and the IMO (2010–2012), and the Climate Conferences (2013–2016).

Conclusions

This chapter has explored the main concepts and contours of the analytical framework that sustains this study, delving into the methodology and method that the book uses to answer the research questions. While engaging with the main literature on law-making, fragmentation and regime interaction in international law, this chapter has provided an account of typologies and notions that the monograph adheres to, identifying for the different research steps what is included and what is not included with regard to the concepts and sources used. More importantly, this chapter has provided arguments to support the suitability of the chosen theoretical approach to examine the research questions, also explaining the analytical framework that will be used to answer the sub-questions in Chapters 3, 4, 5 and 6.

Notes

1 ILC, *Fragmentation of International Law: Difficulties Arising from the Diversification and Expansion of International Law. Report of the Study Group of the International Law Commission.* UN Doc. A/CN.4/L.682. (2006). Paragraph 8.
2 See, James Boyle, 'Ideals and Things: International Legal Scholarship and the Prison-House of Language', *Harvard International Law Journal*, 26, (1985). 330.
3 See, Vaughan Lowe, *International Law* (Oxford University Press, 2007). 1. International law is an evolving framework, where *'the international community has slowly been moving away from the classic state responsibility approach to damage caused towards a regime of international cooperation'*. *See*, Malcolm N. Shaw, *International Law* (Cambridge University Press 6th ed., 2008). 844–845. In the same vein see the reference to international law as a 'law of cooperation, not subordination' in C. Rousseau, 'De la compatibilité des norms juridiques contradictories dans l'ordre international' cited in Christina Voigt, *Sustainable Development as a Principle of International Law: Resolving Conflicts between Climate Measures and WTO Law* (Martinus Nijhoff Publishers, 2009). 195.
4 International environmental law comprises 'substantive, procedural and institutional rules of international law which have as their primary objective the protection of the environment'. This definition is offered in Philippe Sands, *Principles of International Environmental Law* (Cambridge University Press 2nd ed., 2003).15. See further on what international environmental law is and the different perspectives – doctrinal, policy and explanatory approaches- of it, Daniel Bodansky, *The Art and Craft of International Environmental Law* (Harvard University Press, 2010). 1–17.
5 See, D. Bodansky, *The Art and Craft of International Environmental Law.* (2010). 13–15.
6 On the term 'sources' see, Ian Brownlie, *Principles of Public International Law* (Oxford University Press 7th ed., 2008). 3–4. He posits that, in international law, the dichotomy

between formal and material sources of law breaks, since the term 'formal source' misleads the reader towards the type of 'constitutional' machinery of law-making that exists within states which doesn't exist in international law.

7 See, D. Bodansky, *The Art and Craft of International Environmental Law.* (2010). 13.

8 UN, Statute of the International Court of Justice, 18 April 1946. Available at: www. refworld.org/docid/3deb4b9c0.html. The Statute of the International Court of Justice is the basic instrument of the court dealing with its composition and functioning. Although annexed to the Charter of the United Nations it forms an integral part of it.

9 International treaties can be convened between States, States and international organizations or international organizations. They can have a bilateral, plurilateral or multilateral character and come in various forms. They are defined and governed by the Vienna Convention on the Law of Treaties. Vienna, adopted 23 May 1969, in force 27 January 1980. 8 ILM 679, (1969). And, also the Vienna Convention on the Law of Treaties Between States and International Organizations or Between International Organizations, concluded 21 March 1989. UN Doc. A/CONF.129/15, 25 ILM 543, (1989).

10 Customary international law entails a continuous state practice, reassured by opinion iuris.

11 The general principles of the law come mostly from national legal systems.

12 Article 59 of the ICJ Statute expresses that ICJ decisions imply no binding precedent, since they only have force between parties in a particular case.

13 This list of sources was previously upheld in the Statute of the Permanent Court of Justice.

14 However, this provision has not been applied by the ICJ.

15 Christian Tomuschat, *How Relevant Is the Copenhagen Accord? A Legal Perspective* (2010), 3'er Berlin Climate Law Conference. From Bonn to Cancun and Beyond: New Dimensions in Climate Regulation. At his presentation, Professor Tomuschat described Article 38 as 'far from perfect' for these two lacunae.

16 The creation of legal obligations from unilateral declarations was established in Australia & New Zealand v. France, I.C.J. 253, 457. Nuclear Test Case, (International Court of Justice).

17 International Law Commission, Draft Articles on State Responsibility, Part 2, Art 5(1), Report of the ILC to the UNGA, UN Doc. A/44/10, 218 (1989) as cited in P. Sands, *Principles of International Environmental Law.* (2003). 123.

18 José E. Alvarez, *International Organizations as Law-Makers* (Oxford University Press, 2005). 68.

19 The term is borrowed from Hilary Charlesworth, 'Law Making and Sources', in *The Cambridge Companion to International Law* (James Crawford and Martti Koskenniemi eds., 2012). 189.

20 Ibid. at. 189.

21 Treaties, customary norms and the general principles are considered 'hard law' whereas other norms such as resolutions from international organizations or declarations lack the legal character of the former although they are normative and intend to guide behaviour. The latter are under the rubric of 'soft law'. See D. Bodansky, *The Art and Craft of International Environmental Law.* (2010). 96–102. See also C.M. Chinkin, 'The Challenge of Soft Law: Development and Change in International Law', *International and Comparative Law Quarterly*, 38, (1989). 850.

22 For an account of the creation, forms, content and legal effects of 'soft law' in the field of international environmental law see Pierre-Marie Dupuy, 'Soft Law and the International Law of the Environment', *Michigan Journal of International Law* 12, (1990–1991). 420.

23 Alan E. Boyle and Christine M. Chinkin, *The Making of International Law* (Oxford University Press, 2007).

24 Jan Klabbers, *An Introduction to International Institutional Law* (Cambridge University Press 2nd ed., 2009). 179. He is using Jose Alvarez's ideas on how what law is 'playing down the role of formalities' and highlighting the 'sense of being under a legal obligation', taken from J.E. Alvarez, *International Organizations as Law-Makers*. (2005). 153–157.

25 H. Charlesworth, 'Law Making and Sources'. (2012). 189.

26 'Soft law' may become 'hard law' by incorporation to a treaty or custom; in the words of Daniel Bodansky, 'soft law' 'represents a kind of purgatory'. D. Bodansky, *The Art and Craft of International Environmental Law*. (2010). 99.

27 The attractiveness of soft law derives from the ease in reaching agreements, avoiding the ratification process, and to have them amended and replaced. Boyle defines soft law as *'simply another tool in the professional lawyer's armoury.'* Alan E. Boyle, 'Some Reflections on the Relationship of Treaties and Soft Law. ', *International and Comparative Law Quarterly*, 48(4), (1999). 901–913.

28 See below, section 5 on method.

29 Duncan B. Hollis, 'Why State Consent Still Matters: Non-State Actors, Treaties, and the Changing Sources of International Law', *Berkeley Journal of International Law*, 23(1), (2005). 137–174. The debate around state consent and moral values is summarized here.

30 J.E. Alvarez, *International Organizations as Law-Makers*. (2005). 217–222.

31 P.-M. Dupuy, (1990–1991). 420.

32 P. Sands, *Principles of International Environmental Law*. (2003). 124.

33 On the increasing use of non-binding agreements in the climate regime see, Harro van Asselt, 'From UN-ity to Diversity? The UNFCCC, the Asia-Pacific Partnership, and the Future of International Law on Climate Change', *Carbon and Climate Law Review*, 1, (2007). 17–28. Also, Antto Vihma, 'Friendly Neighbor or Trojan Horse? Assessing the Interaction of Soft Law Initiatives and the UN Climate Regime', *International Environmental Agreements: Politics, Law and Economics*, 9(3), (2009). 239–262.

34 Gennadiĭ Mikhaĭlovich Danilenko, *Law-Making in the International Community* (M. Nijhoff, 1993). 1–15 offers a summary of the conceptual aspects of the term "law-making". Here, the author posits a broad definition which, while helpful in legal theory studies, may present some difficulties for technical purposes, where a narrow definition confined to the pure normative mechanism would be more suitable.

35 A.E. Boyle and C.M. Chinkin, *The Making of International Law*. (2007).

36 Boyle & Chinkin's work is used for instance in James Harrison, *Making the Law of the Sea: A Study in the Development of International Law* (Cambridge University Press, 2011). See also, in Annalisa Savaresi, *An International Framework for Reducing Emissions from Deforestation and Forest Degradatiom in Developing Countries*. (University of Copenhagen, 2013).

37 H. Charlesworth, 'Law Making and Sources'. (2012). 187.

38 State sovereignty is one of the founding concepts of international law. It entails that States enjoy exclusive jurisdiction in their territories and over their resources. Such exclusivity is not without limits imposed by international law or derived from international agreements.

39 Vienna Convention on the Law of Treaties. (1969). Article 7(2).

40 Alexandre Charles Kiss and Dinah Shelton, *Guide to International Environmental Law* (Martinus Nijhoff Publishers, 2007). 12.

41 See H. Charlesworth, 'Law Making and Sources'. (2012). 187–201.

42 For an overview on the rising role of international institutional law see J.E. Alvarez, *International Organizations as Law-Makers*. (2005). Also Jan Klabbers, 'International Institutions', in James Crawford and Martti Koskenniemi, *The Cambridge Companion to International Law* (Cambridge University Press, 2012). 228–242.

43 J.E. Alvarez, *International Organizations as Law-Makers*. (2005). 6. A definition is found also in the Article 2 of the UN International Law Commission on the draft

Articles on the Responsibility of International Organizations. Organizations are *'established by a treaty or other instrument governed by international law and possessing its own international legal personality. International organizations may include as members, in addition to States, other entities'*

44 For an overview on international actors see A.C. Kiss and D. Shelton, *Guide to International Environmental Law*. (2007). 47–71.

45 Such premises are laid in their founding instruments. Such charters also usually contain substantive obligations for signatory states as well as the establishment of the organization. On international organizations' charters see J.E. Alvarez, *International Organizations as Law-Makers*. (2005). 65–108. See also, J. Klabbers, *An Introduction to International Institutional Law*. (2009). 38–73.

46 Such as the International Labour Organization.

47 On the relationship between various organs of the same organization, see Jan Klabbers, 'Checks and Balances in the Law of International Organizations', in *Autonomy in the Law: Ius Gentium* (M. N. S. Sellers, University of Baltimore, Center for International and Comparative Law eds., 2007).

48 J.E. Alvarez, *International Organizations as Law-Makers*. (2005). 9.

49 J. Klabbers, *An Introduction to International Institutional Law*. (2009). 176.

50 J.E. Alvarez, *International Organizations as Law-Makers*. (2005). 10.

51 See e.g. Barry E. Carter, 'Making Progress in International Institutions and Law', in Russell A. Miller and Rebecca M. Bratspies, *Progress in International Law* (Martinus Nijhoff Publishers, 2008). 55–58.

52 For example, during the KP negotiation over 200 NGOs were accredited as observers.

53 An overview of legal international environmental governance is offer in P. Sands, *Principles of International Environmental Law*. (2003). 70–122.

54 A.E. Boyle and C.M. Chinkin, *The Making of International Law*. (2007). 98–162.

55 J.E. Alvarez, *International Organizations as Law-Makers*. (2005). 218.

56 Ibid. at.121. The idea that this soft law is an alternative to treaty-making and also part of the multilateral treaty-making process can be found in A.E. Boyle, (1999).

57 J.E. Alvarez, *International Organizations as Law-Makers*. (2005). 220.

58 A definition is found in Joost; Pauwelyn et al., 'The Exercise of Public Authority through Informal International Lawmaking: An Accountability Issue?', Global Governance as Public Authority: Structures, Contestation and Normative Change. Jean Monnet Working Paper 06/11 (2011). *'Cross-border cooperation between public authorities, with or without the participation of private actors and/or international organizations, in a forum other than a traditional international organization (process informality), and/or as between actors other than traditional diplomatic actors (such as regulators or agencies) (actor informality) and/or which does not result in a formal treaty or traditional source of international law (output informality).'* For a deeper analysis on the concept see, Joost Pauwelyn, 'Informal International Law-Making: Framing the Concept and the Research Questions', in *Informal International Law-Making* (Joost Pauwelyn et al. eds., 2012). 13–31.

59 Ayelet Berman et al., *Informal International Lawmaking: Case Studies* (Torkel Opsahl Academic EPublisher, 2012). 3–4. For a critical view on this, Ramses A. Wessel, 'Informal International Law-Making as a New Form of World Legislation?', *International Organizations Law Review*, 8, (2011). 253–265. And J. Klabbers, *An Introduction to International Institutional Law*. (2009). 311–313.

60 Arnold McNair, 'International Legislation', *Iowa Law Review*, 19(2), (1934). 178. Cited in C. Wilfred Jenks, 'Conflict of Law-Making Treaties', *British Year Book of International Law*, 30, (1953). 401. They pointed out that the use of the term '*international legislation*' is a metaphorical one, since there is not such a thing as an authority whose rules bind all persons under a jurisdiction.

61 A.E. Boyle and C.M. Chinkin, *The Making of International Law*. (2007). 233–259.

62 Margaret A. Young, 'Introduction: The Productive Friction between Regimes', in *Regime Interaction in International Law: Facing Fragmentation* (Margaret A. Young ed., 2012). 2–4.

63 C. Wilfried Jenks, 'The Conflict of Law-Making Treaties', *BYBIL*, 30, (1953). 403, cited in ILC Report (2006).
64 The International Law Commission was established by General Assembly of the United Nations in 1947 to develop and codify international law. Among its tasks are the drafting of treaties and guidelines and the preparation of reports and studies on topical issues.
65 ILC Report (2006).
66 See, C. Voigt, *Sustainable Development as a Principle of International Law: Resolving Conflicts between Climate Measures and WTO Law*. (2009). 197.
67 ILC prefers the use of special regime, since no regime can be truly self-contained. See a different view in, Anja Lindroos and Michael Mehling, 'Dispelling the Chimera of "Self-Contained Regimes" International Law and the WTO', *The European Journal of International Law*, 16(5), (2006). 857–877.
68 As Christina Voigt has noted, '*Social complexity lead to legal complexity, making it pointless to insist on unity.*' C. Voigt, *Sustainable Development as a Principle of International Law: Resolving Conflicts between Climate Measures and WTO Law*. (2009). 197. The proliferation of international institutions over time is part of a broader trend that has evolved from a territorial differentiation, based on national boundaries, to sectoral differentiation, based on the boundaries of specific issue areas. See Harro van Asselt, *The Fragmentation of Global Climate Governance: Consequences and Management of Regime Interactions* (2013). 14. See also, Andreas Fischer-Lescano and Gunther Teubner, 'Regime-Collisions: The Vain Search for Legal Unity in the Fragmentation of Global Law', *Michigan Journal of International Law* 25 (2004).1009 states:

> The traditional differentiation in line with the political principle of territoriality into relatively autonomous national legal orders is thus overlain by a sectoral differentiation principle: the differentiation of global law into transnational legal regimes, which define the external reach of their jurisdiction along issue-specific rather than territorial lines, and which claim a global validity for themselves.

69 For an overview on the concept of fragmentation see, Harro van Asselt, 'Managing the Fragmentation of International Climate Law', in *Climate Change and the Law* (Erkki J. Hollo et al. eds., 2013). 334–339.
70 These can be regional or issue-area based, substantive or institutional, in relation to different interpretations of general international law or between general international law and specialized regimes or two or more overlapping specialized regimes. For a summary on the typology of fragmentation see Harro van Asselt, *The Fragmentation of Global Climate Governance: Consequences and Management of Regime Interactions* (Edward Elgar, 2014). 44–59.
71 Ibid. at. 22.
72 This study does not distinguish between substantive fragmentation and institutional fragmentation, since they are interrelated: there is a correlation between the extent to which norms and authority are fragmented since '*an increase in normative* [i.e. substantive] *integration generally results in a corresponding increase in authority* [i.e. institutional] *integration, and vice versa*'. For an overview on fragmentation see ibid. at. 46–48 and Harro van Asselt, 'Managing the Fragmentation of International Climate Law', in *Climate Change and the Law, Ius Gentium: Comparative Perspectives on Law and Justice 21* (E.J. Hollo et al. eds., 2013). 334–336.
73 See below section 2.3.1.
74 Margaret A. Young, 'Climate Change Law and Regime Interaction', *Climate Change Law Review*, (2011). 2, 147; Cinnamon Piñón Carlarne, 'Good Climate Governance: Only a Fragmented System of International Law Away?', *Law & Policy*, 30(4), (2008). 450–480.
75 M.A. Young, (2011). H.v. Asselt, 'Managing the Fragmentation of International Climate Law'. (2013).

76 Kati Kulovesi, 'Exploring the Landscape of Climate Law and Scholarship: Two Emerging Trends', in *Climate Change and the Law: Ius Gentium: Comparative Perspectives on Law and Justice* (Erkki J. Hollo et al. eds., 2013).

77 M.A. Young, 'Introduction: The Productive Friction between Regimes'. (2012). 1.

78 This is prominent in International Relations as an object of study of Political Science and International Law.

79 M.A. Young, 'Introduction: The Productive Friction between Regimes'. (2012). 1–19.

80 In particular the study commits to the term 'special regimes'. See, ILC Report (2006). The report provides three notions of regimes.

81 This comes mainly from International Relations literature where the concept was first used. Traditionally, studies into regimes were not engaged with interactions but in assessing variables within regimes, such as effectiveness.

82 Margaret Young states that regimes *'include or depend upon an institutionalized system'*. Although the ILC Report does not include institutions in its study, some of the concepts of regimes put forward the acceptance of some institutional background. Other studies, more in line with this monograph, recognize the normative influence of institutions, see J.E. Alvarez, *International Organizations as Law-Makers*. (2005). Institutions are also considered in the literature on linkages, global administrative law and governance and fragmentation, as pointed out by Young.

83 M.A. Young, (2011). 151.

84 See, M.A. Young, 'Regime Interaction in Creating, Implementing and Enforcing International Law'. (2012). And Jeffrey Dunoff, 'A New Approach to Regime Interaction', in *Regime Interaction in International Law: Facing Fragmentation* (Margaret A. Young ed., 2012). 136–174.

85 Harro van Asselt, 'Legal and Political Approaches in Interplay Management: Dealing with the Fragmentation of Global Climate Governance', in *Managing Institutional Complexity: Regime Interplay and Global Environmental Change: Institutional Dimensions of Global Environmental Change* (Sebastian Oberthür and Olav Schram Stokke eds., 2011). 61.

86 J. Dunoff, 'A New Approach to Regime Interaction'. (2012). The theory proposed there will be used in chapter 4.

87 M.A. Young, 'Introduction: The Productive Friction between Regimes'. (2012). 1–19.

88 Ibid. at. 11. The definition builds up from the definition of Steven Krasner: *'International regimes are defined as principles, norms, rules, and decision-making procedures around which actor expectations converge in a given issue-area.*" Stephen D. Krasner, *International Regimes* (Cornell University Press, 1983). 3.

89 The author thanks Margaret A. Young, via email exchanges in September and October of 2013, for help in establishing the terminology.

90 Similar lexica are used in the literature, such as *'substantive and institutional linkages'* but their reach is different. See for example, Kati Kulovesi, 'Climate Change and Trade: At the Intersection of Two International Legal Regimes', in *Climate Change and the Law* (Erkki J. Hollo et al. eds., 2013). 420.

91 M.A. Young, (2011). 151.

92 H.v. Asselt, *The Fragmentation of Global Climate Governance: Consequences and Management of Regime Interactions*. (2014). 59. However, as the author acknowledges there is a multiplicity of terms used to describe similar realities such as overlaps, inter-linkages, interplay, linkages. Each of these terms can carry different connotations in meaning and as Van Asselt explains, interaction brings along the idea that influence is possible between regimes. On the concept of overlap see also, G. Kristin Rosendal, 'Overlapping International Regimes: The Case of the Intergovernmental Forum on Forests between Climate Change and Biodiversity', *International Environmental Agreements: Politics, Law and Economics, Kluwer Academic Publishers*, 1, (2001). 458–459.

93 G.K. Rosendal, (2001). 458.

94 Margaret A. Young, 'Toward a Legal Framework for Regime Interaction: Lessons from Fisheries, Trade, and Environmental Regimes', *Proceedings of the Annual Meeting (American Society of International Law)*, 105, (2011). 108.
95 Ibid. at. 108.
96 Ibid. at. 108.
97 She argues for a new interpretation of the principle of implied powers in international institutional law. Ibid. at. 109–110.
98 J. Dunoff, 'A New Approach to Regime Interaction'. (2012). 158.
99 Martti Koskenniemi, 'Hegemonic Regimes', in *Regime Interaction in International Law: Facing Fragmentation* (Margaret A. Young ed., 2012). 305–324.
100 See, Thomas Gehring and Sebastian Oberthur, 'Exploring Regime Interaction: A Framework of Analysis', in *Regime Consequences: Methodological Challenges and Research Strategies* (Arild Underdal and Oran R. Young eds., 2004). 247–277; Sebastian Oberthür and Thomas Gehring, 'Conceptual Foundations of Institutional Interaction', in *Institutional Interaction in Global Environmental Governance: Synergy and Conflict among International and EU Policies: Global Environmental Accord: Strategies for Sustainability and Institutional Innovation* (Sebastian Oberthür and Thomas Gehring eds., 2006). And also, Sebastian Oberthür and Thomas Gehring, 'Institutional Interaction: Ten Years of Scholarly Development', in *Managing Institutional Complexity: Regime Interplay and Global Environmental Change* (Sebastian Oberthür and Olav Schram Stokke eds., 2011). This follows the idea of each case of interaction as a one way process.
101 T. Gehring and S. Oberthur, 'Exploring Regime Interaction: A Framework of Analysis'. (2004).
102 See chapter four.
103 S. Oberthür and T. Gehring, 'Conceptual Foundations of Institutional Interaction'. (2006). 32–33. Causal mechanism is a concept that has largely been studied and established in the social sciences. They use the work of Tomas Schelling and others when defining a causal mechanism as '*a set of statements that are logically connected and provide plausible account for how a given cause creates an observed effect*'. It would involve a macro level and a micro level in the sense that actors within a regime will promote a change of perception, preference or behaviour in the source regime that will lead to a change in actors in the target regime.
104 T. Gehring and S. Oberthur, 'Exploring Regime Interaction: A Framework of Analysis'. (2004).
105 See, Sebastian Oberthür, 'Institutional Interaction to Address Greenhouse Gas Emissions from International Transport: ICAO, IMO and the EU Burden-Sharing Agreement', *Project Deliverable No. D 3, Final Draft. Ecologic: Institute for International and European Policy*, (2003). 3–6. Although not exhaustive, he lists 17 cases of institutional interaction.
106 H.v. Asselt, *The Fragmentation of Global Climate Governance: Consequences and Management of Regime Interactions*. (2014). And Margaret A. Young, *Regime Interaction in International Law: Facing Fragmentation* (Cambridge University Press, 2012).
107 T. Gehring and S. Oberthur, 'Exploring Regime Interaction: A Framework of Analysis'. (2004). 255–267. Oberthür and Gehring present seven dimensions of regime interaction related to significant factors, whose variation have an impact in the causal pathways. They intend to shed light over the specific causes and effects. Also see S. Oberthür and T. Gehring, 'Institutional Interaction: Ten Years of Scholarly Development'. (2011). 35–42. Here, they distinguish between four mutually exclusive types of mechanism: cognitive interaction, interaction through commitment, behavioural interaction and impact-level interaction.
108 On fragmentation of international environmental law in terms of courts and tribunals, see Tim Stephens, *International Courts and Environmental Protection* (Cambridge University Press, 2009). 304–344.

109 'A theory of regime interaction that concentrates solely on the paradigmatic case of con-
     flicting norms before a tribunal is under-inclusive' M.A. Young, 'Regime Interaction in
     Creating, Implementing and Enforcing International Law'. (2012). 91. Also see her
     study on regime interaction in the area of fisheries, where she provides examples of
     interaction in fisheries governance in the different stages, Margaret A. Young, *Trad-
     ing Fish, Saving Fish: The Interaction between Regimes in International Law* (Cambridge
     University Press, 2011). 288–289.
110 This includes the work of the ILC, ILC REPORT (2006).
111 See, J. Dunoff, 'A New Approach to Regime Interaction'. (2012). 157.
112 See also, ILC REPORT (2006).
113 J. Dunoff, 'A New Approach to Regime Interaction'. (2012). 137.
114 See, ibid.
115 See, ibid. at. 136–174.
116 M.A. Young, 'Introduction: The Productive Friction between Regimes'. (2012).
117 J. Dunoff, 'A New Approach to Regime Interaction'. (2012).
118 In that connection, it is worth noting that the questions that arise from the ATAA
     Case are relevant not only from the perspective of 'transactional relations', but
     through the lens of 'relational interactions' and the effect on international law.
119 J. Dunoff, 'A New Approach to Regime Interaction'. (2012). 137.
120 Including international relations studies.
121 See below.
122 Sebastian Oberthür, 'Institutional Interaction to Address Greenhouse Gas Emissions
     from International Transport: ICAO, IMO and the Kyoto Protocol', *Climate Policy*,
     3(3), (2003). 191–205. And, Sebastian Oberthür, 'The Climate Change Regime:
     Interactions of the Climate Change Regime with ICAO, IMO and the EU Burden-
     Sharing Agreement', in *Institutional Interaction in Global Environmental Governance:
     Synergy and Conflict among International and EU Policies: Global Environmental
     Accord: Strategies for Sustainability and Institutional Innovation* (Sebastian Oberthür
     and Thomas Gehring eds., 2006).
123 Fariborz Zelli, 'Regime Conflicts in Global Environmental Governance: A Frame-
     work for Analysis', Global Governance Working Paper No. 36, (2008).
124 He refers to examples such as the study of Margaret Young on the interaction between
     UNCLOS, FAO and WTO in the area of fisheries and also to the case of interaction
     between ICAO and the International Telecommunications Union apropos of the use
     of electronic devices and laptops during flight. See J. Dunoff, 'A New Approach to
     Regime Interaction'. (2012). 162–163.
125 Ibid. at. 159.
126 Here Dunoff clarifies that his approach differs from those pursued by Global Admin-
     istrative Law. While Global Administrative Law has a regime specific focus, regime
     interaction takes the 'across regimes' as the focus.
127 M.A. Young, *Trading Fish, Saving Fish: The Interaction between Regimes in International
     Law*. (2011).
128 J. Dunoff, 'A New Approach to Regime Interaction'. (2012).
129 See, ibid. at. 158–163. And also, M.A. Young, *Trading Fish, Saving Fish: The Interac-
     tion between Regimes in International Law*. (2011).
130 J. Dunoff, 'A New Approach to Regime Interaction'. (2012). 164.
131 Ibid. at. 166.
132 M.A. Young, (2011). 108.
133 Andrew T. F. Lang, 'Legal Regimes and Professional Knowledges: The Internal Poli-
     tics of Regime Definition', in *Regime Interaction in International law: Facing Fragmen-
     tation* (Margaret A. Young ed., 2012).
134 Dunoff acknowledges the fact that some conceptual interactions can be very dif-
     fuse and provides an example of the climate change and human rights regimes.
     Actors in the human rights community are provoking an ongoing set of conceptual

interactions intended to change how we come to understand climate change. This can lead to 'forum shopping', regime shifting and the creation of what Koskenniami calls '*regime hybrids*'.

135 J. Dunoff, 'A New Approach to Regime Interaction'. (2012).167.

136 Ibid. at. 166.

137 As Fariborz Zelli has acknowledged, overlapping does not necessarily mean conflictive. F. Zelli, (2008). And Fariborz Zelli, 'Regime Conflicts and Their Management in Global Environmental Governance', in *Managing Institutional Complexity: Regime Interplay and Global Environmental Change: Institutional Dimensions of Global Environmental Change* (Sebastian Oberthür and Olav Schram Stokke eds., 2011).

138 ICAO, A38-WP/430. Report of the Executive Committee on Agenda Item 17, Section on Climate Change. 3 October 2013 (2013).

139 M.A. Young, 'Introduction: The Productive Friction between Regimes'. (2012). 11.

140 M. Koskenniemi, 'Hegemonic Regimes'. (2012). 305–324.

141 Universalization strategy is explained by Koskenniemi as the effort of a particular regime to appear as a representative of the universal values or knowledge, and assuming this role on behalf of the international community.

142 M. Koskenniemi, 'Hegemonic Regimes'. (2012). 318.

143 H.v. Asselt, *The Fragmentation of Global Climate Governance: Consequences and Management of Regime Interactions*. (2013). 67–69.

144 Neutral outcomes are also possible.

145 S. Oberthür and T. Gehring, 'Conceptual Foundations of Institutional Interaction'. (2006). 44–46. A similar division is found in H.v. Asselt, *The Fragmentation of Global Climate Governance: Consequences and Management of Regime Interactions*. (2014). 52–58; F. Zelli, (2008). See also the same idea of conflict versus synergy in Sebastian Oberthür and Thomas Gehring, *Institutional Interaction in Global Environmental Governance: Synergy and Conflict among International and EU Policies* (MIT Press, 2006).

146 See, H.v. Asselt, *The Fragmentation of Global Climate Governance: Consequences and Management of Regime Interactions*. (2014). This duality is expressed in different terms in F. Zelli, (2008). He refers to subjective consequences, as in manifest, and objective consequences, as in latent.

147 An account on the literature review on the concept of conflict is found in, H.v. Asselt, 'Managing the Fragmentation of International Climate Law'. (2013). 67–71.

148 C.W. Jenks, (1953). 425.

149 Authors arguing for wider conceptions include Joost Pauwelyn, *Conflict of Norms in Public International Law: How WTO Law Relates to Other Rules of International Law* (Cambridge University Press, 2003). 166–175. Pauwelyn argues for the inclusion of both obligations and rights. And Erich Vranes, 'The Definition of "Norm Conflict" in International Law and Legal Theory', *European Journal of International Law*, 17(2), (2006). 19–21, cited in H.v. Asselt, *The Fragmentation of Global Climate Governance: Consequences and Management of Regime Interactions*. (2013). 68.

150 C. Voigt, *Sustainable Development as a Principle of International Law: Resolving Conflicts between Climate Measures and WTO Law*. (2009). 201–202. She argues that the climate regime allow for a high degree of discretion to parties, for example, the KP flexible mechanisms as a means of compliance are not mandatory but a way to fulfil with the obligations under article 3.

151 H.v. Asselt, *The Fragmentation of Global Climate Governance: Consequences and Management of Regime Interactions*. (2014). 52–53.

152 ILC Report, (2006). 17. Also see H.v. Asselt, 'Managing the Fragmentation of International Climate Law'. (2013). 346–348.

153 Tensions can be legal or non-legal but also they can have a legal or non-legal root.

154 See, H.v. Asselt, *The Fragmentation of Global Climate Governance: Consequences and Management of Regime Interactions*. (2014). 55. He includes both legal and political conflicts.

155 ILC Report, (2006). 17.
156 Harro van Asselt et al., 'Global Climate Change and the Fragmentation of International Law', *Law & Policy*, 30(4), (2008). 430. Since, different ways, '*may also lead to mutually supportive and complementary outcomes*'.
157 H.v. Asselt, *The Fragmentation of Global Climate Governance: Consequences and Management of Regime Interactions*. (2014). 52–54. In his work, he argues that the conflictive outcomes of regime interaction can comprise two types of tensions: legal and political. For the sake of conducting research in the area of regime interaction, it is useful to distinguish between the legal and political approaches to understanding the tensions between regimes. He differentiates between 'normative conflicts' from 'policy conflicts' arguing that such a distinction '*captures the fact that from an international lawyer's point of view not all tensions between regimes should be regarded as "conflicts", while at the same time conceding that those broader tensions also deserve attention*'. H.v. Asselt, *The Fragmentation of Global Climate Governance: Consequences and Management of Regime Interactions*. (Vrije Universiteit, 2013). 27.
158 H.v. Asselt, *The Fragmentation of Global Climate Governance: Consequences and Management of Regime Interactions*. (2014). 52–55.
159 See conclusions of this study, for example, M.A. Young, *Trading Fish, Saving Fish: The Interaction between Regimes in International Law*. (2011).
160 G. Kristin Rosendal, 'Impacts of Overlapping International Regimes: The case of biodiversity', *Global Governance*, 7, (2001). 95–117.
161 The term synergy follows the common definition, that is, '*the increased effectiveness that results when two or more people or businesses work together*'. Available at: www.merriam-webster.com/dictionary/synergy. In this sense it refers to cooperation, joint work, assistance, help, working together or combined activities. The scholarship on regime interaction has used the term with this common meaning. For an overview on the concept of synergy, see H.v. Asselt, *The Fragmentation of Global Climate Governance: Consequences and Management of Regime Interactions*. (2014). 55–58. Also, H.v. Asselt, *The Fragmentation of Global Climate Governance. Consequences and Management of Regime Interactions*. (2013). 72–76.
162 M.A. Young, *Trading Fish, Saving Fish: The Interaction between Regimes in International Law*. (2011).
163 The author is aware of the fact that not all the scholarship would agree on this statement. For instance, Koskenniemi critiques management as neither possible nor desirable. See, Martti Koskenniemi, 'The Politics of International Law – 20 Years Later', *European Journal of International Law*, 20(1), (2009). 7–19. However, the study is aligned with the idea put forward by others such as Oberthür, Stokke, Van Asselt and Zelli on the possibilities of managing of interaction. And, furthermore, this author is of the view that, as stated by Margaret Young, accountable regime interaction is something to be strived for. In this connection she identifies the need for transparency, participation and ongoing scrutiny in order to legitimize interaction.
164 Sebastian Oberthür, 'Interplay Management: Enhancing Environmental Policy Integration among International Institutions', *International Environmental Agreements: Politics, Law and Economics*, 9(4), (2009). 377–378.
165 The boundaries of what is legal and non-legal can be blurred since legal techniques may have political consequences, and likewise institutional coordination may have legal implications. For example, the role of international law in institutional relationships is explored in H.v. Asselt, 'Legal and Political Approaches in Interplay Management: Dealing with the Fragmentation of Global Climate Governance'. (2011). It is stated that although it is insufficient to deal with fragmentation, international law can complement political efforts to improve coordination and cooperation between regimes. Conversely, the opposite, that is, that political approaches can complement legal techniques, as posited in H.v. Asselt, 'Managing the Fragmentation of International Climate Law'. (2013).
166 Vienna Convention on the Law of Treaties. (1969).

167 See, I. Brownlie, *Principles of Public International Law*. (2008). 607–638.
168 ILC Report, (2006).
169 Treaty interpretation can be used by courts but also at the law-making stage.
170 Vienna Convention on the Law of Treaties. (1969). Articles 31.
171 Article 30 VCLT. The latest expression of state consent prevails. See discussion in, C. Voigt, *Sustainable Development as a Principle of International Law: Resolving Conflicts between Climate Measures and WTO Law*. (2009). 301–303.
172 The special provision prevails over the general because special provisions are deemed to be more detailed expression of state consent. See, J. Pauwelyn, *Conflict of Norms in Public International Law: How WTO Law Relates to Other Rules of International Law*. (2003). 388. For a critical review on the principle of lex specialis related to fragmentation see, Anja Lindroos, 'Addressing Norm Conflicts in a Fragmented Legal System: The Doctrine of Lex Specialis', *Nordic Journal of International Law*, 74, (2005). 27.
173 Art 53VCLT. Jus cogens, however, is acceptable only for a limited group of norms. Giorgio Gaja 'Jus cogens beyond the Vienna Convention' 1981. Cited in Jan Klabbers, 'Beyond the Vienna Convention: Conflicting Treaty Provisions', in *The Law of Treaties beyond the Vienna Convention* (Enzo Cannizzaro et al. eds., 2011). 202.
174 Vienna Convention on the Law of Treaties. (1969). Art. 30.
175 J. Klabbers, 'Beyond the Vienna Convention: Conflicting Treaty Provisions'. (2011). 194–195. However, some authors have defended the value of interpretative provisions of the VCLT See, Mark E. Villiger, 'The Rules on Interpretation: Misgivings, Misunderstandings, Miscarriage? The "Crucible" Intended by the International Law Commission', in *The Law of Treaties beyond the Vienna Convention* (Enzo Cannizzaro et al. eds., 2011).
176 H.v. Asselt, 'Managing the Fragmentation of International Climate Law'. (2013). 339–343. The reasons are the specific characteristics of the law-making and implementation of the climate regime.
177 Vienna Convention on the Law of Treaties. (1969). Article 31.3(c). This principle does not have a clear status as a recognized principle in general international law.
178 Campbell Mclachlan, 'The Principle of Systemic Integration and Article 31(3)(C) of the Vienna Convention', *International & Comparative Law Quarterly*, 54(2), (2005). 318. As the author suggested, the principle of systemic integration '*is not equipped on its own to resolve true conflicts of norms in international law. No principle which relies on techniques of interpretation alone can do that. The principle of systemic integration must take its place alongside a wider set of techniques which resolve such conflicts by choosing between two rival norms.*'
179 M.A. Young, (2011). Some potential for management is also recognized in H.v. Asselt, 'Managing the Fragmentation of International Climate Law'. (2013). 349.
180 H.v. Asselt, 'Legal and Political Approaches in Interplay Management: Dealing with the Fragmentation of Global Climate Governance'. (2011). 61.
181 Also called collective interplay management in Sebastian Oberthür and Olav Schram Stokke, *Managing Institutional Complexity: Regime Interplay and Global Environmental Change* (MIT Press, 2011).
182 Churchill and Ulfstein 2002 and Jordan and Schout 2006, cited in H.v. Asselt, *The Fragmentation of Global Climate Governance: Consequences and Management of Regime Interactions*. (2014). 91, 94.
183 H.v. Asselt, 'Managing the Fragmentation of International Climate Law'. (2013). 356, see also, M.A. Young, *Trading Fish, Saving Fish: The Interaction between Regimes in International Law*. (2011). 267–287.
184 Olav Schram Stokke and Sebastian Oberthür, 'Introduction: Institutional Interaction in Global Environmental Change', in *Managing Institutional Complexity: Regime Interplay and Global Environmental Change: Institutional Dimensions of Global Environmental Change* (Sebastian Oberthür and Olav Schram Stokke eds., 2011). 9–10.

185 Sebastian Oberthür and Olav Schram Stokke, 'Conclusions: Decentralized Inter-play Management in an Evolving Interinstitutional Order', in *Managing Institutional Complexity: Regime Interplay and Global Environmental Change: Institutional Dimensions of Global Environmental Change* (Sebastian Oberthür and Olav Schram Stokke eds., 2011). 314.

186 O.S. Stokke and S. Oberthür, 'Introduction: Institutional Interaction in Global Environmental Change'. (2011). 9–10. See also, S. Oberthür, (2009).

187 A similar example regarding hypothetical environmental trade restrictions is given in O.S. Stokke and S. Oberthür, 'Introduction: Institutional Interaction in Global Environmental Change'. (2011). 9–10.

188 Robert Cryer et al., *Research Methodologies in EU and International Law* (Hart, 2011). 5–10.

189 Ibid. at. 5–10.

190 Elizabeth Fisher et al., 'Maturity and Methodology: Starting a Debate about Environmental Law Scholarship', *Journal of Environmental Law*, 21(2), (2009). 213–250. In their article, International Environmental Law is described as the 'Peter Pan' of the Legal Scholarship, *'the discipline that never grew up'*, where the lack of focus on methodology is generating much of the problem. Fisher et al. describe how the poor quality of some research in the discipline of environmental law has contributed to the idea of incoherence and lack of analytical rigour.

191 It has been noted that environmental law is in need of coordination between different areas: '*Indeed, by creating a field that encourages scholars to develop expertise in issue-specific as well as jurisdiction-specific environmental laws, the gaps and inter-linkages in and between environmental problems, between these specialist regimes and general public international law, and between international environmental law and other areas of law, are frequently left unaddressed in scholarship. This creates intellectual blind spots and a lack of co-ordinated analysis about the nature of international environmental law.*' Ibid. at. 240.

192 See, K. Kulovesi, 'Exploring the Landscape of Climate Law and Scholarship: Two Emerging Trends'. (2013).

193 Such as discussions on global administrative law, governance, legal pluralism or transnational environmental law.

194 Mainly, Sebastian Oberthür, Olav Schram Stokke, Harro van Asset and Margaret Young.

195 Jeffrey L. Dunoff and Mark A. Pollack, 'International Law and International Relations: Introducing an Interdisciplinary Dialogue', in *Interdisciplinary Perspectives on International Law and International Relations: The State of the Art* (Jeffrey L. Dunoff and Mark A. Pollack eds., 2012). Or Stepan Wood et al., 'International Law and International Relations Theory: A New Generation of Interdisciplinary Scholarship', *American Journal of International Law*, 92(3), (1998). 367–397.

196 See, Anne-Marie Slaughter et al., 'International Law and International Relations Theory: A New Generation of Interdisciplinary Scholarship', *The American Journal of International Law*, 92(3), (1998). 367–397; J. Dunoff, 'A New Approach to Regime Interaction'. (2012). Detlef F. Sprinz and Yael Wolinsky, *Cases, Numbers, Models: International Relations Research Methods* (The University of Michigan Press, 2002). International law and international relations are two linked disciplines and in some universities they operate within the same department. With regards to international organizations, academic studies focus on '*the particular rules that define or issue from a specific legal body*', however other approaches such as global governance allow for the inclusion of '*a broad range of rules and actors that make up the international regime on an issue*'. On the relationship between global governance and international organizations see, Ian Hurd, *International Organizations: Politics, Law and Practice* (Cambridge University Press, 2011). 11–12.

197 An approach based on these two disciplines of international law and international relations can, in turn, be influenced by various theories such as theories on

governance or legal pluralism. See, R. Cryer et al., *Research Methodologies in EU and International Law*. (2011). 76–83, 55–57.

198 H.v. Asselt, *The Fragmentation of Global Climate Governance: Consequences and Management of Regime Interactions*. (2014). 7–9; H.v. Asselt, *The Fragmentation of Global Climate Governance: Consequences and Management of Regime Interactions*. (2013). 29.

199 H.v. Asselt, *The Fragmentation of Global Climate Governance: Consequences and Management of Regime Interactions*. (2013). xxix.

200 M.A. Young, *Trading Fish, Saving Fish: The Interaction between Regimes in International Law*. (2011). She selected some cases for study of regime interactions in the area of fisheries.

Bibliography

A38-WP/430. Report of the Executive Committee on Agenda Item 17, Section ono Climate Change (3 October 2013).

Alvarez, José E. (2005). *International Organizations as Law-Makers*, Oxford, England; New York, Oxford University Press.

Asselt, Harro van (2007). 'From UN-ity to Diversity? The UNFCCC, the Asia-Pacific Partnership, and the Future of International Law on Climate Change', *Carbon and Climate Law Review*, 1, 17–28.

Asselt, Harro van (2011). 'Legal and Political Approaches in Interplay Management: Dealling with the Fragmentation of Global Climate Governance', in, Sebastian Oberthür and Olav Schram Stokke (eds.), *Managing Institutional Complexity: Regime Interplay and Global Environmental Change: Institutional Dimensions of Global Environmental Change*, Cambridge, MA, MIT Press.

Asselt, Harro van (2013). 'Managing the Fragmentation of International Climate Law', in, Erkki J. Hollo, Kati Kulovesi and Michael Mehling (eds.), Ius Gentium: Comparative Perspective on Law and Justice v. 21 *Climate Change and the Law*, Dordrecht; New York, Springer.

Asselt, Harro van (2014). *The Fragmentation of Global Climate Governance: Consequences and Management of Regime Interactions*, Cheltenham, UK, Edward Elgar.

Asselt, Harro van, Sindico, Francesco and Mehling, Michael A. (2008). 'Global Climate Change and the Fragmentation of International Law', *Law & Policy*, 30(4), 423–449.

Berman, Ayelet, Duquet, Sanderijn, Pauwelyn, Joost, Wessel, Ramses A. and Wouters, Jan (eds.) (2012). *Informal International Lawmaking: Case Studies*, The Hague, The Netherlands, Torkel Opsahl Academic EPublisher.

Bodansky, Daniel (2010). *The Art and Craft of International Environmental Law*, Cambridge, MA, Harvard University Press.

Boyle, Alan E. (1999). 'Some Reflections on the Relationship of Treaties and Soft Law', *International and Comparative Law Quarterly*, 48(4), 901–913.

Boyle, Alan E. and Chinkin, Christine M. (2007). *The Making of International Law*, Oxford; New York, Oxford University Press.

Boyle, James (1985). 'Ideals and Things: International Legal Scholarship and the Prison-House of Language', *Harvard International Law Journal*, 26, 327.

Brownlie, Ian (2008). *Principles of Public International Law*, 7th ed., Oxford; New York, Oxford University Press.

Charlesworth, Hilary (2012). 'Law Making and Sources', in, James Crawford and Martti Koskenniemi (eds.), *The Cambridge Companion to International Law*, Cambridge; New York, Cambridge University Press.

Chinkin, C.M. (1989). 'The Challenge of Soft Law: Development and Change in International Law', *International and Comparative Law Quarterly*, 38, 850.

Crawford, James and Koskenniemi, Martti (2012). *The Cambridge Companion to International Law*, Cambridge; New York, Cambridge University Press.

Cryer, Robert, Hervey, Tamara K., Sokhi-Bulley, Bal and Böhm, Alexandra (2011). *Research Methodologies in EU and International Law*, Oxford; Portland, OR, Hart.

Danilenko, Gennadiĭ Mikhaĭlovich (1993). *Law-Making in the International Community*, Dordrecht; Boston, M. Nijhoff.

Dunoff, Jeffrey (2012). 'A New Approach to Regime Interaction', in, Margaret A. Young (ed.), *Regime Interaction in International Law: Facing Fragmentation*, Cambridge; New York, Cambridge University Press.

Dunoff, Jeffrey L. and Pollack, Mark A. (2012). 'International Law and International Relations: Introducing an Interdisciplinary Dialogue', in, Jeffrey L. Dunoff and Mark A. Pollack (ed.), *Interdisciplinary Perspectives on International Law and International Relations: The State of the Art*, New York, Cambridge University Press.

Dupuy, Pierre-Marie (1990–1991). 'Soft Law and the International Law of the Environment', *Michigan Journal of International Law*, 12, 420.

Fischer-Lescano, Andreas and Teubner, Gunther (2004). 'Regime-Collisions: The Vain Search for Legal Unity in the Fragmentation of Global Law', *Michigan Journal of International Law*, 25, 999–1046.

Fisher, Elizabeth, Lange, Bettina, Scotford, Eloise and Carlarne, Cinnamon (2009). 'Maturity and Methodology: Starting a Debate about Environmental Law Scholarship', *Journal of Environmental Law*, 21(2), 213–250.

Gehring, Thomas and Oberthur, Sebastian (2004). 'Exploring Regime Interaction: A Framework of Analysis', in, Arild Underdal and Oran R. Young (eds.), *Regime Consequences: Methodological Challenges and Research Strategies*, Dordrecht, The Netherlands, Kluwer Academic Publishers.

Harrison, James (2011). *Making the Law of the Sea: A Study in the Development of International Law*, Cambridge; New York, Cambridge University Press.

Hollis, Duncan B. (2005). 'Why State Consent Still Matters: Non-State Actors, Treaties, and the Changing Sources of International Law', *Berkeley Journal of International Law*, 23(1), 137–174.

Hurd, Ian (2011). *International Organizations: Politics, Law and Practice*, Cambridge, Cambridge University Press.

ILC (2006). *Fragmentation of International Law: Difficulties Arising from the Diversification and Expansion of International Law. Report of the Study Group of the International Law Commission*. UN Doc. A/CN.4/L.682.

Jenks, C. Wilfred (1953). 'Conflict of Law-Making Treaties', *British Year Book of International Law*, 30, 401.

Kiss, Alexandre Charles and Shelton, Dinah (2007). *Guide to International Environmental Law*, Boston, Martinus Nijhoff Publishers.

Klabbers, Jan (2007). 'Checks and Balances in the Law of International Organizations', in, M.N.S. Sellers, University of Baltimore, Center for International and Comparative Law (ed.), *Autonomy in the Law: Ius Gentium*, Dordrecht, The Netherlands, Springer.

Klabbers, Jan (2009). *An Introduction to International Institutional Law*, 2nd ed., Cambridge, UK; New York, Cambridge University Press.

Klabbers, Jan (2011). 'Beyond the Vienna Convention: Conflicting Treaty Provisions', in, Enzo Cannizzaro, Mahnoush H. Arsanjani and Giorgio Gaja (eds.), *The Law of Treaties beyond the Vienna Convention*, Oxford; New York, Oxford University Press.

Koskenniemi, Martti (2009). 'The Politics of International Law: 20 Years Later', *European Journal of International Law*, 20(1), 7–19.

Koskenniemi, Martti (2012). 'Hegemonic Regimes', in, Margaret A. Young (ed.), *Regime Interaction in International Law: Facing Fragmentation*, Cambridge; New York, Cambridge University Press.

Krasner, Stephen D. (1983). *International Regimes*, Ithaca, Cornell University Press.

Kulovesi, Kati (2013). 'Climate Change and Trade: At the Intersection of Two International Legal Regimes', in, Erkki J. Hollo, Kati Kulovesi and Michael Mehling (eds.), Ius Gentium: Comparative Perspective on Law and Justice v. 21 *Climate Change and the Law*, Dordrecht; New York, Springer.

Kulovesi, Kati (2013). 'Exploring the Landscape of Climate Law and Scholarship: Two Emerging Trends', in, Erkki J. Hollo, Kati Kulovesi and Michael Mehling (eds.), Ius Gentium: Comparative Perspectives on Law and Justice *Climate Change and the Law*, Dordrecht; New York, Springer.

Lang, Andrew T.F. (2012). 'Legal Regimes and Professional Knowledges: The Internal Politics of Regime Definition', in, Margaret A. Young (ed.), *Regime Interaction in International Law: Facing Fragmentation*, Cambridge; New York, Cambridge University Press.

Lindroos, Anja (2005). 'Addressing Norm Conflicts in a Fragmented Legal System: The Doctrine of Lex Specialis', *Nordic Journal of International Law*, 74, 27.

Lindroos, Anja and Mehling, Michael (2006). 'Dispelling the Chimera of "Self-Contained Regimes" International Law and the WTO', *The European Journal of International Law*, 16(5), 857–877.

Lowe, Vaughan (2007). *International Law*, Oxford; New York, Oxford University Press.

Mclachlan, Campbell (2005). 'The Principle of Systemic Integration and Article 31(3) (C) of the Vienna Convention', *International & Comparative Law Quarterly*, 54(2), 279–320.

Miller, Russell A. and Bratspies, Rebecca M. (2008). *Progress in International Law*, Leiden; Boston, Martinus Nijhoff Publishers.

Oberthür, Sebastian (2003). 'Institutional Interaction to Address Greenhouse Gas Emissions from International Transport: ICAO, IMO and the EU Burden-Sharing Agreement', *Project Deliverable No. D 3, Final Draft. Ecologic: Institute for International and European Policy*.

Oberthür, Sebastian (2003). 'Institutional Interaction to Address Greenhouse Gas Emissions from International Transport: ICAO, IMO and the Kyoto Protocol', *Climate Policy*, 3(3), 191–205.

Oberthür, Sebastian (2006). 'The Climate Change Regime: Interactions of the Climate Change Regime with ICAO, IMO and the EU Burden-Sharing Agreement', in, Sebastian Oberthür and Thomas Gehring (eds.), *Institutional Interaction in Global Environmental Governance: Synergy and Conflict among International and EU Policies: Global Environmental Accord: Strategies for Sustainability and Institutional Innovation*, Cambridge, MA, MIT Press.

Oberthür, Sebastian (2009). 'Interplay Management: Enhancing Environmental Policy Integration among International Institutions', *International Environmental Agreements: Politics, Law and Economics*, 9(4), 371–391.

Oberthür, Sebastian and Gehring, Thomas (2006). 'Conceptual Foundations of Institutional Interaction', in, Sebastian Oberthür and Thomas Gehring (eds.), *Institutional Interaction in Global Environmental Governance: Synergy and Conflict among International and EU Policies: Global Environmental Accord: Strategies for Sustainability and Institutional Innovation*, Cambridge, MA, MIT Press.

Oberthür, Sebastian and Gehring, Thomas (2011). 'Institutional Interaction: Ten Years of Scholarly Development', in, Sebastian Oberthür and Olav Schram Stokke (eds.), *Managing Institutional Complexity: Regime Interplay and Global Environmental Change*, Cambridge, MA, MIT Press.

Oberthür, Sebastian and Stokke, Olav Schram (2011). 'Conclusions: Decentralized Interplay Management in an Evolving Interinstitutional Order', in, Sebastian Oberthür and Olav Schram Stokke (eds.), *Managing Institutional Complexity: Regime Interplay and Global Environmental Change: Institutional Dimensions of Global Environmental Change*, Cambridge, MA, MIT Press.

Oberthür, Sebastian and Stokke, Olav Schram (2011). *Managing Institutional Complexity: Regime Interplay and Global Environmental Change*, Cambridge, MA, MIT Press.

Pauwelyn, Joost (2003). *Conflict of Norms in Public International Law: How WTO Law Relates to Other Rules of International Law*, Cambridge, UK; New York, Cambridge University Press.

Pauwelyn, Joost (2012). 'Informal International Law-Making: Framing the Concept and the Research Questions', in, Joost Pauwelyn, Ramses A. Wessel and Jan Wouters (eds.), *Informal International Law-Making*, Oxford, UK, Oxford University Press.

Pauwelyn, Joost, Wessel, Ramses A. and Wouters, Jan (2011). 'The Exercise of Public Authority through Informal International Lawmaking: An Accountability Issue?', Global Governance as Public Authority: Structures, Contestation and Normative Change. Jean Monnet Working Paper 06/11.

Piñón Carlarne, Cinnamon (2008). 'Good Climate Governance: Only a Fragmented System of International Law Away?', *Law & Policy*, 30(4), 450–480.

Rosendal, G. Kristin (2001). 'Impacts of Overlapping International Regimes: The Case of Biodiversity', *Global Governance*, 7, 95–117.

Rosendal, G. Kristin (2001). 'Overlapping International Regimes: The Case of the Intergovernmental Forum on Forests between Climate Change and Biodiversity', *International Environmental Agreements: Politics, Law and Economics, Kluwer Academic Publishers*, 1, 447–468.

Sands, Philippe (2003). *Principles of International Environmental Law*, 2nd ed., Cambridge; New York, Cambridge University Press.

Shaw, Malcolm N. (2008). *International Law*, 6th ed., Cambridge, UK; New York, Cambridge University Press.

Slaughter, Anne-Marie, Tulumello, Andrew S. and Wood, Stepan (1998). 'International Law and International Relations Theory: A New Generation of Interdisciplinary Scholarship', *The American Journal of International Law*, 92(3), 367–397.

Sprinz, Detlef F. and Wolinsky, Yael (2002). *Cases, Numbers, Models: International Relations Research Methods*, Ann Arbor, MI, The University of Michigan Press.

Stephens, Tim (2009). *International Courts and Environmental Protection*, Cambridge, UK; New York, Cambridge University Press.

Stokke, Olav Schram and Oberthür, Sebastian (2011). 'Introduction: Institutional Interaction in Global Environmental Change', in, Sebastian Oberthür and Olav Schram Stokke (eds.), *Managing Institutional Complexity: Regime Interplay and Global Environmental Change: Institutional Dimensions of Global Environmental Change*, Cambridge, MA, MIT Press.

Tomuschat, Christian (2010). *How Relevant Is the Copenhagen Accord? A Legal Perspective*, 3'er Berlin Climate Law Conference. From Bonn to Cancun and Beyond: New Dimensions in Climate Regulation.

Vienna Convention on the Law of Treaties between States and International Organizations or between International Organizations, concluded 21 March 1989. UN Doc. A/ CONF.129/15, 25 ILM 543.

Vienna Convention on the Law of Treaties. Vienna, adopted 23 May 1969, in force 27 January 1980. 8 ILM 679.

Vihma, Antto (2009). 'Friendly Neighbor or Trojan Horse? Assessing the Interaction of Soft Law Initiatives and the UN Climate Regime', *International Environmental Agreements: Politics, Law and Economics*, 9(3), 239–262.

Villiger, Mark E. (2011). 'The Rules on Interpretation: Misgivings, Misunderstandings, Miscarriage? The "Crucible" Intended by the International Law Commission', in, Enzo Cannizzaro, Mahnoush H. Arsanjani and Giorgio Gaja (eds.), *The Law of Treaties beyond the Vienna Convention*, Oxford; New York, Oxford University Press.

Voigt, Christina (2009). *Sustainable Development as a Principle of International Law: Resolving Conflicts between Climate Measures and WTO Law*, Leiden; Boston, Martinus Nijhoff Publishers.

Vranes, Erich (2006). 'The Definition of "Norm Conflict" in International Law and Legal Theory', *European Journal of International Law*, 17(2), 395–418.

Wessel, Ramses A. (2011). 'Informal International Law-Making as a New Form of World Legislation?', *International Organizations Law Review*, 8, 253–265.

Wood, Stepan, Slaughter, Anne-Marie and Tulumello, Andrew S. (1998). 'International Law and International Relations Theory: A New Generation of Interdisciplinary Scholarship', *American Journal of International Law*, 92(3), 367–397.

Young, Margaret A. (2011). 'Climate Change Law and Regime Interaction', *Climate Change Law Review*, 2, 147–157.

Young, Margaret A. (2011). 'Toward a Legal Framework for Regime Interaction: Lessons from Fisheries, Trade, and Environmental Regimes', *Proceedings of the Annual Meeting (American Society of International Law)*, 105, 107–110.

Young, Margaret A. (2011). *Trading Fish, Saving Fish: The Interaction between Regimes in International Law*, Cambridge, UK; New York, Cambridge University Press.

Young, Margaret A. (2012). 'Introduction: The Productive Friction between Regimes', in, Margaret A. Young (ed.), *Regime Interaction in International Law: Facing Fragmentation*, Cambridge; New York, Cambridge University Press.

Young, Margaret A. (2012). 'Regime Interaction in Creating, Implementing and Enforcing International Law', in, Margaret A. Young (ed.), *Regime Interaction in International Law: Facing Fragmentation*, Cambridge; New York, Cambridge University Press.

Young, Margaret A. (2012). *Regime Interaction in International Law: Facing Fragmentation*, Cambridge; New York, Cambridge University Press.

Zelli, Fariborz (2008). 'Regime Conflicts in Global Environmental Governance: A Framework for Analysis', Global Governance Working Paper No. 36.

Zelli, Fariborz (2011). 'Regime Conflicts and Their Management in Global Environmental Governance', in, Sebastian Oberthür and Olav Schram Stokke (eds.), *Managing Institutional Complexity: Regime Interplay and Global Environmental Change: Institutional Dimensions of Global Environmental Change*, Cambridge, MA, MIT Press.

3 Law-making at the climate, ICAO and IMO regimes

> Theoretically the resistance to change is explained in what is termed the double embedding attitudes – i.e. that attitudes are lodged in logical lattices as well as in social networks simultaneously. This makes for mutual reinforcement, continuity and stability: Opinions come in ensembles, friends come in clusters – and both come together. Thus the reason why broad attitude change is event-driven is because, simply put, dramatic events may simultaneously attack personal beliefs as well as social relations. Rather than being changed by the force of argument, attitudes are changed by the force of circumstance, so to speak. Event-generated change is potent because the two structures are simultaneously impacted: one at the level of conceptualization and experience – the logical lattice; the other at the level of human relations and interactions – the social network.[1]

This chapter explores and critiques the legal framework for the regulation of emissions of IBF and gives an account of the state of affairs, divided into three sections dedicated to the climate, ICAO and IMO regimes, respectively. It is important to survey the existing legal framework, the tools available and the actions taken so far for the regulation of emissions from IBF in the three selected regimes in order to identify the tensions that impede progress in this area. This survey also enables an understanding of the channels of interaction between the regimes. This involves a descriptive account of the variables of law-making that were explained in the second chapter, that is, of the *actors, instruments and processes*[2] in the regimes.

The climate regime

An overview

Before focusing on the treatment of GHG emissions from international aviation and maritime transport under the climate change convention and related instruments, a brief summary of the climate regime and the current negotiations within it is provided here in order to outline the legal and institutional frameworks for both sectors.

In the mid-1980s the international community became aware of the climate problem, and decided to pursue an agreement to curb the warming trend.[3] As

Bodansky has described,[4] the agenda-setting[5] phase took place between 1985 and 1988, when climate change went from the scientific to the policy arena, followed by a pre-negotiation period with governments involved in the process, resulting in the establishment of the formal negotiating committee. It was in 1988 when the issue of climate change was recognized by the UN General Assembly[6] as a *'common concern of mankind'*[7] and backed the establishment of the IPCC[8] to provide technical assessments on the causes, impacts and responses to climate change. Global efforts took a firm step forward when the UNGA prompted definitive action by establishing an intergovernmental negotiating process, under its auspices and supported by the United Nations Environment Program (UNEP) and the World Meteorological Organization (WMO), with the mandate of preparing an effective legal instrument,[9] a framework convention on climate change.[10] The Intergovernmental Negotiating Committee for a Framework Convention on Climate Change[11] carried out its work[12] until 1992, when the first international treaty attempting to deal with climate change was adopted. Under the auspices of the 1992 Rio Conference,[13] the UNFCCC was concluded in New York. It has a near-universal character; with a membership of 195 parties, 194 of which are countries and one regional economic integration organization, the European Union (EU).[14] Parties opted for the formula of a framework convention-protocol, familiar to other environmental regimes, which allows for flexibility and the inclusion of all parties.[15]

The Convention established a common, ultimate, objective for the parties in achieving *'the stabilization of greenhouse gas*[16] *concentrations in the atmosphere at a level that would prevent dangerous anthropogenic*[17] *interference with the climate system'*.[18] And, as stated at the end of Article 2, the stabilization level is to be achieved within a certain time frame *'sufficient to allow ecosystems to adapt naturally to climate change, to ensure that food production is not threatened and to enable economic development to proceed in a sustainable manner'*. As such, the convention does not propose an absolute ban on the emissions of greenhouse gases or on the activities causing such emissions, but to stabilize them. In this way the UNFCCC establishes an environmental threshold in order to prevent dangerous interference with the climate system or, in other words, it sets an environmental quality standard similar to those used in different environmental areas by other multilateral environmental agreements.[19] In terms of articulating a legal obligation, the provision can be regarded as *'an ill-defined obligation'*.[20] However, some authors have argued that the agreement at the Copenhagen Accord (2009) and Cancun Agreements (2010)[21] to keep global temperature under 2°C over pre-industrialized levels means the 'quantification' of the convention's objective.[22]

This overarching objective applies to the climate regime as a whole, that is, to the Convention and any related legal instruments that the COP may adopt. As a framework convention, the UNFCCC does not specifically state how to achieve its objective and the commitments are phrased with a language that lacks strength[23] but allows for flexibility. More importantly, the convention establishes the necessary legal and institutional setting for the future negotiations on commitments by the parties and the long-term dialogues, which successfully led to the development of a more specific regime and set of commitments in the KP.[24]

In any further development of the climate regime, the guiding principles that the convention embraces play an essential role, since they should guide parties *'in their actions to achieve the objective of the Convention and to implement its provisions'*.[25] These guiding principles are located in the Preamble and in Article 3 of the Convention and although the legal status of these principles is not necessarily binding, Article 3 is not without legal effect for interpretation, implementation and future negotiation issues.[26] They are, namely: the principle of intra- and inter-generational equity and CBDRRC,[27] especially in connection with most vulnerable countries,[28] the precautionary principle,[29] cost-effectiveness,[30] sustainable development and growth.[31] It has been argued that together, the precautionary principle,[32] the principle of sustainable development[33] and the CBDRRC principle *'form a basis for the substantive provisions of the Convention'*.[34]

The CBDRRC principle combines two elements, namely: a common responsibility of the states to fulfil the objective of the convention and an understanding of the different responsibilities and capabilities of states. Thus different national circumstances lead to differential treatment. Although differential treatment is present in other international legal regimes, CBDRRC has found in the climate regime a fertile ground in which to develop.[35] It is embodied in both the Climate Convention and the KP and it casts a shadow over the whole law-making process both within and beyond the climate regime. It is not only a key principle but the *'most important among the principles that frame the climate regime'*,[36] although it's exact content and meaning is contested.[37] This underpinning principle implies that *'the developed country Parties should take the lead in combating climate change and the adverse effects thereof.'* As such, the convention differentiates obligations and rights for three different categories of country parties: Annex I Parties, Non-Annex I Parties and Annex II Parties. Annex I is composed of developed countries that were members of the OECD in 1992[38] and the economies in transition[39] which have the biggest burden in achieving the objective of the convention. Annex II is a group composed only by OECD members in 1992.[40] Parties that don't feature in Annex I to the Convention (i.e. Non-Annex I Parties) is the largest group of parties that includes all developing countries, although within this group disparate development, economic and social situations can be found[41] as well as different vulnerability to climate change.[42] The convention establishes certain obligations for all countries[43] such as the development, updating and publishing of national inventories of anthropogenic emissions by sources, and their removal through sinks of all greenhouse gases not controlled by the Montréal Protocol,[44] using comparable methodologies.[45] The Convention states that all parties shall also formulate, implement, publish and regularly update national and regional programmes containing measures to mitigate climate change, and measures to facilitate adequate adaptation,[46] and to communicate to the COP information on implementation, pursuant to Article 12.[47]

Despite the fact that these obligations apply to all countries, *'the extent to which developing country Parties will effectively implement their commitments under the Convention will depend on the effective implementation by developed country Parties of their commitments under the Convention related to financial resources and transfer of technology.'*[48] Some flexibility was given to countries with economies in transition.[49] The convention also calls for *'full consideration'* of the specific needs arising from the adverse effects and impacts that measures would have for certain groups of developing country parties,[50] as well as the specific needs and special situations of the least developed countries in their actions with regard to funding and the transfer of technology.[51] In regards to parties with economies that are highly dependent on income generated from the production, processing, export and consumption of fossil fuels and energy-intensive products or with serious difficulties in switching to alternatives.[52]

Based on the differential treatment that guides the climate regime, the convention establishes an extra set of obligations for the parties included in Annex I.[53] This involves the adoption of national policies and measures for mitigation purposes[54] to limit anthropogenic emissions and protect and enhance sinks and reservoirs *'to demonstrate that developed countries are taking the lead'*. The communication of such PAMs, as well as the projected GHG emissions, have *'the aim of returning individually or jointly to their 1990 levels'*.[55] Further differential treatment is reflected in the special obligations of Annex II country parties[56] that *'shall provide new and additional financial resources to meet the agreed full costs incurred by developing country Parties in complying with their obligations under Article 12, paragraph 1'*. This refers to the communication obligations and also to meeting the cost of implementing measures from Article 4.1.[57] Moreover, Annex II countries shall also assist the developing country parties that are particularly vulnerable to the adverse effects of climate change in meeting their costs of adaptation,[58] and shall promote, facilitate and finance the transfer of, or access to, environmentally sound technologies and know-how to other parties, particularly developing country parties, and assist in facilitating the transfer of such technologies.[59]

In addition to the regulatory provisions detailed above, and in order to fulfil its objective, the Convention also establishes an institutional and administrative framework. Multilateral environmental agreements usually result in the setting up of a threefold institutional framework, based on a decision-making body, some expert bodies and a secretariat. This pattern is followed in the climate regime. Although this institutional setup was established under the UNFCCC, the institutions are shared with the KP. The parties to the UNFCCC meet at the COP, while it also serves as a meeting for parties to the KP (CMP). Their role in the active evolution of MEAs has been acknowledged.[60]

The COP[61] is the supreme body of the Convention, which meets annually.[62] It is the place where State actors converge to take decisions. A diplomatic delegation representing each country party attends the COP to negotiate on behalf of their governments. The number of members in the delegations varies greatly depending on the resources that countries can allocate to this end. The COP's functions are to *'keep under regular review the implementation of the Convention and any related legal instruments that the Conference of the Parties may adopt, and shall make, within its mandate, the decisions necessary to promote the effective implementation of the Convention'*,[63] including the adoption of methodologies and the establishment of bodies to achieve its mandate.

A relevant issue here is the lack of procedural rules in the regime; however, the rules set out in the Convention and KP, the failed draft rules of procedure[64] and other unwritten practices of the regime guide the procedures. The COP works on consensus for decision-making; despite extended use, it is not exempt of problems.[65] Nonetheless, limited-membership bodies have their own procedural rules and make use of majority voting.[66]

Two subsidiary bodies were established in the Convention to assist the COP/CMP, namely: a Subsidiary Body for Implementation (SBI)[67] and a Subsidiary Body on Scientific and Technological Advice (SBSTA).[68] These bodies provide assistance in implementing the Convention and scientific issues, respectively. Membership of these bodies is open to representatives of all party governments, with specific knowledge. They meet twice a year, independently, at the COP and at the secretariat. The sessions of the COP and subsidiary bodies admit observers. These could be representatives of the United Nations, specialized agencies and related organizations, IGOs and NGOs.

Another key figure in the institutional climate architecture is the Secretariat,[69] a permanent, neutral and independent body of international civil servants located in Bonn, Germany. It acts under the COP and

> provides organizational support and technical expertise to the UNFCCC negotiations and institutions and facilitates the flow of authoritative information on the implementation of the Convention and its Kyoto Protocol. This includes the development and effective implementation of innovative approaches to mitigate climate change and drive sustainable development.[70]

Among its functions is the coordination with the secretariats from other international bodies and other conventions, whose work relates to the issue of climate change. It is linked to the UN[71] and staffed by almost 500 employees and governed by United Nations Rules and Regulations. The executive secretary reports directly to the UN secretary general, who called for institutional linkage at the first COP, and is directed in its work by the Bureau of the COP.[72] A particularity of the regime is the considerations of membership in this bureau, where a seat is reserved for SIDS in '*recognition of their urgent stake in the regime's work*'.[73]

Another intergovernmental subsidiary body relevant to the regulation of IBF is the ADP. This was established in 2011[74] to develop a legal instrument under the Convention, applicable to all parties, and to identify and explore options for enhancing mitigation. Not only parties, but observer organizations such as IGOs and NGOs can also contribute to discussions and submit documents to the ADP.

At COP1 (Berlin, 1995), an awareness about the insufficiency of the Convention's commitments[75] led to the adoption of the Berlin Mandate, an agreement to initiate talks towards further commitments for developed countries. Such talks culminated in December 1997, at the third COP, held in Kyoto, Japan. It was at COP3 where the first international agreement including binding reduction targets of GHGs for developed countries and countries in transition to a market economy[76] was adopted. However the KP did not come into force until 2005, owing not only to the formal requirements[77] of the instrument itself but also to the political negotiations that lay behind it.[78] Currently 191 countries, plus the EU, are signatories to the KP; however it lacks the membership of a mayor player, namely the United States.[79] The KP can be regarded as an overall framework for further development through its institutions.[80]

At Kyoto, parties agreed to establish quantified emissions limitations and reduction objectives for Annex I country parties. The principle target and time-table was an overall reduction of GHG emissions of 5% below the 1990 emission levels for the first commitment period, that is, from 2008 to 2012.[81] In order to achieve this reduction in a cost-effective manner, the KP established different flexibility mechanisms, namely emissions trading,[82] Joint Implementation,[83] the Clean Development Mechanism (CDM)[84] and the possibility for countries to fulfil their commitments jointly.[85]

Negotiations in the climate change arena operated on two separate tracks, namely a track under the KP and a track under the Convention. At the first meeting of the parties to the KP,[86] the Ad Hoc Working Group on the KP (AWG-KP) was put in place to fulfil the mandate established by the protocol, to consider and negotiate parties' commitments beyond 2012.[87] The work of the AWG-KP has recently led to the adoption of the Doha Amendment,[88] which establishes new commitments for Annex I countries in the second commitment period 2013–2020 of the KP.[89] Separate to that process, an Ad Hoc Working Group on Long-term Cooperative Action (AWG-LCA) under the Convention was launched at COP13,[90] as part of the Bali Action Plan. Its aim was to foster the implementation of the Convention through a new negotiating process for all parties based on long-term cooperative action,[91] presenting an agreed outcome to the COP for adoption.[92] The two-track negotiation paths envisioned a deadline for 2009, although their existence and work was extended successively in 2009, 2010 and 2011. In 2011, the COP held in Durban decided to bring the work of the AWG-LCA to an end by the following year, so in December 2012 its outcomes were published and the group was formally dismantled.[93] AWG-LCA's negotiations were characterized by a division between parties in favour of a top-down and a bottom-up approach. In the AWG-LCA, the negotiation gap between developing and developed countries widened, towards a polarization in discussions. As a consequence, establishing a '*shared vision*' was an almost impossible task and the final outcome of the group was limited to the endorsement of the 2°C target.

As Bodansky has pointed out in connection with the negotiation process in the climate regime, from the beginning

> parties have struggled to choose between two competing models: a top-down 'contractual' approach favoring binding targets and timetables, and a bottom-up 'facilitative' approach favoring voluntary actions defined unilaterally. In the course of the regime's evolution to date, parties have in fact produced examples of both: the binding Kyoto Protocol, and the parallel voluntary framework that emerged at the 2009 Copenhagen summit and was formally adopted a year later in Cancún.[94]

Indeed, the 2009 Copenhagen Accord,[95] a political declaration of which the COP simply took note, rolled out, in the negotiating process, a bottom-up approach where parties, on a voluntary and unilateral basis, committed themselves with emissions reduction pledges.[96] A year later, the Cancun Agreements[97] successfully brought the Copenhagen Accord into the UNFCCC process. However, the role of the regime was just to bear witness of the voluntary mitigation efforts.[98]

The negotiations in Durban 2011 lead to a consensus that a new agreement, which aims to bring together the current patchwork of arrangements under the climate regime into a single comprehensive instrument, is needed and the establishment of a new subsidiary body to deal with this, namely the Ad Hoc Working Group on the Durban Platform for Enhanced Action (ADP).[99] In connection with the contentious issue of CDBR, a '*recasting of differentiation*' in the Durban Outcomes has occurred, since reference to this principle was not included in the text.[100] Furthermore, mention was made to '*all parties*' in the text, which implies that the original significance of equity and differentiation, as guiding principles for instruments emerging under the convention, is diluted.[101] However, the launch of a new commitment period under the KP, at COP 18 in Doha 2012, highlighted that the differential treatment and the obligation of developed countries to lead the way is still relevant.[102] At the same time, the number of countries willing to commit themselves to a second KP period, and the level of their commitments, casts doubts over its reach and future.[103]

Progress in the COP 19 held in Warsaw in November 2013, although limited, were seen as '*an intermediate stop on the way to a global climate agreement to be adopted in Paris in 2015*',[104] where the parties committed to advance the ADP agenda.[105] Similarly, the COP 20 held in Lima brought progress towards the preparation of a negotiating text, due to be presented at COP 21 next year. The Lima Call for Climate Action[106] made evident that, although 'watered down', the agreement for all parties was likely to be achieved in Paris.[107] Notably, the outcomes of Warsaw and Lima were crucial for the development and communication of the Intended Nationally Determined Contributions (INDCs) by each party to the UNFCCC, which formed the basis of negotiations for the global agreement.

Historically, in December 2015, the Paris Agreement, an agreement with legally binding[108] commitments for all Parties under the Climate Convention, was adopted.[109] In implementing the Convention's objective, parties to the Paris Agreement agreed to hold '*the increase in the global average temperature to well below 2°C above pre-industrial levels*' and, even, to pursue a 1.5°C stabilization target.[110] To achieve this temperature goal, '*Parties aim to reach global peaking of greenhouse gas emissions as soon as possible*'.[111] To meet this goal, a flexible bottom-up framework has been established where parties summit their pledges (i.e. Nationally Determined Contributions [NDCs]) every five years and these are reviewed towards the global goal, with a view to ensure that ambition is ratcheted over time.[112] Parties are given leeway in choosing the domestic mitigation measures for their NDCs.[113]

With regards to CBDRRC, the Paris Agreement, an agreement for all parties with commitments for all parties,[114] *'provides an historical U-turn in international climate governance on the vexed question of differentiation'*[115] with a new nuanced form of differentiation between developed and developing countries.[116]

The implementation of the agreement is now in the hands of the COP serving as the meeting of the Parties to the Paris Agreement (CMA1), which held its first session in Marrakech, Morocco in November 2016 at the COP 22. In Marrakech, it was agreed that the 'rule book' detailing and putting flesh into the bones of the Paris Agreement will be developed by December 2018.[117]

Law-making in the climate regime

Actors

Although party delegations usually converge in five groups representing the regions of the world,[118] interests of parties are better represented, in regards to climate change, through specific grouping; developing countries generally form their negotiation positions through the G-77, although individual countries and other clusters such as the Alliance of Small Island States (AOSIS)[119] and the group of least developed countries (LDC)[120] or the African UN Regional Group can diverge on certain matters and work on their own. The Umbrella Group is composed of developed countries excluding the EU[121] and the EU countries usually hold the same position. There are other smaller groupings such as the Environmental Integrity Group (EIG)[122] or the Organization of Petroleum Exporting Countries (OPEC).[123] Aside from country parties, non-state actors are likely to be present and try to lobby the discussions.[124]

Non-state participants in the climate regime include public and private environmental, industry and research NGOs.[125] According to Kal Raustiala, *'States have incorporated NGOs because their participation enhances the ability, both in technocratic and political terms, of states to regulate through the treaty process.'*[126] In a later work, the same author lists the main tasks carried out by non-state actors in the climate regime, namely: agenda setting and awareness raising, policy recommendations, advice and information, political pressure to influence negotiation, monitoring actions and assessing implementation.[127]

NGOs have been organized in constituencies, each of them with a focal point, to make possible the interaction of all stakeholders (over 1,400 observers) to the climate negotiations with the Secretariat.[128] There are currently nine constituencies: business and industry non-governmental organizations (BINGOs), environmental non-governmental organizations (ENGOs), indigenous peoples organizations (IPOs), local government and municipal authorities (LGMAs), research and independent non-governmental organizations (RINGOs), trade unions non-governmental organizations (TUNGOs), farmers and agricultural NGOs, women and gender, and youth (YOUNGO).[129] There are generally no consensual positions within the environmental or business NGOs; divergences result from the north-south origin of the NGOs in the case of ENGOs and from the degree of 'greenness' in the case of BINGOs.[130]

In connection with IBF, and in terms of environmental NGOs, the biggest ENGO is the Climate Action Network-International (CAN-International)[131] which has been highly involved in IBF, through submissions, statements, interventions, presentations and participation at COP side events.[132] There are also ENGOs with a specific focus on IBF: with regard to aviation, the most important is the International Coalition for Sustainable Aviation (ICSA),[133] which is associated with the Aviation Environment Federation (AEF), the International Council for Clean Transportation (ICCT) and Transport and Environment (T&E). In connection with shipping, there is the Clean Shipping Coalition (CSC),[134] where T&E, the Environmental Defense Fund (EDF) and Clean Air Task Force (CATF) are among the member groups. Some important BINGOs comprise relevant industry for aviation and maritime transport, such is the case for example of the Pew Center on Global Climate Change, to which Boeing is a member.[135] However, as Depledge has noted,[136] BINGOS are less active than ENGOS because BINGOS' viewpoints are more diverse and it is more difficult for them to agree in the one or two statements that they are allowed for their constituency. Additionally, in the SBSTA process, it is more frequent to find statements and interventions from ENGOS since matters of their interest are dealt with there, such as IBF.

Epistemic communities in the climate regime are foremost connected with the research coordinated and published by the IPCC. However, other scientist groups participate in the negotiation process, such as the Foundation of International Environmental Law and Development (FIELD), the International Institute for Sustainable Development (IISD) and the Stockholm Environmental Institute, contributing to the debate and the quest for solutions with research and publications. IGOs also partake in the negotiations as non-state actors. This includes the World Bank, OECD, and UN organizations, bodies and agencies; in this connection ICAO and the IMO are also participants in the regime, through their secretariats.

Additionally, initiatives of non-state participants of the regime have developed within the climate regime, such as the NAZCA Climate Portal[137] (which emerged from the COP20 in Lima), a platform where non-state participants, including aviation and maritime business, make available their specific actions and commitments. The COP decision adopting the Paris Agreement explicitly recognized the contribution of non-party stakeholders, including the private sector, in addressing and responding to climate change.[138] Parties invite non-state actors to scale up effort, and specifically to register them at the NAZCA platform,[139] while acknowledging the role of private actors in providing incentives for emission reduction activities.[140] The Paris Agreement itself recognizes '*the importance of the engagements of all levels of government and various actors, in accordance with respective national legislations of Parties, in addressing climate change*'.[141] Also, in the context of the mechanism to transfer mitigation credits, Article 6 mentions the relevance of public and private participation.

Instruments

The UNFCCC is the umbrella instrument for the regulation of GHG emissions, its objective, guiding principles and obligations, that is, the substantive part of the Convention in Articles 2, 3 and 4. These provisions also relates to emissions from IBF.

The commitments established for all parties[142] in Article 4.1(a) and 4.1(c) are specifically relevant to IBF. First, Article 4.1(a) asks countries to:

> Develop, periodically update, publish and make available to the Conference of the Parties, in accordance with Article 12,[143] national inventories of anthropogenic emissions by sources and removals by sinks of all greenhouse gases not controlled by the Montreal Protocol, using comparable methodologies to be agreed upon by the Conference of the Parties.

The regime distinguishes between the domestic and the international sphere when it comes to bunker fuels. While emissions from domestic aviation and domestic maritime transport are included in their national totals as part of the country's transport emissions, the international ones are reported separately and do not count towards national totals.[144]

The obligation to submit annual national inventories has an attached sub-obligation related to the use of similar methodologies, in order to compile the inventories. It was agreed at COP1 (Berlin, 1995) to use the IPCC Guidelines for National Greenhouse Gas Inventories[145] to calculate and report national GHG emissions, removal and sinks. With regards to emissions from IBF, these are calculated based on the place where the fuel was sold. The reason for the choice of this criterion was that the estimations of mobile sources present difficulties in compiling data, accuracy, consistency between inventories and trans-boundary issues on fuel that is moved across borders.[146] The agreed criteria were also consistent with the parties' wishes in the INC-UNFCCC discussions, where it was the preferred option.[147]

Addressing GHG emissions from IBF has been problematic in connection with three different matters: the development of adequate and consistent inventories, the allocation of emissions and the policy options to control these emissions.[148] The development of adequate inventories and finding a way for allocation was entrusted to subsidiary bodies in 1995.[149] From these three issues, the problem of allocation has proved to be the most contentious one, because '*international transport by definition raises international competitiveness issues and some countries are reluctant to count emissions from fuels sold for international aviation or maritime transportation towards their national totals, particularly given the dramatic increase in these emissions since 1990.*'[150] In that connection, the third COP held in Kyoto had to leave allocation issues for later and urged the SBSTA '*to further elaborate on the inclusion of these emissions in the overall greenhouse gas inventories of Parties*'.[151]

The second provision in the convention that relates to IBF emissions is Article 4.1(c), which prompts parties to:

> promote and cooperate in the development, application and diffusion, including transfer, of technologies, practices and processes that control, reduce or prevent anthropogenic emissions of greenhouse gases not controlled by the Montreal Protocol in all relevant sectors, including the energy, transport, industry, agriculture, forestry and waste management sector.

The enhancement of the implementation of this article was pursued under the work of the AWG-LCA.

THE KYOTO PROTOCOL (KP)

Among other decisions on emissions from IBF[152] at Kyoto it was agreed that these emissions would not fall within the scope of the protocol. As such, Article 2.2 of the KP excluded both international aviation emissions and international maritime transport emissions from its coverage and appointed ICAO and the IMO, respectively, as the specific fora where Annex I Parties shall continue the negotiations:

> The Parties included in Annex I shall pursue limitation or reduction of emissions of greenhouse gases not controlled by the Montreal Protocol from aviation and marine bunker fuels, working through the International Civil Aviation Organization and the International Maritime Organization, respectively.

Article 2.2 was built upon the consolidated negotiating text, elaborated by the chairman[153] and with the proposal of EU, Switzerland and New Zealand.[154] The exclusion was based on a few elements; mainly the difficulty of determining the allocation and responsibility for emissions, at the national level, for international emissions as well as the difficulty of defining an instrument to deal with them. The provision recognizes the existence and expertise of both international authorities (i.e. ICAO and IMO), with specialized knowledge in specific areas of international law and law-making and arguably intends to clarify the '*international division of labor between the climate regime and the ICAO and the IMO*'.[155] However, the main reasons for its exclusion of the KP can be found in the lack of agreement on how to distribute responsibility for those international emissions, so the adoption of Article 2.2 '*was intended to lessen the need for the climate regime to be proactive in the controversial policy issues surrounding allocation and control options*'.[156]

COP DECISIONS AND OTHER OUTCOMES ON IBF

The legal nature of COP decisions is contested on the grounds of their autonomy and legitimacy. COP decisions are rarely based on unanimous voting, rather on majority, and the expression of consensus does not constitute formal or explicit consent, such as in the adoption of technical details of obligations that already exist.

Therefore '*the treatment of consent appears to be the most significant difference between law-making operating through COP decisions as opposed to more traditional systems.*'[157]

Few COP decisions have so far been produced regarding the issue of emissions from IBF, and none of them on substantive matters. Nonetheless they provide a framework for law-making in this issue area. The first one, Decision 4/CP.1,[158] relates to the development of adequate inventories and entrusts allocation to subsidiary bodies of the Convention.[159] The second one is the Decision 2/CP.3,[160] which *recalls* IBF not to be included in national totals according to the IPCC Guidelines and *urges* the SBSTA to further elaborate on the inclusion of these emissions in the parties' inventories. Previously, the work of SBSTA revealed that the data '*was incomplete and hampered consideration of the politically thorny issue of emissions allocation*'.[161] Also, in Decision 2/CP.17,[162] parties agreed '*to continue its consideration of issues related to addressing emissions from international aviation and maritime transport*'.

OUTCOMES OF THE AWG-LCA

In 2008, some parties to the AWG-LCA identified the possibility of including the emissions from IBF in the work of the body, under the rubric of cooperative sector-specific approaches and actions envisioned in Bali.[163] A negotiating text with three options was put forward in 2009[164] and IBF was formally included in the chapter on Enhanced Action on Mitigation. The text options were progressively expanded and reservations and objections were voiced.[165] Most discussions orbited around the role of ICAO and IMO, the level or reductions, the allocation not to countries but to the sector as a whole, and treatment of developing countries.[166] The issue of differential treatment was the most contentious, while there was an increasing agreement among parties on the primary role ICAO and IMO for regulation with guidance from the UNFCCC.[167] Due to a lack of agreement, the text options regarding IBF were not included in the document reported to COP16 for consideration. Despite the establishment of a contact group in 2011 with the purpose of facilitating agreement in the AWG-LCA, there were similar discrepancies around the proposed text in 2012. Consequently, IBF did not figure in the final output of the AWG-LCA,[168] awarding the dubious honour of being the only agenda item of the BAP closed without '*a decision text nor a follow-up process*'.[169] Disagreements within the AWG-LCA revealed the same tensions as the general discussions on the specific reach of CBDRRC. Submissions by parties and organizations contributing to the work of the group, and the links established between the climate regime and ICAO and IMO, are apparent.

THE PARIS AGREEMENT

In 2011, the ADP was entrusted to develop '*a protocol, another legal instrument or an agreed outcome with legal force under the Convention applicable to all Parties*' for adoption at the COP21 in Paris,[170] where a clause on IBF was considered but didn't make it to the final text.[171]

While the Paris Agreement was adopted without a specific mention to IBF, references that all sources of anthropogenic GHG emissions imply that the sectors are not excluded from the aims of the agreement. However, while the Paris Agreement does not exclude IBF from its long-term mitigation aims,[172] the mitigation tools, namely national pledges, chosen to achieve these goals are not thought to address IBF.

Nevertheless, even considering that IBF fall outside its scope,[173] the Paris Agreement modifies core aspects of the climate change regime, which, in turn, are likely to have indirect consequences in the regulation of IBFs.[174]

Processes

SUBSIDIARY BODY FOR SCIENTIFIC AND TECHNOLOGICAL ADVICE (SBSTA)

At the first COP, held in Berlin in 1995, it was decided to give a mandate to the SBSTA and the SBI to address the issue of allocation and control of emissions from IBF, and report to the COP, '*taking fully into account on-going work in Governments and international organizations, including the IMO and ICAO*'.[175] The allocation and management of IBF was initially included in the SBSTA agenda,[176] but after inconsistencies were found in inventories, they shifted most of their efforts, especially after the KP was agreed upon,[177] towards improving reporting methodologies.[178]

The SBSTA has held discussions on how to allocate emissions from IBF to particular countries. The options envisioned range from no allocation to allocation to parties based on different criteria, namely: in proportion to their national emissions; according to the place where the fuel was sold; according to nationality of the transporting company or country of register or country of operator; according to the country of departure or destination of the aircraft or vessel; according to country of departure or destination of passengers or cargo; according to country of origin of passenger or owner of the cargo; or according to emissions generated within the national space.[179] Over time these eight options have been narrowed down[180] and it seems that the most likely choice would be to divide the emissions between the countries of origin and destination.[181]

Close cooperation has been established between the SBSTA and ICAO and the IMO by providing reports on their progress, statements and information through the secretariats,[182] and other actors, such as the IPCC.[183] This cooperation was enforced by the mandate given by the COP to its secretariat to '*continue to develop his cooperation with the secretariats of the International Civil Aviation Organization and the International Maritime Organization and participate in their meetings on climate change related issues*'.[184]

The work of the SBSTA is not restricted to scientific and technological issues and there is scope in the mandate of the UNFCCC article 9.2 for '*other disciplines*'.[185] Its sessions are open to all members,[186] and non-state actors, although '*in practice it is rare that all the 190-plus parties and thousands of delegates are intimately involved in a negotiation on a particular topic, with active participants usually confined to 20–30 core individuals, often fewer.*'[187] Usually, the SBSTA makes use of smaller contact groups with no delegated power for drafting and informal consultations. Despite this, the negotiating process at the SBSTA is not eased:

first, because the need to report back to coalitions makes the process '*lengthy and complicated*',[188] and second, because of the effort required to build consensus in the decision-making practice.[189]

ADP

The ADP, a subsidiary body under the Convention established in 2011,[190] held its first session in 2012 establishing its work under two work streams.[191] Work Stream 1 aims to develop '*a protocol, another legal instrument or an agreed outcome with legal force under the Convention applicable to all Parties*' by 2015, to be implemented in 2020.[192] The second Work Stream aims to enhance mitigation ambitions by exploring options to bridge the gap between parties' emission reduction pledges by 2020 and the target of not exceeding 2°C global warming above pre-industrial levels.

In the document containing the outcome of the AWG-LCA's work,[193] parties agreed to '*continue its consideration of issues related to addressing emissions from international aviation and maritime transport*'.[194] This task was transferred to the ADP, although there were no substantive discussions on the issue in the ADP Work Stream 1 until the run-up to Paris. In Doha, parties could not agree on how to conciliate differential and equal treatment especially with regards to distortion of competition, so IBF were not included in the negotiating agenda. However, some parties, such as the EU, allude to IBF in the context of the ADP Work Stream 2 as to be considered for the pre-2020 ambition. It was indicated that IBF could enhance climate change mitigation to bridge the emissions gap and also contribute to the finance by generating finance flows. All parties agree to regulate international aviation and shipping through ICAO and IMO initiatives before 2015.[195]

Within the ADP Work Stream 2, and in connection with initiatives in the thematic areas of transportation, certain workshops on the pre-2020 ambitions were held and parties raised concerns over unilateralism.[196] A technical paper[197] was prepared for COP 19 (2014), gathering information on the options to enhance mitigation ambition in different areas, one of them being aviation and maritime transport. The document is based on submissions from parties and other organizations. With regards to emissions from IBF, some countries pointed out the mitigation potential of the sector[198] as well as some co-benefits in air quality and job creation. The work of ICAO and the IMO was acknowledged under the cooperative initiatives[199] and at the meeting which took place in Bonn in May 2013[200] where the EU '*identified the need to address bunker fuels also through the ICAO and IMO*'.[201] Also, CAN-international voiced the need for the ADP '*to put emissions from international transport firmly on its agenda in both Work streams, and send the signal to the IMO and ICAO that action is expected in 2013*'.[202] Despite these calls the ADP meetings resulted in limited progress.

As part of the ADP negotiating agenda, IBF could have been incorporated in the Paris Agreement. Some beneficial aspects of including IBF in the agreement include the resolution of a problematic issue that has tormented the climate regime for decades, the reduction of global emissions, the improvement of equity in the regime, and the use of potential revenue from IBF towards implementing parties' financial commitments.[203]

However, the road to Paris for IBF was fraught with uncertainties, with both sectors coming in and out of the negotiating text on various occasions. The negotiating text shaped in Geneva in February 2015[204] contained two references to IBF: the first one, in connection with the 2°C target, where the text acknowledges the need for: 1) global sectoral emission reduction targets for the sectors; and 2) all parties to work through ICAO and the IMO to develop global policy frameworks to achieve the target.[205] In the second one, concerning IBF as a source of finance for adaptation, the text included a provision encouraging ICAO and IMO to adopt a levy scheme to provide financial support for the Adaptation Fund. Also, the text requested ICAO and IMO to take into account special needs of developing countries with regards to tourism and the international transport of traded goods, specifically the least developed countries, small island developing states and countries in Africa.[206] The Bonn negotiating text[207] produced in June 2015 maintained the same options. However, these preliminary negotiating articles did not make it to the COP21 and the non-paper noted by the chairs at the Bonn conference in October 2015[208] erased IBF from the draft. Finally, the sectors came back to the text presented by the ADP at the climate negotiations in Paris, which included a mention to IBF but exclude the reference to the sectors as sources for financing adaptation.

The option to include IBF in the context of Article 3 (mitigation) read as follows:

> Parties [shall][should][other] pursue the limitation or reduction of greenhouse gas emissions from international aviation and marine bunker fuels, working through the International Civil Aviation Organization and the International Maritime Organization, respectively, with a view to agreeing concrete measures addressing these emissions, including developing procedures for incorporating emissions from international aviation and marine bunker fuels into low-emission development strategies.[209]

This text was kept in the negotiating draft until Thursday the 9th of December, four days before the closure of the COP21, when the sectors dropped off the draft agreement.[210] IBF remained out of the text on the next day's version[211] and in the final Agreement.[212]

CMA

Since the Paris Agreement does not exclude any sector from its long-term mitigation aims, it is theoretically possible for the CMA to consider work on IBF emissions. However this possibility seems rather unrealistic given the negotiations history and the pressing deadline to finish a basic rule book of the implementation of the Paris Agreement.

The ICAO regime

An overview

ICAO is the global regulatory entity in the field of international aviation, with quasi-universal State-level membership. The ICAO's constitutive instrument is the Convention on International Civil Aviation.[213] The organization was established in 1944[214] with the aim of developing '*the principles and techniques of international air navigation and to foster the planning and development of international air transport*'.[215] These aims involve pursuing the safe and orderly development of international civil aviation throughout the world, the development of airways, airports, and air navigation facilities and in general all aspects of civil aeronautics. Furthermore the ICAO seeks to prevent economic waste owed to '*unreasonable competition*', ensuring that contracting States' rights, fair opportunities and non-discrimination are fully respected and that flight safety is promoted, as stated in the Convention.[216]

ICAO is an autonomous agency linked to the UN system through special agreements. The Charter of the United Nations[217] in its Chapter IX on International Economic and Social Co-operation makes provision for bringing the specialized agencies into the UN fold[218] and also allows these organizations to '*make recommendations for the co-ordination of the policies and activities of the specialized agencies*'.[219] The main organ vested with power to carry out such tasks is the Economic and Social Council (ECOSOC).[220] ICAO signed a relationship agreement with the United Nations in 1946,[221] which mainly implies that the United Nations recognizes ICAO as a specialized agency.[222]

The aims and objectives of ICAO set in the Chicago Convention are '*to develop the principles and techniques of international air navigation and to foster the planning and development of international air transport*'.[223] However, this objective has been revised to include sustainability.[224]

The convention contains some fundamental principles. In the preamble to the convention the following principles are identified; the first of those principles is that every State has complete and exclusive sovereignty over the airspace above its territory. It also highlights the principle of good faith and equal opportunity and participation in air transport. However, the latest principle has found challenges, with countries traditionally trying to favour their own airlines and impose demands on foreign airlines.[225]

There are some characteristics that define the international air transport regime set by the Chicago Convention and the subsequent development under ICAO. First, the so-called 'nine freedoms of the air', which includes transit rights, traffic right and cabotage rights for scheduled air transport.[226] These freedoms are a concession to the principle of state sovereignty that posits that every State is sovereign over its airspace. Second, the regime draws upon the division established in the United Nation Convention on the Law of the Sea with regard to the freedom of overflight in the high seas and contiguous zones, and the autonomy from State sovereignty. Third, the issue of jurisdiction and nationality of aircraft, where

'Aircraft have the nationality of the State in which they are registered'[227] and their appropriate nationality and registering marks shall be displayed when engaged in international air navigation.[228] The convention declares invalid dual registration (i.e. registration in more than one country), though registration may be changed from one State to another.[229] Such registration or transferal of registration is governed by national laws[230] and the information concerning the registration and ownership of any particular aircraft registered in that State shall be made available and reported to the ICAO or to any contracting State on demand.[231] Although the Chicago Convention does not consider an aircraft as part of the territory of the State of nationality,[232] the protection of the State of nationality guarantees the functioning of international air activity. Fourth, international air transport has been subject to the forces of market liberalization[233] while subject to tight regulation,[234] in other words: '*One of the most unique features of the aviation industry is the unprecedented amount of regulatory and operational control that the industry is subject to.*'[235] Finally, in its quest to foster the growth and development of aviation, the sector has enjoyed a favourable framework of exemptions, such as zero taxation on aircraft fuel.

In order to achieve the aims and objectives set up by the Chicago Convention, ICAO is entrusted to adopt and amend '*from time to time as may be necessary*'[236] international standards and regulations for the safety, security, efficiency and regularity of air transport, as well as to ensure environmental protection and serve as the coordinator for international cooperation in all fields of civil aviation for its member States.[237]

The Chicago Convention, as the constituent charter, confers various powers to ICAO. These powers can be divided between rule-making powers granted for the organization's internal functioning and normative standard-setting powers, through hortatory recommendations within its field of expertise. While the first group of powers is of minimal relevance for the purpose of this monograph, the second category warrants further analysis. Law-making power in ICAO is granted in Article 12 of the Chicago Convention for the regulation of air transport over the high seas, but also from other instruments such as standards with '*qualified legal force*'.[238] ICAO has developed a body of law that governs the actions of the organization. This law, and the processes that led to its creation, will be explored in this chapter.[239]

The institutional setting that the Chicago Convention established for ICAO is composed of three main bodies, following a similar structure to other international organizations. ICAO's governing bodies are the Assembly, the Council and the Secretariat.[240] The Convention also allows for the establishment of '*such other bodies as may be necessary*'[241] and two other bodies, namely the Air Transport Committee and the Air Navigation Commission.[242] These assist the Council in technical and economic matters, respectively, as do the Committee on Joint Support of Air Navigation Services and the Finance Committee.

The Assembly[243] is the sovereign plenary body of ICAO, where all contracting States are equally represented and entitled to one vote each.[244] Although extraordinary meetings of the Assembly may be held at any time,[245] as a general rule, the Assembly meets at least once every three years.[246] The Assembly's quorum is made up of a majority of the contracting States and decisions are taken by majority vote, unless otherwise stated in the Convention.[247] Some decisions taken by the Assembly require different voting, such as the requirement of a two-thirds majority vote for adopting amendments to the Convention.[248] However, the Assembly usually adopts its recommendations by consensus.

The powers and duties of the Assembly include the election of its president and other officers, and the election of the contracting States to be represented on the Council.[249] The Assembly is also empowered to determine its own rules of procedure and the establishment of subsidiary commissions[250] if convenient, the voting of annual budgets and determination of the organization's financial arrangements,[251] including oversight of its expenditures and approval of the organization's accounts. More importantly, the Assembly examines and takes action on the reports of the Council and decides on any matters referred to it by the Council. The Assembly can also refer to the Council, to subsidiary commissions or to any other body regarding matters within its sphere of action, and can delegate to the Council the powers and authority necessary or desirable for the discharge of the duties of the Organization and revoke or modify the delegation of authority. The Assembly can consider proposals for the modification or amendment of the Convention[252] and, moreover, the Assembly can deal with any matter within the sphere of action of the Organization not specifically assigned to the Council.[253]

The Council,[254] composed of 36[255] contracting States, is elected with an adequate representation[256] by the Assembly for a period of three years and is the permanent body responsible to the Assembly.[257] At the head of the Council is the president,[258] who is elected by the Council for a term of three years and has no voting powers. Her duties include convening meetings of the Council, the Air Transport Committee and the Air Navigation Commission; serving as representative of the Council; and carrying out on behalf of the Council the functions assigned to her by the Council.[259]

The functions assigned to the Council include an array of administrative, legislative,[260] supervisory[261] and judiciary or quasi-judiciary tasks, some being mandatory and others permissive. The mandatory functions of Council include the submission of reports to the Assembly, the appointment of a secretary general, the establishment of an Air Navigation Commission, the administration of the finances in the Organization, and the discharge of the duties of the Assembly. The Council shall also report to the Assembly and to contracting States on infractions of the Convention, failures to carry out recommendations or determinations of the Council and failures to take appropriate action by States. The mandatory legislative function is to '*Adopt, in accordance with the provisions of Chapter VI of this Convention, international standards and recommended practices; for convenience, designate them as Annexes to this Convention; and notify all contracting States of the action taken*'. It is also in charge of considering recommendations of the Air Navigation Commission to amend the Convention's Annexes and matters relating to the Convention, to which any contracting State refers.[262]

The Council may[263] create subordinate air transport commissions and define groups of States or airlines to help carrying out the aims of the Convention, delegate duties to the Air Navigation Commission and revoke or modify such delegations. It is also responsible for commissioning research into all aspects of air transport and air navigation and to communicate the results to contracting States, facilitating the exchange of information between contracting States. Finally, the Council is charged with studying any matters affecting the organization and operation of international air transport and to investigate and report upon any situation which may present obstacles to the development of international air navigation, at the request of any State.

Decisions taken by the Council require the approval of a majority of its members. With respect to particular matters, authority may be delegated to a committee of Council members and the decisions of these committees can be appealed to the Council, backed by any interested contracting State. The members of the Council involved in a dispute cannot vote. It is possible for any contracting State to participate without a vote in the Council or in its committees and commissions, if the matter has a particular impact on the State's interests.[264] Also, the Council is invested with quasi-judiciary functions, since it is able to perform a dispute-settlement role between States on the interpretation of the convention.[265]

From the above it can be inferred that the Council is the 'real power' within ICAO. Its legitimacy derives from the fact that its members include those with greatest interest in (and influence over) international civil aviation. In other words, its legitimacy is a product of its power in a specific domain.[266]

As the world's primary organization for the regulation of global aviation, ICAO seems particularly well placed to tackle the sector's GHG emissions. However, so far the organization has been very slow and unambitious in adopting any meaningful measures. Nevertheless, the adoption of the KP stimulated the ICAO to assume a more cooperative role by improving the availability of data on emissions from international aviation and by regularly reporting on its work on potential policy options. ICAO has commissioned studies looking into a range of possibilities[267] to address aviation emissions and has set up working groups and committees to inform discussions in its governing bodies.

Law-making at the ICAO regime

Actors

Although all countries have representation in the ICAO Assembly, not all of them are part of the Council. The functions attributed to the Council reflect the fact that most of the work on climate change occurs under the Council umbrella, not only with CAEP but through the creation of other groups that report to it. The membership of the Council is therefore crucial to the way matters are approached in ICAO. Given the structure of the international air transport industry, a fundamental balance of power has traditionally occurred between the United States and European countries. As previously noted,[268] for example, the

United States would never cede its seat in the reduced council, given the economic and political stakes of the international aviation regime.

Another relevant issue here is the fact the EU,[269] as a bloc, is not a member of ICAO, since according to Article 92 of the Chicago Convention membership of ICAO is open exclusively to individual States. For the EU to become a member, it would be necessary to amend of the Convention which would require a two-thirds majority vote in the Assembly, under Article 94. However, the EU has a permanent observer status at ICAO through the EU Commission.[270] Although observers cannot generally take the floor, special prerogatives to do so can be given at the ICAO Council. With regards to the EU, it is worth mentioning the existence of an IGO, the European Civil Aviation Conference (ECAC),[271] which works '*in close liaison*' with ICAO.[272] The ECAC '*supports its Member States in the development and delivery of a pan-European approach*' by preparing common European positions for presentation at ICAO.[273] With regards to environmental issues the organization aims for the '*promotion of European positions and priorities at ICAO, ensuring that they are well represented there, including through close coordination with European members of the ICAO Council*'.[274]

Other participants in the ICAO regime include IGOs and NGOs which are observers at the CAEP and other subsidiary bodies, and which contribute in different ways to the work undertaken in these groups and interact with the Secretariat of ICAO. One of the longest-standing NGOs representing the air industry at ICAO is the International Air Transport Association (IATA), which represents over 240 airlines, covering 84% of total global air traffic.[275] The influence of IATA, dating from the days of the Chicago Conference, over the regulation of air transport is uncontested. For example, the worldwide system of slot allocation has been guided by the work of IATA, which developed the Scheduling Procedures Guide[276] or the establishment of airline rates.[277] With regards to climate, IATA focuses on '*developing sensible environmental policies to enable and promote sustainable and eco-efficient air transport*'[278] and has lobbied for voluntary measures over compulsory and global solutions over national and regional patchworks.[279] IATA has fiercely opposed the inclusion of aviation in the EU ETS; after the retreat of the EU, IATA's CEOs finally endorsed the idea of developing a global MBM.[280]

A second organization is the Air Transport Action Group (ATAG), a coalition of companies, NGOs and other groups representing the aviation industry, which aims to promote 'sustainable growth'. It members come from all industries related to aviation, including airports, airlines, manufacturers, service and communication providers, pilot and traffic controller unions, chambers of commerce, tourism and trade partners and ground transportation.[281] They have sought to influence international decision-making on climate change issues by commissioning reports, organizing events, supporting and making commitments in conjunction to ICAO.[282] In 2009, the aviation industry set itself some climate goals.[283]

As for environmental NGOs, the International Coalition for Sustainable Aviation (ICSA), which is a network of NGOs providing observer status to the Aviation Environment Federation (AEF), the International Council for Clean Transportation (ICCT) and Transport and Environment (T&E) at all present at

ICAO. This group has observer status not only in the CAEP and subsidiary bodies but also contribute to their work on technical and market-based measures by '*supporting economic and environmental analysis, modelling and forecasting*' and presenting '*its views at ICAO workshops on carbon markets and bio-fuels, and has presented to the high-level Group on International Aviation and Climate Change (GIACC)*'.[284]

Instruments

THE CONVENTION ON INTERNATIONAL CIVIL AVIATION

As previously expressed, the Chicago Convention is the fundamental source granting regulatory powers to the international community on matters relating to international civil aviation[285] and has been described as '*the backbone of the international legal regulation of civil aviation*'.[286] The contracting parties to this multilateral treaty have agreed on certain principles and provisions in order to pursue the goal of developing international aviation '*in a safe and orderly manner*'.[287] While the first and third part of the Chicago Convention contains obligations and rights for states parties regarding air navigation and air transport, respectively, the second part is devoted to the establishment of a permanent organization, ICAO.

The process for modifying and amending the Convention is laid out in its Article 94. As with other treaties, the requirements for amendment are thorough and the process is uphill. Specifically, proposed amendments

> must be approved by a two-thirds vote of the Assembly and shall then come into force in respect of States which have ratified such amendment when ratified by the number of contracting States specified by the Assembly. The number so specified shall not be less than two thirds of the total number of contracting States.[288]

Furthermore,

> [i]f in its [*the Assembly's*] opinion the amendment is of such a nature as to justify this course, the Assembly in its resolution recommending adoption may provide that any State which has not ratified within a specified period after the amendment has come into force shall thereupon cease to be a member of the Organization and a party to the Convention.[289]

ANNEX 16 TO THE CHICAGO CONVENTION

To date, 19 Annexes to the Chicago Convention have been agreed, covering a wide range of topics such as the rules of the air, nationality and registration marks of aircraft and environmental protection. However, no annexes were included in the original draft of the Convention at the Chicago Conference[290] and so these do not form an integral part of the Convention; that is, they do not have the same force and effect as the Convention itself, meaning that they aren't legally binding.[291] While this can be viewed as a legal weakness, it has *de facto* allowed the organization to develop stricter, and timelier, regulation of international air navigation. This non-binding/non-compulsory character has provided benefits, in that the 'opting out' from compliance[292] *'frees the ICAO legislative process of the legal, political, and economic complications'*[293] and has enabled a body of regulations to be developed without much opposition from member States.

The first initiatives taken to tackle environmental issues in ICAO were linked to the local impacts of aviation and came hand in hand with an increasing global awareness of human impacts on the environment in the late 1960s and early 1970s. In 1971, environmental Standards and Recommended Practices and Procedures (SARPs) on aircraft noise were adopted in Annex 16 to the Convention[294] and aircraft emissions were first considered in the same year.[295] The first SARPs were adopted in 1981 and have become two well-defined areas under Annex 16, divided into two volumes: Volume I on aircraft noise and Volume II on aircraft engine emissions.[296] This distinction was also evident by the division of work in the environmental arena around two separate committees: the Committee on Aircraft Noise (CAN) and the Committee on Aircraft Engine Emissions (CAEE).[297] However, in 1983 these committees were replaced by one single technical committee reporting to the Council: the Committee on Aviation Environmental Protection (CAEP).[298] Previously, and after participating in the UN Conference on the Human Environment in Stockholm (1972), ICAO stated its awareness of the adverse environmental impacts of aviation, as well as its responsibility to achieve the *'maximum compatibility between the safe and orderly development of civil aviation and the quality of the human environment'*.[299] Furthermore, the Assembly requested the Council to work towards the development of standards, recommended practices and procedures and guidance material dealing with the human environment.[300] As a result, the Action Program Regarding the Environment was established, including a Study Group on emissions to assist the Secretariat. The fruit of that work was a Circular on Control of Aircraft Engine Emissions published in 1997.[301] However, a new volume dealing with CO_2 emissions (Volume III) was due to be adopted by 2016. This will include a CO_2 certification standard for new aircraft.[302]

ICAO ASSEMBLY RESOLUTIONS

ICAO's Assembly Resolutions have been classified as soft law or quasi-law in the academic literature, meaning that although they are not legally binding, it is expected for a contracting State, that hasn't expressed reservations, to follow them.[303] In this connection, although the Chicago Convention does not invest Assembly Resolutions with a legally binding character, they have a value in developing the law.[304]

ICAO's first concerns with the impact of aviation on the climate led them to request a technical report from the IPCC, which resulted in the 1999 special report on aviation.[305] Specific actions to tackle climate change started emerging around the time of ICAO's 33rd, 34th and 35th Assemblies (held in 2001, 2003 and 2004, respectively).[306] In particular, Assembly resolution 33–7 endorsed the development of a voluntary open emissions trading system and requested the Council to develop guidelines for it, providing flexibility and consistency with the UNFCCC.[307] Assembly Resolution 35–5 initiated the process of developing technological and operational measures, and singled out MBMs, and elaborated further on international emissions trading as promising instruments, while urging states '*to refrain from unilateral implementation of greenhouse gas emissions charges prior to the next regular session of the Assembly in 2007, where this matter will be considered and discussed again*'.[308]

At the 36th session of the ICAO Assembly in 2007, climate change played a prominent role. Among others, Assembly Resolution A36–22[309] requested the ICAO Council to form a special group to address greenhouse gas emissions, namely the Group on International Aviation and Climate Change (GIACC),[310] technically supported by the CAEP.[311] Its purpose was to develop and recommend to the Council an '*aggressive*' Programme of Action on aviation and climate change. The Council was further requested to convene a High-level Meeting on International Aviation and Climate Change,[312] in the run-up to the Copenhagen COP, which took place in December 2009.

Driven by developments with the imminent inclusion of aviation in the EU ETS, the Assembly resolution A36–22 urged '*Contracting States not to implement an emissions trading system on other Contracting States' aircraft operators except on the basis of mutual agreement between those States*'.[313] However, 42 EU countries reserved their position regarding this element of the Resolution.[314] Another issue that emerged at this time was the tension between differential and equal treatment with regards to MBMs. The resolution acknowledged

> the principles of non-discrimination and equal and fair opportunities to develop international civil aviation set forth in the Chicago Convention, as well as the principles and provisions on common but differentiated responsibilities and respective capabilities under the UNFCCC and the Kyoto Protocol.[315]

At the same time A36–22 recognized that '*other Contracting States consider that any open emissions trading system should be established in accordance with the principle of non-discrimination.*'[316]

The GIACC held four meetings during 2008 and 2009, and its final report incorporated a Programme of Action,[317] which was presented to the Council, and welcomed by the HLM-ENV/09[318] and endorsed by ICAO's 37th Assembly in 2010.[319] The Programme of Action agreed in A37–19 included a global commitment to improve annual fuel efficiency by 2% per year up until 2020, which was further extended by the Assembly to an aspirational 2% annual improvement up until 2050, as well as an aspirational goal to achieve carbon-neutral growth in the sector from 2020 onwards.[320] This would imply a stabilization of CO_2 emissions of between 682 and 755 megatons.[321] The carbon-neutral growth path is envisioned to be achieved through a '*basket of measures*',[322] which includes technical and operational improvements, the development of alternative fuels,[323] and the establishment of a global MBM for international aviation,[324] which is estimated to fill a gap of at least 1039 megatons of CO_2 emissions by 2050.[325] The ICAO Council followed by putting a set of recommendations before the 38th Assembly, held in the autumn of 2013. The measures that the Assembly eventually agreed upon through Resolution 38–18 include a CO_2 certification standard for new aircraft, the preparation of member States' action plans on reduction activities and the enhancement of capacity building and assistance, plus mechanisms to facilitate access to financial resources.[326]

Crucially, in 2013, ICAO members agreed to work on developing a global MBM (GMBM) at the global level by the next ICAO session in 2016, with a view to implement it by 2020.[327] The CORSIA was agreed at the 39th ICAO Assembly in October 2016 through Assembly Resolution.[328] Although there were other possibilities available, mainly an international treaty or SARPs, the legal instrument of CORSIA is an Assembly Resolution. While the non-binding characteristics allow for flexibility and quick adoption and review, this legal vehicle for CORSIA presents challenges with: first, the effective enforcement of the measure; and second, the Assembly Resolution is not enough; that is, the specific implementation details will still need to be developed either through a treaty or standards.[329] This second option is likely to be the way forward.[330]

In a nutshell, CORSIA is based in offsetting of emissions outside the sector from the 2020 levels. This means that aviation will grow carbon neutral from that year. The coverage of the scheme is based on routes, with exceptions for LDC, SIDS and landlocked developing countries.[331] The implementation of the mechanism comes in three phases: 1) a pilot voluntary phase from 2021 to 2023; 2) a first phase with voluntary participation from 2023–3026; and 3) a second phase from 2027 to 2035 when all states above the threshold[332] will be obliged to participate.

As for the CO_2 certification standard for new aircraft,[333] the 39th Assembly also requested the ICAO Council to '*adopt the CO_2 emissions certification Standard for aeroplanes as soon as possible*'.[334]

Processes

ICAO AS A FORUM FOR MULTILATERAL AGREEMENTS

In addition to the legislative powers conferred to the ICAO Council for the adoption of SARPs and the amendment of Annexes to the Convention, and the Assembly Resolutions and other outcomes from the Council, ICAO also has the capacity to serve as a venue for multilateral treaty-making. This capacity is not discussed in the constitutional charter of ICAO where no reference to delegated treaty-making power can be found,[335] but it has been exercised *de facto* since ICAO has served as a venue for international conventions dealing with issues such as terrorism, security and liability.[336]

The role of ICAO in facilitating discussions and debate and as an arena where international politics take place is reinforced by, for example, holding symposiums or colloquiums, where information on developments are shared, usually preceding the Assembly sessions.[337] These are opportunities for information exchange in order to facilitate discussion and decision-making. For example, ICAO has arrogated the status of being the competent forum in which to deal with GHG emissions from international aviation.

Leaving aside that ICAO can adopt internal institutional law,[338] ICAO is a law-maker in the external law facet through different processes: 1. the adoption of SARP though the Council's conferred powers, by the amendment of annexes that do not involve a formal treaty process or amending the constituent instrument; 2. the enactment of air regulations out outside the Convention's Annexes; 3. the adoption of soft law in the form of assembly resolutions; 4. being a forum for multilateral treaty-making; and 5. enjoying judicial law-making by the settle of aviation disputes.[339]

THE ADOPTION OF STANDARDS AND RECOMMENDED PRACTICES AND PROCEDURES (SARPS)

Traditionally, the legislative functions of ICAO have been mainly confined to very technical issues of a non-political character, providing minimal scope for disagreement.[340] Of these functions, '*the adoption and amendment of international standards and recommended practices and procedures*' (SARPs)[341] have been most relevant. ICAO's Council can establish SARPs by circumventing the formal treaty process or amending the constituent instrument of the organization.[342] The Chicago Convention dedicates its Chapter VI[343] to them, and states that SARPs will deal with the following issues: communications systems and air navigation aids, the characteristics of aerodromes, rules of the air and air traffic control practices, licensing of operating and mechanical personnel, airworthiness of aircraft, registration and identification of aircraft, collection and exchange of meteorological information, journey log books, aeronautical maps and charts, customs and immigration procedures, aircraft in distress and investigation of accidents and '*other matters concerned with the safety, regularity, and efficiency of air navigation as may from time to time appear appropriate*'.[344]

Although the Chicago Convention does not define what SARPs are, a definition of what the standards and recommended practices adopted by the Council under the Chicago Convention's provisions can be found in the Convention's Annexes:

> [A] Standard is any specification for physical characteristics, configuration, material, performance, personnel or procedure, the uniform application of which is recognized as necessary for the safety and regularity of international air navigation and to which Contracting States will conform in accordance with the Convention; in the event of impossible compliance, notification to the Council is compulsory under article 38.

And:

> [A] Recommended Practice is any specification for physical characteristics, configuration, material, performance, personnel or procedure, the uniform application of which is recognized as desirable in the interest of safety, regularity or efficiency of international navigation, and to which Contracting States will endeavour to conform in accordance with the Convention.

SARPs are promulgated as Annexes to the Chicago Convention[345] by the Council, whose authority has been expressly conferred in ICAO's constitution to adopt and amend Annexes, with the requirement of '*the vote of two-thirds of the Council at a meeting called for that purpose*'.[346]

With some exceptions,[347] member States that aim to the '*highest practicable degree*' of uniformity in SARPs[348] can ignore the ICAO Annexes if they '*find it impracticable to comply*'[349] but they shall notify immediately and in due manner[350] to ICAO's Council about the differences between their own national practice and the practice established by SARPs. Furthermore, to inform on future differences, which means that member States could even adopt norms directly in conflict with SARPs, whether or not they have previously committed themselves to them.[351] The obligation for States to notify the Council is compulsory with regard to differences with International Standards and their amendments. However, contracting States are invited to extend such notification of any difference from the Recommended Practices and their amendments, when the notification of such differences is important for the safety of air navigation.[352] If a State that is unable to comply with certain standards fails to notify the differences to ICAO under Article 38, it would be in breach of this legally binding duty under the convention. In the absence of notification, full compliance with the SARP is presumed.[353] In addition to this obligation, contracting States shall publish the differences between national regulations and SARPS through the Aeronautical Information Service.[354]

Besides the establishment of SARPs through the adoption and amendment of Annexes, ICAO can also enact air regulations outside the Convention's Annexes. These regulations are '*hierarchically inferior to the Annexes*'[355] and intend to supplement them. The issue of implementation of SARPs at the domestic level presents challenges on how the actual provisions of the Annexes are incorporated into national legal systems[356] and effectively executed. ICAO facilitates this implementation by assisting States with administrative problems they may encounter. To date, the level of implementation has been characterized as unsatisfactory,[357] especially in relation with the economic and technological differences between developed and developing countries, but two positive synergies and incentives have been observed regarding implementation: first, the aeronautical experts that participate in the elaboration of annexes are often also responsible for their domestic implementation; therefore a natural alliance between ICAO and aeronautical authorities occurs in many cases. Second, it's in the interest of national agencies to implement the ICAO provisions as this enables them to gain in size, relevance and status.[358]

The forthcoming aircraft CO_2 emissions standard[359] will apply to all new airplanes, will come in the form of a SARP and will conform to the third volume of Annex 16 of the Chicago Convention. It has completed its first phase, where the aspect of certification requirements has been agreed upon, and a second phase, where the setting of regulatory levels, applicability dates and stringency, was decided upon. The finalized standard was presented at the 39th ICAO Assembly and is waiting Council approval at the time of this writing. This standard will be mandatory for all contracting States since SARPs are, in essence, equal treatment norms.

CAEP AND OTHER GROUPS

The CAEP's mission is to assist the Council in formulating new policies and adopting new standards on aircraft noise and aircraft engine emissions through the development of Annex 16. It is composed of three working groups, namely: WG1 on technical aspects of aircraft noise, WG2 on aircraft noise and emissions issues linked to operations and WG3 on the technical aspects of aircraft emissions. Furthermore, four supporting groups cover a variety of issues from the cost-benefit analyses of options, models and databases, the ICAO Carbon Calculator and scientific understanding of aviation's environmental impacts.[360] The CAEP meets as a Steering Group to review and provide guidance on the progress of the activities of the working groups, producing a report with specific recommendations for consideration at the Council.[361]

The bodies involved in the development of environmental regulations are mainly the Assembly, the Council and the CAEP. The Air Navigation Committee and the Air Transport Committee, in certain cases, are also involved in the process by providing comments on the recommendations made to the Council by the CAEP. Consultation can also be sought from contracting States through special procedures when the recommendations concern the introduction or amendment of SARPs. After these consultations, the final decision rests with the Council. The Assembly considers the policy issues brought up by the Council or by contracting States, reviews and takes action on the proposals presented for consideration, commonly by endorsing them.

The ongoing work on climate change issues at ICAO has been mainly linked to the CAEP, which includes a group dealing with the establishment of CO_2 standards[362] and a group dealing specifically with MBMs[363] and the defunct GIACC.[364] The GIACC[365] was a politically oriented group created to develop and recommend a Program of Action for the Council, which was accomplished in 2009. GIACC held four meetings during 2008 and 2009,[366] which resulted in a final report[367] and a Program of Action[368] which was approved by ICAO's Council in 2009 and endorsed by the High Level Meeting on International Aviation and Climate Change.[369]

However, since 2012, in order to quicken the development of a framework for MBMs, other clusters have entered into play. First, a steering group of Council members, experts and international organizations was set up by the Council's president, whose work was reviewed by an Ad Hoc Working Group on Climate Change.[370] Second, a High-level Group on International Aviation and Climate Change (HGCC) was established in November 2012 to provide political recommendations to the Council.[371] The groups have assessed the role, purpose, main elements and guiding principles of a number of mechanisms, narrowing them down to three options, namely, a global emission trading system and two global mandatory offsetting schemes, one of which would be accompanied by revenue generation.

In the run-up to the 39th ICAO Assembly, the work to develop a GMBM for international aviation, intensified including not only CAEP but also the Council's Environment Advisory Group (EAG), and the GMBM Technical Task Force (GMTF), Global Aviation Dialogues (GLADs),[372] the High-level Group on a GMBM.[373] In particular, CAEP, EAG and GMTF will remain very busy with detailing the mechanism. Specifically, putting in place an MRV system by 2019, agreeing on the Emission Unit Criteria (EUC) – the type of credits that would be eligible under CORSIA – a registry system, and delivering of capacity building and assistance. The deadline for detailing CORSIA is 2018, coinciding with the deadline for the PA's rule.

The IMO regime

An overview

Given the increasing number of shipping agreements adopted since the second half of the 19th century, the need for a permanent body to cater for the needs of global shipping[374] became increasingly apparent. However, the adoption of a convention establishing an international maritime organisation[375] was not free from disagreements over whether the role of the organisation should be exclusively technical or include economic aspects.[376] Eventually, in 1959, a year after the Convention on the International Maritime Organization[377] entered into force, the IMCO became linked to the UN system as a specialized agency,[378] on a similar basis to how the ICAO also became part of the UN system.[379] Part XII of the IMO Convention provided the premise for this agreement.[380]

The purposes of the IMO can be divided into three sections: first, to provide '*machinery for co-operation*' in the regulation and practices relating to technical matters affecting shipping engaged in international trade, encouraging and facilitating the general adoption of the highest practicable standards[381] and dealing with related administrative and legal matters. Second, the removal of '*discriminatory action and unnecessary restrictions*' affecting shipping engaged in international trade.[382] Third, to be a forum where members can discuss matters concerning unfair restrictive practices by shipping, in accordance with Part II. This includes any matters concerning the effects of shipping on the marine environment[383] that may be referred to it by any organ or specialized agency of the United Nations, and providing for the exchange of information among governments on matters under consideration by the organization.[384]

In order to achieve these aims, Part II of the IMO Convention establishes the functions of the organization. Originally, the convention gave no powers to the IMCO to adopt regulations, where in the original Article 2 it was stated that *'the functions of the convention shall be consultative and advisory'*[385] and Article 3 explicitly prevented the IMO from adopting treaties. However, IMO functions include making recommendations referred to it under Article 1 to provide for the drafting of conventions, agreements or other suitable instruments; to provide machinery for consultation and the exchange of information; to facilitate technical cooperation; and to *'perform functions arising in connexion with paragraphs (a), (b) and (c) of the Article, in particular those assigned to it by or under international instruments relating to maritime matters and the effect of shipping on the marine environment'*.[386] The IMO may also recommend settlement through the normal processes of international shipping, and if this doesn't work to consider the matter.[387]

The IMO follows the same threefold organizational structure as ICAO, as stated in its founding charter.[388] It consists of an Assembly, which meets every two years and contains representation from all member States, and a governing body (i.e. the Council and a Secretariat). The Assembly can meet in extraordinary sessions, when adequately convened.[389] The quorum for a meeting is the majority of members, where each member has one vote. The main functions of the Assembly are the election of the assembly president, vice president members of the Council[390] and the Maritime Safety Committee (MSC); the establishment of its rules of procedure; the establishment of necessary temporary or permanent subsidiary bodies; and approving financial arrangements, budgets and accounts for the organization. The Assembly also considers reports and decides on questions referred by the Council; performs the functions of the Organization in connection with Article 3; can recommend the adoption of regulations to members; and may delegate to the Council matters that fall within the scope of the Organization, except in the function of making recommendations, which cannot be delegated.[391]

The 40 members of the Council are elected by the Assembly for a period of two years, under pre-defined criteria. This includes a representation of the States with greatest interest in providing international shipping services,[392] States with the largest interest in international seaborne trade[393] and States representing all geographic areas of the world, not eligible under the previous criteria but with special interests in maritime transport or navigation.[394] The Council manages the work of the IMO between the Assembly sessions and takes over most of the Assembly's functions.[395] Among its functions are the coordination of the activities of the IMO's different bodies, including the consideration of the draft work programme and the budgets, reports and proposals from the different bodies for submission to the Assembly and members, providing comments and recommendations as appropriate. The Council can also enter into agreements or arrangements with other international organizations.

The Secretariat[396] is based in London and has around 300 staff members working under the direction of a secretary general, who is appointed by the Council with the approval of the Assembly. There are also five regional offices for technical cooperation activities around the world.[397] The duties of the Secretariat include administrative functions and serving the main bodies and the members of the organization. It is also the depository of legal instruments.[398]

The organization structure of the IMO is made up of five committees, namely the MSC, the Marine Environment Protection Committee (MEPC), the Legal Committee, the Technical Co-operation Committee and the Facilitation Committee. Some sub-committees have also been established to assist the main committees.[399]

Law-making at the IMO regime

Actors

IMO has wide international participation from member States[400] but also from NGOs that can be granted a consultative status,[401] under certain circumstances,[402] by the Council and subject to approval by the Assembly. Meanwhile IGOs may enter into cooperation agreements with IMO and can be granted observer status.[403]

Although all countries are represented in the Assembly, '*the composition of the Council is dominated by shipping states*', in a similar way to how the ICAO Council is dominated by countries with a major stake in global aviation.[404] It is also worth noting that States that have the capabilities to control the agenda in the IMO, because they have influence in the different relevant issues, '*shape the outcomes*'.[405] Aware of this, some of the industry champions in these shipping nations often feed the debates with technical studies and reports.[406] On the question of how rules to prevent pollution from ships have been agreed, De la Rue and Anderson have highlighted that this is usually the outcome of a compromise between the desire for more stringent rules expressed by coastal states and the preferences of flag States[407] and the major shipping nations for less burdensome obligations.[408] In an effort to balance these interests, the latter group of nations has shown a keen desire for uniform global regulations, instead of unilateral measures.[409] However, when it comes to climate change, this traditional division of country interests varies; for example, the desire of coastal states to regulate emissions does not necessarily reflect their position regarding other environmental problems. Instead, a new pattern of negotiations has opened up, where divisions between developed and developing countries reflect other concerns such as differentiating principles.[410]

Another feature that the IMO has in common with ICAO is that the European Union is not a member of the IMO since membership is only open to States, which raises concerns regarding adequate representation of the Union's collective interests.[411] However, as with ICAO, the European Commission enjoys an observer status, which allows for participation in IMO processes.[412] Similarly to the aviation case, the EU exerts influence through its own legislation, so the potential regulation of emission from international shipping can be seen as a driver to action in IMO.[413]

It is also worth noting the fact that the contributions of member States to the organization's budget are based on the tonnage of their merchant fleet. This criterion differs from other UN agencies, where contributions are usually made on the basis of GDP. Therefore, in 2012, the biggest contributions to the IMO budget came from Panama, Liberia, the Marshall Islands, the United Kingdom, the Bahamas, Singapore, Malta, Greece, China and Japan, where Panama contributed five times more than Japan.

The importance of the role of non-state transnational actors has been widely acknowledged in international law. As early as 1979, the relevance of these actors in the IMO was made evident by M'Gonigle and Sacher.[414] They pointed out the fact that the activity of non-state transnational actors is 'beyond any single national control' and also because, as a consequence of their control over information and technologies, non-state actors can lobby within national capitals and at the IMCO. Furthermore, due to their ability to provide their own solutions, these actors have an important influence over the outcome of IMO negotiations.

The most relevant NGOs related to climate issues, active at the IMO, are the CSC (which is the only global international environmental NGO focused exclusively on shipping issues), the World Wildlife Fund (WWF), Friends of the Earth International (FOEI), International Union for Conservation of Nature (IUCN) and Greenpeace. The NGO Transport & Environment, part of the CSC, is also recognized as an individual NGO with Special Consultative Status in the ECO-SOC of the United Nations. Overall, the environmental NGOs argue in favour of the establishment of stringent regulation and are heavily involved in efforts to overcome negotiation problems and impasses.[415]

In general, the industry NGOs defend the IMO as the only forum in which to deal with climate change issues, through global measures,[416] although they tend to promote the narrative of maritime transport as being the most carbon-efficient form of transport. This position translates into resistance to the pressure received from governments to reduce emissions and their fierce opposition to mandatory instruments, particularly to MBMs, but also to technical and operational efficiency indexing systems, based on market distortions. One of the most relevant industry NGOs is the International Chamber of Shipping (ICS),[417] which is the principal trade association representing shipowners and operators in all sectors and trades, accounting for over 80% of the global merchant tonnage.[418] ICS *'takes the view and has argued strongly that the only acceptable MBM – if one is required at all – is a fuel levy'*.[419] In the same vein, the Baltic International Maritime Council (BIMCO) has deemed MBMs as unsuitable and furthermore has stated that *'the concept of an ETS is unworkable for the shipping industry'*, arguing that if other market-based instruments are introduced then these *'should apply globally and should completely address the nine IMO principles – effective; binding and equally applicable; cost-effective; limit distortion; not penalizing trade and growth; goal based; promote R&D; accommodating energy-efficient technology; practical, transparent, fraud-free and easy to administer'*.[420] Similar positions are held by the Oil Companies International Marine Forum (OCIMF) and the International Association of Independent Tanker Owners (INTERTANKO). Other industry groups active in climate issues include the Community of European Shipyard Associations (CESA), the International Association of Classification Societies (IACS), the

International Association of Dry Cargo Shipowners (INTERCARGO) and the World Shipping Council (WSC). Recently, some of these groups have called and offered support for coming up with an emissions reduction target at the IMO.[421]

Instruments

THE CONVENTION ON THE INTERNATIONAL MARITIME ORGANIZATION

Article 1 of the IMO Convention contains two important premises for the regulation of GHG emissions from maritime transport. This first article includes a reference to the '*prevention and control of marine pollution from ships*'[422] as a purpose of the organization and in doing so establishes a working principle, which has been further embraced by all treaties and rules adopted under the IMO auspices. Article 1(b) states that, among others, the purpose of the IMO is:

> To encourage the removal of discriminatory action and unnecessary restrictions by Governments affecting shipping engaged in international trade so as to promote the availability of shipping services to the commerce of the world without discrimination; assistance and encouragement given by a Government for the development of its national shipping and for purposes of security does not in itself constitute discrimination, provided that such assistance and encouragement is not based on measures designed to restrict the freedom of shipping of all flags to take part in international trade.

This article translates into a practice where all regulations emanating from the IMO apply to all ships engaged in maritime transport, regardless their flag, operator or ownership. This reflects the fact that '*under the IMO's regulatory framework, an individual ship in the world's fleet is the legal subject and the obligation for the flag State refers mainly to implementation of the regulations in their domestic legislation.*'[423]

Amendments to the Convention, if needed to accommodate other requirements on the regulation of GHG, require the support of a two-thirds majority vote of the Assembly, entering into force 12 months after the acceptance by two-thirds of IMO members.[424] However, it is unlikely that Article 1(b) would be amended since there is no precedent of differentiation, or selective flag application, of the law in any treaty or regulation within the IMO sphere.[425]

Furthermore, Article 15 (j) of the Convention on the functions of the Assembly states that it is within its competence to pursue regulations and guidelines concerning the prevention and control of marine pollution from ships and other matters concerning the effect of shipping on the marine environment.

UNCLOS

UNCLOS[426] also has a role in the regulation of environmental matters since it establishes a general framework for legislative and jurisdictional rights and obligations for states with regards to marine issues. The provisions on environmental protection are found in Part XII[427] and specifically on the pollution from ships in article 211. UNCLOS 'has elevated international convention such as MARPOL to the status of international standards within a global regime potentially applicable to all states'. The Convention differentiates five zones in which countries have different rights and jurisdiction, namely: internal waters, territorial waters, contiguous zones, exclusive economic zones and the high seas.[428] From these, only the high seas are beyond the jurisdiction of any State.[429] While UNCLOS reaffirms the main role of flag States in the protection of the environment by warranting that ships under their registry comply with international standards, it also allows for jurisdictional and enforcement rights of coastal States and port States. In this connection, UNCLOS establishes flag States' jurisdiction over all ships flying their flag or registry in the high seas. Nonetheless regulations in flag States cannot go beneath the internationally agreed standards.[430] However, the role of flag States is crucial, especially in connection to the areas beyond national jurisdiction.[431]

UNCLOS contains a provision, Article 212, on the pollution from or through the atmosphere (i.e. atmospheric-based pollution),[432] which requires UNCLOS signatories to adopt laws and regulations to prevent atmospheric pollution that will result in pollution of the marine environment. In accordance with this provision the IMO developed legally binding measures to reduce air pollution from ships through Annex VI to MARPOL.[433] It is argued that this provision refers also to ICAO.[434]

The IMO is also related to UNCLOS since the latter has recognized the IMO's activities and competences in dealing with maritime issues.[435] Various UNCLOS provisions[436] establish obligations for parties[437] to follow and apply IMO rules and standards. Two types of instruments contain these provisions, namely: recommendations adopted by the IMO Assembly, MSC and MEPC,[438] and provisions in the IMO conventions.[439] However, even if internationally accepted regulations adopted at the IMO acquire indirect legal force through UNCLOS, it does not mean an automatic breach of UNCLOS.[440]

Additionally, UNCLOS embraces the principle of non-discrimination, since it proclaims that States cannot discriminate between vessels on the basis of nationality: 'In exercising their rights and performing their duties under this Part, States shall not discriminate in form or in fact against vessels of any other State.'[441] However, the convention allows for prerogatives for developing countries.[442]

THE INTERNATIONAL CONVENTION FOR THE PREVENTION OF POLLUTION FROM SHIPS (MARPOL). ANNEX VI: REGULATIONS FOR THE PREVENTION OF AIR POLLUTION FROM SHIPS

Pollution from ships is either caused by accidents where quantities of oil or other dangerous substances are spilled into the sea or by operational causes, mainly due to routine discharges, emissions and operations. From this division (i.e. between accidental and non-accidental pollution) is derived the two main regulations regarding pollution from ships (i.e. ship safety standards), such as the Safety of

Life at Sea Convention (SOLAS),[443] and the prevention and control of pollution from ships. The regulation of vessel-sourced environmental pollution, routine discharges and emissions, is mostly[444] covered under MARPOL, which was modified by the Protocol of 1978.[445] MARPOL aims to eliminate pollution caused by ship operations and to minimize unintentional discharges.[446] It covers all types of pollution resulting from ships, except the issue of waste dumping, which is a major issue covered under a separate agreement. To date, MARPOL contains six annexes of a technical nature. Annexes I and II, on the prevention of pollution by oil and the control of pollution by noxious liquid substances, are compulsory for parties to the MARPOL Convention, while Annex III on the prevention of pollution by harmful substances in packaged form, Annex IV on the prevention of pollution from sewage from ships, Annex V on the prevention of pollution by garbage from ships and Annex VI on the prevention of air pollution from ships are optional.[447]

In the early days of drafting environmental regulation, the IMO was focused on the more visible aspects of water pollution, so the need to prevent air pollution from ships did not entered the organization's agenda until the late 1980s[448] and was not fully recognized until the 1990s,[449] when it was agreed to enlarge the MARPOL Convention with a new Annex on air pollution. MARPOL Annex VI[450] was adopted in 1997 with the aim to '*preserve the marine environment through the complete elimination of pollution by oil and other harmful substances and the minimization of accidental discharge of such substances*'.[451] Annex VI was adopted in 1997 and entered into force in 2005.[452] The Convention has been subsequently amended to include new substances. It regulates the following emissions from ships: sulphur oxide (SOx), nitrogen oxide (NOx), ozone depleting substances, Volatile Organic Compounds (VOCs) and other Atmospheric particulates.[453]

Crucially, Annex VI did not cover the emission of GHGs, but the conference where Annex VI was adopted[454] alluded to them and agreed to conduct a study with the view to informing future action.[455] At the 60th session of the MEPC, it was agreed that MARPOL Annex VI was the appropriate vehicle for enacting mandatory energy efficiency requirements for ships.[456] In July 2011, the latest amendments to MARPOL Annex VI added a new chapter (Chapter 4 on *Regulations on Energy Efficiency for Ships*) on regulations for energy efficiency of ships over 400 tonnage by making mandatory the Energy Efficiency Design Index (EEDI), and the Ship Energy Efficiency Management Plan (SEEMP), thus confronting the emission of CO_2.[457] The EEDI is a technical measure, applied to new ships from 2013. A 10% improvement is set for the first phase, becoming more stringent from 2025. Since the EEDI is based on performance, the way in which the target should be achieved is left to industry. The SEEMP is an operational measure applying to all ships, which establishes a mechanism for monitoring ship and fleet energy efficiency and promotes the optimization of the efficiency performance. It focuses on shipowners and operators by reviewing the technologies and practices used to optimise the performance of ships. The guidance on the development of the SEEMP makes use of 'best practices' for fuel efficient ship operation and the voluntary use of the Energy Efficiency Operational Indicator

(EEOI) as a monitoring tool. Developing countries have been allowed to delay their compliance to both measures until 2019.[458]

Chapter 4 of MARPOL Annex VI has been acclaimed as 'the first legally bind-ing climate change treaty to be adopted since the Kyoto Protocol'[459] and *'first ever mandatory global GHG reduction regime for an international industry sector'*.[460] How-ever, the adoption of these instruments was not free from controversy, and objec-tions[461] exist to the absence of differentiation for developing countries and to the lack of *'capacity building, technical assistance and transfer of technology* [which] *was not ready for adoption'*.[462] However the chapter contains also a regulation on the 'promotion of Technical Co-operation and Transfer of Technology Relating to the Improvement of Energy Efficiency of Ships'. In negotiating Annex VI it proved impossible to achieve a consensus, and the EEDI and SEEMP were adopted against the vote of five key countries, namely, Brazil, China, Chile, Kuwait and South Arabia.[463] Controversy around these energy efficiency measures dates back to when the amendments were first proposed by Australia, Belgium, Canada, Denmark, Germany, Japan, Liberia, Norway and the United Kingdom and circu-lated by the secretary general in 2010.[464]

IMO RESOLUTIONS

IMO Resolutions can be adopted by the Assembly or the committees.[465] They are decisions from the organization's organs, whose content can include techni-cal codes and guidelines. They lack binding force, since the IMO Convention did not provide for them.[466] However, resolutions can incorporate recommenda-tions on the implementation of technical rules and standards not included in IMO treaties. Resolutions containing technical codes and recommendations[467] become mandatory when incorporated into national legislation, though some-times codes and guidelines contained in non-mandatory IMO resolutions also become part of the IMO conventions acquiring a hard-law form.[468] In other words, *'[t]he law-making process at the IMO is directed to both the creation of binding and non-binding instruments'*.[469]

All IMO States are entitled to participate in their adoption, which normally occurs by consensus. Each IMO member State is entitled to one vote. The IMO's decision-making processes are usually subject to consensus. However, in cases where consensus is not possible, majority voting can be used, since this is, in fact, the official process set up in Article 57 of the IMO Convention. Even when rul-ing by consensus, the chair of a given committee can disregard an objection put forward by a party in order to advance in the negotiation.

The resolutions relevant to the issue of GHG emissions include: the Assembly resolution urging the MEPC to identify and develop the mechanisms needed to achieve a limitation or reduction of GHG emissions from ships,[470] the MEPC reso-lution adopting the EEDI and the SEEMP[471] and a subsequent number of MEPC resolutions on guidelines for the development of the EEDI and SEEMP from the 63rd, 64th and 65th MEPC Sessions.[472] At the 65th MEPC, a landmark Resolution which provides a framework for the promotion of technical cooperation and the transfer of technology for these energy efficiency measures was adopted.[473] Crucially, at the 70th MEPC, a new requirement for ships to record and report data on their fuel oil consumption was adopted, as amendments to MARPOL Annex VI.[474]

Processes

THE MEPC

All members of the IMO are part of the MEPC,[475] which was established in 1975[476] in response to rising awareness about environmental damage from shipping activities. Until 1985 it was a subsidiary body of the Assembly, but since then the MEPC has been fully invested with the power to '*consider any matter within the scope of the Organization concerned with prevention and control of pollution from ships*'.[477] This includes GHG emissions. It can adopt and amend all types of environmental regulation, including conventions and other measures. Revisions to MARPOL are carried out by the adoption of resolutions. The MEPC usually meets twice a year and reports to the Council.

In 1997 the Air Pollution Conference[478] invited the IMO, in cooperation with the UNFCCC, to develop a study on CO_2 emissions from the maritime sector,[479] which resulted in the IMO Study on Greenhouse Gas Emissions from Ships.[480] The Conference also called on the MEPC to consider feasible CO_2 reduction strategies related to other atmospheric pollutants, such as NOx. However, work on GHGs in the MEPC started later, after the mandate given by the assembly in 2004,[481] which urged the Committee '*to identify and develop the mechanism or mechanisms needed to achieve the limitation or reduction of GHG emissions from international shipping*'.[482]

Two differentiated paths for emissions reductions have been pursued by the MEPC: one focuses on technical and operational measures and another is centred on MBMs. With regards to technical and operational initiatives, it was agreed at the 60th session of the MEPC that MARPOL Annex VI was the appropriate means for enacting mandatory energy efficiency measures for ships.[483] A correspondence group on energy efficiency measures for ships was established at the next session to further improve the EEDI and the SEEMP, whose outcome was assessed by the Working Group on GHG-related issues.[484] At MEPC 66 a correspondence group on Further Technical and Operational Measures for Enhancing Energy Efficiency was established, in addition to an Ad Hoc Expert Working Group on Facilitation of Technology Transfer for Ships,[485] designed to discuss the implementation of resolution MEPC.229(65).

After the Second IMO Study was published at the 59th session of the MEPC, there was a common understanding on the insufficiency of technical and operational measures,[486] and wide agreement on the need to develop market-based instruments to address GHG emissions from the sector. A few proposals were put forward.[487] Subsequent work has been delegated within the MEPC to a number of groups dealing with different aspects of the puzzle. In 2010, at the 60th session, members of the MEPC agreed to launch an Expert Group on MBMs[488] to assess the feasibility and impact assessment of the measures against nine criteria provided by the Committee.[489] A total of 10 proposals were analyzed, ranging from a GHG Fund to various emissions trading options and a rebate mechanism.[490] In the same year, at the 61st session of the MEPC, the outcomes of the MBM-EG stimulated significant debate and so the Committee decided to establish an Intersessional Meeting of the Working Group on GHG Emissions from Ships,[491] whose work was due to be submitted in the next session.[492] However, the 62nd session of the MEPC decided to postpone discussion on the outcomes until the next session. The 63rd MEPC took over the dialogue on market-based measures, although the next session of the MEPC decided to focus on the need of an updated study on the impact of international maritime emissions, and an Expert Workshop was held in 2013 to organize this work.

The 64th MEPC was due to agree on an impact assessment of the proposed market-based instruments. However, objections were raised over the terms of reference for the impact assessment, particularly the position of developing countries in relation to the UNFCCC, and so discussions were postponed. At the 65th session, discussions on MBMs were again postponed. However, some progress was made regarding the conflict between the principles of CBDRRC and non-discrimination; in the preamble to the Resolution on Promotion of Technical Co-operation and Transfer of Technology relating to the Improvement of Energy Efficiency of Ships, under the expression of 'being cognizant', acknowledgement is given to both principles:[493]

> BEING COGNIZANT of the principles enshrined in the Convention on the Organization, including the principle of non-discrimination, as well as the principle of no more favourable treatment enshrined in MARPOL and other IMO Conventions.
>
> BEING COGNIZANT ALSO of the principles enshrined in the UNFCCC and its Kyoto Protocol including the principle of common but differentiated responsibilities and respective capabilities.

Prompted by the results of the Third IMO GHG Study 2014 and the adoption of a MRV at the regional level by the EU, a global data collection system for fuel was agreed at the 69th MEPC and adopted at 70th MEPC.[494] This mandatory system will apply to all ships from 5,000 GT that will have to report annually. This data collection system is seen as a first step towards an MBM for the sector.[495]

One of the key issues, in this connection is to set a target, objective or cap for the sector. The issue has been debated at the 61st session of the MEPC,[496] but it was subsequently postponed from at the 62nd and 63rd session of the MEPC, and put in standby at the 64th MEPC.[497] At the 68th session of the MEPC the Marshall Islands put forward a proposal to set up a *fair share* – that is, a global sectoral CO_2 emissions target for international maritime transport. Again, the issue was left aside until COP21. The fair share made a comeback to the discussions at the MEPC 70 through some submissions, but included in a different shape ('levels of ambition') in the IMO a Roadmap for a '*comprehensive IMO Strategy on reduction of GHG emissions from ships*',[498] which was approved at the 70th MEPC. The

Roadmap foresees an initial GHG reduction strategy to be adopted in 2018,[499] under which the debate on MBMs might be reinitiated. This task is envisioned to require establishing intersessional working groups reporting to the MEPC.

IMO AS A FORUM FOR MULTILATERAL AGREEMENTS

Since its establishment, the IMO has provided a venue and support to over 40 conventions and protocols that the organization regularly updates.[500] IMO conventions – conventions adopted under the auspices of the IMO or for which the Organization is otherwise responsible – address various aspects of maritime transport such as maritime safety, marine pollution and liability and compensation for damage, facilitation, tonnage measurement, unlawful acts against shipping and salvage.[501] Among these, the conventions that relate to the environment are the International Convention for the Prevention of Pollution of the Sea by Oil,[502] the International Convention relating to Intervention on the High Seas in Cases of Oil Pollution Casualties,[503] the Convention on the Prevention of Marine Pollution by Dumping of Wastes and Other Matter[504] and the International Convention for the Control and Management of Ships' Ballast Water and Sediments.[505]

Proposals to develop a new environmental convention are usually generated by individual States, and are first discussed and considered in the MEPC. If an agreement on a recommendation is reached, the Assembly will decide whether to endorse it through a resolution. This is followed by a diplomatic conference. Okumara describes this process as a '*slow negotiating process*', where Members have to '*consider the administrative, financial and other implications against the possible benefit of the proposed international agreement, often in consultation with the relevant industries*'.[506]

The rapid development of the commercial and technological needs of the shipping industry tends to drive the adoption of new environmental conventions, but it also influences the updating of the existing conventions, through amendments. The process of amending conventions usually requires the approval of two-thirds of member States, which, in the past, often meant delays and difficulties in adapting to changing business and technological regimes.[507] Therefore the two-thirds majority approval was dropped in favour of a faster and easier process, that is, the 'tacit acceptance of amendments procedure',[508] where after a set period of time the amendments are in force, if they have not been objected to by a particular number of parties, though this varies from instrument to instrument. However, this tacit acceptance procedure was not incorporated via an amendment to the IMO Convention itself but by revising the conventions where the IMO has a role.[509] Flexibility is now part of the IMO modus operandi in order '*to facilitate the process of modifying IMO instruments.*'[510]

Conclusions

This chapter has assessed, in detail, the legal framework and the state of affairs at the climate, ICAO and the IMO regimes with regards to the regulation of

IBF. It has provided a general overview of law-making in these regimes, discussed in terms of the participants or actors, the processes and the outcomes or instruments. This has been conducted with a view to answer the first research question of this study: *Why have IBF emissions remained largely unregulated?* In attempting to answer that, this chapter has provided responses to the following sub-questions: *How does the existing legal framework work? What are the tools available to address them? What have been the developments towards tackling the problem? What are the tensions impeding progress?*[511]

Although the legal framework in the three regimes presents opportunities for the regulation of IBF, we can identify two main types of challenges that are slowing down progress: those that are internal to the regimes and those that concern 'inter-regime' issues. The first group of challenges refers to the contradictions/tensions faced by any given regime when encountering a new matter that requires action and whose existence is independent of the existence of other regimes. Here, the regulation of new environmental problems, in this case climate change from IBF, will inevitably encounter differing views and conflicting interests among the actors within a regime, regarding if and how to regulate. These 'internal' challenges reflect the structure of regimes and the processes in place to address them, especially when it comes to accommodating the potential new regulation alongside existing legal instruments, so as to avoid conflicts or disruptions in the regulatory status quo. In the climate regime, this manifests itself with the fundamental dilemmas of how to deal with climate change in general, and specifically a lack of political will to agree on global emissions reduction targets. The same fundamental tensions can be found in ICAO and the IMO regimes where, even in the case of non-interaction with other regimes, the proposed regulations tend not to be very stringent or ambitious. To a large extent we can see that this is due to the strong influence of certain States, combined with the strong influence that the aviation and shipping industries have exerted over the regimes.

In the climate regime the law-making process around emissions from IBF has its own particularities and also suffers from the same problems that concern the general process of the climate regime, namely: disagreements over how much and who should bear the burden of the emissions reductions, linked to disparities in the understanding the CBDRRC principle. These difficulties have translated into slowness and uncertainty in reaching outcomes, where the general lack of political will seems insurmountable. After the PA, progress is confined to the work of the SBSTA, and potentially the CMA, where all parties to the Convention can participate, and whose outcomes are referred to the COP for final decisions. Non-state actors can participate in the work of these bodies in various ways, as observers, expressing their views through reports, statements and workshops. The involvement of ICAO and the IMO in the SBSTA is fully established and cooperation among the regimes has been encouraged from the COP. Indeed, inter-regime cooperation and observance in each other's processes has been strengthened, where: '*In order to address questions on bunker fuel emissions, the Convention's bodies cooperate closely with the relevant international organizations.*'[512] The decision-making processes of these bodies centre on the legal instruments and normative setup of the Climate Convention, the KP, the PA and the decisions adopted by the COP and other subsidiary bodies. In that connection, this chapter has highlighted the relevance of these specific instruments, including the provisions in the convention related to the objectives, guiding principles and commitments of the UNFCCC, and in particular the principle of CBDRRC.

With regards to ICAO and the IMO, as Buergenthal explains,[513] specialized international organizations share many similarities in terms of structure, constitution and processes. However, they have followed divergent paths and developed their own specific institutional personalities. This institutional personality or *modus operandi* is derived from a variety of factors, among them the history, functions and membership of the organization, but also the predominant political or economic power within them. As a consequence of that *modus operandi*, the resolution of legal problems and the articulation of rules are shaped and defined.[514]

The fact that ICAO and the IMO are organizations characterized as dealing with mostly technical issues does not preclude these organizations from political and commercial quagmires and influences. As Alvarez points out:

> [e]ven internal decisions within such regimes, such as whether to delegate authority to an expert body composed of governmental representatives or one that includes members of industry, is a political, contested question. Even technocratic organizations and organs within them serve strategic, and possible hegemonic interests.[515]

It has been pointed out that ICAO *'is a typical of a "technocratic" body that is responsive to particular agencies within governments, is dominated by a specific expertise'*.[516] This functionality and speciality imprints the regimes with a degree of autonomy in their law-making processes. A good test of this is to observe how the participants in the law-making processes are chosen on the basis of technical knowledge. However, the composition of the council, the most powerful body in ICAO, reveals that the technocracy is subordinate to political and economic power (e.g. from the United States). Although technocratic, ICAO has found itself in *'serious contested matters of high politics'*.[517] Similar concerns can be raised about the technical character of the IMO and the politics between flag States and shipping nations, although the composition of the Council has evolved from six members to 40, balancing the traditional domination of shipping nations.

According to Milde, the fact that ICAO has had only a small number of presidents in its history is in fact a quest for stability that *'may also translate into a lack of innovative courage and an overanxious preservation of the status quo'*.[518] One of the barriers to the lack of progress in the ICAO forum on regulating GHG emissions from international aviation is the structure of the international aviation regime itself, whose main function is to facilitate the growth of safe air transport. As it has been pointed out, the legal framework that has so successfully promoted the expansion of the sector, and its market liberalization, might not be *'so well equipped to deal with climate change'*.[519] Indeed, the Chicago Convention *'stands now up as a monument of stagnation; no substantive amendment entered into force 50 years since its adoption*' and the few administrative and constitutional amendments were '*purely cosmetic and could be seen as rather harmful*' namely, a *de facto* reduction of the role of the Assembly by the introduction of the triennial rather than annual cycle, and an increase in the composition of the council and air navigation commission, '*not motivated by efficiency but rather to preserve the quasi-permanent representation and vested interest of some member States*'.[520] '*Stagnation in the developments of the legal framework has been accompanied by stagnation in the working methods of ICAO.*'[521] Other authors have also pointed out the need for a renewal of the Chicago Convention, arguing that while the role of ICAO has been essential to the development of aviation since its inception, the organization is '*losing ground in tackling the main challenges posed by modern aviation, in the context of growing complexity*'.[522] In his article, Olivier Onidi argues that this holds true with regard to addressing climate change.

On the other hand, the IMO is deemed to contain a more flexible and adaptive structure since the IMO Convention has been revised many times, demonstrating a willingness to adapt to new realities and processes. Another example of how the IMO has adjusted to fit its circumstances is the 'tacit acceptance procedure' that the organization uses at the MEPC for the amendment of IMO treaties, which have given *de facto* prerogatives to the IMO bodies to streamline the legal machinery. All in all, the role of the IMO in addressing environmental matters, which has been praised in the literature as being successful, is argued to have '*shown the flexibility and responses necessary to keep pace with new developments, and has successfully provided a forum in which competing interest can be balanced*'.[523] However, it has been highlighted that the speed of the IMO's law-making process is dependant, more than anything else, on the will of the member States.[524]

The second group of challenges identified in this chapter allude to the tensions arising from the overlap between regimes, which will be explored in Chapter 5. Some barriers to progress in tackling the aviation sector's contribution to climate change has been identified by the literature[525] and include the political position of States, specifically in relation to who should undertake mitigation actions and how. This also connects with the question of principles and international rights and obligations under the Chicago Convention and other associated agreements. This chapter has identified and discussed three main challenges that would need to be overcome if the ICAO is to assume the leadership in reducing the aviation sector's contribution to climate change. These are:

> To marry the unified approach of the Chicago Convention that guides ICAO with the principle of common but differentiated responsibility that is a cornerstone of the UNFCCC process. [. . .] to preserve the sectoral approach for international aviation that was established by Kyoto [. . .] to develop economic measures that are effective in reducing aviation's emissions.[526]

Meanwhile, the regulation of emissions from international maritime transport may present even more challenges, not only due to the complex matrix of actors[527] involved in the maritime activity, but also because there are nearly eight times more ocean-going vessels than international aircraft.[528] Furthermore, the IMO perceives itself as being part of the climate solution rather than the problem, since shipping is the least energy-intensive means of transport.[529]

Notes

1 Gudmund Hernes, *Hot Topic – Cold Comfort: Climate Change and Attitude Change* (Nordforsk, 2012). 13.
2 Alan E. Boyle and Christine M. Chinkin, *The Making of International Law* (Oxford University Press, 2007). Their work offers a structure to be used in order to analyze law-making processes in international law. See Chapter 2.
3 An array of conferences and declarations was key to developing such awareness and determination, for example the conference on Changing Atmosphere: Implications for Global Security, the Noordwijk Declaration on Atmospheric Pollution and Climate Change or the Declaration on Global Warming and Sea Level Rise. An important milestone was the International Meeting of Legal and Policy Experts on the Protection of the Atmosphere (Ottawa, 1989), which recommended taking international action through a legal instrument. Another element in the raise of awareness was the Brundtland Report of 1987.
4 See, Daniel Bodansky, 'The History of the Global Climate Change Regime', in *International Relations and Global Climate Change: Global Environmental Accord* (Urs Luterbacher and Detlef F. Sprinz eds., 2001).
5 In international law-making the setting of the agenda can come from a variety of situations including responses to unilateral claims made by one country or a group of countries, proposals from principal political organs of the United Nations or United Nations' subsidiary bodies or UN specialized agencies. Individuals, NGOs and expert bodies can spur states to take action. Although some processes can arise from specific disasters or accidents, such as the Torre Canyon oil spill, or dramatic situations, mostly it is mostly a policy-driven process, and the climate change issue is an example of that. For a full explanation on how new topics reach the law-making agenda see A.E. Boyle and C.M. Chinkin, *The Making of International Law*. (2007). 98.
6 Although UNGA Resolutions have a non-legally binding character, they are highly relevant. They are recommendations in pursuant of the authority conferred by the UN Charter on the promotion of economic, social- and health-related issues. The UNGA has been an important actor in the development of environmental matters in general and in connection to the climate change in particular, not only by adopting resolutions but also by convening environmental conferences including Rio (1992), initiating the intergovernmental negotiations on environmental matters, including climate change.
7 UNGA Resolution on the Protection of Global Climate for Present and Future Generations of Mankind, UN Doc. A/RES/43/53, 6 December 1988. It recognized '*that climate change is a common concern of mankind*'. The implications of such recognition are that there is a common legal interest of all states to protect and enforce rules towards the protection of the climate since it is an essential condition which sustains life on earth and that given that climate change is a global problem that affects the community of states as a whole, artificial territorial boundaries are inadequate to deal with it, so necessary action should be taken within a global framework. The same status applies to the ozone layer and the atmosphere in general. For further explanations see Patricia W. Birnie et al., *International Law and the Environment* (Oxford University Press 3rd ed., 2009). 129–130 and 338–339. See also GA Resolution 44/207 in 1989.
8 Developing countries felt that their concerns were not properly addressed by the scientifically focused IPCC process and rejected the proposal of a negotiating committee that would work under the auspices of the WMO and UNEP. See

explanation in D. Bodansky, 'The History of the Global Climate Change Regime'. (2001).

9 Although the option of elaborating an umbrella legislative instrument similar to that of UNCLOS (i.e. a kind of 'law of the atmosphere') was considered, it was ruled out for reasons of flexibility and time. Instead the framework convention was pursued. See Elli Louka, *International Environmental Law: Fairness, Effectiveness, and World Order* (Cambridge University Press, 2006). 358.

10 United Nations General Assembly, UNGA Resolution on the Protection of Global Climate for Present and Future Generations of Mankind, UN Doc. A/RES/45/212, 21 December 1990.

11 In order to fulfil its mandate, the INC/FCCC held five sessions where participants discussed all important issues of the convention, where the outcome was a final text reflected the broad participation and prioritization of consensus. The dialectic of developed versus developing countries was present at the outset of the work of the INC/FCCC, which was also a matter subject to negotiation and compromise. Due to political objections from developing countries, the convention failed to secure a common position, hence countries were finally divided in groups. A.E. Boyle and C.M. Chinkin, *The Making of International Law*. (2007). 107. Also, The Work of the INC/UNFCCC Is. Available at: http://ccsr.aori.u-tokyo.ac.jp/old/unfccc4/lists/all_by_date_1991.html

12 The work of the INC towards the elaboration of the UNFCCC has been described as '*a further two years of strenuous negotiations*' in David Freestone and Charlotte Streck, *Legal Aspects of Carbon Trading: Kyoto, Copenhagen, and Beyond* (Oxford University Press, 2009). 5.

13 The United Nations Conference on Environment and Development took place in Rio de Janeiro in 1992 and was considered a success in terms of participation and outcome. Under its auspices, the UNFCCC was adopted, together with the Rio Declaration on Environment and Development, a collection of 27 principles regarding environment and socio-economic development and Agenda 21, a work program for the forthcoming century.

14 The membership, as of May 2013, totals 195 parties, of which 165 were signatories. See status of ratification in: http://unfccc.int/essential_background/convention/status_of_ratification/items/2631.php. States and regional economic integration organizations may become parties to the Climate Convention at any time through ratification, acceptance, approval or accession, according to its Article 22.

15 The purpose of the UNFCCC '*is to set the general tone for the future climate change discussions and to compromise in a single text the often irreconcilable interests and ideologies of state parties. Because of this reality – a reality for every framework convention – the convention straddles the world of firm commitments and vague hortatory articulations.*' E. Louka, *International Environmental Law: Fairness, Effectiveness, and World Order* (Cambridge University Press, 2006). 361.

16 The convention covers all GHGs not covered by the Montréal Protocol on the depletion of the ozone layer.

17 The IPCC has established a strong positive relationship between human activity and global warming in the last century. There are three working groups within it: WGI dealing with the physical science; WGII assessing vulnerability, consequences and adaptation; and WGIII, which focuses on mitigation actions.

18 UNFCCC, Article 2.

19 See Farhana Yamin and Joanna Depledge, *The International Climate Change Regime: A Guide to Rules, Institutions and Procedures* (Cambridge University Press, 2004). 60–65; P.W. Birnie et al., *International Law and the Environment*. (2009). 358.

20 Alexander Zahar, 'The Climate Change Regime', in *Routledge Handbook of International Environmental Law* (Shawkat Alam ed., 2013). 352.

21 The goal of keeping global warming below 2°C above pre-industrial levels was agreed upon in COP15 and assimilated to the UNFCCC process in COP16. In the

light of the IPCC Fifth Assessment Report in 2014, the goal could be tightened to 1.5°C.

22 Jutta Brunnée, 'An Agreement in Principle? The Copenhagen Accord and the Post-2012 Climate Regime', in *Law of the Sea in Dialogue* (Holger Hestermeyer et al. eds., 2011). 51–53. As stated: '*With this central concept quantified, the Article 1 objective provides not just general direction to states' efforts, but sets a bar against which the credibility of emissions reduction commitments can be measured.*'

23 For example the soft aim of returning the GHGs emission to 1990 levels for developed countries by 2000.

24 For a detailed description of the climate regime see F. Yamin and J. Depledge, *The International Climate Change Regime: A Guide to Rules, Institutions and Procedures.* (2004).

25 UNFCCC, Article 3 expresses that the Parties shall be guided by the principles contained in it.

26 For a discussion on the legal value and status of the principles see Daniel Bodansky, 'The United Nations Framework Convention on Climate Change: A Commentary', *Yale Journal of International Law*, 18, (1993). 501–503; P.W. Birnie et al., *International Law and the Environment.* (2009). 359; Chris Wold et al., *Climate Change and the Law* (LexisNexis Matthew Bender, 2009). 150–154.

27 UNFCCC, Article 3.1 states that '*The Parties should protect the climate system for the benefit of present and future generations of humankind, on the basis of equity and in accordance with their common but differentiated responsibilities and respective capabilities. Accordingly, the developed country Parties should take the lead in combating climate change and the adverse effects thereof.*'

28 UNFCCC Article 3.2 states that '*The specific needs and special circumstances of developing country Parties, especially those that are particularly vulnerable to the adverse effects of climate change, and of those Parties, especially developing country Parties, that would have to bear a disproportionate or abnormal burden under the Convention, should be given full consideration.*'

29 UNFCCC Article 3.3 states that '*The Parties should take precautionary measures to anticipate, prevent or minimize the causes of climate change and mitigate its adverse effects. Where there are threats of serious or irreversible damage, lack of full scientific certainty should not be used as a reason for postponing such measures.*'

30 UNFCCC, Article 3.3 '*that policies and measures to deal with climate change should be cost-effective so as to ensure global benefits at the lowest possible cost*'.

31 UNFCCC Article 3.3 and 3.4. The former states that '*The Parties have a right to, and should, promote sustainable development. Policies and measures to protect the climate system against human-induced change should be appropriate for the specific conditions of each Party and should be integrated with national development programmes, taking into account that economic development is essential for adopting measures to address climate change.*' See also, UNFCCC, Article 5, which states that '*The Parties should cooperate to promote a supportive and open international economic system that would lead to sustainable economic growth and development in all Parties, particularly developing country Parties, thus enabling them better to address the problems of climate change. Measures taken to combat climate change, including unilateral ones, should not constitute a means of arbitrary or unjustifiable discrimination or a disguised restriction on international trade.*'

32 The precautionary principle stated in principle 15 of the Rio Declaration implies that the lack of full scientific certainty cannot be used as a reason for inaction when there is an environmental threat.

33 Sustainable development is '*the development that meets the needs of the present without compromising the ability of future generations to meet their own needs*'. As defined in the Brundtland Report.

34 Paolo Galizzi, 'Air, Atmosphere and Climate Change', in *Routledge Handbook of International Environmental Law* (Shawkat Alam ed., 2013). 345.

35 Lavanya Rajamani, *Differential Treatment in International Environmental Law* (Oxford University Press, 2006). 176–215.

36 J. Brunnée, 'An Agreement in Principle? The Copenhagen Accord and the Post-2012 Climate Regime'. (2011). 53. Also, Jutta Brunnée and Stephen J. Toope, *Legitimacy and Legality in International Law: An Interactional Account* (Cambridge University Press, 2010).

37 Different parties put the accent on different aspects of the principle, responsibility for historical emissions, responsibility for current emissions, capabilities of countries. See further Chapter 5.

38 List of Annex I Parties to the Convention: Australia; Austria; Belarus; Belgium; Bulgaria; Canada; Croatia; Cyprus; Czech Republic; Denmark; Estonia; European Union; Finland; France; Germany; Greece; Hungary; Iceland; Ireland; Italy; Japan; Latvia; Liechtenstein; Lithuania; Luxembourg; Malta; Monaco; the Netherlands; New Zealand; Norway; Poland; Portugal; Romania; the Russian Federation; Slovakia; Slovenia; Spain; Sweden; Switzerland; Turkey; Ukraine; the United Kingdom; the United States of America. Source: http://unfccc.int/parties_and_observers/parties/annex_i/items/2774.php

39 The term 'economies in transition' comprises the Russian Federation and some states from Eastern Europe (i.e. the ex-members of the Soviet Union).

40 List of Annex II Parties to the Convention: Australia; Austria; Belgium; Canada; Denmark; European Economic Community; Finland; France; Germany; Greece; Iceland; Ireland; Italy; Japan; Luxembourg; the Netherlands; New Zealand; Norway; Portugal; Spain; Sweden; Switzerland; the United Kingdom; the United States of America. Source: http://unfccc.int/essential_background/convention/background/items/1348.php

41 China, the world's second largest economy and one of the fastest growing, is thus featured in the same category as the Democratic Republic of Congo, one of the world's poorest countries. Although emerging economies and least developed countries are under the Non-Annex I group, the Convention does distinguish between groups, in terms of obligations, implementation and assistance, such as small island developing states, developing countries with economies particularly dependent on fossil fuel production or developing countries with fragile mountainous ecosystems. Lavanya Rajamani, 'The Cancun Climate Agreements: Reading the Text, Subtext and Tea Leaves', *International Affairs*, 60(2), (2011). 617.

42 For example, the LDC Group includes 48 countries that are especially vulnerable to droughts or floods.

43 UNFCCC Article 4.1 '*All Parties, taking into account their common but differentiated responsibilities and their specific national and regional development priorities, objectives and circumstances, shall*'.

44 UNFCCC, Article 4.1 (a). For a summary of obligations and right of states under UNFCCC article 4, see: A. Zahar, 'The Climate Change Regime'. (2013). 353–356.

45 According to UNFCCC Article 12 and using comparable methodologies agreed upon by the Parties.

46 *UNFCCC, Article 4.1 (b). Other exhortative provisions include: to promote and cooperate in the field of technologies, practices and processes that control, reduce or prevent GHG emissions in all sectors (Article 4.1 (c)), to promote the sustainable management of sinks and reservoirs (Article 4.1 (d)), to cooperate in the field of adaptation (Article 4.1 (e)), to take into account and integrate climate change into their relevant social, economic and environmental policies and actions with appropriate methods (Article 4.1 (f)), to promote and cooperate in the fields of research (Article 4.1 (g)), exchange of information and education (Article 4.1 (h)) and training and public awareness encouraging wide participation (Article 4.1 (i)).*

47 UNFCCC, Article 4.1 (j).

48 UNFCCC, Article 4.7.

49 UNFCCC, Article 4.2.

50 UNFCCC, Article 4.8. Those countries are: small island countries, countries with low-lying coastal areas, countries with arid and semi-arid areas, forested areas and areas

liable to forest decay, countries with areas prone to natural disasters, countries with areas liable to drought and desertification, countries with areas of high urban atmospheric pollution, countries with areas with fragile ecosystems, including mountainous ecosystems, countries whose economies are highly dependent on income generated from the production, processing and export, and/or on consumption of fossil fuels and associated energy-intensive products, and landlocked and transit countries.

51 UNFCCC, Article 4.9.
52 UNFCCC, Article 4.10 – in connection with article 10.
53 UNFCCC, Article 4.2.
54 UNFCCC, Article 4.2 (a) The so-called PAMs can be implemented jointly with other Parties.
55 UNFCCC, Article 4.2 (b) The previous level and the way to return to it are not provided in the convention.
56 UNFCCC, Articles 4.3, 4.4 and 4.5.
57 This refers to the cost of implementing the measures agreed between developing countries and the Financial Mechanism established in Article 11.
58 UNFCCC, Article 4.4.
59 UNFCCC, Article 4.6.
60 Robin R. Churchill and Geir Ulfstein, 'Autonomous Institutional Arrangements in Multilateral Environmental Agreements: A Little-Noticed Phenomenon in International Law', *The American Journal of International Law*, 94(4), (2000). 623–659.
61 UNFCCC, Article 7.
62 Climate Convention, article 7
63 Ibid.
64 UNFCCC Draft Rules of Procedure, FCCC/CP/1996/2, (1996). The COP failed to adopt the rules of procedure, mainly because of divergences on the voting rules.
65 Consensus usually leads to lowest common denominator results. On the challenges of rule-making in the climate regime see for example, Arunabha Ghosh and Ngaire Woods, 'Governing Climate Change: Lessons from Other Governance Regimes', in *The Economics and Politics of Climate Change* (Dieter Helm and Cameron Hepburn eds., 2009). 455–463.
66 Limited-membership institutions include the Compliance Committee of the KP, Executive Board of the CDM and the Supervisory Committee of the Joint Implementation and the Adaptation Board and other experts groups. See, Joanna Depledge and Farhana Yamin, 'The Global Climate Change Regime: A Defense', in *The Economics and Politics of Climate Change* (Dieter Helm and Cameron Hepburn eds., 2009). 438–442.
67 UNFCCC, Article 10.
68 UNFCCC, Article 9.
69 UNFCCC, Article 8.
70 UNFCCC home website: http://unfccc.int/bodies/items/6241.php
71 FCCC/CP/1995/7/Add.1 Decision14/CP.1.
72 The COP Bureau is a limited-membership committee that provides advice to the COP.
73 J. Depledge and F. Yamin, 'The Global Climate Change Regime: A Defense'. (2009). 438–439.
74 decision 1/CP.17.
75 See, Lorraine M. Elliott, *The Global Politics of the Environment* (New York University Press 2nd ed., 2004). 86.
76 The reduction targets were assumed only by the Annex I countries. Parties agreed to reduce their overall emissions of six GHGs by 5% below 1990 levels by the end of the first commitment period from 2008 to 2012.
77 Requirements for the approval of the KP are specified in its Article 23. It states that it shall be entered into force on the ninetieth day after the date on which not less

than 55 Parties to the UNFCCC (incorporating Parties included in Annex I, which accounted in total for at least 55% of the total carbon dioxide emissions in 1990 of the Parties included in Annex I) have deposited their instruments of ratification, acceptance, approval or accession. This process took over seven years and the KP finally entered into force in February 2005.

78 The EU negotiated with Russia to allow the Protocol to enter into force.

79 The United States had a very proactive role in the negotiation process, pushing hard for the adoption of MBMs in the Kyoto model, and President Clinton signed the Protocol in 1998. However the Clinton administration could not secure the support of the Senate, which was required for ratification. Indeed the Senate had already, in 1997, voted 95–0 in support of the non-binding Byrd-Hagel Resolution that opposed any international agreement that did not require developing countries to make emission reductions. This position was supported by the two Bush administrations (2000–2008). See the explanation provided in J. Brunnée and S.J. Toope, *Legitimacy and Legality in International Law: An Interactional Account.* (2010). 135. The United States is not the only case; Canada withdrew from the KP in 2011.

80 Ibid. at. 137. This idea is put forward because it is in fact an enabling framework for the mechanisms to be developed in subsequent COPs/MOPs.

81 The commitment was further redistributed among countries. The negotiated emission targets for each Annex I country can be found in the Annex B to the KP.

82 KP, Article 17.

83 KP, Article 6.

84 KP, Article 12.

85 KP, Article 4. It allows countries to aggregate and reduce their emissions together. The emissions bubbles were design after a request of the EU.

86 The COPs serve as meetings of the Parties to the Kyoto Protocol. (Hereinafter COP/MOP). The first meeting took place in Montréal in 2005.

87 Decision 1/CMP.1 Consideration of commitments for subsequent periods for Parties included in Annex I to the Convention under Article 3, paragraph 9, of the Kyoto Protocol. UN Doc. FCCC/FP/CMP/2005/8/Add.1, 30 March 2006. The AWG-KP is *'an open-ended ad hoc working group of Parties to the Kyoto Protocol'* that reports to the COP/MOP on the status of the process.

88 UNFCCC, Decision 1/CMP.8, Amendment to the Kyoto Protocol pursuant to its Article 3, paragraph 9 (the Doha Amendment) UN Doc. FCCC/KP/CMP/2012/13/Add.1, 28 Febrero 2013 (2013).

89 Annex B of the KP has been replaced.

90 Decision 1/CP.13, Bali Action Plan. UN Doc. FCCC/CP/2007/6/Add.1*, 14 March 2008. The AWG-LCA is a subsidiary body under the convention. At COP11 a process with a focus on long-term cooperation was opened under the name of the Convention Dialogue. This process ended up with the adoption of the Bali Action Plan and the creation of the AWG-LCA two years later. The Bali Roadmap was agreed to enhance the commitments of the parties on long-term issues.

91 This comprehensive process aimed to agree on a shared vision for long-term cooperative action, on enhancement of national and international mitigation and adaptation, financial and technology transfer actions.

92 The work of the AWG-LCA was scheduled to finish in two years but the group has had its mandate renewed three times since 2009.

93 Decision 1/CP.18 Agreed outcome pursuant to the Bali Action Plan. UN Doc. FCCC/CP/2012/8/Add.1, 28 February 2013.

94 Daniel Bodansky, 'The Durban Platform: Issues and Options for a 2015 Agreement' (Centre for Climate and Energy Solutions, 2012).

95 Decision 2/CP.15, The Copenhagen Accord, UN Doc. FCCC/CP/2009/7/Add.1, 30 March 2010, (2009).

96 Over 140 States joined the accord. Developed countries pledged quantified economy-wide reduction targets while developing countries committed to Nationally Appropriate

Mitigation Actions (NAMAs). For an overview on the Copenhagen outcomes see, Matthieu Wemaere, 'State of Play of the International Climate Negotiations: What Are the Results of the Copenhagen Conference?', *Carbon and Climate Law Review*, 4(1), (2010). 106; Meinhard Doelle, 'The Legacy of the Climate Talks in Copenhagen: Hopenhagen or Brokenhagen?', *Carbon and Climate Law Review*, 4(1), (2010). 86.

97 The Cancun Agreements include an outcome under the AWG-LCA and another under the KP: Decision 1/CP.16 The Cancun Agreements: Outcome of the work of the Ad Hoc Working Group on Long-term Cooperative Action under the Convention. UN Doc. FCCC/CP/2010/7/Add.1, 15 March 2011; Decision 1/CMP.6 The Cancun Agreements: Outcome of the work of the Ad Hoc Working Group on Further Commitments for Annex I Parties under the Kyoto Protocol at its 15th session, UN Doc. FCCC/KP/CMP/2010/12/Add.1, 15 March 2011.

98 L. Rajamani, (2011). For a more positive evaluation on the Copenhagen Accord see, Fred L. Morrison, 'The Reluctance of the United States to Ratify Treaties', in *Law of the Sea in Dialogue* (Holger Hestermeyer et al. eds., 2011).

99 Decision 1/CP.17, Establishment of an Ad Hoc Working Group on the Durban Platform for Enhanced Action, UN Doc. FCCC/CP/2011/9/Add.1. 11 December 2011, (2011).

100 Lavanya Rajamani, 'The Durban Platform for Enhanced Action and the Future of the Climate Regime', *International & Comparative Law Quarterly*, 61(2), (2012). 501–518.

101 Ibid.

102 UNFCCC, The Doha Amendment, (2013).

103 Ibid.

104 For a summary of the Warsaw outcomes see, Harro van Asselt and Pieter Pauw, 'Beyond Warsaw: Finding New Hope for International Climate Policy', *Outreach*, (2013). *'Warsaw offered an opportunity to develop rules for this agreement. Parties made only modest progress on this front, adopting a rather flexible timeline for the submission of "contributions" (rather than "commitments") in 2015, and postponing any serious discussion on how to review these contributions to the next conference, in Lima. In some specific issue areas, such as reducing emissions from deforestation and forest degradation (REDD+), and monitoring, reporting and verification of emission reductions, Parties booked notable progress, whereas in other areas, such as climate finance, the lack of agreement and ambition was more concerning.'* Another relevant element was the establishment of the Warsaw international mechanism for loss and damage, aiming to provide for the consequences of climate impacts in most vulnerable countries.

105 UNFCCC, Decision 1/CP.19 Further Advancing the Durban Platform. FCCC/CP/2013/10/Add.1, (2013).

106 UNFCCC, Decision -/CP.20, Lima Call for Climate Action, (2014).

107 Robert N. Stavins, 'COP-20 in Lima: A New Way Forward. (Conference of the Parties of the UN Framework Convention on Climate Change)', *The Environmental Forum*, 32, (2015). 14.

108 For an analysis of the binding elements of the PA, see Daniel Bodanski, 'The Legal Character of the Paris Agreement', *Review of European, Comparative, and International Environmental Law*, (2016).

109 UNFCCC, Paris Agreement (Paris, 12 December 2015, in force 4 November 2016) FCCC/CP/2015/L.9. (2015).

110 Ibid. at. Article 2.1(a).

111 Ibid. at. Article 4.1.

112 For an analysis see, Harro van Asselt, 'International Climate Change Law in a Bottom-Up World', *Questions of International Law*, Zoom-in 26, (2016).

113 Paris Agreement. Article 4.2.

114 Ibid. at. Article 3 and 4.1.

115 Annalisa Savaresi, 'The Paris Agreement: A New Beginning?', *Journal of Energy & Natural Resources Law*, 34(1), (2016). 16–26. At 22.

116 Lavanya Rajamani, 'Ambition and Differentiation in the 2015 Paris Agreement: Interpretative Possibilities and Underlying Politics', *International and Comparative Law Quarterly*, 65, (2016) 493–514.

117 A rather ambitious deadline since it took four years to develop the rules for the KP.

118 African States, Asian States, Eastern European States, Latin American and the Caribbean States, and the Western European and Other States (the 'Other States' include Australia, Canada, Iceland, New Zealand, Norway, Switzerland and the United States of America, but not Japan, which is in the Asian Group).

119 Forty-three low-lying and small island countries, most of which are members of the G-77, that are particularly vulnerable to sea level rise.

120 The list of 49 least developed countries: Afghanistan; Angola; Bangladesh; Benin; Bhutan; Burkina Faso; Burundi; Cambodia; Central African Republic; Chad; Comoros; Democratic Republic of the Congo; Djibouti; Equatorial Guinea; Eritrea; Ethiopia; Gambia; Guinea; Guinea-Bissau; Haiti; Kiribati; Lesotho; Liberia; Madagascar; Malawi; Maldives; Mali; Mauritania; Mozambique; Myanmar; Nepal; Niger; Rwanda; Samoa; São Tomé and Principe; Senegal; Sierra Leone; Solomon Islands; Somalia; Sudan; Timor-Leste; Togo; Tuvalu; Uganda; United Republic of Tanzania; Lao People's Democratic Republic; Vanuatu; Yemen; Zambia. Source: http://unfccc.int/files/cooperation_and_support/ldc/application/pdf/ldc-list-31jan08.pdf

121 Australia, Canada, Japan, New Zealand, Norway, the Russian Federation, Ukraine and the United States.

122 Formed in 2000, comprises Mexico, Liechtenstein, Monaco, the Republic of Korea and Switzerland.

123 UNFCCC website: http://unfccc.int/parties_and_observers/parties/negotiating_groups/items/2714.php

124 For example, the negotiations on the KP '*attracted extensive non-state activity from environmentalist and from industry*'. See, L.M. Elliott, *The Global Politics of the Environment.* (2004). 88.

125 For an overview on participation of NGOs in the climate regimes see, Joanna Depledge, *The Organization of Global Negotiations: Constructing the Climate Change Regime* (Taylor & Francis, 2013). 209–230.

126 Kal Raustiala, 'States, NGOs, and International Environmental Institutions', *International Studies Quarterly*, 41, (1997). 376.

127 Kal Raustiala, 'Nonstate Actors in the Global Climate Regime', in *International Relations and Global Climate Change: Global Environmental Accord* (Urs Luterbacher and Detlef F. Sprinz eds., 2001). See an account of the regime participants in F. Yamin and J. Depledge, *The International Climate Change Regime: A Guide to Rules, Institutions and Procedures.* (2004). 30–59.

128 These informal arrangements '*[do] not preclude other ways of communicating*'. See, Daniel Blobel et al., *United Nations Framework Convention on Climate Change: Handbook* (Intergovernmental and Legal Affairs, Climate Change Secretariat, 2006). 63. Available at: http://unfccc.int/files/parties_and_observers/ngo/application/pdf/constituency_2011_english.pdf

129 Naghmeh Nasiritousi et al., 'The Roles of Non-State Actors in Climate Change Governance: Understanding Agency Through Governance Profiles', *International Environmental Agreements: Politics, Law and Economics*, (2014).

130 Joyeeta Gupta, 'On Behalf of My Delegation: A Survival Guide for Developing Country Climate Negotiators', *International Institute for Sustainable Development & Center for Sustainable Development in the Americas*, (2000).

131 CAN-International is the biggest NGO coalition and has regional branches, including Climate Network Europe (CNE), Climate Network Africa (CNA), Climate Action Network South-East Asia (CANSEA), Climate Action Network-South Asia (CANSA) and a US branch. There is a group within CAN dealing with IBF.

132 For a list of actions on IBF by CAN-International. Available at: www.climatenet-work.org/policy-information/publication/topics/1432 (last accessed 1 August 2014).

133 Established in 1998, it also has observer status in CAEP. It is the biggest civil society voice in ICAO.

134 CSC has observer status at the IMO.

135 Other relevant BINGOs include the International Climate Change Partnership or the International Chamber of Commerce.

136 J. Depledge, *The Organization of Global Negotiations: Constructing the Climate Change Regime.* (2013). 221–222.

137 Global Climate Action, NAZCA. Available at: http://climateaction.unfccc.int/

138 FCCC/CP/2015/L.9 Adoption of the Paris Agreement. Proposal by the President, section V, paragraphs 134–137. Also, paragraph 118.

139 Global Climate Action, NAZCA. Available at: http://climateaction.unfccc.int

140 Joshua Busby, 'After Paris: Good Enough Climate Governance', *Current History*, January 2016, (2016). 3-9. At 7–9.

141 FCCC/CP/2015/L.9 Adoption of the Paris Agreement. Proposal by the President, section V, paragraphs 134–137.

142 '*[T]aking into account their common but differentiated responsibilities and their specific national and regional development priorities, objectives and circumstances*'. This is translated in differ-ent content and timetables for the reporting obligation of Non-Annex I countries.

143 UNFCCC, Article 12 contains the obligation of communicating to the COP, among other issues, parties' national inventories. Art 12.1 (a). '*In accordance with Article 4, paragraph 1, each Party shall communicate to the Conference of the Parties, through the secretariat, the following elements of information: (a) A national inventory of anthropo-genic emissions by sources and removals by sinks of all greenhouse gases not controlled by the Montreal Protocol, to the extent its capacities permit, using comparable methodologies to be promoted and agreed upon by the Conference of the Parties.*'

144 See Chapter 1.

145 The *IPCC Guidelines for National Greenhouse Gas Inventories* (1996) were first released in 1994 and revised in 1996. In 2000 and 2003 'good practices' for the revised guide-lines were added and in 2006 they were revised again. However, this guidance still leaves room for 'a number of definitional and methodological problems' that arise from the split between domestic and international. See F. Yamin and J. Depledge, *The International Climate Change Regime: A Guide to Rules, Institutions and Procedures.* (2004). 84.

146 1996 *IPCC Guidelines for National Greenhouse Gas Inventories* and IPCC, Guidelines for National Greenhouse Gas Inventories (2006).

147 INC-UNFCCC 2 Decision9/2. It concluded that the country where the fuel was sold was the best criteria for the purposes of reporting emissions from IBF.

148 F. Yamin and J. Depledge, *The International Climate Change Regime: A Guide to Rules, Institutions and Procedures.* (2004). 83.

149 UNFCCC, FCCC/CP/1995/7/Add.1 Decision 4/CP.1 on Methodological issues, (1995).

150 F. Yamin and J. Depledge, *The International Climate Change Regime: A Guide to Rules, Institutions and Procedures.* (2004). 83–87.

151 Decision 2/CP3 Methodological issues related to the Kyoto Protocol. UN Doc. FCCC/CP/1997/7/Add.1, (1997).

152 Mainly the decision to follow the reporting practices of the Convention for Kyoto parties and the agreement to pursue the inclusion of IBF in national inventories.

153 For a drafting history of Article 2.2, see: FCCC/AGBM/1997/7 13 October 1997. Consolidated negotiating text by the Chairman. It was based on the work of the 7th meeting of the Ad hoc Group of the Berlin Mandate, reflecting Parties preferences and a compromise text envisioned by the Chairman.

154 Joanna Depledge, 'Tracing the Origins of the Kyoto Protocol: An Article-Byarticle Textual History. Prepared under Contract to UNFCCC by Joanna Depledge August 1999/August 2000. UN Doc. FCCC/TP/2000/2 25 November 2000', (2000). 27.

155 F. Yamin and J. Depledge, *The International Climate Change Regime: A Guide to Rules, Institutions and Procedures.* (2004). 85.

156 Ibid. at. 85.

157 Paul Govind, 'International Environmental Institutions', in *Routledge Handbook of International Environmental Law* (Shawkat Alam ed., 2013). 118.

158 Decision 4/CP.1 Methodological issues UN Doc. FCCC/CP/1995/7/Add.1, (1995).

159 Ibid. at. Paragraph 1(f).

160 .Decision 2/CP.3, FCCC/CP/1997/7/Add.1.

161 F. Yamin and J. Depledge, *The International Climate Change Regime: A Guide to Rules, Institutions and Procedures.* (2004). 85.

162 Decision 2/CP.17, UNFCCC, FCCC/CP/2011/9/Add.1 Report of the Conference of the Parties on its seventeenth session, held in Durban from 28 November to 11 December 2011 (2011).

163 Bali Action Plan paragraph 1b(IV).

164 FCCC/AWGLCA/2009/8, (2009).

165 FCCC/AWGLCA/2009/14, (2009).

166 Herold Anke et al., 'The Development of Climate Negotiations in View of Cancun (COP 16): Study Requested by the EU Directorate General for Internal Policies: Policy Department A: Economic and Scientific Policy', (2010). 44.

167 Herold Anke et al., 'The Development of Climate Negotiations in View of Warsaw (COP 19): Study Requested by the EU Directorate General for Internal Policies: Policy Department A: Economic and Scientific Policy', (2013). 67.

168 Decision1/CP.18. UN Doc. FCCC/CP/ 2012/8/Add1, (2012).

169 A.e.a.Ö.-I.e.V. Herold, (2013). 67.

170 Decision 1/CP.17. Paragraph 2.

171 See further in the next section on the ADP process.

172 Paris Agreement. Article 2.1(a) and 4.1.

173 While the Paris Agreement, above, does not exclude IBF from its long-term mitigation aims (Article 2.1(a) and 4.1), the mitigation tools (national pledges) chosen to achieve this goals are not thought to address IBFs.

174 In an analysis of the Paris Agreement, Meinhard Doelle stated that the failure to address emissions from IBF 'will likely continue to plague the regime', see M. Doelle, 'The Paris Agreement: Historic Breakthrough or High Stakes Experiment?', *Climate Law* (December 22, 2015). Forthcoming, Special Issue 6(1–2), (2016). Available at: https://ssrn.com/abstract=2708148. 17. See also, Beatriz Martinez Romera, 'The Paris Agreement and the Regulation of International Bunker Fuels', *Review of European Comparative & International Environmental Law*, 25(2), (2016). 215–227 and further in this thesis Chapter 4.

175 FCCC/CP/1995/7/Add.1 The mandate to the SBSTA included an invitation to international organizations to contribute to the SBSTA's work. Paragraph f.

176 FCCC/SBSTA/ 1995/3. A year later, the SBSTA4 highlighted the existence of three different issues in regards to IBF, namely: adequate and consistent inventories, allocation of emissions to countries and control possibilities. See: FCCC/SBSTA/1996/9/ Add1.

177 FCCC/CP/1997/7/Add.1. Decision 2/CP.3 Methodological issues related to the Kyoto protocol. para. 4. *'urges the Subsidiary Body for Scientific and Technological Advice to further elaborate on the inclusion of these emissions in the overall greenhouse gas inventories of Parties'.*

178 With regards to reporting, the SBSTA11 acknowledged the need for improvement in the reporting by Annex I Parties and referred to *'the forthcoming IPCC good practice guidance, as well as in the new UNFCCC reporting guidelines on annual inventories'.* See

D. Blobel et al., *United Nations Framework Convention on Climate Change: Handbook.* (2006). 186.

179 FCCC/SBSTA/1996/9/Add1, FCCC/SBSTA/1996/9/Add2.
180 For example the option of allocating responsibility according to the national space criteria was ruled out since most of the emissions occur outside national airspace.
181 Faber, J., B. Boon et al. 2007. Aviation and Maritime transport in a post 2012 climate policy regime, Netherlands Environmental Assessment Agency.
182 FCCC/SBSTA/1997/14, FCCC/SBSTA/2000/10, FCCC/SBSTA/2001/2.
183 FCCC/SBSTA/1999/6. SBSTA welcomes the IPCC Report on Aviation and the Global Atmosphere. (Joyce E. Penner et al., *Aviation and the Global Atmosphere: A Special Report of IPCC Working Groups I and III in Collaboration with the Scientific Assessment Panel to the Montreal Protocol on Substances That Deplete the Ozone Layer* (Cambridge University Press, 1999).
184 FCCC/CP/1999/6/Add.1. Decision 18/CP.5 Emissions based upon fuel sold to ships and aircraft engaged in international transport. parag.3.
185 F. Yamin and J. Depledge, *The International Climate Change Regime: A Guide to Rules, Institutions and Procedures.* (2004). 416–417.
186 'government representative competent in the relevant field of expertise'.
187 J. Depledge, F. Yamin, 'The Global Climate Change Regime: A Defense'. (2009). 447.
188 Ibid. at. 447.
189 Clark A. Miller, 'Challenges in the Application of Science to Global Affairs', in *Changing the Atmosphere: Expert Knowledge and Environmental Governance* (C.A. Miller and P.N. Edwards eds., 2001). 247–286.
190 Decision 1/CP.17.
191 FCCC/ADP/2012/2.
192 Decision 1/CP.17. paragraphs 4 and 6.
193 FCCC/CP/2011/9/Add.1. 16.
194 Ibid. at. P16, Paragraph 78.
195 E. Haites et al., 'Possible Elements of a 2015 Legal Agreement on Climate Change', Working Paper No. 16/13, IDDRI, (2013).
196 ADP.2013.14.Informal Note. p3, paragraph 20.
197 'Technical Paper FCCC/TP/2013/4 Compilation of information on mitigation benefits of actions, initiatives and options to enhance mitigation ambition'. 21–23.
198 This refers to the '0.3–0.5 Gt CO_2 eq in 2020' reduction provided in UNEP, *The Emissions Gap Report 2012* (UNEP, 2012).
199 While cooperative actions at all levels can support the enhancement of mitigation ambition by facilitating action by parties, they should not impose new or additional commitments.
200 The Bonn Meeting took place from 29th April to 3rd May 2013. The Ad Hoc Working Group on the Durban Platform for Enhanced Action dealt with the Work Stream 1 on finding the way for an agreement in 2015 and the Work Stream 2 on the pre-2020 ambitions.
201 Earth Negotiations Bulletin Vol. 12 No. 568. Available at: www.iisd.ca/climate/adp/adp2. 7.
202 Editorial/Production: Kyle Gracey, *Closing the Gap on Aviation and Shipping* (ECO, 2013). 1–2.
203 E. Haites et al., (2013).
204 AD HOC WORKING GROUP ON THE DURBAN PLATFORM FOR ENHANCED ACTION, FCCC/ADP/2015/1 Geneva Negotiating text (2015).
205 Ibid. at. Paragraph 40.
206 Ibid. at. Paragraph 116.5 (b) and (c).
207 AD HOC WORKING GROUP ON THE DURBAN PLATFORM FOR ENHANCED ACTION, FCCC/ADP/2015/1 Version of 11 June 2015. Bonn Negotiating text (2015).

208 AD HOC WORKING GROUP ON THE DURBAN PLATFORM FOR ENHANCED ACTION, ADP. 2015.8. Informal Note. Non-paper. Note by the Co-Chairs 5 October 2015 (2015).

209 Draft agreement and draft decision on workstreams 1 and 2 of the Ad Hoc Working Group on the Durban Platform for Enhanced Action Work of the ADP contact group. Version of 3 December 2015 at 08:00hrs. (2015). Paragraph 20. AD HOC WORKING GROUP ON THE DURBAN PLATFORM FOR ENHANCED ACTION UNFCCC, Draft agreement and draft decision on workstreams 1 and 2 of the Ad Hoc Working Group on the Durban Platform for Enhanced Action. Work of the ADP Contact Group incorporating bridging proposals by the Co-facilitators. Version of 4 December 2015 at 10.00 hrs (2015). Paragraph 20. And, AD HOC WORKING GROUP ON THE DURBAN PLATFORM FOR ENHANCED ACTION UNFCCC, FCCC/ADP/2015/L.6, Draft Paris Agreement. 5th December 2015 (2015). Paragraph 20.

210 UNFCCC, Draft Paris Outcome. Proposal by the President. Draft Text on COP 21 agenda item 4 (b) Durban Platform for Enhanced Action (decision 1/CP.17) Adoption of a protocol, another legal instrument, or an agreed outcome with legal force under the Convention applicable to all Parties. Version 1 of 9 December 2015 at 15:00 (2015).

211 UNFCCC, Draft Paris Outcome. Proposal by the President. Draft Text on COP 21 agenda item 4 (b) Durban Platform for Enhanced Action (decision 1/CP.17) Adoption of a protocol, another legal instrument, or an agreed outcome with legal force under the Convention applicable to all Parties. Version 2 of 10 December 2015 at 21:00 (2015).

212 Paris Agreement.

213 Convention on International Civil Aviation, adopted 7 December 1944, entered into force 4 April 1947. 15 UNTS 295, as amended, ICAO Doc. 7300/9 (2006), (hereinafter Chicago Convention), (1944). Available at: www.unhcr.org/refworld/docid/3ddca0dd4.html [accessed 12 April 2013] The convention entered into force on 4 April 1947 and has been revised in various occasions, being the last one 2006. It has 191 members to date. www.icao.int/MemberStates/Member%20States.Multilingual.pdf

214 The Provisional International Civil Aviation Organization (PICAO) was established by the Chicago Convention as a temporary arrangement to perform a technical and advisory role in the field of international civil aviation, and as a replacement for the International Commission for Air Navigation (ICAN), while waiting for the permanent ICAO to be established after the necessary number of countries had ratified the convention. The PICAO operated from 1945 to 1947 when it was replaced by ICAO. Since its establishment the ICAO's headquarters have been based in Montréal.

215 Chicago Convention, Article 44. The Chicago Convention builds upon previous aviation treaties, especially the Convention Relating to the Regulation of Aerial Navigation (Paris Convention). League of Nations Treaty Series. October 13, 1919. 11 LNTS 173.

216 Convention on International Civil Aviation, 7 December 1944, No. 15 U.N.T.S. 295. Article 44. ICAO's objectives and aims are set in Article 44 of the Chicago Convention: '*The aims and objectives of the Organization are to develop the principles and techniques of international air navigation and to foster the planning and development of international air transport so as to: (a) Insure the safe and orderly growth of international civil aviation throughout the world; (b) Encourage the arts of aircraft design and operation for peaceful purposes; (c) Encourage the development of airways, airports, and air navigation facilities for international civil aviation; (d) Meet the needs of the peoples of the world for safe, regular, efficient and economical air transport; (e) Prevent economic waste caused by unreasonable competition; (f) Insure that the rights of contracting States are fully respected and that every contracting State has a fair opportunity to operate international airlines; (g) Avoid*

discrimination between contracting States; (h) Promote safety of flight in international air navigation; (i) Promote generally the development of all aspects of international civil aeronautics.'

217 United Nations, Charter of the United Nations, 24 October 1945, 1 UNTS XVI (hereinafter UN Charter).

218 United Nations, UN Charter. Article 57 states that *'The various specialized agencies, established by intergovernmental agreement and having wide international responsibilities, as defined in their basic instruments, in economic, social, cultural, educational, health, and related fields, shall be brought into relationship with the United Nations in accordance with the provisions of Article 63.'* In this article, the Charter confers the Economic and Social Council (ECOSOC) with the power of entering into agreements with specialized agencies, defining the terms on which the agency concerned shall be brought into relationship with the United Nations. The agreements shall be approved by the General Assembly. Also ECOSOC *'may co-ordinate the activities of the specialized agencies through consultation with and recommendations to such agencies and through recommendations to the General Assembly and to the Members of the United Nations.'* (Article 63.2).

219 United Nations, UN Charter. Article 58.

220 See supra nota 2. Also the ECOSOC may also, according to art 62.1, *'make or initiate studies and reports with respect to international economic, social, cultural, educational, health, and related matters and may make recommendations with respect to any such matters to the General Assembly to the Members of the United Nations, and to the specialized agencies concerned'* and, according to article 64, *'take appropriate steps to obtain regular reports from the specialized agencies. It may make arrangements with the Members of the United Nations and with the specialized agencies to obtain reports on the steps taken to give effect to its own recommendations and to recommendations on matters falling within its competence made by the General Assembly.'* The ECOSOC, in pursuit of the goal to *'discharge effectively its responsibility to coordinate the activities of the specialized agencies'*, took steps to establish the Administrative Committee on Coordination.

221 Draft agreement between the UN and ICAO. GA Draft Agreement A/106–30 September 1946, (1946). In October 1947, ICAO became an agency of the United Nations linked to ECOSOC. Article 64 and 65 of the Convention on International Civil Aviation provides ICAO with the possibility of enter into agreements with other international organizations and international bodies.

222 The agreement includes an array of provisions on: application for membership in ICAO by certain States; reciprocal representation; proposal of agenda items; recommendations of the UN; reporting and coordination, exchange of information and documents; cooperation and assistance; relations with the International Court of Justice; headquarters and regional offices; personnel arrangements; statistical services; administrative and technical services; financial, budgetary arrangements; and the financing of special services, inter-agency agreements and liaison arrangements.

223 Chicago Convention, Article 44.

224 Ruwantissa Abeyratne, *Convention on International Civil Aviation: A Commentary* (Springer, 2014). 515–524. See further chapter five.

225 I. H. Philepina Diederiks-Verschoor, *An Introduction to Air Law* (Kluwer Law International 6th rev. ed., 1997). 12.

226 See a summary in Steven Truxal, *Competition and Regulation in the Airline Industry: Puppets in Chaos* (Routledge, 2012). 11.

227 Chicago Convention, Chapter III Nationality of Aircraft (article 17–21). Article 17 maintains the same approach as its predecessors in the Paris Convention, the Iberoamerican Convention and Panamerican Convention. However, in the Paris Convention, registration could only happen in the state where the owners are nationals, while in Chicago the only limit is the prohibition of dual nationality. An explanation to this phenomenon is given in Ian Brownlie, *Principles of Public International Law* (Oxford University Press 7th ed., 2008). 425–426: *'in the absence of flags of convenience*

> in air traffic, it may be that the issue was left on one side by the authors, the assumption being that registration in practice depend on the existence of substantial connections.'

228 Chicago Convention, Article 20.
229 Ibid. at. Article 18.
230 Ibid. at. Article 19.
231 Ibid. at. Article 21.
232 I.H.P. Diederiks-Verschoor, *An Introduction to Air Law.* (1997). 22–26. The author acknowledges that a treaty rule could establish that aircraft over the high seas is part of the state of nationality, as, for example, does Article 23 (2) of the 1952 Rome Convention on damage caused by foreign aircraft to third parties.
233 Some of the market practices include interlining practice, franchise, cabotage, code-share agreements (airline designator code is shared so one airline is allowed to fly under other designator code, although it does operate that service), Global Airline Alliances (sky alliance, one world, sky team) cargo alliances, joint ventures, stock investments, mergers or loyalty programmes.
234 On the regulations of markets rather than the regulation of operations of the airline industry see, S. Truxal, *Competition and Regulation in the Airline Industry: Puppets in Chaos.* (2012). The treatise reflects upon the changing structure of the air transport sector through more airlines entering into horizontal and vertical arrangements and their integration through various types of agreements, mergers and alliances, and elaborates on the process undergone in the EU and United States of deregulation, liberalization and self-regulation and regulation through competition and antitrust.
235 Vasigh, Fleming and Tacker, Introduction to Air Transport Economics, 107 as cited in Ibid. at. 15.
236 Chicago Convention, Article 44.
237 ICAO website, www.icao.int/about-icao/Pages/default.aspx (last accessed December 2016).
238 Edward Yemin, *Legislative Powers in the United Nations and Specialized Agencies* (A. W. Sijthoff, 1969). 146–147, cited in Jan Klabbers, *An Introduction to International Institutional Law* (Cambridge University Press 2nd ed., 2009). 187.
239 This study looks into the law and law-making processes of ICAO and compares its constitutive instruments and institutional practices. For more information on the membership, legislation, settlement of disputes and amendments to the Chicago Convention see: Thomas Buergenthal, *Law-Making in the International Civil Aviation Organization* (Syracuse University Press 1st ed., 1969).
240 The Secretariat consists of five main divisions: the Air Navigation Bureau, the Air Transport Bureau, the Technical Co-operation Bureau, the Legal Affairs and External Relations Bureau, and the Bureau of Administration and Services. The head of the Secretariat is the secretary general.
241 Chicago Convention. Art 43.
242 Ibid. at. Arts 54 (d) y 56, 57, respectively.
243 Aspects related to the Assembly are regulated in Chapter VIII of the Chicago Convention, art 48 and 49 CC.
244 Ibid. at. Art 48 b *'Delegates representing contracting States may be assisted by technical advisers who may participate in the meetings but shall have no vote.'*
245 This can happen upon the request of the Council or if not less than one-fifth of the total number of contracting States agree upon.
246 Chicago Convention. Art 48 a. This article was amended in 1954, before the Assembly met once a year.
247 Ibid. at. Art 48 b and c, on Meetings of the Assembly and voting.
248 Other exceptions are the four-fifths vote for admission of enemy states to the organizations and three-fifths of the total number of ICAO members to relocate the ICAO's headquarters.

249 Chicago Convention. Article 49 b. Every three years the 36 members of the Council are elected by the Assembly and hold office until the next election. They represent adequately the States of chief importance in air transport, the States not otherwise included which make the largest contribution to the provision of facilities for international civil air navigation and the States not otherwise included whose designation will insure that all the major geographic areas of the world are represented. Provisions of art 50.

250 These are the committees and commissions created *ad hoc* at the session to assist the Assembly, such as an executive or administrative group.

251 In accordance in accordance with the provisions of Chapter XII.

252 Requiring two-thirds voting.

253 Chicago Convention. Art 49 on powers and duties of the Assembly.

254 Provisions on the Council are in ibid. at. Chapter IX, art 50 to 55.

255 See council members here: www.icao.int/about-icao/Council/Pages/council-states-2016-2019.aspx

256 Chicago Convention. Article 50(b).The adequate representation includes some members from the States of chief importance in air transport, from the States, not otherwise included, which make the largest contribution to the provision of facilities for navigation, and from the States, not otherwise included, whose designation will ensure that all major geographic areas of the world are represented.

257 Ibid. at. Article 50 (a).

258 Ibid. at. Art 51 – The President can be re-elected and need not be selected from among the representatives of the members of the Council but, if a representative is elected, his seat shall be deemed vacant and it shall be filled by the State which he represented. If one or more Vice Presidents shall be elected by the council from among its members, they retain their right to vote when serving as acting President.

259 Ibid. at. Article 51.

260 Ibid. at. Article 37, 54 and 80.

261 For example, under Chicago Convention article 15, '*the Council is entitled not only to make recommendations but also to report on any infringement of the duties incumbent on member states.*' See, Bin Cheng, *The Law of International Air Transport* (Stevens Oceana Publications, 1962).

262 Chicago Convention. Article 54.

263 Ibid. at. Article 55 defines the permissive functions of the Council.

264 Ibid. at. Art 52 and 53 on voting issues.

265 Frederic L. Kirgis, *International Organizations in Their Legal Setting* (West Pub. Co. 2nd ed., 1993). 443–479.

266 José E. Alvarez, *International Organizations as Law-Makers* (Oxford University Press, 2005). 261 and Peter Ateh-Afac Fossungu, 'The ICAO Assembly: The Most Unsuprente of Supreme Organs in the United Nations System? A Critical Analysis of Assembly Sessions', *Transportation Law Journal*, 26(3), (1999).

267 These usually include operational and technological measures, a shift to low carbon fuels (e.g. biofuels) and the use of MBMs.

268 P.A.-A. Fossungu, (1999). 27. See also, Christer Jönsson, Sphere of flying: The politics of international aviation, 35 International Organization. (1981). And E. Sochor, *The Politics of International Aviation* (University of Iowa Press, 1991).

269 The EU was provided with legal personality by article 47 TEU. Before the Treaty of Lisbon only the European Community had legal personality under article 281 EC treaty.

270 SEC/2002/0381 final. Recommendation from the Commission to the Council in order to authorise the Commission to open and conduct negotiations with the International Civil Aviation Organization (ICAO) on the conditions and arrangements for accession by the European Community, (2002).

271 Established in 1955, it has 44 Members to date. It seeks the '*promotion of the continued development of a safe, efficient and sustainable European air transport system*'. Available at: www.ecac-ceac.org//about_ecac/mission

272 B. Cheng, *The Law of International Air Transport*. (1962). The ECAC has an intermediate independent status from ICAO: while it has its own work programme, meetings and agenda, it works closely with ICAO and makes use of the ICAO Secretariat. See ICAO Assembly Resolution A10–5: '*members of ICAO, have constituted the European Civil Aviation Conference (ECAC) – whose constitution, objectives and rules of procedure are set forth in ICAO Document 7676, ECAC/1 – with the particular purpose, among other things, of promoting the co-ordination and better utilisation of intra-European air transport*'.

273 European Civil Aviation Conference, ECAC's Strategy for the Future – A Policy Statement. Endorsed by ECAC Directors General of Civil Aviation at DGCA/137, (2011). 5.

274 Ibid. at. 7. ECAC has a number of groups dealing with environmental aspects, such as the EuroCAEP, a group on climate change (ACCAPEG), the MBM Expert Group, and on sustainable aviation fuels (ECAFA).

275 Low cost carriers are not represented there.

276 S. Truxal, *Competition and Regulation in the Airline Industry: Puppets in Chaos*. (2012). 92.

277 David Clark MacKenzie, *ICAO: A History of the International Civil Aviation Organization* (University of Toronto Press, 2010). 63–64.

278 See IATA website. Available at www.iata.org/policy/environment/Pages/default.aspx

279 IATA, IATA 69th Annual General Meeting . Resolution on the Implementation of the Aviation CNG2020 Strategy, (2013).

280 Transport and Environment, 'Global Deal or No Deal? Your Free Guide to ICAO's 38th Triennial Assembly'. (2013). 6. Also, Michael Gill, 'Aviation and the Impacts of Climate Change Aviation and the Climate: An ATAG Perspective', *Carbon & Climate Law Review*, 10(2), (2016).

281 See ATAG website. Available at: www.atag.org/about-us/what-we-do.html Air Transport Association Group. Statutes, adopted 2002, amended 2007, (2007).

282 See, for example the joint action statement delivered by ICAO and ATAG at the Climate Summit 2014. ICAO & ATAG, Action Statement. Climate Summit 2014. New York. (2014).

283 'Environmental Efficiency: Aviation: Benefits Beyond Borders'. Available at: www.enviro.aero/

284 See ICSA website. Available at: www.icsa-aviation.org/

285 Ruwantissa Abeyratne, *Legal and Regulatory Issues in International Aviation* (Transnational Publishers, 1996). 279.

286 Michael Milde, 'Future Perspective of Air Law', in Karl-Heinz Böckstiegel et al., *Perspectives of Air Law, Space Law, and International Business Law for the Next Century* (C. Heymanns, 1996). 13–18.

287 Chicago Convention. Preamble.

288 Ibid. at. Article 94(a).

289 Ibid. at. Article 94(b).

290 '*However, because of lack of time, the attempt to adopt a final set of Annexes at Chicago was abandoned shortly before the conference adjourned.*' T. Buergenthal, *Law-Making in the International Civil Aviation Organization*. (1969). 90, referring to the Resolution 11 (Draft Technical Annexes), 1 Proceedings, 123–124 and also the *travaux preparatoires* of the Convention do not provide the Annexes with compulsory force.

291 Chicago Convention. Art 54. This was the case of the 1919 Paris Convention Relating to the Regulation of Aerial Navigation. League of Nations Treaty Series, October 13, 1919.

292 In the Chicago Convention, many articles focus on the idea of optional compliance based on practicability.

293 T. Buergenthal, *Law-Making in the International Civil Aviation Organization.* (1969). 120.
294 Work on Annex 16 was started in 1968 at the 16th session of the ICAO Assembly when Assembly Resolution A16–3 called for a conference to consider the problem of aircraft noise in the vicinity of airports and take measures against it.
295 At the 18th session of the ICAO Assembly when Assembly Resolution A18–11 requested action. Alexandre Charles Kiss and Dinah Shelton, *Guide to International Environmental Law* (Martinus Nijhoff Publishers, 2007). 54. ICAO's efforts on policies in air quality control were done through an engine certification scheme.
296 The first measures contained in Volume I were developed in the 1960s, while the measures in volume II were included in the 1980s, reflecting changes in environmental concerns. Annex 16 Volume II contains three parts: Part I contains definitions and symbols, Part II regards the SARPs on vented fuel and Part III SARPs on emissions certification for different engines.
297 The CAEE was established in 1977 after the Council agreed on the need of a specific committee given that '*the subject of aircraft emissions was not one that was solely confined to objective technical issues but was one that needed consideration by experts in many fields and included the direct views of member states.*' Annex 16 to the *Convention on International Civil Aviation*, 2, (2008). (Foreword).
298 On CAEP see next section.
299 A18–11, clause 2.
300 A18–12.
301 Circular 134, 1997.
302 See further in next section.
303 See for example, Brian F. Havel and Gabriel S. Sanchez, *The Principles and Practice of International Aviation Law.* 58–60 or R. Abeyratne, *Legal and Regulatory Issues in International Aviation.* (1996).
304 For debates around the binding force and relevance of ICAO's regulations, also see T. Buergenthal, *Law-Making in the International Civil Aviation Organization.* (1969). 57–122; Michael Milde, *International Air Law and ICAO* (Eleven International Publishing, 2008). 129–170 and J.E. Alvarez, *International Organizations as Law-Makers.* (2005). 111, 223–224.
305 IPCC 1999, Aviation and the Global Atmosphere. Cambridge, UK, Cambridge University Press.
306 Although the ICAO Assembly is usually convened each three years, an extraordinary assembly was convened in 2003.
307 Assembly Resolution A33–7: Consolidated Statement of Continuing ICAO Policies and Practices Related to Environmental Protection. Appendix I, (2001).
308 ICAO, Assembly Resolution A35–5: Consolidated Statement of Continuing ICAO Policies and Practices Related to Environmental Protection, (2004). Appendix H and I.
309 Assembly Resolution A36–22: Consolidated Statement of Continuing ICAO Policies and Practices Related to Environmental Protection. Appendix K of ICAO Program of Action on International Aviation and Climate Change.
310 Group on International Aviation and Climate Change (GIACC). Its members are senior government officials representing all ICAO regions. It came to an end in 2009.
311 CAEP is a technical committee formed in 1983 to assist the ICAO Council on environmental matters such as the formulation of policies and adoption of SARPs. It is comprised of 23 members and 15 observers, and involves over 400 international experts.
312 The High Level Meeting on International Aviation and Climate Change, HLM-ENV/09 was attended by ministers and other high-level officials from 73 ICAO members, representing 94% of global aviation traffic and 26 international organizations.
313 Assembly Resolution A36–22: Consolidated Statement of Continuing ICAO Policies and Practices Related to Environmental Protection (2007). However,

considerations on 'mutual consent' between countries with regards to charges and levies were already given in A35–5 and reaffirmed in A36–22.

314 Written statement of reservation on behalf of the member States of the European Community (EC) and the other states members of the European Civil Aviation (ECAC) [made at the 36th Assembly of the International Civil Aviation Organization in Montreal, 18–28 September 2007], (2007).

315 Assembly Resolution A36–22. Apendix J, K and L.

316 Ibid. at. Apendix L.

317 The ICAO Program of Action on International Aviation and Climate Change. Group on International Aviation and Climate Change Report, 2009, ICAO. For an overview on the Program of Action see the contribution of the ICAO's Secretariat to the ICAO. Environment Branch of ICAO, *ICAO Environmental Report 2010: Aviation and Climate Change* (ICAO, 2010). 8–12.

318 ICAO, Declaration by the High-level Meeting on International Aviation and Climate Change (HLM-ENV/09) in October 2009, (ICAO, 2009).

319 Assembly Resolution A37–19: Consolidated Statement of Continuing ICAO Policies and Practices related to Environmental Protection. Climate Change, 2010.

320 Ibid.

321 ICAO, Environment Branch of ICAO, *ICAO Environmental Report 2013: Aviation and Climate Change* (ICAO, 2013). 23–25.

322 See further in Section VI.

323 Alternative fuels can provide emissions reductions by substituting traditional kerosene jet fuel. ICAO has established a Global Framework for Aviation Alternative Fuels (GFAAF) to promote them. Since 2008, pilot flights have been performed by different airlines and in 2012 'drop-in' sustainable biofuel, blended with conventional jet fuel, was used in over 1800 commercial flights. See ICAO's Environmental Report 2013. P. 122–137. Work in ICAO has been established under the Sustainable Alternative Fuels for Aviation (SUSTAF) experts group.

324 ICAO, Assembly Resolution A37–19 (2010). This resolves to '*explore the feasibility of a global MBM scheme*' and report to the 38th Assembly. The ICAO Council meeting in November 2012 further agreed to make significant progress towards such an MBM for the 38th Assembly.

325 I.E.B.o. ICAO, *ICAO Environmental Report 2013: Aviation and Climate Change*. (2013). 25.

326 ICAO, Assembly Resolution A38–18: Consolidated Statement of Continuing ICAO Policies and Practices Related to Environmental Protection – Climate Change (2013). Paragraph 33(e), 11–15.

327 Ibid. at. Paragraph 18–24.

328 ICAO, Assembly Resolution A39–3: Consolidated statement of continuing ICAO policies and practices related to environmental protection – Global Market-based Measure (MBM) scheme (2016).

329 Alejandro Piera, 'Compliance Tools for a Global Market Based Measure for Aviation Designing the Legal Form of a Global Aviation Market Based Measure', *Carbon & Climate Law Review*, 10(2), (2016). 144–152.

330 As reported by the ICAO Secretary General Dr Fang Liu at the UNFCCC COP22 facilitative dialogue in Marrakech November 2016. Available at: www.icao.int/News room/Pages/cop22-icao-secretary-general-emphasizes-next-steps-for-corsia.aspx

331 Still these countries can decide to participate on a voluntary basis.

332 0.5 % of total RTK.

333 See: 'ICAO CAEP Recommends Emissions Standards, Lays Groundwork for Market-Based Measure' IISD news (12 February 2016). Available at: http://energy-l.iisd.org/news/icao-caep-recommends-co2-emissions-standards-lays-groundwork-for-market-based-measure

334 ICAO, Assembly Resolution A39–2: Consolidated statement of continuing ICAO policies and practices related to environmental protection – Climate Change (2016). Paragraph 19.

335 For an overview on international organizations as treaty-makers see J.E. Alvarez, *International Organizations as Law-Makers*. (2005). 273–337. Alvarez underlines that the negotiation and conclusion of treaties under the auspices of international organizations means that such activity is no longer a domain limited to States, and highlights the change from a system of *ad hoc* conferences to a more established and improved multilateral system.

336 Some international instruments adopted with ICAO serving as a venue are: the International Conference on Air Law, the Diplomatic Conference to Consider Amending the Tokyo Convention of 1963 (2014) the Convention of the Marking of Plastic Explosives for the Purpose of Detention (1991), The Convention on Offenses and Certain Other Acts Committed on Board Aircraft (Tokyo Convention of 1963), the Convention for the Suppression of the Unlawful Seizure of Aircraft (Hague Convention of 1970), the Convention for the Suppression of Unlawful Acts Against the Safety of Civil Aviation (Montreal Convention of 1971) or the Convention on Compensation for Damage to Third Parties, Resulting from Acts of Unlawful Interference Involving Aircraft, the Convention on Damage Caused by Foreign Aircraft to Third Parties on the Surface (Rome Convention of 1952), the Convention on the International Recognition of Rights in Aircraft (the Geneva Convention of 1948), the Convention on the Unification of Certain Rules Relating to International Carriage by Air (Warsaw Convention of 1929). See list at: www.icao.int/secretariat/legal/Pages/default.aspx

337 ICAO Colloquium on Environmental Aspects of Aviation 9–11 April 2001, ICAO Colloquium on Aviation Emissions – 16 May 2007, ICAO Colloquium on Aviation and Climate Change 11–14 May 2010 and a pre-symposium seminar on States Action Plans on the 13 May and a ICAO Symposium on Aviation and Climate Change, "Destination Green" 14–16 May 2013. This author attended the Colloquium on Aviation and Climate Change in 2010.

338 In matters such as voting, financing, procedure and membership.

339 J.E. Alvarez, *International Organizations as Law-Makers*. (2005). 111.

340 T. Buergenthal, *Law-Making in the International Civil Aviation Organization*. (1969). 57.

341 Chicago Convention. Article 37 gives ICAO the power and the legal basis for the adoption of international standards and recommended practices, hereinafter SARPS.

342 J.E. Alvarez, *International Organizations as Law-Makers*. (2005).

343 Chicago Convention. Article 37–42.

344 Ibid. at Article 37.

345 Chicago Convention, Article 54 (L) When enumerating the functions of the Council: '*Adopt, in accordance with the provisions of Chapter VI of this Convention, international standards and recommended practices; for convenience, designate them as Annexes to this Convention; and notify all contracting States of the action taken.*'

346 Chicago Convention, Article 54 (m): '*Consider recommendations of the Air Navigation Commission for amendment of the Annexes and take action in accordance with the provisions of Chapter XX*' and Chapter XX on Annexes (article 90).

347 Chicago Convention, Article 12 states that over the high seas the rules of the air established under the convention (i.e. that ICAO has a power to adopt according to Article 37, including the SARPs that Annex 2 contains) are mandatory. ICAO members are obliged to comply with rules over high seas that are periodically updated in the Annexes. Also, SARPs on log books of Annex 6 are mandatory under Article 29 and 34 and SARPs contained in Annex 1 and 8, on recognition of certificates and licenses are made mandatory by Article 33.

348 Chicago Convention, Article 37.

349 Chicago Convention, Article 38. States can opt out and the Annexes would be binding for those that decide to.
350 ICAO has issued guidelines with the criteria and principles for the reporting of differences for international standards and for recommended practices.
351 T. Buergenthal, *Law-Making in the International Civil Aviation Organization*. (1969).
78–79.
352 All these differences notified by the contracting States are published in Supplements
to Annexes.
353 Michael Milde clarifies that the number of differences reported has been low but it
has been apparent that many states do not comply and do not notify. K.-H. Böckstiegel et al., *Perspectives of Air Law, Space Law, and International Business Law for the
Next Century*. (1996). 16.
354 Chicago Convention, Article 15.
355 T. Buergenthal, *Law-Making in the International Civil Aviation Organization*. (1969).
114. The author refers to the possibility of upgrading their status to the same that
the Annexes enjoys through incorporation by reference, pointing out that the lack
of action in that direction can be understood from the complicated process that the
enactment of annexes entails compared channels outside the convention.
356 In the early days of ICAO, the Council adopted a resolution stating the desirability
of using in national regulations the precise language of the Annexes and the incorporation of the text without changes.
357 T. Buergenthal, *Law-Making in the International Civil Aviation Organization*. (1969). 121.
358 Ibid. at 120–121.
359 ICAO, Assembly Resolution A38–18 (2013). Paragraph 33(e), 11–15.
360 More details on CAEP's work and structure are available at: www.icao.int/environmental-
protection/documents/Caep_Structure.pdf (last accessed December 2016).
361 The CAEP held meetings in 1986 (CAEP/1), 1991 (CAEP/2), 1995 (CAEP/3),
1998 (CAEP/4,) 2001 (CAEP/5), 2004 (CAEP/6), 2007 (CAEP/7), 2010 (CAEP/8).
2013 (CAEP/9) and 2016 (CAEP/10).
362 For the CAEP/10 cycle running from 2013 to 2016 there was a Working Group on
Emissions Technical Issues (WG3).
363 The group runs under the name the Global MBM Technical Task Force (GMTF).
364 Side-lining the role played by other ICAO bodies, such as the Secretariat in facilitating and providing assessments, most work is carried out under the Council
structure.
365 The Council formed the GIACC upon the request of the 36th Assembly. It was
composed of around 15 representatives of States of all regions and was assisted on the
technical side by the CAEP. Appendix K.
366 The four meetings took place at the ICAO Headquarters, Montréal, Canada: the
First Meeting of the GIACC (hereinafter GIACC/1) was held from 25 to 27 February 2008, the Second Meeting of the GIACC (hereinafter GIACC/2) from 14 to
16 July 2008, the Third Meeting of the GIACC (hereinafter GIACC/3) from 17 to
19 February 2009 and the Fourth Meeting of the GIACC (hereinafter GIACC/4)
from 25 to 27 May 2009.
367 Group on International Aviation and Climate Change Report, 2009, ICAO.
368 Recommendations of the programme took the approach that individual countries
act according to their preferences guided by an aspirational goal of 2% annual fuel
efficiency improvement. This goal would slow but not offset growth in emissions.
The group did not achieve consensus in this proposal.
369 High-level Meeting on International Aviation and Climate Change, (hereinafter
HLM-ENV/09). It was the '*first ever ICAO meeting exclusively dedicated to aviation
and climate change*' in Ruwantissa Abeyratne, *Aviation and the Carbon Trade* (Nova
Science Publishers, 2011). P42 It was attended by ministers and other high-level

officials representing the 73 contracting States responsible for 94% of the global international aviation traffic and 26 international organizations.

370 Ad Hoc Working Group on Climate Change composed of ICAO Council Representatives from each of the six ICAO regions was on active up until June 2012.

371 The HGCC was set up by the ICAO Council in November 2012. It is composed of high-level government officials tasked to examine and provide policy recommendations on MBMs.

372 Two rounds in 2015 and 2016.

373 Also held meetings in 2016.

374 The idea was already discussed in 1889 at the international maritime conference in Washington DC. For a contextual overview see Ademun-Odeke's article: 'From the "Constitution of the Maritime Safety Committee" to the "Constitution of the Council": Will the IMCO Experience Repeat Itself at the IMO Nearly Fifty Years On? The Juridical Politics of an International Organization', *Texas International Law Journal*, 43. 55–113.

375 Initially the organization received the name of Inter-governmental Maritime Consultative Organization (IMCO). In 1982 it changed its name to International Maritime Organization (IMO).

376 Samir Mankabady, *The International Maritime Organization § 1: International Shipping Rules* (Croom Helm, 1986). P2. It took 10 years to get the necessary number of countries on board for the convention to enter into force.

377 Convention on the Inter-Governmental Maritime Consultative Organization, adopted on 6 March 1948, entered into force 17 March 1958. 289 UNTS 48, amended and renamed as Convention on the International Maritime Organization, 14 November 1975, 9 UTS 61, (1948). Hereinafter referred to as the IMO Convention.

378 Draft Agreement between the UN and IMCO (IMO). ECOSOC Resolution 165 (VII) – 27 August 1948, (1948). The implications of this agreement include: recognition by the United Nations of the actions of the IMO as an specialized agency; the establishment of an array of provisions on reciprocal representation, the proposal of agenda items, formal consideration of UN recommendations, the exchange of information and documents and cooperation and assistance. It also enabled relations with the International Court of Justice, UN headquarters and regional offices, personnel arrangements, access to statistical services, administrative, technical and financial services, budgetary arrangements and the financing of special services, inter-agency agreements and liaison arrangements.

379 Chapter IX of The Charter of the United Nations provides for bringing the specialized agencies into a relationship with the United Nations through the ECOSOC.

380 IMO Convention, article 45 provides that the organization shall be brought into relationship with the United Nations as one of the specialized agencies referred to in article 57 and 63 of the UN Charter, according to the procedure laid in article 26; that is, the IMO Council can enter into agreements subject to approval by the Assembly.

381 IMO Convention, Article 1(a) refers specifically to '*matters concerning the maritime safety, efficiency of navigation and prevention and control of marine pollution from ships*'.

382 IMO Convention, Article 1(b).

383 The convention text of 1948 made no mention of marine pollution and the environment, which was included in the 1975 and 1997 amendments and entered into force in 1984.

384 IMO Convention, Article 1(c), (d) and (e).

385 In 1977 the consultative and advisory character was removed from Article 2.

386 IMO Convention, Article 2.

387 Ibid. at. Article 3.

388 Ibid. at. Article 11.

389 Providing a 60-day notice period.

390 The election of members of the council is done according to the rules of Article 17.

391 IMO Convention, Article 15.
392 For the current Council (2014–2015), 10 states are included in this category, namely: China, Greece, Italy, Japan, Norway, Panama, Republic of Korea, Russian Federation, the United Kingdom and the United States.
393 For the current Council (2014–2015), 10 states fall under this group, namely: Argentina, Bangladesh, Brazil, Canada, France, Germany, India, the Netherlands, Spain and Sweden.
394 For the current Council (2014–2015), 20 states are in this category: Australia, Bahamas, Belgium, Chile, Cyprus, Denmark, Indonesia, Jamaica, Kenya, Liberia, Malaysia, Malta, Mexico, Morocco, Peru, Philippines, Singapore, South Africa, Thailand and Turkey.
395 The exception, as pointed out before, is the making of recommendations reserved for the Assembly under Article 15, IMO Convention.
396 IMO Convention, Articles 47–52.
397 They are in Côte d'Ivoire, Ghana, Kenya, Philippines and Trinidad and Tobago.
398 S. Mankabady, *The International Maritime Organization*. (1986). 11–12.
399 These committees have been successively included in system through IMO Convention amendments. See, Andrew Serdy, 'Public International Law Aspect of Shipping regulation', in *Maritime Law* (Y. Baatz ed., 2014). 326.
400 As of September 2014 there are 170 member States and three associate members: Faroes, Hong Kong and Macao.
401 Which means that they can '*participate in the work of various bodies in an observer capacity*' and '*contribute to the work of various organs and committees through the provision of information, documentation and expert advice*'. See, IMO, IMO What Is It?. Brochure. London, IMO. 22.
402 Such as expertise, capacity to contribute to the work of IMO and an international character in its membership. There are 77 international non-governmental organizations in consultative status. See IMO website: www.imo.org/About/Membership/Pages/Default.aspxx (last accessed December 2016).
403 To date there are 63 intergovernmental organizations which have signed agreements of cooperation. (September 2014).
404 A.E. Boyle and C.M. Chinkin, *The Making of International Law*. (2007).
405 R. Michael M'Gonigle and Mark W. Zacher, *Pollution, Politics, and International Law: Tankers at Sea* (University of California Press, 1979). 346–347. On the composition of the Council see also, Frank Biermann and Bernd Siebenhüner, *Managers of Global Change: The Influence of International Environmental Bureaucracies* (MIT Press, 2009).
406 For example, the report on finding a fair share contribution for the shipping sector commissioned by the Danish Shipowners Association. T. Smith et al., 'CO$_2$ Emissions from International Shipping: Possible Reduction Targets and their Associated Pathways. Prepared by UMAS, London', (2016).
407 Flag States are the States whose flag a vessel flies. Ships fly the flag of the country where they are registered. The phenomenon of 'flags of convenience' is a '*well-known fact of international maritime law that ships have been registered in accommodating states (notably Panama, Liberia, Honduras and Greece) to avoid certain national legislation, usually labour and tax laws in the countries of their owners. The ships have little genuine link with the states whose flags they fly, and the states have correspondingly little incentive or ability to apply various international rules and standards to them.*' See: Jonathan I. Charney and American Society of International Law, *The New Nationalism and the Use of Common Spaces: Issues in Marine Pollution and the Exploitation of Antarctica* (Allanheld, Osmun, 1982). 20; I. Brownlie, *Principles of Public International Law*. (2008). 422–425. Ships have the nationality of the state whose flag they are entitled to fly. To that end there should be a genuine link between vessel and country; that is, it is not a mere administrative formality. See, Convention of the High Seas 1958 article 5 and UNCLOS article 91.

408 Colin M. de la Rue and Charles B. Anderson, *Shipping and the Environment: Law and Practice* (Informa Law 2nd ed., 2009). 816.

409 See, for instance Paul Gilbert, Alice Bows, and Richard Starkey, 'Shipping and Climate Change: Scope for Unilateral Action', *The University of Manchester* (August 2010). 22–24.

410 Some of these insights come from an interview with Eivind S. Vagslid, Head of Chemical and Air Pollution Prevention Section at the Marine Environment Division of the IMO. April 2011.

411 Given that the EU, through the Commission, cannot negotiate at the IMO on behalf of EU member States, a process of coordination of positions is followed. Although this process is not binding, the European Court of Justice has supported the idea that not following the coordinated positions puts States in breach of European law, owed to the duty of loyalty. However, following such common positions is '*not easy sometimes for member States, especially those with strong shipping interests*'. For an overview see, Nengye Liu, 'The Relations between the European Union and the International Maritime Organization: An Analysis', Working Paper Annual Legal Research Network Conference 2010, (2010); Nengye Liu and Frank Maes, 'The European Union and the International Maritime Organization: EU's External Influence on the Prevention of Vessel-Source Pollution', *Journal of Maritime Law and Commerce*, 41(4), (2010). Also, V. Frank, *The European Community and Marine Environmental Protection in the International Law of the Sea: Implementing Global Obligations at the Regional Level* (Martinus Nijhoff Publishers, 2007). 261–263.

412 The Agreement of Mutual Co-operation concluded by the Commission and the IMO secretary general was first signed in 1974.

413 Doris Koenig, 'Global and Regional Approaches to Ship Air Emissions Regulations: The International Maritime Organization and the European Union', in *Regions, Institutions, and Law of the Sea Regions, Institutions, and Law of the Sea: Studies in Ocean Governance* (Harry N. Scheiber and Jin-Hyun Paik eds., 2013). 317–336.

414 R.M. M'Gonigle and M.W. Zacher, *Pollution, Politics, and International Law: Tankers at Sea.* (1979). 346–347.

415 See for instance the proposals to the IMO from CSC and WWF with regards to MBM. GHG-WG 3/3/3. Review of Proposed MBMs. The IMO, global MBMs that reduce emissions and the question of Principles. Submitted by Clean Shipping Coalition (CSC) and World Wide Fund for Nature (WWF), (2011).

416 See for instance the International Chamber of Shipping, Preliminary ICS Comments on Draft EU Regulation on MRV. Brief for EU Member States and Members of the European Parliament on the Proposal for a Regulation of the European Parliament and of the Council on the Monitoring, Reporting and Verification of Carbon Dioxide Emissions from Maritime Transport and Amending Regulation (EU) No. 525/2013 (2013).

417 Kamil A. Bekiashev and Vitali V. Serebriakov, 'International Chamber of Shipping (ICS)', in *International Marine Organizations* (1981).

418 www.ics-shipping.org/about-ics/about-ics The European Community Shipowners' Associations (ECSA) and the Asian Shipowners' Forum (ASF) are a Regional Partner to ICS.

419 Peter Hinchliffe, secretary general of the ICS at the Conference on Climate Change of the Tyndall Centre for Climate Change Research June 2014.

420 See, BIMCO, *GHG and Market Based Measures (MBMs): BIMCO's Position* (BIMCO). Available at: www.bimco.org/About/Viewpoint/04_Greenhouse_Gases_and%20Market_Based_Measures.aspx

421 See for example, MEPC 69/7/4. Establishing a Process for Considering Shipping's Appropriate Contribution to Reducing CO_2 Emissions. Submitted by WSC, CLIA, INTERTANKO, and IPTA; MEPC 70/7/8, Development of a Road Map to

Determine a Possible IMO Fair Share Contribution. Submitted by BIMCO, ICS, INTERCARGO, INTERTANKO and WSC.

422 IMO Convention, article 1(a).

423 Andreas Chrysostomou and Eivind S. Vagslid, 'Climate Change: A Challenge for IMO Too', in *Maritime Transport and the Climate Change Challenge* (R. Asariotis and Hassiba Benamara eds., 2012). 85.

424 IMO Convention, Article 66–68.

425 This is further explored in Chapter 4 and 5.

426 United Nations Convention on the Law of the Sea, Montego Bay, adopted 10 December 1982, in force 16 November 1994, 21 International Legal Materials (1982), 1261. 1833 UNTS 3, (1982). The UN Convention on the Law of the Sea was adopted in 1982 and entered into force in 1994. It pursues the establishment of a legal system to promote the peaceful uses of the seas, the utilization of its resources and the preservation of the marine environment. See preamble. It codifies partly existing customary and conventional law.

427 UNCLOS, Part XII on the Protection and Preservation of the Marine Environment, articles 192–237.

428 For an overview see, P.W. Birnie et al., *International Law and the Environment*. (2009). 379–423.

429 UNCLOS Article 89 states that '*No State may validly purport to subject any part of the high seas to its sovereignty.*'

430 UNCLOS Article 211(2) reads: '*States shall adopt laws and regulations for the prevention, reduction and control of pollution of the marine environment from vessels flying their flag or of their registry. Such laws and regulations shall at least have the same effect as that of generally accepted international rules and standards established through the competent international organization or general diplomatic conference.*'

431 For an overview on the role of the UNCLOS in regulating the high seas, see: Robin Warner, *Protecting the Oceans beyond National Jurisdiction: Strengthening the International Law Framework* (Martinus Nijhoff Publishers, 2009). 27–65. For an analysis of the implications of the LOS port state jurisdiction and control for the regulation of international maritime emissions, see Yoshifumi Tanaka, 'Regulation of Greenhouse Gas Emissions from International Shipping and Jurisdiction of States, Review of European', *Comparative & International Environmental Law* 25(3), (2016). 333–346.

432 UNCLOS, article 212.

433 IMO, Resolution A.719(17). Adopted on 6 November 1991. Prevention of Air Pollution from Ships (1991).

434 G.K. Walker, *Definitions for the Law of the Sea: Terms Not Defined by the 1982 Convention* (Brill, 2011). 144.

435 Generally, UNCLOS does not refer to the IMO by name but rather as '*the competent international organization*'.

436 UNCLOS articles 21, 210, 211, 217 or 219.

437 Such obligations are expressed in a variety of forms, such as 'to take account of', 'to conform to', 'to give effect to' or 'to implement'.

438 Louise de La Fayette, 'The Marine Environment Protection Committee: The Conjunction of the Law of the Sea and International Environmental Law', *The International Journal of Marine and Coastal Law*, 16(2), (2001). 155–238.

439 IMO Secretariat, Implications of the United Nations Convention on the Law of the Sea for the International Maritime Organization. Study by the Secretariat of the International Maritime Organization (IMO)LEG/MISC. 7, (19 January 2012), (2012).

440 Yvonne Baatz, *Maritime Law 3e* (Informa Law Routledge, 2014); A. Serdy, 'Public International Law Aspect of Shipping Regulation'. (2014); ibid. 297–326. Also, Agustín Blanco-Bazán, 'IMO Interface with the Law of the Sea Convention', Paper

Presented at the *Twenty-Third Annual Seminar of the Center for Ocean Law and Policy, University of Virginia School of Law*, (2000).

441 UNCLOS, Article 227.

442 UNCLOS, Article 202 on scientific and technical assistance to developing States, and 203 on preferential treatment for developing States.

443 The Safety of Life at Sea Convention (SOLAS Convention) was adopted in 1974 with the main objective of protecting human lives, but environmental protection is also a stated aim. Amendment to the SOLAS Convention falls under the work of the Maritime Safety Committee of the IMO.

444 Also the Convention on the Prevention of Marine Pollution by Dumping of wastes and other Matter (hereinafter London Convention), the International Convention on the Control of Anti-fouling Systems, the International Convention for the Control and Management of Ships' Ballast Water and Sediments (2004) and the International Convention for the Prevention of Pollution of the Sea by Oil (1954).

445 International Convention for the Prevention of Pollution From Ships, adopted 2 November 1973 as modified by the Protocol of 1978, adopted on 17 February 1978, entered into force in 1983. MARPOL 73/78. 1340 UNTS 61; 17 ILM 546 (1978). (Hereinafter MARPOL Convention). The Convention and the Protocol were merged into one legal instrument. The Protocol came after a series of disasters that proved a lack of uniform application of MARPOL 73. For a concise overview see, Douglas Brubaker, *Marine Pollution and International Law: Principles and Practice* (Belhaven Press; Distributed in North America by CRC Press, 1993). 122–129. As explained in S. Mankabady, *The International Maritime Organization.* (1986). 321, some of the reason why the MARPOL Convention had difficulties was that *'the original text was badly drafted as the control measures were expressed in a general way.'*

446 MARPOL Convention Preamble.

447 MARPOL Annex VI has 69 parties covering 93.29 % of world shipping gross tonnage.

448 See, foreword in IMO, *Revised MARPOL Annex VI. Regulations for the Prevention of Air Pollution from Ships and NOx Technical Code 2008* (International Maritime Organization 2009 ed., 2009).

449 IMO, Resolution A.719(17).

450 Annex VI to the Convention for the Prevention of Pollution from Ships: Regulations for the Prevention of Air Pollution from Ships (Adopted 26 September 1997, in force 19 May 2005). This includes a mandatory code in NOx from engines. It followed the decision to adopt a new Annex taken by IMO, Resolution A.719(17).

451 MARPOL Convention, Article 1.

452 A revision of this annex was agreed in 2008 and entered into force in 2010. IMO, *Revised MARPOL Annex VI: Regulations for the Prevention of Air Pollution from Ships and NOx Technical Code 2008.* (2009).

453 For an analysis of the different emissions controls under MARPOL Annex VI, see: C.M.d.l. Rue and C.B. Anderson, *Shipping and the Environment: Law and Practice.* (2009). 840–847.

454 International Conference on Air Pollution from Ships, 1997. It was convened by the IMO who adopted the 1997 Protocol that includes Annex VI.

455 C.M.d.l. Rue and C.B. Anderson, *Shipping and the Environment: Law and Practice.* (2009). 845–846.

456 MEPC 60/22, (2010). Paragraph 4.34.

457 MEPC.203(62) on Amendments to the annex of the protocol of 1997 to amend the international convention for the prevention of pollution from ships, 1973, as modified by the protocol of 1978 relating thereto (Inclusion of regulations on energy efficiency for ships in MARPOL Annex VI) Adopted 15 July 2011. (2011). It was also necessary to add new definitions and requirements, such as the International Energy Efficiency Certificate in support of chapter 4.

458 For a detailed description on the measures see, A. Chrysostomou and E.S. Vagslid, 'Climate Change: A Challenge for IMO Too'. (2012). 91–95.

459 See IMO website www.imo.org/OurWork/Environment/PollutionPrevention/Air-Pollution/Pages/Technical-and-Operational-Measures.aspx

460 MEPC Press briefing cited in Aldo Chircop, *The Regulation of International Shipping: International and Comparative Perspectives. Essays in Honor of Edgar Gold* (Martinus Nijhoff Publishers, 2012). 275–276.

461 MEPC 62/24. Report of the Marine Environment Protection Committee on its 62nd Session. (26 July 2011), (2011). Annex 8. Brazil, India, Peru and Poland made statements on matters of principle or policy concerning the reduction of GHG emissions from ships.

462 Ibid. at. Paragraph 6.103–6.106.

463 An overwhelming majority were in favour (49 parties) and there were three abstentions from Jamaica, Saint Vincent and the Grenadines. The Islamic Republic of Iran, Kenya, and Syrian Arab Republic were not present.
     Ibid. at. Paragraph 6.110.

464 Circular letter No.3128 of 24 November 2010 (2010).

465 MEPC Resolutions are included as an Annex to the Reports of the MEPC meetings, where the resolutions were adopted.

466 See further in, P. Ehlers and Rainer Lagoni, *International Maritime Organisations and Their Contribution towards a Sustainable Marine Development* (Lit, 2006).

467 List of codes and recommendations, guidelines and other safety- and security- related non-mandatory instruments; for an overview see, IMO, IMO What Is It? 16–18.

468 For example, the International Code for the Construction and Equipment of Ships carrying Dangerous Chemicals in Bulk is now incorporated to MARPOL and SOLAS.

469 Ekaterina Anianove, 'The International Maritime Organization: Tanker or Speedboat?', in *International Maritime Organisations and Their Contribution towards a Sustainable Marine Development* (P. Ehlers and Rainer Lagoni eds., 2006).

470 IMO, Assembly Resolution A.963(23) on IMO Policies and Practices Related to the Reduction of Greenhouse Gas Emissions from Ships (2004).

471 MEPC.203(62).

472 Specifically: MEPC.212(63) on 2012 Guidelines on the Method of Calculation of the Attained Energy Efficiency Design Index (EEDI) for New Ships, (2012); MEPC.213(63) on 2012 Guidelines for the Development of a Ship Energy Efficiency Management Plan (SEEMP), (2012); MEPC.214(63) on 2012 Guidelines on Survey and Certification of the Energy Efficiency Design Index (EEDI), (2012); MEPC.215(63) on Guidelines for Calculation of Reference Lines for Use with the Energy Efficiency Design Index (EEDI), (2012); MEPC.224(64) on Amendments to the 2012 Guidelines on the Method of Calculation of the Attained Energy Efficiency Design Index (EEDI) for new ships, (2012); MEPC.231(65) on 2013 Guidelines for Calculation of Reference Lines for Use with the Energy Efficiency Design Index (EEDI), (2013); MEPC.233(65) on 2013 Guidelines for Calculation of Reference Lines for Use with the Energy Efficiency Design Index (EEDI) for Cruise Passenger Ships Having Non-Conventional Propulsion, (2013); MEPC.234(65) on Amendments to the 2012 Guidelines on Survey and Certification of the Energy Efficiency Design Index (EEDI) (Resolution MEPC.214(63)), as amended, (2013); and the latest, MEPC.245(66) on 2014 Guidelines on the Method of Calculation of the Attained Energy Efficiency Design Index (EEDI) for New Ships (2014).

473 MEPC.229(65) on Promotion of Technical Co-Operation and Transfer of Technology Relating to the Improvement of Energy Efficiency of Ships (2013).

474 IMO, MEPC.278(70) Amendments to Marpol Annex VI – Data Collection System for Oil Consumption (2016).

475 IMO Convention, Articles 37–41.

476 IMO, Resolution A.358(IX). Adopted at the 9th IMO Assembly 1975, (1975).
477 IMO Convention, Article 38(a) on the functions of the MEPC conferred upon it by international conventions for the prevention and control of marine pollution from ships. The structure of the IMO is available in their website: www.imo.org/About/Pages/Structure.aspx (last accessed December 2016).
478 MARPOL Conference of the Parties 1997, where Annex VI was adopted.
479 MARPOL Conference of the Parties 1997, Resolution 8.
480 First published in 2000. The second study is from 2009. A third study came out in 2014.
481 Assembly Resolution A.963(23).
482 Ibid. at. 1.
483 MEPC 60/22, Paragraph 4.34.
484 MEPC 62/WP.15.
485 The AHEWG-TT held two meetings, the latest in October 2014.
486 However, they are not without value; the adoption of environmental instruments, even if they are weak, is considered to greatly influence innovation processes within the industry. See the example of MARPOL and NOx in Heli Hyvättinen and Mikael Hilden, 'Environmental Policies and Marine Engines: Effects on the Development and Adoption of Innovations', *Marine Policy*, 28 (2004). 491–502.
487 MEPC 59/24 (2009).
488 The MBM-EG was established by the secretary general to evaluate 10 proposals and their value in reducing GHG emissions from international shipping. See work at www.imo.org/OurWork/Environment/PollutionPrevention/AirPollution/Pages/Feasibility-Study-and-Impact-Assessment.aspx
489 See: MEPC 60/22. Report of the Marine Environment Protection Committee 60th Session.
490 For a summary on the proposal see, A. Chrysostomou and E.S. Vagslid, 'Climate Change: A Challenge for IMO Too'. (2012). 97–99.
491 MEPC 61/24. Report of the Marine Environment Protection Committee on its Sixty-First Session, (2010). The two previous Intersessional Meetings took place in June 2008. The first Intersessional Meeting of IMO's Working Group on Greenhouse Gas Emissions from ships (GHG-WG1), and March 2009, the Second intersessional meeting of IMO's Working Group on Greenhouse Gas Emissions from ships (GHG-WG2)
492 The Third Intersessional Meeting of IMO's Working Group on Greenhouse Gas Emissions from ships (GHG-WG 3) was held in March 2011. The meeting concluded that, first, no incompatibilities existed with customary international law and UNCLOS: second, it called for an impact study building upon the work of the MBM-EG; and. third, it acknowledged the lack of detail and maturity of the proposal, urging proponents to continue working on the improvement of the proposals. The meeting reported to the MEPC 62 on the measures, highlighting their strengths and weaknesses, their relation to relevant international conventions and possible impacts. See, MEPC 62/5/1 Report of the third Intersessional Meeting of the Working Group on Greenhouse Gas Emissions from Ships, (2011).
493 MEPC.229(65).
494 MEPC.278(70).
495 The so called three-step approach consists of 1. data collection, 2. analysis and 3. decision-making.
496 IMO, Report of the Marine Environment Protection Committee on Its Sixty-First Session (IMO Doc. MEPC 61/24, 6 October 2010). 43–44.
497 See IMO, Report of the Marine Environment Protection Committee on Its Sixty-Second Session (IMO Doc. MEPC 62/24, 26 July 2011); Report of the Marine Environment Protection Committee on Its Sixty-Third Session (IMO Doc. MEPC 63/23,

14 March 2012); and Report of the Marine Environment Protection Committee on Its Sixty-Fourth Session (IMO Doc. MEPC 64/23, 11 October 2012).

498 MEPC70/WP.7

499 See IMO Press Briefing (28/10/2016). Available at: www.imo.org/en/MediaCentre/PressBriefings/Pages/28-MEPC-data-collection--.aspx

500 A.C. Kiss and D. Shelton, *Guide to International Environmental Law.* (2007). 52–53.

501 A list of the IMO Conventions can be found at the organization website: www.imo.org/About/Conventions/ListOfConventions/Pages/Default.aspx

502 International Convention for the Prevention of Pollution of the Sea by Oil, 1954, as amended (OILPOL 1954).

503 International Convention Relating to Intervention on the High Seas in Cases of Oil Pollution Casualties, 1969 (INTERVENTION 1969).

504 Convention on the Prevention of Marine Pollution by Dumping of Wastes and Other Matter, 1972, as amended (LC (amended) 1972).

505 International Convention for the Control and Management of Ships' Ballast Water and Sediments, 2004.

506 Bin Okumara, 'Proposed IMO Regulations for the Prevention of Air Pollution from Ships', *Journal of Maritime Law and Commerce*, 26(2), (1995) 183–195.

507 *'this normally meant that more acceptances were required to amend a convention than were originally required to bring it into force in the first place, especially where the number of States which are Parties to a convention is very large'* see, www.imo.org/About/Conventions/Pages/Home.aspx

508 The first Council proposal looking into this issue examines the procedures of other UN agencies, including ICAO, concluding that amendment of technical and other regulations became binding on member States without a further ratification or acceptance. The requirement can vary from one amendment to another. For example for the 2008 revision of Annex VI, it is stated that *'The amendments enter into force six months after the deemed acceptance date, 10 July 2010, unless within the acceptance period an objection is communicated to the Organization by not less than one third of the Parties or by the Parties the combined merchant fleets of which constitute not less than 50 per cent of the gross tonnage of the world's merchant fleet.'* See also: S. Mankabady, *The International Maritime Organization.* (1986). 321–322.

509 This is a reminder of the fact that before 1977 amendments of the IMO Convention and its functions were limited to *'consultative and advisory'* (deleted Article 2). This mandate allowed it only to *'provide for the drafting of conventions, agreements or other instruments and to recommend these to Governments and to intergovernmental organizations and to convene such conferences as may be necessary'.* The Organization could arrange a conference – but it was up to the conference to decide whether the Convention under discussion should or should not be adopted and to decide how it should be amended.

510 C.M.d.l. Rue and C.B. Anderson, *Shipping and the Environment: Law and Practice.* (2009). 817, 824.

511 See Chapter 1.

512 D. Blobel et al., *United Nations Framework Convention on Climate Change: Handbook.* (2006). 186.

513 T. Buergenthal, *Law-Making in the International Civil Aviation Organization.* (1969). 1.

514 Ibid. at. 1.

515 J.E. Alvarez, *International Organizations as Law-Makers.* (2005). 2.252–253.

516 Ibid. at. 111.

517 For example in the use of force against civilian airlines, see ibid. at. 253.

518 M. Milde, 'Future Perspective of Air Law'. (1996). 13–18.

519 Andrew Macintosh, 'Overcoming the Barriers to International Aviation Greenhouse Gas Emissions Abatement', *Air and Space Law*, 33(6), (2008). 403–429.

520 M. Milde, 'Future Perspective of Air Law'. (1996). 13–18 Milde highlights that the only two substantive amendments were made for practical needs. He refers to article 83 bis and 3 bis.

521 M. Milde, 'Future Perspective of Air Law'. (1996). 13–18.

522 Olivier Onidi, 'A Critical Perspective on ICAO', *A Critical Perspective on ICAO, Air & Space Law*, 33(1), (2008). 38.

523 P.W. Birnie et al., *International Law and the Environment*. (2009). 441.

524 E. Anianove, 'The International Maritime Organization: Tanker or Speedboat?'. (2006). 77–106.

525 A. Macintosh, (2008).

526 Giovanni Bisignani, 'Think Again: Airlines', *Foreign Policy* (4 January 2006). Cited in Ruwantissa Abeyratne, *Aviation and the Carbon Trade*. (Nova Science Publishers, 2011). 196.

527 Shipowners, registering states, crew, ship chartered or even sub-chartered, ship management, based in a differing country.

528 Duncan Brack et al., *International Trade and Climate Change Policies* (Earthscan, 2000). 106–107.

529 This idea was also put forward in Sebastian Oberthür, 'The Climate Change Regime: Interactions of the Climate Change Regime with ICAO, IMO and the EU Burden-Sharing Agreement', in *Institutional Interaction in Global Environmental Governance: Synergy and Conflict among International and EU Policies: Global Environmental Accord: Strategies for Sustainability and Institutional Innovation* (Sebastian Oberthür and Thomas Gehring eds., 2006). 66. Since then, the idea hasn't changed. See for example, the IMO submission to the climate regime: IMO, Update on IMO's Work to Address Emissions from Fuel Used for International Shipping. Note by the International Maritime Organization to the fortieth session of the Subsidiary Body for Scientific and Technological Advice (SBSTA 40) Bonn, Germany, 4 to 15 June 2014. Agenda item 11(c) Emissions from fuel used for international aviation and maritime transport (2014). Paragraph 30: '*Although international maritime transport is the most energy efficient mode of mass transport and only a modest contributor to worldwide CO_2 emissions*'.

Bibliography

Abeyratne, Ruwantissa (1996). *Legal and Regulatory Issues in International Aviation*, Irvington-on-Hudson, NY, Transnational Publishers.

Abeyratne, Ruwantissa (2011). *Aviation and the Carbon Trade*, New York, Nova Science Publishers.

Abeyratne, Ruwantissa (2014). *Convention on International Civil Aviation: A Commentary*, Switzerland, Springer International Publishing.

Ademun-Odeke (2007). 'From the "Constitution of the Maritime Safety Committee" to the "Constitution of the Council": Will the IMCO Experience Repeat Itself at the IMO Nearly Fifty Years On? The Juridical Politics of an International Organization', *Texas International Law Journal*, 43, 55–113.

ADP. 2015.8. Informal Note. Non-Paper. Note by the Co-Chairs 5 October 2015.

Air Transport Association Group. Statutes. Adopted 2002, amended 2007.

Alvarez, José E. (2005). *International Organizations as Law-Makers*, Oxford, England; New York, Oxford University Press.

Anianove, Ekaterina (2006). 'The International Maritime Organization: Tanker or Speedboat?', in, Peter Ehlers and Rainer Lagoni (eds.), *International Maritime Organisations and Their Contribution towards a Sustainable Marine Development*, Hamburg, Germany, Lit Verlag.

Asselt, Harro van (2016). 'International Climate Change Law in a Bottom-Up World', *Questions of International Law*, Zoom-in 26, 5–15.

Asselt, Harro van and Pauw, Pieter (2013). 'Beyond Warsaw: Finding New Hope for International Climate Policy', *Outreach*. Available at: http://outreach.stakeholderforum.org/index.php/previous-editions/cop-19/200-cop19wrapup/11651-beyond-warsaw-finding-new-hope-for-international-climate-policy

Assembly Resolution A33–7: Consolidated Statement of Continuing ICAO Policies and Practices Related to Environmental Protection: Appendix I.

Assembly Resolution A35–5: Consolidated Statement of Continuing ICAO Policies and Practices Related to Environmental Protection.

Assembly Resolution A36–22: Consolidated Statement of Continuing ICAO Policies and Practices Related to Environmental Protection.

Assembly Resolution A37–19: Consolidated Statement of Continuing ICAO Policies and Practices Related to Environmental Protection: Climate Change.

Assembly Resolution A38–18: Consolidated Statement of Continuing ICAO Policies and Practices Related to Environmental Protection: Climate Change.

Assembly Resolution A39–2: Consolidated Statement of Continuing ICAO Policies and Practices Related to Environmental Protection: Climate Change.

Assembly Resolution A39–3: Consolidated Statement of Continuing ICAO Policies and Practices Related to Environmental Protection: Global Market-Based Measure (MBM) Scheme.

Assembly Resolution A.963(23) on IMO Policies and Practices Related to the Reduction of Greenhouse Gas Emissions from Ships.

Baatz, Y. (2014). *Maritime Law 3e*, Taylor & Francis.

Bekiashev, Kamil A. and Serebriakov, Vitali V. (1981). 'International Chamber of Shipping (ICS)', in, *International Marine Organizations*, Netherlands, Springer.

Biermann, Frank and Siebenhüner, Bernd (2009). *Managers of Global Change: The Influence of International Environmental Bureaucracies*, Cambridge, MA, MIT Press.

Birnie, Patricia W., Boyle, Alan E. and Redgwell, Catherine (2009). *International Law and the Environment*, 3rd ed., Oxford; New York, Oxford University Press.

Blanco-Bazán, Agustín (2000). 'IMO Interface with the Law of the Sea Convention', *Twenty-Third Annual Seminar of the Center for Ocean Law and Policy, University of Virginia School of Law*.

Blobel, Daniel, Meyer-Ohlendorf, Nils, Schlosser-Allera, Carmen and Steel, Penny (2006). *United Nations Framework Convention on Climate Change: Handbook*, Bonn., Germany, Intergovernmental and Legal Affairs, Climate Change Secretariat.

Böckstiegel, Karl-Heinz, Universität zu Köln. Institut für Luft- und Weltraumrecht. and Universität zu Köln. Lehrstuhl für Internationales Wirtschaftsrecht. (1996). *Perspectives of Air Law, Space Law, and International Business Law for the Next Century*, Köln, C. Heymanns.

Bodansky, Daniel (1993). 'The United Nations Framework Convention on Climate Change: A Commentary', *Yale Journal of International Law*, 18, 451.

Bodansky, Daniel (2001). 'The History of the Global Climate Change Regime', in, Urs Luterbacher and Detlef F. Sprinz (eds.), *International Relations and Global Climate Change: Global Environmental Accord*, Cambridge, MA, MIT Press.

Bodanski, Daniel (2012). 'The Durban Platform: Issues and Options for a 2015 Agreement', Centre for Climate and Energy Solutions.

Bodanski, Daniel (2016). 'The Legal Character of the Paris Agreement', *Review of European, Comparative, and International Environmental Law*.

Boyle, Alan E. and Chinkin, Christine M. (2007). *The Making of International Law*, Oxford; New York, Oxford University Press.

Brack, Duncan, Grubb, Michael and Windram, Craig (2000). *International Trade and Climate Change Policies*, London, Earthscan.

Brownlie, Ian (2008). *Principles of Public International Law*, 7th ed., Oxford; New York, Oxford University Press.

Brubaker, Douglas (1993). *Marine Pollution and International Law: Principles and Practice*, London; Boca Raton, FL, Belhaven Press; Distributed in North America by CRC Press.

Brunnée, Jutta (2011). 'An Agreement in Principle? The Copenhagen Accord and the Post-2012 Climate Regime', in, Holger Hestermeyer, Nele Matz-Lück, Anja Seibert-Fohr and Silja Vöneky (eds.), *Law of the Sea in Dialogue*, Berlin; Heidelberg, Max-Planck-Gesellschaft zur Förderung der Wissenschaften e.V., Springer.

Brunnée, Jutta and Toope, Stephen J. (2010). *Legitimacy and Legality in International Law: An Interactional Account*, Cambridge; New York, Cambridge University Press.

Buergenthal, Thomas (1969). *Law-Making in the International Civil Aviation Organization*, 1st ed., Syracuse, NY, Syracuse University Press.

Busby, Joshua (2016). 'After Paris: Good Enough Climate Governance', *Current History*. January 2016, 3–9.

Charney, Jonathan I. and American Society of International Law (1982). *The New Nationalism and the Use of Common Spaces: Issues in Marine Pollution and the Exploitation of Antarctica*, Totowa, NJ, Allanheld, Osmun.

Cheng, Bin (1962). *The Law of International Air Transport*, London; New York, Stevens; Oceana Publications.

Chircop, Aldo, Letalik, N., McDorman, T.L., Rolston, S. (2012). *The Regulation of International Shipping: International and Comparative Perspectives. Essays in Honor of Edgar Gold*, Leiden, The Netherlands, Martinus Nijhoff Publishers.

Chrysostomou, Andreas and Vagslid, Eivind S. (2012). 'Climate Change: A Challenge for IMO Too', in, R. Asariotis and Hassiba Benamara (eds.), *Maritime Transport and the Climate Change Challenge*, 1st ed., New York, Earthscan.

Churchill, Robin R. and Ulfstein, Geir (2000). 'Autonomous Institutional Arrangements in Multilateral Environmental Agreements: A Little-Noticed Phenomenon in International Law', *The American Journal of International Law*, 94(4), 623–659.

Circular Letter No. 3128 of 24 November 2010 ECAC's Strategy for the Future: A Policy Statement. Endorsed by ECAC Directors General of Civil Aviation at DGCA/137.

Convention on the Inter-Governmental Maritime Consultative Organization, Adopted on 6 March 1948, entered into force 17 March 1958. 289 UNTS 48, amended and renamed as Convention on the International Maritime Organization, 14 November 1975, 9 UTS 61.

Convention on International Civil Aviation, adopted 7 December 1944, entered into force 4 April 1947. 15 UNTS 295, as amended, ICAO Doc. 7300/9 (2006), (hereinafter Chicago Convention).

Decision 1/CMP.8, Amendment to the Kyoto Protocol Pursuant to Its Article 3, Paragraph 9 (the Doha Amendment) UN Doc. FCCC/KP/CMP/2012/13/Add.1 (28 February 2013).

Decision -/CP.20, Lima Call for Climate Action.

Decision 1/CP.17, Establishment of an Ad Hoc Working Group on the Durban Platform for Enhanced Action, UN Doc. FCCC/CP/2011/9/Add.1 (11 December 2011).

Decision 1/CP.18, UN Doc. FCCC/CP/ 2012/8/Add1.

Decision 1/CP.19, Further Advancing the Durban Platform. FCCC/CP/2013/10/Add.1.

Decision 2/CP.3, Methodological Issues Related to the Kyoto Protocol. UN Doc. FCCC/CP/1997/7/Add.1.

Decision 2/CP.15, The Copenhagen Accord, UN Doc. FCCC/CP/2009/7/Add.1 (30 March 2010).

Decision 4/CP.1, Methodological Issues UN Doc. FCCC/CP/1995/7/Add.1.

Declaration by the High-level Meeting on International Aviation and Climate Change (HLM-ENV/09) in October 2009.

De La Fayette, Louise (2001). 'The Marine Environment Protection Committee: The Conjunction of the Law of the Sea and International Environmental Law', *The International Journal of Marine and Coastal Law*, 16(2), 155–238.

Depledge, Joanna (2000). 'Tracing the Origins of the Kyoto Protocol: An Article-By article Textual History. Technical Paper. UNFCCC. UN Doc. FCCC/TP/2000/2 25 November 2000.

Depledge, Joanna (2013). *The Organization of Global Negotiations: Constructing the Climate Change Regime*, London, Earthscan.

Depledge, Joanna and Yamin, Farhana (2009). 'The Global Climate Change Regime: A Defense', in, Dieter Helm and Cameron Hepburn (eds.), *The Economics and Politics of Climate Change*, Oxford; New York, Oxford University Press.

Diederiks-Verschoor, I.H. Philepina (1997). *An Introduction to Air Law*, 6th rev. ed., The Hague; Boston, Kluwer Law International.

Doelle, Meinhard (2010). 'The Legacy of the Climate Talks in Copenhagen: Hopenhagen or Brokenhagen?', *Carbon and Climate Law Review*, 4(1), 86–100.

Draft Agreement and Draft Decision on Workstreams 1 and 2 of the Ad Hoc Working Group on the Durban Platform for Enhanced Action. Work of the ADP Contact Group Incorporating Bridging Proposals by the Co-Facilitators. Version of 4 December 2015 at 10.00 hrs.

Draft Agreement between the UN and ICAO. GA Draft Agreement A/106 (30 September 1946).

Draft Agreement between the UN and IMCO (IMO). ECOSOC Resolution 165 (VII) (27 August 1948).

Draft Paris Outcome. Proposal by the President. Draft Text on COP 21 Agenda Item 4 (b) Durban Platform for Enhanced Action (decision 1/CP.17) Adoption of a Protocol, another Legal Instrument, or an Agreed Outcome with Legal Force Under the Convention Applicable to all Parties. Version 1 of 9 December 2015 at 15:00.

Draft Paris Outcome. Proposal by the President. Draft Text on COP 21 Agenda Item 4 (b) Durban Platform for Enhanced Action (decision 1/CP.17) Adoption of a Protocol, another Legal Instrument, or an Agreed Outcome with Legal Force Under the Convention Applicable to all Parties. Version 2 of 10 December 2015 at 21:00.

Ehlers, Peter and Lagoni, Rainer (2006). *International Maritime Organisations and Their Contribution towards a Sustainable Marine Development*, Hamburg, Germany, Lit Verlag.

Elliott, Lorraine M. (2004). *The Global Politics of the Environment*, 2nd ed., Washington Square, NY, New York University Press.

FCCC/ADP/2015/1 Geneva Negotiating Text.

FCCC/ADP/2015/1 Version of 11 June 2015. Bonn Negotiating Text.

FCCC/ADP/2015/L.6, Draft Paris Agreement (5th December 2015).

FCCC/AWGLCA/2009/8.

FCCC/AWGLCA/2009/14.

FCCC/CP/1995/7/Add.1 Decision 4/CP.1 on Methodological Issues.

FCCC/CP/1997/7/Add.1. Decision 2/CP.3 Methodological Issues Related to the Kyoto Protocol.

FCCC/CP/1999/6/Add.1. Decision 18/CP.5 Emissions Based Upon Fuel Sold to Ships and Aircraft Engaged in International Transport.

FCCC/CP/2011/9/Add.1 Report of the Conference of the Parties on its Seventeenth Session, held in Durban from 28 November to 11 December 2011.

FCCC/SBSTA 40. Emissions from Fuel Used for International Aviation and Maritime Transport. Submission by the International Civil Aviation Organization.

Fossungu, Peter Ateh-Afac (1999). 'The ICAO Assembly: The Most Unsuprente of Supreme Organs in the United Nations System? A Critical Analysis of Assembly Sessions', *Transportation Law Journal*, 26(3). 1–49

Frank, Veronica (2007). *The European Community and Marine Environmental Protection in the International Law of the Sea: Implementing Global Obligations at the Regional Level*, Leiden, The Netherlands, Martinus Nijhoff Publishers.

Freestone, David and Streck, Charlotte (2009). *Legal Aspects of Carbon Trading: Kyoto, Copenhagen, and Beyond*, Oxford; New York, Oxford University Press.

Galizzi, Paolo (2013). 'Air, Atmosphere and Climate Change', in, Shawkat Alam (ed.), *Routledge Handbook of International Environmental Law*, New York, Routledge.

GHG-WG 3/3/3. Review of Proposed MBMs: The IMO, Global MBMs That Reduce Emissions and the Question of Principles. Submitted by Clean Shipping Coalition (CSC) and World Wide Fund for Nature (WWF).

Ghosh, Arunabha and Woods, Ngaire (2009). 'Governing Climate Change: Lessons from Other Governance Regimes', in, Dieter Helm and Cameron Hepburn (eds.), *The Economics and Politics of Climate Change*, Oxford; New York, Oxford University Press.

Gilbert, Paul, Bows, Alice and Starkey, Richard (2010). 'Shipping and climate change: Scope for Unilateral Action', *The University of Manchester and Tyndall Centre for Climate Change Research*.

Gill, Michael (2016). 'Aviation and the Impacts of Climate Change, Aviation and the Climate: An ATAG Perspective', *Carbon & Climate Law Review*, 10(2), 118–119.

Govind, Paul (2013). 'International Environmental Institutions', in, Shawkat Alam (ed.), *Routledge Handbook of International Environmental Law*, New York, Routledge.

Gupta, Joyeeta (2000). 'On Behalf of My Delegation: A Survival Guide for Developing Country Climate Negotiators', *International Institute for Sustainable Development & Center for Sustainable Development in the Americas*.

Haites, E., Yamin, F. and Höhne, N. (2013). 'Possible Elements of a 2015 Legal Agreement on Climate Change', Working Paper N°16/13, IDDRI.

Havel, Brian F. and Sanchez, Gabriel S. (2014) *The Principles and Practice of International Aviation Law*. New York, Cambridge University Press.

Hernes, Gudmund (2012). *Hot Topic – Cold Comfort: Climate Change and Attitude Change*, Oslo, Nordforsk.

Herold, Anke, Cames, Martin and Cook, Vanessa (2010). 'The Development of Climate Negotiations in View of Cancun (COP 16)). Study Requested by the EU Directorate General for Internal Policies. Policy Department A: Economic and Scientific Policy'.

Herold, Anke, Cames, Martin, Siemons, Anne, Emele, Lukas and Cook, Vanessa (2013). 'The Development of Climate Negotiations in View of Warsaw (COP 19). Study Requested by the EU Directorate General for Internal Policies. Policy Department A: Economic and Scientific Policy'.

Hilden, Mikael and Heli Hyvättinen (2004). 'Environmental Policies and Marine Engines: Effects on the Development and Adoption of Innovations', *Marine Policy*, 28, 491–502.

ICAO. Environment Branch of ICAO (2010). *ICAO Environmental Report 2010: Aviation and Climate Change*, Montreal, ICAO.

ICAO. Environment Branch of ICAO (2013). *ICAO Environmental Report 2013: Aviation and Climate Change*, Montreal, ICAO.

ICAO & ATAG, Transport and Aviation Action Statement. Climate Summit 2014. New York. IMO, Resolution A.358(IX). Adopted at the 9th IMO Assembly 1975.

IMO, Resolution A.719(17).

IMO (2009). *Revised MARPOL Annex VI: Regulations for the Prevention of Air Pollution from Ships and NOx Technical Code 2008*, 2009 ed., London, International Maritime Organization.

INC-UNFCCC 2 Decision9/2.

International Convention for the Prevention of Pollution From Ships, adopted 2 November 1973 as modified by the Protocol of 1978, adopted on 17 February 1978, entered into force in 1983. MARPOL 73/78. 1340 UNTS 61; 17 ILM 546 (1978).

IPCC (2006). *2006 IPCC Guidelines for National Greenhouse Gas Inventories*, Prepared by the National Greenhouse Gas Inventories Programme, H.S. Eggleston, L. Buendia, K. Miwa, T. Ngara and K. Tanabe (eds). IGES, Japan.

Kirgis, Frederic L. (1993). *International Organizations in Their Legal Setting*, 2nd ed., St. Paul, MN, West Pub. Co.

Kiss, Alexandre Charles and Shelton, Dinah (2007). *Guide to International Environmental Law*, Boston, Martinus Nijhoff Publishers.

Klabbers, Jan (2009). *An Introduction to International Institutional Law*, 2nd ed., Cambridge, UK; New York, Cambridge University Press.

Koenig, Doris (2013). 'Global and Regional Approaches to Ship Air Emissions Regulations: The International Maritime Organization and the European Union', in, Harry N. Scheiber and Jin-Hyun Paik (eds.), *Regions, Institutions, and Law of the Sea Regions, Institutions, and Law of the Sea: Studies in Ocean Governance*, Leiden; Boston, Martinus Nijhoff Publishers.

Liu, Nengye (2010). 'The Relations between the European Union and the International Maritime Organization: An Analysis', Working Paper Annual Legal Research Network Conference 2010.

Liu, Nengye and Maes, Frank (2010). 'The European Union and the International Maritime Organization: EU's External Influence on the Prevention of Vessel-Source Pollution', *Journal of Maritime Law and Commerce*, 41(4). 581–894.

Louka, Elli (2006). *International Environmental Law: Fairness, Effectiveness, and World Order*, Cambridge; New York, Cambridge University Press.

Macintosh, Andrew (2008). 'Overcoming the Barriers to International Aviation Greenhouse Gas Emissions Abatement', *Air and Space Law*, 33(6), 403–429.

MacKenzie, David Clark (2010). *ICAO: A History of the International Civil Aviation Organization*, Toronto; Buffalo, University of Toronto Press.

Mankabady, Samir (1986). *The International Maritime Organization*, § 1: International Shipping Rules, London; Wolfeboro, NH, Croom Helm.

Martinez Romera, B. (2016). 'The Paris Agreement and the Regulation of International Bunker Fuels', *Review of European Comparative & International Environmental Law*, 25(2). 215–227.

MEPC.59/24. Report of the Marine Environment Protection Committee on its 59th Session

MEPC.60/22. Report of the Marine Environment Protection Committee 60th Session.

MEPC.61/24. Report of the Marine Environment Protection Committee on its 61st Session.

MEPC.62/5/1. Report of the Third Intersessional Meeting of the Working Group on Greenhouse Gas Emissions from Ships.

MEPC.62/24. Report of the Marine Environment Protection Committee on its 62nd Session (26 July 2011).

MEPC.203(62) on Amendments to the Annex of the Protocol of 1997 to Amend the International Convention for the Prevention of Pollution from Ships, 1973, as Modified by the Protocol of 1978 Relating Thereto (Inclusion of regulations on energy efficiency for ships in MARPOL Annex VI) Adopted 15 July 2011.

MEPC.212(63) on 2012 Guidelines on the Method of Calculation of the Attained Energy Efficiency Design Index (EEDI) for New Ships.

MEPC.213(63) on 2012 Guidelines for the Development of a Ship Energy Efficiency Management Plan (SEEMP).

MEPC.214(63) on 2012 Guidelines on Survey and Certification of the Energy Efficiency Design Index (EEDI).

MEPC.215(63) on Guidelines for Calculation of Reference Lines for Use with the Energy Efficiency Design Index (EEDI).

MEPC.224(64) on Amendments to the 2012 Guidelines on the Method of Calculation of the Attained Energy Efficiency Design Index (EEDI) for New Ships.

MEPC.229(65) On Promotion of Technical Co-Operation and Transfer of Technology Relating to the Improvement of Energy Efficiency of Ships.

MEPC.231(65) on 2013 Guidelines for Calculation of Reference Lines for Use with the Energy Efficiency Design Index (EEDI).

MEPC.233(65) on 2013 Guidelines for Calculation of Reference Lines for Use with the Energy Efficiency Design Index (EEDI) for Cruise Passenger Ships Having Non-Conventional Propulsion.

MEPC.234(65) on Amendments to the 2012 Guidelines on Survey and Certification of the Energy Efficiency Design Index (EEDI) (Resolution MEPC.214(63), as Amended.

MEPC.245(66) on 2014 Guidelines on the Method of Calculation of the Attained Energy Efficiency Design Index (EEDI) for New Ships.

MEPC.278(70) Amendments to Marpol Annex VI – Data Collection System for Oil Consumption.

M'Gonigle, R. Michael and Zacher, Mark W. (1979). *Pollution, Politics, and International Law: Tankers at Sea*, Berkeley; London, University of California Press.

Milde, Michael (2008). *International Air Law and ICAO*, Utrecht, Netherlands, Eleven International Publishing.

Miller, Clark A. (2001). 'Challenges in the Application of Science to Global Affairs', in, C.A. Miller and P.N. Edwards (eds.), *Changing the Atmosphere: Expert Knowledge and Environmental Governance*, Cambridge, MIT Press.

Morrison, Fred L. (2011). 'The Reluctance of the United States to Ratify Treaties', in, Holger Hestermeyer, Nele Matz-Lück, Anja Seibert-Fohr and Silja Vöneky (eds.), *Law of the Sea in Dialogue*, Berlin, Heidelberg, Max-Planck-Gesellschaft zur Förderung der Wissenschaften e.V., Springer.

Nasiritousi, Naghmeh, Hjerpe, Mattias and Linnér, Björn-Ola (2014). 'The Roles of Non-State Actors in Climate Change Governance: Understanding Agency through Governance Profiles', *International Environmental Agreements: Politics, Law and Economics*, 16(1) 109–126.

Oberthür, Sebastian (2006). 'The Climate Change Regime: Interactions of the Climate Change Regime with ICAO, IMO and the EU Burden-Sharing Agreement', in, Sebastian Oberthür and Thomas Gehring (eds.), *Institutional Interaction in Global Environmental Governance: Synergy and Conflict among International and EU Policies: Global Environmental Accord: Strategies for Sustainability and Institutional Innovation*, Cambridge, MA, MIT Press.

Okumara, Bin (1995). 'Proposed IMO Regulations for the Prevention of Air Pollution from Ships', *Journal of Maritime Law and Commerce*, 26(2) 183–195.

Onidi, Olivier (2008). 'A Critical Perspective on ICAO', *A Critical Perspective on ICAO, Air & Space Law*, 33(1), 38.

Paris Agreement (Paris, 12 December 2015, in force 4 November 2016) FCCC/CP/2015/L.9.

Penner, Joyce E., Intergovernmental Panel on Climate Change. Working Group I. and Intergovernmental Panel on Climate Change. Working Group III. (1999). *Aviation and the Global Atmosphere: A Special Report of IPCC Working Groups I and III in Collaboration with the Scientific Assessment Panel to the Montreal Protocol on Substances That Deplete the Ozone Layer*, Cambridge, Cambridge University Press.

Piera, Alejandro (2016). 'Compliance Tools for a Global Market Based Measure for Aviation · Designing the Legal Form of a Global Aviation Market Based Measure', *Carbon & Climate Law Review*, 10(2). 144–152.

Preliminary ICS Comments on Draft EU Regulation on MRV. Brief for EU Member States and Members of the European Parliament on the Proposal for a Regulation of the European Parliament and of the Council on the Monitoring, Reporting and Verification of Carbon Dioxide Emissions from Maritime Transport and Amending Regulation (EU) No 525/2013.

Rajamani, Lavanya (2011). 'The Cancun Climate Agreements: Reading the Text, Subtext and Tea Leaves', *International Affairs*, 60(2), 499–519.

Rajamani, Lavanya (2012). 'The Durban Platform for Enhanced Action and the Future of the Climate Regime', *International & Comparative Law Quarterly*, 61(2), 501–518.

Rajamani, Lavanya (2016). 'Ambition and Differentiation in the 2015 Paris Agreement: Interpretative Possibilities and Underlying Politics', *International and Comparative Law Quarterly*, 65, 493–514.

Raustiala, Kal (1997). 'States, NGOs, and International Environmental Institutions', *International Studies Quarterly*, 41, 719–740.

Raustiala, Kal (2001). 'Nonstate Actors in the Global Climate Regime', in, Urs Luterbacher and Detlef F. Sprinz (eds.), *International Relations and Global Climate Change: Global Environmental Accord*, Cambridge, MA, MIT Press.

Resolution A.719(17). Adopted on 6 November 1991. Prevention of Air Pollution from Ships.

Rue, Colin M. de la and Anderson, Charles B. (2009). *Shipping and the Environment: Law and Practice*, 2nd ed., London, Informa Law.

Savaresi, Annalisa (2016). 'The Paris Agreement: A New Beginning?', *Journal of Energy & Natural Resources Law*, 34(1), 16–26.

SEC/2002/0381 final. Recommendation from the Commission to the Council in Order to Authorise the Commission to Open and Conduct Negotiations with the International Civil Aviation Organization (ICAO) on the Conditions and Arrangements for Accession by the European Community.

Serdy, Andrew (2014). 'Public International Law Aspect of Shipping Regulation', in, Yvonne Baatz (ed.), *Maritime Law*, London, Informa Law Routledge.

Smith, Tristan., Raucci, C., Haji Hosseinloo, S., Rojon, I., Calleya, J., Suárez de la Fuente, S., Wu, P. and Palmer, K. (2016). 'CO$_2$ Emissions from International Shipping: Possible Reduction Targets and Their Associated Pathways.' Prepared by UMAS. London.

Sochor, Eugene (1991). *The Politics of International Aviation*, London, Palgrave Macmillan UK.

Stavins, Robert N. (2015). 'COP-20 in Lima: A New Way Forward.(conference of the Parties of the UN Framework Convention on Climate Change)', *The Environmental Forum*, 32, 14.

Tanaka, Yoshifumi. (2016). Regulation of Greenhouse Gas Emissions from International Shipping and Jurisdiction of States, *Review of European, Comparative & International Environmental Law*, 25(3), 333–346.

FCCC/TP/2013/4. Technical Paper. 'Compilation of Information on Mitigation Benefits of Actions, Initiatives and Options to Enhance Mitigation Ambition'.

Transport and Environment (2013). 'Global Deal or No Deal? Your Free Guide to ICAO's 38th Triennial Assembly'. Published online on September 24, 2013. www.transportenvironment.org/publications/global-deal-or-no-deal-your-free-guide-icao-assembly

Truxal, Steven (2012). *Competition and Regulation in the Airline Industry: Puppets in Chaos*, Abingdon, Oxon, UK; New York, Routledge.

UNEP (2012). *The Emissions Gap Report 2012*, Nairobi, UNEP.

UNFCCC Draft Rules of Procedure, FCCC/CP/1996/2.

UNGA Resolution on the Protection of Global Climate for Present and Future Generations of Mankind, UN Doc. A/RES/45/212, 21 December.

United Nations Convention on the Law of the Sea, Montego Bay, adopted 10 December 1982, in force 16 November 1994, 21 International Legal Materials (1982), 1261. 1833 UNTS 3.

Update on IMO's Work to Address Emissions from Fuel Used for International Shipping. Note by the International Maritime Organization to the fortieth session of the Subsidiary Body for Scientific and Technological Advice (SBSTA 40) Bonn., Germany, 4–15 June 2014. Agenda Item 11(c) Emissions from Fuel Used for International Aviation and Maritime Transport.

Walker, George K. (2011). *Definitions for the Law of the Sea: Terms Not Defined by the 1982 Convention*, Leiden, Martinus Nijhoff Publishers.

Warner, Robin (2009). *Protecting the Oceans beyond National Jurisdiction: Strengthening the International Law Framework*, Leiden; Boston, Martinus Nijhoff Publishers.

Wemaere, Matthieu (2010). 'State of Play of the International Climate Negotiations: What Are the Results of the Copenhagenn Conference?', *Carbon and Climate Law Review*, 4(1), 106–111.

Wold, Chris, Hunter, David and Powers, Melissa (2009). *Climate Change and the Law*, Newark, NJ, LexisNexis Matthew Bender.

Written Statement of Reservation on behalf of the Member States of the European Community (EC) and the other States Members of the European Civil Aviation (ECAC) [made at the 36th Assembly of the International Civil Aviation Organization in Montreal, 18–28 September 2007].

Yamin, Farhana and Depledge, Joanna (2004). *The International Climate Change Regime: A Guide to Rules, Institutions and Procedures*, Cambridge, UK; New York, Cambridge University Press.

Yemin, Edward (1969). *Legislative Powers in the United Nations and Specialized Agencies*, Leyden, A. W. Sijthoff.

Zahar, Alexander (2013). 'The Climate Change Regime', in, Shawkat Alam (ed.), *Routledge Handbook of International Environmental Law*, New York, Routledge.

4 Bunker fuels at the intersection of international legal regimes

This chapter critically explores how IBF are at the juncture of the climate, ICAO and IMO regimes, elaborating on the interaction among these regimes in terms of norms and institutions, and highlights the main tensions surrounding the regulation of this overlapping area. In order to map the interaction among the selected regimes, this chapter aims to understand how overlaps and connections between the selected regimes occur, through what means (both in terms of hard law and soft law), through what channels (both formal and informal), what type of interaction takes place, and whether it entails tensions and leaves room for synergies.

This chapter first analyzes the real-world relationship between climate change, aviation and shipping before analyzing the relationship between the climate, ICAO and IMO regimes. An array of 'interacting objects'[1] are identified, as well as their connections. The drivers and aims of such interactions are also considered here. These interactions are then disaggregated in different cases following the typology proposed by various scholars,[2] in particular the scheme proposed by Dunoff on regulatory and administrative interaction, operational interaction and conceptual interactions,[3] which allows for a more nuanced and rich characterization of the interaction. The consequences of these interactions and how to manage them is the focus of Chapters 5 and 6.

Climate change, ICAO and the IMO: overlapping regimes?

The impacts and costs of climate change on aviation and maritime transport

The increase in volume of international aviation and maritime transport has lead inevitably to an escalation in the sectors' GHG emissions, with concomitant impact on the climate. At the same time, the consequences of climate change also affect the development of international transport, by disrupting their performance and challenging the sectors' resilience.[4] Rising sea levels, the increased frequency and severity of storms, flooding and other extreme weather events all disturb and pose operational risks to airports, ports and associated transport infrastructure and facilities.[5] Other ways in which maritime transport can be affected is with regards to trade routes, ships and cargo, in cases of storms at sea.[6] In fact, awareness of the impacts of climate change on shipping transport reveals not only the need for mitigation,[7] but also the need for adapting ports and other coastal structures to the impacts of climate change in the next decades since mitigation will offer limited benefits by 2070.[8] Meanwhile, air transport is also affected by the consequences of global warming. The potential effects would vary greatly geographically and are related to precipitation changes and sea level rise, which may require investment in repairs and new infrastructure, the use of cooling for buildings, drainage for runways and challenges for ground and flight operations related to high wind, freezing rain, heavy precipitation, lightning strikes and heavy snow events.[9] In this connection, ICAO has also recognized the need to consider climate adaptation measures: '*even though there are some uncertainties about the potential impacts of climate change on aviation operations and related infrastructure, clearly there are challenges that will need to be addressed.*'[10]

Although climate change is likely to affect international air and sea transport, disrupting the normal functioning of the industry and involving adaptation costs for these sectors,[11] it would appear that such impacts are not perceived as severe enough to motivate clear and urgent action. Mitigating aviation and shipping emissions stands to indirectly benefit the sectors but adapting to the effect of climate change has an exclusive and direct benefit on the sectors. Furthermore it can be said that the decision to pursue emissions limitations and reductions is 'unnatural' to the purpose and structure of the aviation and shipping business. For example, despite the fact that scientific studies have shown that reducing the speed of ships leads to emission reductions of around 30% at zero abatement cost,[12] there is resistance in the industry to do this. This is due to the economic trade-offs, where the market value of speed often outweighs the fuel cost savings.[13] In the aviation industry, where fuel costs are of greater significance, the inverse of this trade-off may apply.[14] In short, the drivers for the aviation and maritime transport sectors to tackle IBF are more likely to come from externally imposed incentives such as fuel price increases or political and regulatory competition threatening the status quo of the regimes.[15] The lack of such externally imposed incentives and drivers is not uncommon in situations of overlap between environmental and non-environmental areas, and also between public and private interests. In addition, especially in the case of aviation, there is an extreme polarization between those that cause the emissions and those that bear its environmental costs. This asymmetry is extreme since only a privileged minority of the global population contributes to climate change through air transport, while a large underprivileged majority suffers the consequences of global warming, mostly in the least developed countries. Consequently, political interest in developing tight regulation of IBF varies between and within different fora.[16]

IBF emissions: connecting the climate, ICAO and IMO regimes

The regulation of GHG emissions from IBF is a matter that, as with climate change and other issues of a global nature, does '*not fit neatly within a single regime*'.[17] As detailed in the previous chapters, tackling emissions from IBF has become an area where different international legal regimes have a legitimate interest and voice.[18] The overlap and relationships generated by it are established below.

The climate change regime, the ICAO and IMO regimes have been established at different points in history, responding to different needs and drivers, with different objectives and functions and have evolved in an independent fashion.[19] However, the overlap between these distinctive fields of international law and governance (i.e. the climate and international transport regimes) does not necessarily imply a direct clash or conflict between them. Furthermore, and in spite of the tensions, overlaps can also create opportunities for cooperation between regimes.

Regime interaction can manifest not only in the form of overlapping norms but in the inter-regime activity and institutional collaboration[20] that has taken place ever since these regimes began to discuss this area of common interest. The interaction between the climate, ICAO and IMO regimes is bi-directional and multifaceted, meaning that, regardless of the triggers of interaction, developments in one arena affect and influence the other. Interaction runs from the climate regime to the ICAO and vice versa, from the climate regime to the IMO and vice versa. Actions in the climate regime towards reducing emissions may lead to restrictions in aviation and shipping, affect competitiveness and disturb the balance and normal modus operandi of the ICAO and IMO regimes, such as by polarizing country positions.

An interface between ICAO and the IMO also exists. Both sectors supply transport and so they can, up to certain point, provide interchangeable forms of commercial and consumer transport. Also, they have exchanged information in workshops and meetings related to climate change in the three fora.[21]

Questions on forum, mandate and competence

When legal regimes coincide in an area of common interest and action, one of the first questions to be asked is about their adequacy as a forum to deal with the issue at hand, the existence of competition between fora to regulate a specific issue (in this case IBF), or if they can prevent the other regime from regulating. These issues bring to light the different mandates and competence of regimes, which is the focus of this section.

While the KP does not cover emissions from IBF, the shipping and aviation sectors were not omitted from the protocol's text. Although the issue of transportation was mentioned in the UNFCCC,[22] Article 2.2 of the KP is the only hard-law provision in the climate regime, which explicitly names and rules for IBF. Article 2.2 urges parties to take action through ICAO and the IMO in regard to emissions from aviation and shipping, with the following words:

> The Parties included in Annex I shall pursue limitation or reduction of emissions of greenhouse gases not controlled by the Montreal Protocol from aviation and marine bunker fuels, working through the International Civil Aviation Organization and the International Maritime Organization, respectively.

However, the text of the article is not clear in various aspects, thus requiring further analysis. The exact role given to ICAO and the IMO by Article 2.2 is imprecise and the relationship of the signatories to the KP with ICAO and the IMO regimes is also unclear. Indeed, there is no guidance in the article on the content, meaning or implications for cooperation between the climate and international transport regimes. Neither is there explicit direction on whether States, individually or jointly, should refrain from acting in this area, or in cases of conflict or in the event of inaction or delays in action within ICAO and the IMO.[23] However, even if a multilateral solution is envisioned in the KP by assigning responsibility to ICAO and the IMO regimes to tackle emissions, it can be inferred that Article 2.2 does not appoint exclusive authority or either preclude action from outside these fora.[24] In this regard, a restrictive interpretation of the article would oppose the objective of limiting emissions, therefore a teleological interpretation is more appropriate.[25]

Eckhard Pache presents two arguments in support of the idea that Article 2.2 lacks any intention to adjudicate the 'sole authority' in tackling IBF to ICAO and the IMO. First, a veto on advancing the regulation in other fora would undermine the aims of the protocol and the climate regime as a whole. Second, two provisions in the UNFCCC support this interpretation; principally Article 7.2 of the UNFCCC,[26] which *'reserves the right to review any legal instrument adopted on the basis of this convention, thus leaving competence for monitoring and implementing to the COP'*.[27] In fact, after COP 13 in Bali (2007), IBF was included in the negotiations under the UNFCCC for a post-2012 agreement, demonstrating that the UNFCCC is also a legitimate authority and fora for action.[28] Third, there is article 4.2(a) of the UNFCCC, which requires developed countries to take the lead in limiting their emissions. Also, the opinion of the Advocate General of the Court of Justice of the European Union (CJEU) regarding the ATAA Case[29] uses pleas of uneven membership to embrace the non-exclusivity authority of the specialized agencies in Article 2.2. She argued that the case of exclusivity would lead to situations where some contracting parties to ICAO would recognize obligations under a treaty they haven't signed, and where some signatories of the KP would not be able to fulfil their obligations of working through ICAO or IMO, since they are not members of these organizations. However, such argumentation does not directly explain the intention of the parties in Article 2.2, but rather reveals a not well-thought-through choice of wording.[30]

Article 2.2 was built upon the consolidated negotiating text elaborated by the chairman,[31] based upon a proposal put forward by the EU, Switzerland and New Zealand,[32] where parties favoured measures that are achieved by *'working through'* ICAO and IMO rather than just by cooperating with the organizations.[33] Looking back to the *travaux préparatoires* and the circumstances of the treaty conclusion, it can be said that Article 2.2 supposes that a compromise solution[34] would be reached with regard to the difficulties of allocating emissions to countries.[35] At the same time, a delegation or transferral of responsibility from the signatories of the KP to ICAO and the IMO on the basis of the expertise and knowledge of both international agencies was recognized. The choice of these fora to advance the negotiations on IBF was intended to provide an *'international division of labour'* between regimes,[36] not only in the hope that reaching an agreement will be easier through them, but also as a way to *'lessen the need for the climate regime to be proactive in the controversial policy issues surrounding allocation and control options'.*[37] However, it can be argued that the exclusion of these sector's emissions from the otherwise economy-wide agreement of the KP[38] also follows the logic that *'no matter how responsibility is assigned, restriction of emissions at a country level creates an incentive for unwanted behavioural change.'*[39]

In any case, Article 2.2 is a commitment of the parties to take subsequent action in limiting the emissions from IBF, given the impossibility of reaching an agreement in Kyoto. This is summed up by Kulovesi who states that

> the wording negotiating history and subsequent practice related to article 2.2 of the Protocol do not seem to support the view that parties to the protocol have conferred on the ICAO [or IMO] the sole authority to address aviation emissions and have prohibited any other multilateral or unilateral measures.[40]

The subsequent practice of Annex I countries reporting their work under ICAO and IMO, and the fact that such commitment is subject to review by experts and the Facilitative Branch of the KP compliance committee, also supports the idea that Article 2.2 was not a full delegation of power.[41]

In this context, the term *'shall pursue'* used in the article points towards a direction for action, involving a request for ICAO and the IMO to find a route forward, rather than an exclusive mandatory requirement, or a prohibition on any work on IBF through different arenas.[42] The other official language versions of the KP (Spanish and French) point towards this interpretation as they use non-strong formulas, in this case the words *'procurarán'* and *'cherchent'*, respectively. Neither of these terms express the sense of obligation that *'shall'* could confer to the provision. The binding force of the provision is also elucidated in the Advocate General Kokott's opinion to the AATA Case.[43] Although Kokott recognized the preference of Article 2.2 for multilateralism, this cannot be understood as an exclusive competence of ICAO or a prohibition for the EU to regulate emissions from aviation. According to Kokott, this is especially relevant in connection with the lack of progress and overall delay of action in ICAO.[44] In the same line of thought, the CJEU ruling considered that Article 2.2 lacks precision and that its assignment of responsibility to ICAO and IMO is not unconditional.[45] However, there is no unanimity among the legal community and some authors question this matter, considering that the mandate of the KP is exclusive.[46]

In any event, the KP's mandate to ICAO and the IMO is not, at least technically, the reason for initiating action in both regimes. Neither ICAO nor IMO's command can come from Kyoto, since there is no hierarchical supremacy of Kyoto as a source of external direction.[47] ICAO and the IMO's mandate must come from the will of their own members, established in their constituency documents, viz., the Chicago Convention and the IMO Convention, and/or expressed in other legal instruments related to the organizations. Therefore any mandate under the KP is not recognized by these organizations as binding for them; their mandates are established internally.[48] However, Oberthür has stated that as '*both ICAO and IMO primarily serve shipping and aviation interests, they may not necessarily be expected to initiate action on climate change of their own accord*'.[49]

These mandates are, in the case of aviation, the assembly Resolution A33–7[50] and A35–5,[51] which request the Council to cooperate with the IPCC and UNFCCC in determining the impact of aviation, to studying policy options to limit or reduce the environmental impact of aircraft engine emissions and to develop concrete proposals. The Council is also urged to continue to assist the SBSTA with regard to methodological issues; and to develop the necessary tools to promote operational measures. In addition, Assembly Resolution 37–19 requests the Council '*to ensure that ICAO exercise continuous leadership on environmental issues relating to international civil aviation, including GHG emissions*'.[52]

In the case of maritime transport, IMO's general mandate to act in GHG emissions derives from the IMO Convention,[53] the LOSC[54] and particularly MARPOL Resolution 8.[55] However, the mandate set in Assembly Resolution A963 (23)[56] is highly relevant since it urges the MEPC to identify and develop the mechanisms for the limitation or reduction of GHG emissions from international shipping. It also requests the MEPC to consider the methodological aspects related to reporting, to develop a work plan with a timetable, review and prepare consolidated statements on continuing policies and related practices. Assembly Resolution A963 (23) also requests the IMO Secretariat to continue cooperating with the Secretariats of UNFCCC and ICAO.

However, the ICAO and IMO regimes have embraced, from the beginning, the regulatory role given to them by the KP and have accroached themselves as the sole organizations with authority to act.[57] Furthermore, pressure caused by forum competition to negotiate in the area of IBF has provoked ICAO and the IMO to repeatedly arrogate themselves as the suitable forum in which to deal with aviation and maritime transport, respectively. In that line of thought, Oberthür foresaw[58] that the trigger towards meaningful action in ICAO and IMO would come either from regulatory competition among the climate, ICAO and IMO regimes, or from '*threats*' associated with unilateral action. In this connection, the EU has proved to be a more effective driver for action in ICAO, following its unilateral action on aviation emissions, than the weak regulatory competition resulting from the climate regime.

Article 2.2 presupposes the suitability of ICAO and the IMO regimes to deal with climate change issues. This issue is considered with regard to the competence of both organizations in this matter and also the powers attributed to their bodies and organs.[59]

While international law offers the only limit to state actions, international organizations are competent to act within their attributed powers by their members, which are found in their constitutive documents or other instruments of international law. Unlike states, international organizations do not enjoy a sovereign power (i.e. '*unlimited powers unconnected to the pursuant of specific objectives*'[60]) and their powers are defined by their '*finalité fonctionnelle*', meaning that they agree to whatever is needed to perform their functions.[61] This principle of speciality or 'conferred powers' governs the scope of action of international organizations (i.e. *'they are invested by the states which create them with powers, the limits of which are a function of the common interests whose promotion those states entrust to them'*).[62] This is also supported by the ICJ when interpreting the UN Charter in the Reparation Case advisory opinion,[63] which understood that an organization must be deemed to have those powers which, though not expressly provided in their charters, are conferred upon it as being essential to the performance of its duties.[64] The attribution of organizational competence is also connected to the division of powers between the organization and their member's legal systems, as well as among the organs of the organization itself. According to their respective charters and other legal documents and practices, ICAO and the IMO have the competence to deal with climate change issues related to their activity and their apparatuses.[65]

In addition to the above topics, Article 2.2 opens questions on two other fronts. First, on the issue of which States should be pursuing measures (i.e. just Annex I countries), all signatory states of KP or all members of the ICAO and IMO. The issue of membership between regimes arises here. Second, there is the issue of whether ICAO and the IMO are somehow bound to work under a differentiated basis when dealing with climate change. Both issues, however, are interrelated.

Regarding the first point, 191 states and the EU are, to date, signatories to the KP,[66] while the Doha Amendment establishing the second commitment period of the KP has only been ratified by 75 countries, and therefore under the threshold to enter into force.[67] It was the will and covenant of all the signatories states[68] to tackle emissions of IBF outside Kyoto, although Article 2.2 states that *'Annex I parties'* are the ones that shall pursue limitations and reductions of emissions in these sectors. Annex I parties refers to the UNFCCC. However, not all parties in the KP are members of ICAO and vice versa, which creates situations of uncertainty with regards to the relationship and interaction between regimes. Also, not all parties to the UNFCCC are parties to the KP.[69]

Article 2.2 calls for a differentiation in commitments, which follows the spirit of the climate regime division in Annex I and Non-Annex I UNFCCC parties. Only countries listed in Annex B of the KP hold limitation and reduction commitments.[70] The climate regime is underpinned by the CBDRRC principle, although the scope and content of the principle is contentious.

It seems from the wording of Article 2.2 that differential treatment with regard to the regulation of IBF is the favoured option. Although the article points towards ICAO and the IMO as the preferred fora for advancing negotiations, it is unclear whether they are obliged to work on the basis of differentiation. The question becomes especially relevant because ICAO and the IMO operate, as a general rule, on the premise of non-discriminatory and equal treatment. Such principles are given in their respective constitutive instrument and have been secured through the regimes' practice. Given that the mandates of ICAO and the IMO come from their own instruments where these principles are established and not from the KP, there is a tension among regimes regarding differentiating and equal treatment for climate change regulation.[71]

Article 2.2 KP: a conflict clause?

A conflict clause can be defined as a segment of a legal document where parties intend to avoid contradictions by giving '*direction as to what to do with subsequent or prior conflicting treaties*'.[72] These clauses can provide a variety of clarifications; for instance they can prohibit the conclusion of incompatible posterior treaties or permit those that are compatible, or establish that they will not be affected.[73] However, conflict clauses suffer from limitations since they cannot affect third parties rights or *jus cogens*, and can be unclear or cause conflict themselves with other treaties.[74] Furthermore, the set of challenges faced by conflict clauses include a lack of dynamism to reflect new developments, difficulties in the delimitation of when a treaty comes into existence and the need of a unifying dispute-settlement system to apply them.[75]

The climate regime contains a number of clauses that aim to regulate the relation of the climate instruments with other treaties.[76] Article 2.2 of the KP contains a conflict clause in relation to the Montréal Protocol, since the provision establishes a limit in the scope of action for IBF to '*the greenhouse gases not controlled by the Montreal Protocol*'. Such a division is in line with other references made by the UNFCCC and the KP in recognizing a previous treaty, the Montréal Protocol, dealing with certain GHGs, and providing clear direction of the relationship between treaties. However, it cannot be said that KP Article 2.2 provides an unequivocal direction with regards to previous or future treaties, as they relate to the ICAO and IMO regimes. Indeed, it does not intend to clarify the relationship between instruments in the regimes or establish a prevailing treaty. The article does not contain a conflict clause in that sense. In the case of containing a conflict clause with regards to the ICAO and IMO regimes, such a clause would refer exclusively to the delegation of the negotiation of rules,[77] since Article 2.2 is '*a provision delimiting the scope of the climate treaties by delegating the negotiation of rules*' on IBF.[78] In any event, given the constant disagreements on the issue of forum and the lack of progress of negotiations within ICAO and IMO, Article 2.2 would have been a rather unsuccessful conflict clause.[79] Even in connection to the delegation of negotiating rules, in the light of the discussion in the previous section, it cannot be inferred that Article 2.2 contains a conflict clause regarding the relationship with ICAO and IMO. First and foremost, there was no intention from parties to fully disaggregate negotiations on IBF from the climate regime, and neither to establish the principles of CBDRRC as the basis for agreements in ICAO and IMO. In any case, since parties are non-identical, Article 30 of the VCLT would allow the '*state that has concluded incompatible obligations to choose which of them to observe*'.[80] Nevertheless, KP Article 2.2 has an interpretative value and provides guidance for successive norms.[81]

The appropriateness of ICAO and the IMO to deal with climate change

Beyond technical issues of mandates and competences, an important question to ask is whether ICAO and the IMO are the adequate fora to regulate the climate change aspects of international aviation and maritime transport, or whether the task of negotiating the regulation of GHG emissions is best dealt with solely within the climate regime. Do ICAO and the IMO have the necessary frameworks and structures to negotiate the regulation of GHG emissions from their respective sectors? At this point the issue becomes highly debatable and is inevitably reduced to a discussion of the criteria for adequate frameworks and structures, and of what are considered to be the necessary tools. Here, it can be assumed that measurable progress towards regulating the sector's emissions would be the key assessment criteria.

Factors of universal participation in the regimes, sector-specific expertise and previous success in regulating environmental matters also support the argument that ICAO and the IMO are the appropriate forums in which to deal with the regulation of IBF emissions.[82] Issues of expertise are also relevant here. Both organizations have a positive record on regulating environmental issues.[83] Indeed, they have been successful in reaching agreements and outcomes partly for the technical aspects they deal in and their sector-specific knowledge, and partly for the relative simplicity of their negotiation and law-making processes. These issues are often seen in the literature as favouring the regulation of IBF in the ICAO and IMO fora, owed to their allegedly *'greater facility for passing resolutions, by comparison with the Climate Change conference'*.[84] However, some authors argue that actions to mitigate climate change are best pursued under the UNFCCC.[85] Bringing IBF into the climate regime would mean that *'the failed Kyoto attempt to task ICAO and IMO could be corrected'*.[86] A similar conclusion was reached by a group of climate NGOs in the prolegomena of COP16.[87]

Divergent primary purposes and normative goals and principles are among the reasons for the failure to achieve progress in this area. As has been pointed out,[88] the main political idea behind the Chicago Convention was the *'development and liberalisation of international aviation'*, which was supported by two types of provisions, namely the strict limitations on taxation affecting international aviation and the principle of non-discrimination. Similar driving forces are to be found in the case of maritime transport, where the main role for the IMO is to create a level playing field and a *'regulatory framework for the shipping industry that is fair and effective, universally adopted and universally implemented'*.[89]

These mandates and principles can conflict when attempts are made to establish a meaningful regulation for IBF under the ICAO and IMO regimes. For example, both organizations have experienced constant difficulties in obtaining consensus among their members.[90] However, such difficulties are linked to specific tensions such as the allocation of emissions, rather than to complicated decision-making systems per se.

The issue of regime bias is also related to the choice of forum for the regulation of IBF. While ICAO and the IMO regimes want to define their role and establish their dominance in regulating IBF, they are likely to be biased in favour of themselves as fora and against a climate-led regulation of GHG emissions. Similar arguments are put forward in connection with non-environmental regimes dealing with environmental issues, such as the WTO in the case of subsidies for fisheries.[91]

Parallel membership

Another relevant aspect regarding the adequacy of fora and regime interaction is the issue of membership. Although the ICAO, IMO and climate regime are systems of universal membership,[92] not all countries are parties to some of the treaties that the regimes are based upon, notably Kyoto, MARPOL or the UNCLOS. There is also an uneven system of membership between the climate regime, ICAO and IMO, where Markus W. Gehring et al.[93] have highlighted that the structures in ICAO and IMO do not allow for a very important player, the EU, to participate. This is problematic since the EU's member States do not necessarily represent the EU position as a whole.[94] However, the issue of parallel membership as a requirement for interaction has been challenged,[95] since 'a *fixation on the need for parallel membership obstructed regime interaction and led to grave problems in the ability of international law to meet new and emerging challenges'.*[96]

Defining interaction between the climate, ICAO and IMO regimes

On the face of it, the relationship between the climate regime, ICAO and the IMO does not appear to be antagonistic or hostile. Although the main purpose and interests pursued by these regimes differs widely, ICAO and the IMO have established, on previous occasions, their authority in other environmental issues and have regulated environmental matters related to air and sea transport, respectively.

Although the explicit request from Article 2.2 of the KP to ICAO and the IMO is generally considered to be the trigger for interaction between the climate regime, ICAO and IMO,[97] two facts challenge this assumption. First, ICAO and the IMO were already aware of climate change and its impacts on their respective sectors before the KP was signed. For example, ICAO initiated a study of the problem in 1996[98] and the IMO also resolved to study climate change in 1997, so it can be argued that at least some interaction started prior to Kyoto. Second, ICAO and the IMO were already interacting with the climate regime as part of the negotiating process, so they also contributed to and influenced the KP.[99]

Oberthür, in his studies on the interaction between the climate regime, ICAO and the IMO,[100] has highlighted that the interaction can be defined in connection with its drivers as '*interaction through commitment*', meaning that commitments made by actors in the climate regime may affect preferences in IMO and ICAO[101] and that there are two main characteristics defining the relationships. First, that the IMO and ICAO were '*far from enthusiastic*' in dealing with climate change, such that any progress made has been driven by two fears: losing regulatory authority to the climate regime and the growth of unilateral actions that would undermine their multilateral functions. Second, Oberthür has characterized the relationship between the climate regime, ICAO and the IMO as disruptive,[102] as has been the case with interactions of the climate regime with other non-environmental institutions. However, he concedes that the '*disruption may turn into synergy if these institutions decide that they can address climate change without harming their primary objective.*'[103] Furthermore Oberthür pointed out the '*lack of coordination*' between regimes as one of the reasons in determining the character of the interaction.[104] In this connection, recent developments in ICAO and the IMO provide an opportunity to assess if such a change of direction has occurred.

However, to assess this relationship, this study focuses not only on the institutional character. There are two different groups of variables or 'ways' through which the selected regimes communicate and influence each other. First, through norms, either rules or principles, including hard-law instruments and soft-law tools. Second, through institutional activities, also established by hard or soft law and that have a formal or informal character. For example communications, reports, workshops and other exchanges among the regimes' participants, States, non-state bodies or bureaucracies. In this connection, this study opts to take a rather novel view on regime interaction, using Dunoff's classification, which is explained and then applied in the following sections.

Interaction from a relational perspective

In order to illustrate the interaction between regimes, concrete examples of interaction between the climate, ICAO and IMO regimes have been selected around the issue of GHG emissions from international aviation and maritime transport. In doing so, the intention is to reveal the most significant aspects of that overlap and of the influence between the selected regimes, exploring the nuances in the type of interaction between regimes. This will enable the following chapters to elaborate upon the consequences and management of interaction between these regimes. Furthermore, this exercise aims to help future research to systematize information on regime interaction, by presenting a case study that follows the scheme proposed by Dunoff.[105]

These interactions occur during the law-making process of international law, that is, how the selected regimes are incorporated when international law is created. Some cases of interaction are very visible, especially if they involve requirements for action or conflicts,[106] while other interactions are less obvious. The following sections discuss these interactions.

Regulatory and administrative interaction

As Dunoff acknowledges, most interaction at the law-making stage occurs when regimes engage the context of regulatory or administrative law-making. These can take the form of decisions of subsidiary bodies, creation of consortia and groups for the participation of various regimes, interactive exchanges provided in a treaty, and the invitation of experts to collaborate from one regime to another, in any form. These forms involve frequent and repetitious collaboration in formal and informal exchanges among participants of different regimes, technical and scientific studies, dialogue among experts and exchanges between civil servants.[107]

'*In order to address questions on bunker fuel emissions, the Convention's bodies cooperate closely*' with ICAO and IMO.[108] The climate regime has used two different channels in which to establish collaboration with ICAO and the IMO: first, by cooperation through the negotiation processes.[109] In that connection, the first COP,[110] the KP and a number of SBSTA decisions recognize the important role of ICAO and IMO in addressing IBF. Second, by cooperating through the secretariats, the importance of cooperation between secretariats has also been highlighted in SBSTA decisions. At the fifth COP, secretariats of the climate, ICAO and IMO regimes were invited to fortify their cooperation.[111] Since then the secretariats have been closely cooperating, based on an *'efficient reciprocal exchange of information'* and *'participation on their meetings'*.[112]

Since 1996, ICAO and IMO have provided reports and information to the SBSTA not only on methodological issues,[113] but also on the ongoing work relevant to GHG emissions from international aviation and maritime transport respectively.[114] Also, the three secretariats have been called to explore opportunities for examining and improving the quality of data reporting and comparability.[115] Additionally, expert meetings including the three regimes to address methodological issues relating to the estimation, compilation and reporting of GHG emissions data from IBF have been organized. For example, joint expert meetings on methodological issues organized by ICAO and IMO in consultation with the UNFCCC Secretariat, were held in their respective headquarters in 2003[116] and 2004.[117] Also, in 2009, the *'three leaders of the UNFCCC, IMO and ICAO held a tripartite meeting to further explore coordination and possible strategies to ensure cooperation in this area.'*[118] In this context, reports and presentations at the meetings are also jointly prepared.

One of the functions of the UNFCCC Secretariat is to regularly inform ICAO and IMO parties at the CAEP and MEPC, respectively, on developments in the climate regime. As stated, *'The UNFCCC secretariat attended several meetings of ICAO and IMO. It made several presentations on the status of the climate change negotiations. The UNFCCC secretariat also provides and maintains a webpage on the issue, where further information can be found.'*[119] At the same time, ICAO and IMO have also shown willingness to enhance cooperation with the UNFCCC, and between secretariats.[120]

Oberthür notes that there is a specific demand for coordination between the ICAO, IMO and climate regimes in setting the level of stringency required from those sectors to achieve the convention's objective, and in the establishment of specific measures, which may require technical coordination, such as market-based instruments connected to the general climate regime or affecting each other's sectors.[121] According to Oberthür, participants of the regimes have responded to this need by *'exchanging information through mutual participation in meetings and reporting on relevant developments and decisions by the respective secretariats'*, which enables parties to the climate regime to review progress in ICAO and IMO and provide guidance. However, in practice, *'the brief reports'* submitted by IMO and ICAO have triggered *'little substantive debate on relevant issues'* under the climate regime and *'very limited feedback'* to the specialized agencies.[122]

However, since Oberthür's last study, this regulatory and administrative interaction has intensified. First, recent work in ICAO and the IMO towards tackling GHG emissions has led to concrete proposals and measures, based on and leading to more detailed debates and reports, covering issues such as the role of CBDRRC and the principle of equal treatment. Second, some of the decisions adopted at the IMO and ICAO have affected unilateral actions of the parties, which has generated more statements from IGOs, NGOs and parties than in previous years. Third, the initial concerns regarding technical and methodological issues have become outdated by political developments, which has expanded the reach of regulatory interaction from the SBSTA to the (now-defunct) AWG-LCA and the ADP, which again multiplies, at least in theory, the sites for exchanges. Nonetheless, it remains to be said that '*a closer coordination of efforts under ICAO, IMO and the climate regime could facilitate and accelerate progress.*'[123]

Operational interaction

Operational activities of international actors are '*another common site of regime interaction*'[124] characterized by being a place where participants from different regimes interact in the course of performing their deeds. Among other examples,[125] Dunoff points to a wide range of international bodies such as regional development banks, the Food and Agriculture Organization (FAO), United Nations Development Programme (UNDP), UNEP, the World Bank and other international agencies working '*with and through*' the GEF, where the use of a funding mechanism improves regime efficiency and is '*an adaptive strategy to respond to the fragmented nature of the international legal order*'.[126]

In this connection two initiatives exist where operational interactions, in the Dunoffian sense, occur between ICAO and the IMO with the climate regime, through the GEF. ICAO and the IMO have established a partnership with climate finance provided by the GEF to implement their adopted policies to achieve GHG reductions.[127] These are the GEF-UNDP-ICAO Project on '*Transforming the Global Aviation Sector: Emissions Reductions From International Aviation*'[128] and the GEF-UNDP-IMO Project on '*Transforming the Global Maritime Transport Industry towards a Low Carbon Future through Improved Energy Efficiency*',[129] so-called Global Maritime Energy Efficiency Partnerships Project (GloMEEP). The legal nature of these projects is not treaty-like in the VCLT sense. Neither are they soft-law instruments. However, they cannot be classified as purely political. It can be argued that these projects belong to the realm of international law, given that they intend to implement agreed-upon measures, and influence and promote States' behaviours towards climate mitigation, with a subsequent potential impact on hard- and soft-law instruments.

A broad definition of climate finance includes all '*financial flows mobilized by industrialized country governments and private entities that support climate change mitigation and adaptation in developing countries*'.[130] This definition covers a variety of funds under the UNFCCC, the KP and the PA.[131] The GEF[132] operates the financial mechanism of the UNFCCC to assist developing countries to implement climate-related projects and reforms,[133] and manages some of the climate change funds, including the Adaptation Fund of the KP,[134] the Special Climate Change Fund and the Least Developed Countries Fund. The GEF is itself a product of regime interaction[135] since it is a partnership between the World Bank, UNEP and the UNDP, founded in 1991. It was established in response to an increasing awareness of the need for a funding mechanism to support international environmental agreements. The GEF now has a unique institutional structure with a Council composed of primarily developing country governments. It also serves as the financial mechanism for the Convention on Biological Diversity, the Convention on Persistent Organic Pollutants, and the United Nations Convention to Combat Desertification, thus working with numerous international organizations. Changes in GEF with regards to its relationship with the climate regime has made '*its policies more climate friendly*'.[136]

Financing climate change actions in developing countries is crucial for the implementation of existing global agreements to reduce GHG emission and for the engagement of developing countries in new commitments.[137] The provision of financial assistance also embodies CBDRRC by allocating part of the cost of mitigation and adaptation actions to developed countries. However, the issue of finance has proved to be contentious, and one that has become central to the climate negotiations, where criticism has been raised on the scarcity of funds and the difficulties and delays in accessing them.[138]

In line with the trend of climate regulation occurring increasingly outside the UNFCCC venue, financial assistance has also evolved in a highly fragmented way.[139] However, in dealing with climate change, international aviation and maritime transport have neither an assigned financing mechanism nor do they have access to the Kyoto 'flexible mechanisms' funding.[140] As such, the interplay between the actions discussed and taken at ICAO and the IMO with regards to finance and those in the climate regime (via the GEF) are central to understanding the operational interactions.

In this vacuum, the ICAO has arrogated the idea of being the '*appropriate institution to deal with aviation financing*',[141] and is putting forward initiatives to facilitate financial support.[142] The IMO has also emphasized its role in climate financing by leading the development of MBMs to reduce GHG emissions.[143] Beyond the technical capacity the organizations purport to have, the interest of ICAO and the IMO in taking an active role in financing can be understood as a response to calls for targeting the maritime and aviation sectors as a possible source of financing for the Green Climate Fund.[144]

In tackling emissions from international aviation, ICAO has set in place voluntary State Action Plans,[145] for which developing countries will be provided with assistance. The 37th ICAO Assembly[146] requested contracting States to submit Action Plans on their emissions reduction activities,[147] including information on their assistance needs.[148] Also, the Council was requested to facilitate assistance and access to existing and new financial resources, technology transfer and capacity building to developing countries. And, furthermore, to initiate specific measures to assist them.[149] Operational activities from ICAO towards the development and fulfilment of its climate programme led to the establishment of the GEF-UNDP-ICAO Project. ICAO has also established a partnership with the EU with regards to State Action Plans.[150]

In early 2013, ICAO, in collaboration with the UNDP, submitted a project proposal to the GEF to help reduce greenhouse gas emissions from the international aviation sector in developing countries.[151] Specifically, this GEF/UNDP/ICAO partnership supports capacity building for technological and operational measures by identifying the 'implementation needs' of ICAO developing country members and providing support to enhance relevant national capacities. While contributing to the implementation of ICAO's State Action Plans, the project also enables the GEF to fulfil its strategic goals of expanding work in the areas of innovation and transport. The project,[152] approved by the GEF Council[153] in August 2013, was awarded 2 million USD,[154] which makes it a medium-sized project by GEF standards.[155] The project aims to stimulate the implementation of low-emission aviation measures in developing States by: identifying implementation needs through State Action Plans; support to States in enhancing national capacities and developing 'processes and mechanisms' for low-emission aviation; establishment of a technical support platform for the implementation of low-emission operational measures; and the demonstration of low-emission aviation measures in developing States.[156] According to the GEF, the project will create a global platform to help transform policy frameworks at the global and regional level, enhancing stakeholder alliances, while contributing to the UNFCCC negotiations. As such, the broad benefit of working with the GEF is that it is likely to increase the '*buy in*' of developing countries to the ICAO's basket of measures.[157]

Achieving emissions reductions in the transportation sector by investing in developing countries is envisioned under the KP. However, to date, these investments have taken place mainly through the CDM and from project financing by the GEF.[158] Nonetheless, those investments were neither targeted towards air transportation or towards emissions that have not been effectively allocated to States under the climate regime, such as those from IBF. Therefore the GEF/UNDP/ICAO venture is innovative in that regard and also from the partnership perspective, since it is the first time the GEF funds a project in the aviation sector and for ICAO to collaborate as executing partner for a GEF project.[159] An additional benefit posited of GEF involvement is that it was likely to increase the chances of an agreement with developing countries.[160]

Similarly, in order to help operationalize the climate and energy efficiency measures (EEDI and SEEMP), agreed at the 62nd MEPC,[161] IMO has focused on issues of technical cooperation and technology transfer[162] but also, through UNDP, submitted a Project Identification Form to the GEF to fund a medium-size project entitled: '*Transforming the Global Maritime Transport Industry towards a Low Carbon Future through Improved Energy Efficiency*'.[163] As stated in the project description its objective is '*to build capacity in developing countries for implementing the technical and operational measures for energy efficient shipping and to catalyse overall reductions in GHG emissions from global shipping*'.[164]

The project was approved in mid-November 2013 and received the GEF's endorsement for funding of 2 million USD to support an additional 11 million

USD in co-financing. The project is due to operate for five years until November 2018.[165] Beneficiary countries will be selected *'based on their level of interest and commitment to undertake a fast-track approach'*[166] with the idea that the tools developed and partnerships created by the project, and the funding provided by the project, will lead to the *'creation of successful models and centres of excellences that can be replicated in other countries around the world'*.[167] The project centres on three main aims:

> 1. legal, policy and institutional reforms for GHG reductions through improved energy efficiency within maritime transport sector in developing countries; 2. maritime sector energy efficiency related capacity building, awareness raising, knowledge creation and dissemination and; 3. public-private partnerships to catalyse maritime sector energy efficiency innovation and R&D.[168]

GloMEEP Marine Technology Cooperation Centres (MTCCs) represent two emerging initiatives. They aim to assist particularly developing countries, both in the development of national strategies and legislation for reduction of shipping GHG emissions, and in the transfer and development of capacity in low carbon technologies for shipping.

In the case of the GloMEEP partnership, it is not the first time that the IMO has worked with and through the GEF. In fact, the three entities have established a project for other environmental concerns, including the GEF/UNDP/IMO Regional Programme on the Prevention and Management of Marine Pollution in the East Asian Seas[169] and the GEF/UNDP/IMO Global Ballast Water Programme (GloBallast).[170] Indeed, in October 2012 at the Aviation and Climate Change Seminar that took place at ICAO, a presentation from the UNDP programme on the GloBallast initiative and the IMO proposal for shipping energy efficiency was given.[171] This is an example of the ongoing informal exchanges of information and collaboration across regimes, enabling mutual learning and influence. Similarly to ICAO,[172] an IMO-European Union project, *Capacity Building for Climate Mitigation in the Maritime Shipping Industry*, funded by the EU was put in place in 2016. It establishes MTCCs in Africa, Asia, the Caribbean, Latin America and the Pacific, with a focus on LDCs and SIDSs.[173] The aim is to support these countries in limiting and reducing GHG emissions from their shipping sectors through technical assistance and capacity building to promote ship energy efficiency.

A series of workshops, meetings and consultations between the 2010 and 2013 assemblies led ICAO to enter into partnership with the GEF, among others, to channel funding to support emissions reductions in the international aviation sector. Furthermore, the GEF and ICAO have hosted a side event and presented the project at COP 19, highlighting the benefits of the cooperation.[174]

Overlaps in operational programmes can risk duplicating efforts and costs but they also create opportunities for scaling-up and synergies. In that connection, the establishment of new ventures and joint programmes can provide mutual support between regimes and also provide a path to integrate international efforts with national approaches.[175] Indeed, these initiatives open up a path for ongoing collaboration between regimes. In particular, coordinated funding affects operational activities of international regimes, since they have to fulfil with certain criteria and modify intra-regime behaviour. The GEF-UNDP-ICAO and the GEF-UNDP-IMO projects fill the vacuum of the climate regime provisions on funding for IBF-related mitigation actions, while operationalizing the principle of CBDRRC.[176]

Differential treatment has played a pivotal role in shaping new legal meaning for the provision of financial assistance in international environmental agreements, especially in those involving common concerns.[177] The CDBRRC principle provides a specific rationale for the provision of financial assistance to developing countries for climate change mitigation and adaptation projects, which can occur through different financial mechanisms and funds, as well as through private investment.[178] As such, the CBDRRC principle has shed new light on the obligation of developed countries to cover the incremental costs of developing countries engaged in environmental projects, aimed at providing global benefits. In the architecture of climate change finance, the GEF plays an essential role as a '*vehicle for assistance*'[179] in facilitating the involvement of developing countries.[180] The country eligibility criteria for GEF financing is linked to the eligibility criteria established by the respective convention or its instruments, and membership to the convention and eligibility to borrow from the World Bank or eligibility as recipients of UNDP technical assistance.[181] However, an important issue is how developing countries are defined for assistance purposes in ICAO or IMO. Taking the case of ICAO, neither the Assembly Resolutions nor other ICAO documents define what developing countries are in this connection. Since there are no specific criteria or characteristics, it is likely that ICAO and IMO would consider developing countries according to the most accepted IMF rules or the World Bank lists, drifting from OECD 1992 criteria to a more flexible and updated listing. However, with regards to least developed countries, ICAO has specifically adhered to the UNCTAD list for other purposes.[182] A similar situation can be said of the IMO. However, in negotiations over other measures to mitigate climate change, such as MBMs, ICAO and the IMO have been unable to agree on prioritizing CBDRRC over equal treatment, non-discrimination and no more favourable treatment. Therefore these projects, which offer financing to assist developing countries, open a way for more meaningful future interventions, manifesting the principle of CBDRRC.

Conceptual interactions

At the same time that the climate, ICAO and the IMO regimes have engaged in regulatory and operational interactions to tackle GHG emissions from IBF, another type of interaction is taking place as a consequence of those encounters: conceptual interactions.[183] Furthermore, channels for conceptual interaction are also linked to studies undertaken by the regimes, through their bodies, and submissions and analyses that actors in the regimes exchange. Especially relevant is the role of '*well-placed experts, policy-makers and academics*' in conceptualizing the debates, generating new concepts or redefining and adapting existing ones.[184]

It can be argued that the concept of IBF is, itself, the outcome of a conceptual interaction among climate change and international aviation and maritime transport, since the category was first conceptualized by the IPCC and then adopted by the climate regime to allude to 'a new reality'.[185] In defining the terms of the allocation and regulation of IBF, at the law-making stage, this research identifies two main conceptual interactions, occurring through regulatory and administrative, and operational activities, but also through the overlap of hard-law norms. This occurs, first, through the shaping of differential treatment, which embodies conflicts among the principles of CBDRRC and equal treatment, non-discrimination and no more favourable treatment. Second, there has been a reconceptualization of taxes and charges for IBF, especially for international aviation in the light of MBMs. These issues are explored in the Chapter 5 as it relates to the consequences of interactions.

Conclusions

This chapter has shed light on the overlapping areas and the connections between the selected regimes, focusing on the ways and channels of interaction. By looking at regime interaction through the lens of the typology proposed by Dunoff it has been possible to consider the issues from a 'relational' perspective, a broader viewpoint which reflects the variety, levels and temporal dimensions of the interactions, which is better suited for interactions at the law-making stage. This choice of typology is relevant in the way the study understands the consequences of that interaction, while widening the options for managing regime interaction.

In answering the second research question: *How does interaction among the selected regimes occur?*, this chapter has responded to the sub-questions set out in Chapter 1: *What are the channels of interaction between these regimes, both formal and informal? What does the interaction entail and what type of interaction has taken place?* This now points towards the conflicts or tensions embedded in the interaction.

In this chapter the intersection of climate, international aviation and maritime transport has been established as well as the channels of interaction between the three regimes, while analyzing some preliminary questions on fora and mandates. This chapter has found that the three regimes have identified sites and ways of interaction beyond their initial mandates for cooperation. As the regimes' respective work on IBF grows and advances, new issues emerge and possibilities appear, allowing for an update of Oberthür's findings, while acknowledging that some of his insights and arguments remain valid.

Notes

1 The term is borrowed from Harro van Asselt, *The Fragmentation of Global Climate Governance: Consequences and Management of Regime Interactions* (Edward Elgar, 2014). 10.
2 Thomas Gehring and Sebastian Oberthur, 'Exploring Regime Interaction. A Framework of Analysis', in *Regime Consequences: Methodological Challenges and Research Strategies* (Arild Underdal and Oran R. Young eds., 2004). And Sebastian Oberthür and Thomas Gehring, 'Conceptual Foundations of Institutional Interaction', in

Institutional Interaction in Global Environmental Governance: Synergy and Conflict among International and EU Policies: Global Environmental Accord: Strategies for Sustainability and Institutional Innovation (Sebastian Oberthür and Thomas Gehring eds., 2006). See also chapter two.

3 The scheme is proposed in Jeffrey Dunoff, 'A New Approach to Regime Interaction', in *Regime Interaction in International Law: Facing Fragmentation* (Margaret A. Young ed., 2012).

4 However, melting of the ice in the Arctic also presents opportunities for new shipping routes; in particular the Northern Sea Route might become viable in the future. See, Miaojia Liu and Jacob Kronbak, 'The Potential Economic Viability of Using the Northern Sea Route (NSR) as an Alternative Route between Asia and Europe', *Journal of Transport Geography*, 18(3), (2010). 434–444.

5 See the example given on disruption of shipping and the damage to a number of ports in Queensland, Australia, in Deanna Grant-Smith, 'Maritime Transport and the Climate Change Challenge', *Australian Planner*, (2013).

6 See for example, Marius Rossouw and Andre Theron, 'Investigation of Potential Climate Change Impacts on Ports and Maritime Operations Around the Southern African Coast', in *Maritime Transport and the Climate Change Challenge* (R. Asariotis and Hassiba Benamara eds., 2012).

7 Gary Howard, *Emissions Reduction a Matter of Survival, Says ICS. Seetrad Global. 18 June 2014. Web.* (2014). The secretary general of the ICS, Peter Hinchliffe recognize that the *'industry's focus on reducing CO_2 emissions is a matter of survival'*.

8 Susan Hanson and Robert J. Nicholls, 'Extreme Flood Events and Port Cities Trough the Twenty-First Century: Implications of Climate Change and Other Drivers', in *Maritime Transport and the Climate Change Challenge* (R. Asariotis and Hassiba Benamara eds., 2012).

9 See, 'Adaptation to Climate Change – Challenges Facing Civil Aviation Stakeholders, Airports', in S. Kahn Ribeiro et al., 'Transport and Its Infrastructure', in *Climate Change 2007: Mitigation: Contribution of Working Group III to the Fourth Assessment Report of the Intergovernmental Panel on Climate Change* (O.R. Davidson et al. eds., 2007). And, Sqn Ldr Sabitha Banu, 'Aviation and Climate Change: A Global Sectored Approach is the Need of the Hour', *International Journal of Low Carbon Technologies*, 7(2), (2012). 137–142. Also, in relation to the impact of climate change and aviation safety see, Herbert Pümpel, 'Aviation and the Impacts of Climate Change Maintaining Aviation Safety: Regulatory Responses to Intensifying Weather Events', *Carbon & Climate Law Review*, 10(2), (2016) 113–117.

10 See, ICAO. Environment Branch of ICAO, *ICAO Environmental Report 2010: Aviation and Climate Change* (ICAO, 2010). Chapter 6. Aviation and Adaptation to Climate Change. See also ICAO website on adaptation of aviation to climate change. See, www.icao.int/environmental-protection/Pages/adaptation.aspx

11 See the N.H. Stern, *The Economics of Climate Change: The Stern Review* (Cambridge University Press, 2007).

12 However, some degree of 'slow steaming' has been implemented by most shipping lines since the 2008 oil price spike and economic crisis, leading to an 11% decrease in CO_2 emissions from container ships since 2008. See, Pierre Cariou, 'Is Slow Steaming a Sustainable Means of Reducing CO_2 Emissions from Container Shipping?', *Transportation Research Part D: Transport and Environment*, 16(3), (2011). 260–264. Also, Haakon Lindstad et al., 'Reductions in Greenhouse Gas Emissions and Cost by Shipping at Lower Speeds', *Energy Policy*, 39(6), (2011). 3456–3464. In their study, they find substantial potential for reducing CO_2 emissions from the maritime sectors: up to a 19% reduction with a negative abatement cost and by 28% at zero abatement cost.

13 See, Harilaos N. Psaraftis and Christos A. Kontovas, 'Balancing the Economic and Environmental Performance of Maritime Transportation', *Transportation Research*

Part D: Transport and Environment, 15, (2010) 458–462. Similar trade-offs occur in regards to changes in the number of vessels in fleet and in-transit inventories.

14 A relevant example is how Concord, the only supersonic commercial aircraft to have operated under market conditions (the other was the Soviet Tupolev Tu-144 nick-named in the West as 'Concordski') always struggled to make a profit for British Airways and Air France.

15 See, Sebastian Oberthür, 'Institutional Interaction to Address Greenhouse Gas Emissions from International Transport: ICAO, IMO and the Kyoto Protocol', *Climate Policy*, 3(3), (2003). 191–205.

16 However, developed countries want tighter regulation while lower-income countries traditionally prefer less strict environmental regulation.

17 Margaret A. Young, 'Regime Interaction in Creating, Implementing and Enforcing International Law', in *Regime Interaction in International Law: Facing Fragmentation* (Margaret A. Young ed., 2012). 85

18 It can be argued that there are other relevant regimes, such as the WTO. For an explanation of why the trade regime has been excluded from the scope of this monograph, see Chapter 1.

19 See Chapter 3 on law-making in the climate, ICAO and IMO regimes.

20 As referenced in the analytical framework (Chapter 2), this book builds upon the work of Young, who sheds lights over this 'underexplored' way of interaction in international law literature, with a view on the legitimacy underpinning it. Such legitimacy is argued to come from alternative authority to representation, based on *'deliberative credentials of the regime participants'*. See: Margaret A. Young, *Trading Fish, Saving Fish: The Interaction between Regimes in International Law* (Cambridge University Press, 2011). And M.A. Young, 'Regime interaction in Creating, Implementing and Enforcing International Law'. (2012).

21 For instance, IMO has participated in the colloquiums and seminars previous to the ICAO Assembly. Additionally, ICAO and IMO have cooperated in other fields such as Joint ICAO and IMO work on Harmonization of Aeronautical and Maritime Search and Rescue (IAMSAR) or the partnership between ICAO, IMO and the World Customs Organization toward harmonizing their respective international frameworks in promoting global supply chain security.

22 UNFCCC, Art 4.1

23 See, in regards to room for State action in 2.2 KP, Malte Petersen, 'The Legality of the EU's Stand-Alone Approach to the Climate Impact of Aviation: The Express Role Given to the ICAO by the Kyoto Protocol', *Review of European Community & International Environmental Law*, 17(2), (2008). 196–204.

24 Eckhard Pache, On the Compatibility with Legal Provisions of Including Greenhouse Gas Emissions from International Aviation in the EU Emission allowance Trading Scheme as a Result of the Proposed Changes to the EU Emission Allowance Trading Directive, (2008). 4–6 Also, in regards to aviation, see, Case-366/10. Opinion of Advocate General Kokott delivered on 6 October 2011.

25 See, Vienna Convention on the Law of Treaties. Vienna, adopted 23 May 1969, in force 27 January 1980. 8 ILM 679, (1969). Section 3 on Interpretation of Treaties. Article 31–33. Art 31 general rules of interpretation, 32 supplementary means, 33, authenticated languages texts. For an overview of means of interpretation in Article 31 and 32 VCLT see, Mark E. Villiger, 'The Rules on Interpretation: Misgivings, Misunderstandings, Miscarriage? The "Crucible" Intended by the International Law Commission', in *The Law of Treaties beyond the Vienna Convention* (Enzo Cannizzaro et al. eds., 2011). And, Luigi Sbolci, 'Supplementary Means of Interpretation', in *The Law of Treaties beyond the Vienna Convention* (Enzo Cannizzaro et al. eds., 2011).

26 UNFCCC, Article 7.2, *The Conference of the Parties, as the Supreme Body of This Convention, Shall Keep under Regular Review the Implementation of the Convention and Any Related Legal Instruments That the Conference of the Parties May Adopt, and Shall Make,*

within Its Mandate, the Decisions Necessary to Promote the Effective Implementation of the Convention.

27 E. Pache, On the Compatibility with Legal Provisions of Including Greenhouse Gas Emissions from International Aviation in the EU Emission Allowance Trading Scheme as a Result of the Proposed Changes to the EU Emission Allowance Trading Directive. 2008. 5.

28 Claybourne Fox Clarke and Thiago Chagas, 'Aviation and Climate Change Regulation', in *Legal Aspects of Carbon Trading: Kyoto, Copenhagen, and Beyond* (David Freestone and Charlotte Streck eds., 2009). 616.

29 Case-366/10. Opinion of Advocate General Kokott delivered on 6 October 2011.

30 Brian F. Havel and John Q. Mulligan, 'The Triumph of Politics: Reflections on the Judgment of the Court of Justice of the European Union Validating the Inclusion of Non-EU Airlines in the Emissions Trading Scheme', *Air and Space Law*, 37(1), (2012). 25. As they state, *While These Observations Do Suggest That It May Not Have been a Good Idea for the KP Parties to Assign Airline Emission Exclusively to ICAO, They Do Not Persuasively Demonstrate That Exclusive Assignment Is Not What the Kyoto Parties Intended: The Use of the Word 'Shall', in Particular, Certainly Implies That the Assignment to ICAO Was Not Intended as Casually as the Advocate General Appears to Believe.*

31 See: FCCC/AGBM/1997/7 13 October 1997. Consolidated negotiating text by the Chairman. It was based on the work of the 7th meeting of the Ad hoc Group of the Berlin Mandate, reflecting parties' preferences and a compromise text envisioned by the Chairman.

32 For a drafting history of article 2.2, see: Depledge, Joanna (2000). 'Tracing the Origins of the Kyoto Protocol: An Article.' Textual History. Technical Paper. UNFCCC. UN Doc. FCCC/TP/2000/2 25 November 2000. 27.

33 Joanna Depledge, 'Tracing the Origins of the Kyoto Protocol: An Article-Byarticle Textual History. Prepared under Contract to UNFCCC by Joanna Depledge August 1999/August 2000. UN Doc. FCCC/TP/2000/2, 25 November 2000', (2000). 27.

34 Verki Michael Tunteng, *Legal Analysis on the Inclusion of Civil Aviation in the European Union Emissions Trading System* (Faculty of Law. McGill University, 2012). 8–9.

35 Sebastian Oberthür and Hermann Ott, *The Kyoto Protocol: International Climate Policy for the 21st Century* (Springer, 1999). 112.

36 Farhana Yamin and Joanna Depledge, *The International Climate Change Regime: A Guide to Rules, Institutions and Procedures* (Cambridge University Press, 2004). 85.

37 Ibid. at. 85.

38 See, Chapter 1.

39 Scott Barrett, 'A Portfolio System of Climate Treaties', in *Post-Kyoto International Climate Policy: Implementing Architectures for Agreement: Research from the Harvard Project on International Climate Agreements* (Joseph E. Aldy et al. eds., 2010). 249–251.

40 Kati Kulovesi, 'Make Your Own Special Song, Even if Nobody Else Sings Along: International Aviation Emissions and the EU Emissions Trading Scheme', *University of Eastern Finland Legal Studies Research Paper No. 1*, (2011). 17.

41 F. Yamin and J. Depledge, *The International Climate Change Regime: A Guide to Rules, Institutions and Procedures.* (2004); K. Kulovesi, (2011).

42 Such explanations can be offered with regards to the legality under international law of the EU's regulation of emissions from aviation.

43 Case-366/10. Opinion of Advocate General Kokott delivered on 6th October 2011. However, the Court did not enter to value the claim in this point.

44 Ibid. at. 174–188.

45 Case C-366/10, (Court of Justice of the European Union).

46 See, Coraline Goron, 'The EU Aviation ETS Caught between Kyoto and Chicago: Unilateral Legal Entrepreneurship in the Multilateral Governance System', Green-Gem Doctoral Working Papers Series, (2012). 19. Also, B.F.a.M. Havel, John Q., (2012). 24–27.

47 See discussion in Yubing Shi, 'Greenhouse Gas Emissions from International Shipping: The Response from China's Shipping Industry to the Regulatory Initiatives of the International Maritime Organization', *International Journal of Marine and Coastal Law*, 29(1), (2014). 4–7. Also, James Harrison, 'Recent Developments and Continuing Challenges in the Regulation of Greenhouse Gas Emissions from International Shipping', *University of Edinburgh School of Law Research Paper 2012/12*, (2012). 3–9.

48 The industry has been especially vocal in this connection. See the IATA statement at the 35th ICAO Assembly. IATA, 'A35-WP/85. Working Paper. Aviation and Climate Change. Presented by the International Air Transport Association (IATA)', (2004). *While the Kyoto Protocol Recognises That ICAO Is the Appropriate Body to Address Aviation Emissions, It Should be Noted That ICAO's Authority in This Regard Does Not Derive from the Kyoto Protocol, Nor Does the Kyoto Protocol Limit ICAO's Authority: ICAO Has Its Own Independent Competence Deriving from the Chicago Convention That Has been Interpreted to Encompass the Environmental Aspects of Aviation: ICAO Has Indeed Established Standards, Recommended Practices and Policies Related to the Environmental Aspects of Aviation for Over 25 Years.*

49 S. Oberthür, (2003). 195.

50 ICAO, Assembly Resolution A33–7: Consolidated Statement of Continuing ICAO Policies and Practices Related to Environmental Protection. Appendix I, (2001).

51 ICAO, Assembly Resolution A35–5: Consolidated Statement of Continuing ICAO Policies and Practices Related to Environmental Protection, (2004).

52 ICAO, Assembly Resolution A37–19: Consolidated Statement of Continuing ICAO Policies and Practices related to Environmental Protection. Climate Change, (2010).

53 IMO Convention Articles 1(a) and 64.

54 United Nations Convention on the Law of the Sea, Montego Bay, adopted 10 December 1982, in force 16 November 1994, 21 International Legal Materials (1982), 1261. 1833 UNTS 3, (1982). Articles 211–212 See Chapter 3

55 IMO, MARPOL Resolution 8 (1997) on 'CO$_2$ Emissions from Ships' (1997), which requested the IMO to work on the study of GHG emissions.

56 IMO, Assembly Resolution A.963(23) on IMO Policies and Practices Related to the Reduction of Greenhouse Gas Emissions from Ships, (2004).

57 ICAO, Assembly Resolution A31–11 (1995). And ICAO, Assembly Resolution A35–5, (2004).

58 S. Oberthür, (2003).

59 Here the term 'competence' means the legal ability 'ratione materiae' and the term 'powers' is used to allude to the means to exercise that competence. See further explanations on, Henry G. Schermers and Niels Blokker, *International Institutional Law: Unity within Diversity* (Martinus Nijhoff Publishers 5th rev. ed., 2011). 155–162.

60 Ibid. at. 158.

61 This functional necessity approach or functionalism is confronted and complemented with constitutionalism, the second mainstream approach towards exploring the limits of powers in international organizations. For an overview, see Jan Klabbers, 'Contending Approaches to International Organization: Between Functionalism and Constitutionalism', in *Research Handbook on the Law of International Organizations: Research Handbooks in International Law* (Jan Klabbers and Åsa Wallendahl eds., 2011). 3–29.

62 ICJ Report 1996, Advisory Opinion on nuclear weapons and WHO 78, 25.

63 ICJ Reports 1949, 174 at 180.

64 Ian Brownlie, *Principles of Public International Law* (Oxford University Press 7th ed., 2008). 679–686

65 See chapter three.

66 See, status of ratification at the UNFCCC website: https://unfccc.int/kyoto_protocol/status_of_ratification/items/2613.php (last accessed December 2016).

67 See, status of ratification at the UNFCCC website: http://unfccc.int/kyoto_protocol/doha_amendment/items/7362.php (last accessed December 2016).
68 E. Pache, On the Compatibility with Legal Provisions of Including Greenhouse Gas Emissions from International Aviation in the EU Emission Allowance Trading Scheme as a Result of the Proposed Changes to the EU Emission Allowance Trading Directive. 2008. 1. '*contains an instruction to the Signatory states to take action*'.
69 The most significant case is the United States.
70 Annex B was modified in Doha with new commitments for the second period of Kyoto (2013–2020). Together with the lack of ratification of the KP from the United States, the withdrawal of Canada from the second period is to be noted.
71 This issue will be further developed in Chapter 5.
72 ILC, *Fragmentation of International Law: Difficulties Arising from the Diversification and Expansion of International Law. Report of the Study Group of the International Law Commission.* UN Doc. A/CN.4/L.682, (2006). Paragraph 267. On conflict clauses see further chapter six.
73 For a complete classification see, ibid. at. Paragraph 268.
74 Ibid. at. Paragraphs 269–271.
75 Harro van Asselt, *The Fragmentation of Global Climate Governance: Consequences and Management of Regime Interactions* (Vrije Universiteit, 2013). 86.
76 The list includes UNFCCC and KP provisions related to the Montréal Protocol, Article 2.1 (a) (ii) KP on '*do not implement climate policies that frustrate the objective of other environmental agreements*'; that is, CBD, UNCDD and the Ramsar Convention on Wetlands, art 2.3 KP and art 3.5 UNFCCC in connection to WTO. See, Harro van Asselt, 'Dealing with the Fragmentation of Global Climate Governance: Legal and Political Approaches in Interplay Management', Global Governance Working Paper No. 30, (2007). While the conflict clauses related to the Montréal Protocol establish a clear division, '*less clear and more contested is the conflict clause character*' of the other articles. In, Harro van Asselt, 'Managing the Fragmentation of International Climate Law', in *Climate Change and the Law* (Erkki J. Hollo et al. eds., 2013). 343–344.
77 H.v. Asselt, 'Managing the Fragmentation of International Climate Law'. (2013). 344.
78 Sebastian Oberthür, 'The Climate Change Regime: Interactions of the Climate Change Regime with ICAO, IMO and the EU Burden-Sharing Agreement', in *Institutional Interaction in Global Environmental Governance: Synergy and Conflict among International and EU Policies: Global Environmental Accord: Strategies for Sustainability and Institutional Innovation* (Sebastian Oberthür and Thomas Gehring eds., 2006).
79 See further Chapter 6.
80 ILC Report (2006) paragraph 272.
81 H.v. Asselt, 'Managing the Fragmentation of International Climate Law'. (2013). 344.
82 Some authors have pointed in this direction, for example, Steven Truxal, 'The ICAO Assembly Resolutions on International Aviation and Climate Change: Historic Agreement, Breakthrough Deal and the Cancun Effect', *Air & Space Law*, 36(3), 217, (2011). 226–230; Ruwantissa Abeyratne, 'Outcome of the 37th Session of the ICAO Assembly', *Air and Space Law*, 36(1), (2011). 20–22.
83 ICAO has established multiple SARPS on environmental related matters for 60 years and the IMO has adopted around 23 environmental instruments since its inception.
84 E. Pache, On the Compatibility with Legal Provisions of Including Greenhouse Gas Emissions from International Aviation in the EU Emission Allowance Trading Scheme as a Result of the Proposed Changes to the EU Emission Allowance Trading Directive. 2008. 5. Other scholars have also posited that '*the improvement of the institutional framework to tackle climate change should be at the forefront of the international negotiations*' See, Massimiliano Montini, 'Reshaping Climate Governance for Post-2012', *European Journal of Legal Studies*, 4(1), (2011). 9.

85 See, Olivier Onidi, 'A Critical Perspective on ICAO', *A Critical Perspective on ICAO, Air & Space Law*, 33(1), (2008). 42. He argues that, given developments in recent years, both aspects are not to be pursued further by ICAO; first, market aspects of air services, which find a better forum in WTO. Second, climate change issues, which should return to the climate umbrella.

86 Markus W. Gehring and Cairo A. R. Robb, 'Addressing the Aviation and Climate Change Challenge: A Review of Options', *ICTSD Programme on Trade and Environment: Trade and Sustainable Energy Series*, (2013).

87 Transport and Environment, *FAQ: Bunker Emissions at Copenhagen December 2009*. (2009). 2.

88 C. Goron, (2012).

89 IMO website. Introduction. Available at: www.imo.org/About/Pages/Default.aspx

90 Adoption of the EEDI Index in IMO was done through voting and the agreement on MBMs in ICAO was done in extremis, by consensus.

91 See, M.A. Young, *Trading Fish, Saving Fish: The Interaction between Regimes in International Law* (2011). 85–133.

92 On the regimes membership see, chapter three.

93 See, M.W. Gehring and C.A.R. Robb, (2013).

94 See, ibid. at. 28. For an explanation on external and internal competence in the EU see, Elisa Morgera, 'Introduction to European Environmental Law from an International Environmental Law Perspective', *Edinburgh Europa Paper Series*, (2012). On EU and international institutions see also, Bart Van Vooren and Ramses A. Wessel, *EU External Relations Law: Text, Cases and Materials*. Cambridge University Press (2013). 246–275. See also Chapter 3.

95 See Young's proposal for a legal framework for interaction, M.A. Young, *Trading Fish, Saving Fish: The Interaction between Regimes In International Law*. (2011). 267–287.

96 Ibid. at. 269.

97 Sebastian Oberthür, 'Institutional Interaction to Address Greenhouse Gas Emissions from International Transport: ICAO, IMO and the EU Burden-Sharing Agreement', *Project Deliverable No. D 3, Final Draft: Ecologic – Institute for International and European Policy*, (2003). And S. Oberthür, 'The Climate Change Regime: Interactions of the Climate Change Regime with ICAO, IMO and the EU Burden-Sharing Agreement'. (2006). 61.

98 In 1996 ICAO requested the IPCC to produce a special report on aviation and the global atmosphere. Joyce E. Penner et al., *Aviation and the Global Atmosphere: A Special Report of IPCC Working Groups I and III in Collaboration with the Scientific Assessment Panel to the Montreal Protocol on Substances That Deplete the Ozone Layer* (Cambridge University Press, 1999).

99 See, J. Depledge, (2000). 27; Michael Grubb et al., *The Kyoto Protocol: A Guide and Assessment* (Energy and Environmental Programme ed., Royal Institute of International Affairs, 1999); S. Oberthür and H. Ott, *The Kyoto Protocol: International Climate Policy for the 21st Century*. (1999).

100 S. Oberthür, (2003). 5.

101 See Chapter 2.

102 Disruptive is used as opposed to synergistic. See typology of interactions in chapter two.

103 S. Oberthür, 'The Climate Change Regime: Interactions of the Climate Change Regime with ICAO, IMO and the EU Burden-Sharing Agreement'. (2006); S. Oberthür, (2003). 5.

104 S. Oberthür, 'The Climate Change Regime: Interactions of the Climate Change Regime with ICAO, IMO and the EU Burden-Sharing Agreement'. (2006). 67.

105 Dunoff's theory has been referred in Chapter 2.

106 See Chapter 2 for a discussion about the value of intentional and unintentional interaction.

107 A definition and characterization of regulatory and administrative interaction has been established in Chapter 2.

108 Daniel Blobel et al., *United Nations Framework Convention on Climate Change: Handbook* (Intergovernmental and Legal Affairs, Climate Change Secretariat, 2006). 186.

109 See for example statements made by ICAO and IMO to the SBSTA, AWG-LCA and COP. For example, ICAO at the SBSTA3. UN Doc. FCCC/SBSTA/1996/13, Paragraph 61, (1996). ICAO delivered a statement in which the organization indicated its willingness to support the IPCC in the development of a special report on aviation, if the IPCC would prepare such a report for the SBSTA. The Chairman of the SBSTA noted the significance of such a report and indicated that he would bring this to the attention of the IPCC. Other examples are found at FCCC/SBSTA/1997/14, paragraph 12, (1997). FCCC/SBSTA/2006/5*; SBSTA24, (2006). Paragraph 71, FCCC/SBSTA/2007/4; SBSTA 26, (2007). Paragraph 67, FCCC/SBSTA/2008/6; SBSTA28, (2008). Paragraph 114; also, FCCC/SBSTA/2008/13; SBSTA29, (2009). Paragraph 68; FCCC/SBSTA/2009/3; SBSTA30, (2009).

110 Decision 4/CP.1 Methodological issues UN Doc. FCCC/CP/1995/7/Add.1, (1995). Paragraph 1.f. *'That the Subsidiary Body for Scientific and Technological Advice and the Subsidiary Body for Implementation, taking fully into account ongoing work in Governments and international organizations, including the International Maritime Organization and the International Civil Aviation Organization, address the issue of the allocation and control of emissions from international bunker fuels, and report on this work to the Conference of the Parties at its second session'.* Together with the issues on cooperation, the same decision provided for the SBSTA to address emissions from IBF, including options for the allocation of emissions, reporting requirements for parties and methodological issues regarding data collection and reporting.

111 Decision 18/CP.5 Emissions Based Upon Fuel Sold to Ships and Aircraft Engaged in International Transport. UN Doc. FCCC/CP/1999/6/Add.1, (1999). Paragraph 3. *'Request the Secretariat to continue to develop its cooperation with the Secretariats of the International Civil Aviation Organization and the International Maritime Organization and participate in their meetings on climate change related issues.'*

112 Ibid. at. Paragraph 3.

113 See for instance, ICAO contributed with a technical paper upon the request of SBSTA. FCCC/TP/2003/3 Compilation of Data on Emissions from International Aviation, (2003).

114 *'The SBSTA invites the secretariats of ICAO and IMO to continue to report, at future sessions of the SBSTA, on relevant work on this issue.'* See, FCCC/SBSTA/2005/MISC.4; SBSTA 22, May 2005. Compilation of data on emissions from international aviation. Submission from the International Civil Aviation Organization, (2005). FCCC/SBSTA/2010/MISC.5; SBSTA 32, June 2010. Information relevant to emissions from fuel used for international aviation and maritime transport. Submissions from international organizations, (2010). FCCC/SBSTA/2010/MISC.14; SBSTA 33, December 2010. Information relevant to emissions from fuel used for international aviation and maritime transport. Submissions from international organizations, (2010). FCCC/SBSTA/2011/MISC.5; SBSTA 34, June 2011. Information relevant to emissions from fuel used for international aviation and maritime transport. Submissions from international organizations, (2011). FCCC/SBSTA/2011/MISC.9; SBSTA 35, December 2011. Information relevant to emissions from fuel used for international aviation and maritime transport. Submissions from international organizations., (2011);FCCC/SBSTA/2012/MISC.7; SBSTA 36, May 2012. Information relevant to emissions from fuel used for international aviation and maritime transport. Submissions from international organizations., (2012). FCCC/SBSTA/2012/MISC.20; SBSTA 37, December 2012. Information relevant to emissions from fuel used for international aviation and maritime transport. Submissions from international organizations., (2012). FCCC/SBSTA/2013/MISC.20; SBSTA 39, December 2013.

Information relevant to emissions from fuel used for international aviation and maritime transport. Submissions from international organizations., (2013).

115 FCCC/SBSTA/2001/8 Paragraph 19 (f), (2001). Invitation recalled at the FCCC/SBSTA/2002/6, (2002). Paragraph 52 (c).

116 FCCC/SBSTA/2003/INF.3, (2003).

117 FCCC/SBSTA/2004/INF.5, (2004).

118 ICAO, Statement from the International Civil Aviation Organization (ICAO) to the Sixth Session of the Ad Hoc Working Group on Long-Term Cooperative Action under the Convention (AWG-LCA6) (Bonn, Germany, 1 to 12 June 2009). (2009).

119 FCCC/SBSTA/2001/INF.1; SBSTA 14. Reports on Intersessional Activities. Emissions resulting from fuel used for international transportation, (2001). paragraph 22.

120 See, ICAO, Assembly Resolution A37-19 (2010). Among others, the Council is requested to report and advise the climate regime on limitation and reduction options and to continue to cooperate with organizations involved in policy-making in this field, namely the UNFCCC.

121 S. Oberthür, (2003). 200–202.

122 Ibid. at. 201.

123 Ibid.

124 J. Dunoff, 'A New Approach to Regime Interaction'. (2012). 163–166. See, chapter two.

125 Some examples are the Joint United Nations Programme on HIV/AIDS (UNAIDS), a joint venture of a number of sponsors such as UNICEF, UNHCR, UNDP, ILO, UNESCO, WHO. A second example is the Collaborative Partnership on Forests (CPF) where various international organizations such as FAO, UNDP, UNEP, World Bank, and UNFCCC organize and complement efforts.

126 J. Dunoff, 'A New Approach to Regime Interaction'. (2012). 166.

127 These projects are executed by ICAO and IMO respectively, in partnership with the UNDP with the financial support from the GEF.

128 GEF Project Concept number 5054 runs under the rubric *"Transforming The Global Aviation Sector: Emissions Reductions From International Aviation"*.

129 GEF. Project Identification Form. Transforming the Global Maritime Transport Industry towards a Low Carbon Future through Improved Energy Efficiency. GEF Project ID:1 5508.

130 There is currently no internationally agreed-upon definition of 'climate finance'. J. Pickering et al., 'Splitting the Difference in Global Climate Finance: Are Fragmentation and Legitimacy Mutually Exclusive?', CCEP Working Paper 1308, November 2013: Crawford School of Public Policy, Australian National University, (2013). 4. The definition is taken from Martin Stadelmann et al., (2013) Difficulties in accounting for private finance in international climate policy, Climate Policy, 13:6, 718–737.

131 For an updated account of climate finance, see 'Final draft Report, dated 17 December 2013, of the Working Group III contribution to the IPCC 5th Assessment Report "Climate Change 2014: Mitigation of Climate Change"', (2014). and Anke Herold et al., 'The Development of Climate Negotiations in View of Warsaw (COP 19): Study Requested by the EU Directorate General for Internal Policies: Policy Department A: Economic and Scientific Policy', (2013). 50–56. In this connection, finance is a key issue in the implementation of the PA.

132 The GEF was created in 1991 by the World Bank in partnership with UNEP and UNDP. It was later amended in 1994 and became an independent institution.

133 For a summary on the UNFCCC's financial mechanism see, Benito Müller Luis Gomez-Echeverri, 'The Financial Mechanism of the UNFCCC: A Brief History', *The Oxford Institute for Energy Studies. ECBI Policy Brief*, (2009).

134 It is funded from the adaptation levy charged for CDM projects.

135 J. Dunoff, 'A New Approach to Regime Interaction'. (2012). 166.

136 S. Oberthür, 'The Climate Change Regime: Interactions of the Climate Change Regime with ICAO, IMO and the EU Burden-Sharing Agreement'. (2006).

137 *'Financing is make or break'* Statement on GHG Issues by the observers of IUCN. IMO MEPC 59, closing plenary, 17 July 2009 (Response to J10 paper & GHG debate; reproduced in the session report MEPC 59/24/Add.1), (2009). Daniel S. Hall et al., 'Policies for Developing Country Engagement', *Discussion Paper 08–15, Harvard Project on International Climate Agreements, Belfer Center for Science and International Affairs, Harvard Kennedy School*, (2008). 25.

138 See for example the Statement of the UN Secretary General at the latest COP 19 in Warsaw. Available at: http://climate-l.iisd.org/news/un-secretary-general-stresses-importance-of-climate-finance/

139 Laurence Boisson de Chazournes, 'Climate Change and Financial Assistance: A Fragmented, Unified or Coordinated Approach?', in *International Law and Developing Countries: Essays in Honour of Kamal Hossain* (P. Sands et al. eds., 2014). 126–152.

140 Namely CDM and the Climate Investment Funds, i.e. excluding neither the Clean Technology Fund nor the Strategic Climate Fund since international aviation was excluded from the Kyoto Protocol.

141 ICAO website. Available at: www.icao.int/environmental-protection/Pages/financing.aspx

142 *'Although international aviation is prepared to implement measures for reducing its climate change impact, it should not be singled out or treated in a discriminatory manner. Any aviation financing mechanism should primarily serve the interests of the sector. This would ensure equity and non-discrimination since international aviation would be responsible for its real impact on climate change.'* Furthermore, *'ICAO is the appropriate institution to deal with aviation financing, as it can adapt the financial instruments to aviation specific goals and at the same time assist developing countries, not only financially, but also through technology transfer and capacity building,'* ICAO website. www.icao.int/environmental-protection/Pages/financing.aspx.

143 MEPC 59/24 (2009).

144 UN, Report of the Secretary-General's High-level Advisory Group on Climate Change Financing. Work Stream 2: Paper on Potential Revenues from International Maritime and Aviation Sector Policy Measures. (2010).

145 See Chapter 3. The objective of action plans is also to assess progress towards countries achieving their aspirational goals and preferred measures. See, ICAO, Assembly Resolution A37–19 (2010). The action plans were envisioned as a tool for States to communicate with ICAO but also as a way for States to identify actions to tackle their aviation emissions. Reiterated in the 38th Assembly. ICAO, Assembly Resolution A38–18: Consolidated Statement of Continuing ICAO Policies and Practices Related to Environmental Protection – Climate Change (2013).

146 The Assembly built upon the recommendations of the HLM-ENV/09 with regards to technical and financial assistance to developing countries for the reporting processes and facilitation of *'access to financial resources, technology transfer and capacity building.'* Recommendations 14 and 7, respectively. See ICAO, HLM-ENV/09-SD/2. Apendix B. High-level Meeting on International Aviation and Climate Change, Montréal, 7 to 9 October 2009. Summary of Discussions (2009). The 38th Assembly asked to further submit state action plans before 2015.

147 ICAO, Assembly Resolution A37–19 (2010). Paragraph 9. The Assembly *'encourages States to submit their action plans outlining their respective policies and actions, and annual reporting on international aviation CO₂ emissions to ICAO.'*

148 Ibid. at. Paragraph 10 invites those States that choose to prepare their action plans to reflect *'their respective national capacities and circumstances, and information on any specific assistance needs'.* Action plans have been regarded as a shift in ICAO's approach to implementation. In other words, *'the delivery of action plans is the first opportunity offered to States to support in concrete terms the implementation of the agreement which was*

reached in ICAO, and to showcase their actions and their own strategy'. Patrick Gandil, DGCA France. 2011.

149 Ibid. at. Paragraph 22. Action plans mean a shift in ICAO's from 'standard policy setting' to an 'implementation mode' or, in other words, the delivery of action plans is the first opportunity offered to States to support in concrete terms the implementation of the agreement which was reached in ICAO, and to showcase their actions and their own strategy.

150 The project, named '*Capacity building for CO$_2$ mitigation from international aviation*' started in January 2014. Negotiations between the EU and ICAO were launched on this assistance project to mitigate emissions from aviation in developing countries, through capacity building. The project specifically targets countries within Africa and the Caribbean area. Beneficiary countries need to be from the African and Caribbean ICAO regions and fulfil two more requirements: to agree to elaborate an ICAO State Action Plan and to have requested ICAO for assistance to do so. The fourteen chosen countries are: Dominican Republic, Trinidad and Tobago, Kenya, Burkina Faso, Angola, Burundi, Cameroon, Central African Republic, Chad, Republic of the Congo, DR Congo, Equatorial Guinea, Gabon and São Tomé and Príncipe. It focuses on the development of reporting programmes, infrastructure and reductions of fuel consumption, through ICAO's State Action Plans on emissions reductions. The EU has pledged financing of €6.5 million over a period of 3.5 years.

151 The Concept Document UNEP 5254.

152 Project Concept number 5054 entitled *"Transforming The Global Aviation Sector: Emissions Reductions From International Aviation"*.

153 See, GEF. Available at: www.thegef.org/gef/project_detail?projID=5450. The GEF Council is in charge of the approval of new projects. It meets twice a year.

154 The grant from GEF is 2 million USD while the entire project costs 10.3 million USD, with co-financing totalling 8.3 million USD.

155 Support provided by the GEF is available in three main categories of projects, namely: full size projects, medium-sized projects and the so-called enabling activities.

156 GEF. Project Identification Form. Transforming the Global Aviation Sector: Emissions Reductions from International Aviation. GEF Project ID:1 5450.

157 The role and value of this project in achieving a final agreement for the CORSIA has been highlighted by Jane Hupe, the chief of the Environmental Unit at ICAO at the COP 22 aviation side event *Climate Action Takes Flight*, which the author attended.

158 Through the UNEP, UNDP and the World Bank. See WCTRS and ITPS, 2003 in Werner Rothengatter, 'Climate Change and the Contribution of Transport: Basic Facts and the Role of Aviation', *Transportation Research Part D: Transport and Environment*, 15(1), (2010). 9.

159 Presentation by GEF and ICAO – side event COP19 Warsaw.

160 Ibid.

161 MEPC.203(62) on Amendments to the annex of the protocol of 1997 to amend the international convention for the prevention of pollution from ships, 1973, as modified by the protocol of 1978 relating thereto (Inclusion of regulations on energy efficiency for ships in MARPOL Annex VI) Adopted 15 July 2011 . (2011). See chapter three.

162 IMO, MEPC.229(65) on Promotion of Technical Co-operation and Transfer of Technology Relating to the Improvement of Energy Efficiency of Ships (2013).

163 GEF. Project Identification Form. Transforming the Global Maritime Transport Industry towards a Low Carbon Future through Improved Energy Efficiency. GEF Project ID:1 5508.

164 Ibid.

165 Implementation is foreseen for the end of 2014, after the detailed project implementation document prepared by the IMO Secretariat get approved by the GEF.

166 See, IMO, Update on IMO's Work to Address Emissions from Fuel Used for International Shipping. Note by the International Maritime Organization to the fortieth session of the Subsidiary Body for Scientific and Technological Advice (SBSTA 40) Bonn, Germany, 4 to 15 June 2014. Agenda item 11(c) Emissions from fuel used for international aviation and maritime transport (2014). paragraph 28.

167 See, ibid. at. Paragraph 27.

168 See, ibid. at. Paragraph 28.

169 The GEF/UNDP/IMO Regional Programme on the Prevention and Management of Marine Pollution in the East Asian Seas, in particular pertaining to the identification of land and sea-based sources of pollution in Malaysia.

170 The GEF/UNDP/IMO GloBallast Partnerships Project assists developing countries and their maritime industries to implement international regulations on ballast water management to prevent the spread of alien invasive species. See a full description in, United Nations Development Programme and Global Environmental Facility, Catalysing Ocean Finance Volume II Methodologies and Case Studies, (2012). 69–73.

171 Andrew Hudson, Greening the Shipping sector through the GEF-UNDP-IMO Globallast Programme – A Model for GHG Reduction in Shipping and Aviation? (2012).

172 There is arguably a learning process between ICAO and the IMO with regards to these initiatives.

173 See further at EU website: http://capacity4dev.ec.europa.eu/climate-mitigation-in-the-maritime-shipping-industry/

174 Side Event COP 19.

175 See, J. Dunoff, 'A New Approach to Regime Interaction'. (2012). 166. Case of HIV/AIDS.

176 Which also entail conceptual interactions, see next section. On CBDRRC see further in Chapter five. See also, Beatriz Martinez Romera and Harro van Asselt, 'The International Regulation of Aviation Emissions: Putting Differential Treatment into Practice', *Journal of Environmental Law*, 25(2) (2015). 259–283.

177 For an insight on financial and technology assistance in environmental law, see Laurence Boisson de Chazournes, 'Technical and Financial Assistance', in *The Oxford Handbook of International Environmental Law: Oxford Handbooks* (Daniel Bodansky et al. eds., 2007).

178 See, L. Boisson de Chazournes, 'Climate Change and Financial Assistance: A Fragmented, Unified or Coordinated Approach?'. (2014).

179 See, ibid.

180 See Jon Hovi et al., *Implementing the Climate Regime: International Compliance* (Earthscan, 2005); Ibid. at. 8–9. 'the main international instrument for capacity enhancement.'

181 GEF Instrument, Paragraph 9th: '(a) *GEF grants that are made available within the framework of the financial mechanisms of the conventions referred to in paragraph 6 shall be in conformity with the eligibility criteria decided by the Conference of the Parties of each convention, as provided under the arrangements or agreements referred to in paragraph 27. (b) All other GEF grants shall be made available to eligible recipient countries and, where appropriate, for other activities promoting the purposes of the Facility in accordance with this paragraph and any additional eligibility criteria determined by the Council. A country shall be an eligible recipient of GEF grants if it is eligible to borrow from the World Bank (IBRD and/or IDA) or if it is an eligible recipient of UNDP technical assistance through its country Indicative Planning Figure (IPF). GEF grants for activities within a focal area addressed by a convention referred to in paragraph 6 but outside the framework of the financial mechanism of the convention, shall only be made available to eligible recipient countries that are party to the convention concerned'*.

182 See the ICAO Fellowship Programme to assist States in developing their safety oversight capabilities or implementing their State Safety Programmes, where priorities for granting fellowships are given to least developed countries according the UNCTAD list.

183 J. Dunoff, 'A New Approach to Regime Interaction'. (2012). 166–173. See also chapter two.
184 Ibid. at. 167. referring to the work of Andrew Lang among others.
185 See UNFCCC website: http://unfccc.int/methods/emissions_from_intl_transport/items/1057.php

Bibliography

Abeyratne, Ruwantissa (2011). 'Outcome of the 37th Session of the ICAO Assembly', *Air and Space Law*, 36(1). 7–22.
AGF(2010). UN Report of the Secretary-General's High-Level Advisory Group on Climate Change Financing. Work Stream 2: Paper on Potential Revenues from International Maritime and Aviation Sector Policy Measures.
Asselt, Harro van (2007). 'Dealing with the Fragmentation of Global Climate Governance: Legal and Political Approaches in Interplay Management', Global Governance Working Paper No. 30.
Asselt, Harro van (2013). 'Managing the Fragmentation of International Climate Law', in, Erkki J. Hollo, Kati Kulovesi and Michael Mehling (eds.), Ius Gentium: Comparative Perspective on Law and Justice v. 21 *Climate Change and the Law*, Dordrecht; New York, Springer.
Asselt, Harro van (2014). *The Fragmentation of Global Climate Governance: Consequences and Management of Regime Interactions*, Cheltenham, UK, Edward Elgar.
Assembly Resolution A31–11. Consolidated Statement of Continuing ICAO Policies and Practices Related to Environmental Protection.
Assembly Resolution A33–7: Consolidated Statement of Continuing ICAO Policies and Practices Related to Environmental Protection: Appendix I.
Assembly Resolution A35–5: Consolidated Statement of Continuing ICAO Policies and Practices Related to Environmental Protection.
Assembly Resolution A37–19: Consolidated Statement of Continuing ICAO Policies and Practices Related to Environmental Protection: Climate Change.
Assembly Resolution A38–18: Consolidated Statement of Continuing ICAO Policies and Practices Related to Environmental Protection: Climate Change.
Assembly Resolution A.963(23) on IMO Policies and Practices Related to the Reduction of Greenhouse Gas Emissions from Ships.
Banu, Sqn Ldr Sabitha (2012). 'Aviation and Climate Change: A Global Sectored Approach Is the Need of the Hour', *International Journal of Low Carbon Technologies*, 7(2), 137–142.
Barrett, Scott (2010). 'A Portfolio System of Climate Treaties', in, Joseph E. Aldy, R.N. Stavins and Harvard Project on International Climate Agreements (eds.), *Post-Kyoto International Climate Policy: Implementing Architectures for Agreement: Research from the Harvard Project on International Climate Agreements*, Cambridge, Cambridge University Press.
Blobel, Daniel, Meyer-Ohlendorf, Nils, Schlosser-Allera, Carmen and Steel, Penny (2006). *United Nations Framework Convention on Climate Change: Handbook*, Bonn, Germany, Intergovernmental and Legal Affairs, Climate Change Secretariat.
Boisson de Chazournes, Laurence (2007). 'Technical and Financial Assistance', in, Daniel Bodansky, Jutta Brunnée and Ellen Hey (eds.), *The Oxford Handbook of International Environmental Law: Oxford Handbooks*, Oxford; New York, Oxford University Press.

Boisson de Chazournes, Laurence (2014). 'Climate Change and Financial Assistance: A Fragmented, Unified or Coordinated Approach?', in, P. Sands, S. Bhuiyan and N. Schrijver (eds.), *International Law and Developing Countries: Essays in Honour of Kamal Hossain*, Leiden, The Netherlands, Martinus Nijhoff Publishers; Brill Academic.

Brownlie, Ian (2008). *Principles of Public International Law*, 7th ed., Oxford; New York, Oxford University Press.

Cariou, Pierre (2011). 'Is Slow Steaming a Sustainable Means of Reducing CO_2 Emissions from Container Shipping?', *Transportation Research Part D: Transport and Environment*, 16(3), 260–264.

Chagas, Thiago and Clarke, Claybourne Fox (2009). 'Aviation and Climate Change Regulation', in, David Freestone and Charlotte Streck (eds.), *Legal Aspects of Carbon Trading: Kyoto, Copenhagen, and Beyond*, Oxford; New York, Oxford University Press.

Decision 4/CP.1 Methodological issues UN Doc. FCCC/CP/1995/7/Add.1.

Decision 18/CP.5 Emissions Based Upon Fuel Sold to Ships and Aircraft Engaged in International Transport. UN Doc. FCCC/CP/1999/6/Add.1.

Depledge, Joanna (2000). 'Tracing the Origins of the Kyoto Protocol: An Article. Technical Paper. UNFCCC. UN Doc. FCCC/TP/2000/2 25 November 2000.

Dunoff, Jeffrey (2012). 'A New Approach to Regime Interaction', in, Margaret A. Young (ed.), *Regime Interaction in International Law: Facing Fragmentation*, Cambridge; New York, Cambridge University Press.

FCCC/SBSTA/1997/14, Paragraph 12.

FCCC/SBSTA/2001/8, Paragraph 19 (f).

FCCC/SBSTA/2001/INF.1; SBSTA 14. Reports on Intersessional Activities. Emissions Resulting from Fuel used for International Transportation.

FCCC/SBSTA/2002/6.

FCCC/SBSTA/2003/INF.3.

FCCC/SBSTA/2004/INF.5.

FCCC/SBSTA/2005/MISC.4; SBSTA 22, May 2005. Compilation of Data on Emissions from International Aviation. Submission from the International Civil Aviation Organization.

FCCC/SBSTA/2006/5*; SBSTA 24.

FCCC/SBSTA/2007/4; SBSTA 26.

FCCC/SBSTA/2008/6; SBSTA 28.

FCCC/SBSTA/2008/13; SBSTA 29.

FCCC/SBSTA/2009/3; SBSTA 30.

FCCC/SBSTA/2010/MISC.5; SBSTA 32, June 2010. Information Relevant to Emissions from Fuel used for International Aviation and Maritime Transport. Submissions from International Organizations.

FCCC/SBSTA/2010/MISC.14; SBSTA 33, December 2010. Information Relevant to Emissions from Fuel used for International Aviation and Maritime Transport. Submissions from International Organizations.

FCCC/SBSTA/2011/MISC.5; SBSTA 34, June 2011. Information Relevant to Emissions from Fuel used for International Aviation and Maritime Transport. Submissions from International Organizations.

FCCC/SBSTA/2011/MISC.9; SBSTA 35, December 2011. Information Relevant to Emissions from Fuel used for International Aviation and Maritime Transport. Submissions from International Organizations.

FCCC/SBSTA/2012/MISC.7; SBSTA 36, May 2012. Information Relevant to Emissions from Fuel used for International Aviation and Maritime Transport. Submissions from International Organizations.

FCCC/SBSTA/2012/MISC.20; SBSTA 37, December 2012. Information Relevant to Emissions from Fuel used for International Aviation and Maritime Transport. Submissions from International Organizations.

FCCC/SBSTA/2013/MISC.20; SBSTA 39, December 2013. Information Relevant to Emissions from Fuel used for International Aviation and Maritime Transport. Submissions from International Organizations.

FCCC/TP/2003/3. Compilation of Data on Emissions from International Aviation.

IPCC (2014). 'Final Draft Report of the Working Group III Contribution to the IPCC 5th Assessment Report "Climate Change 2014: Mitigation of Climate Change"' Chapter 16: Cross-cutting Investment and Finance Issues.

Gehring, Markus W. and Robb, Cairo A.R. (2013). 'Addressing the Aviation and Climate Change Challenge: A Review of Options', *ICTSD Programme on Trade and Environment. Trade and Sustainable Energy Series*.

Gehring, Thomas and Oberthur, Sebastian (2004). 'Exploring Regime Interaction: A Framework of Analysis', in, Arild Underdal and Oran R. Young (eds.), *Regime Consequences: Methodological Challenges and Research Strategies*, Dordrecht, The Netherlands, Kluwer Academic Publishers.

Gomez-Echeverri, Luis and Müller, Benito (2009). 'The Financial Mechanism of the UNFCCC: A Brief History', *The Oxford Institute for Energy Studies. ECBI Policy Brief*.

Goron, Coraline (2012). 'The EU Aviation ETS Caught between Kyoto and Chicago: Unilateral Legal Entrepreneurship in the Multilateral Governance System', Green-Gem Doctoral Working Papers Series.

Grant-Smith, Deanna (2013). Book Review. 'Maritime Transport and the Climate Change Challenge', *Australian Planner* 51, 362–363.

Grubb, Michael, Vrolijk, Christiaan and Brack, Duncan (1999). *The Kyoto Protocol: A Guide and Assessment*, Energy and Environmental Programme (ed.), London; Washington, DC, Royal Institute of International Affairs.

Hall, Daniel S., Levi, Michael, Pizer, William A. and Ueno, Takahiro (2008). 'Policies for Developing Country Engagement', *Discussion Paper 08–15, Harvard Project on International Climate Agreements, Belfer Center for Science and International Affairs, Harvard Kennedy School*.

Hanson, Susan and Nicholls, Robert J. (2012). 'Extreme Flood Events and Port Cities Trough the Twenty-First Century: Implications of Climate Change and Other Drivers', in, R. Asariotis and Hassiba Benamara (eds.), *Maritime Transport and the Climate Change Challenge*, 1st ed., New York, Earthscan.

Harrison, James (2012). 'Recent Developments and Continuing Challenges in the Regulation of Greenhouse Gas Emissions from International Shipping', *University of Edinburgh School of Law Research Paper 2012/12*.

Havel, Brian F. and Mulligan, John Q. (2012). 'The Triumph of Politics: Reflections on the Judgment of the Court of Justice of the European Union Validating the Inclusion of Non-EU Airlines in the Emissions Trading Scheme', *Air and Space Law*, 37(1), 3–33.

Herold, Anke, Cames, Martin, Siemons, Anne, Emele, Lukas and Cook, Vanessa (2013). 'The Development of Climate Negotiations in View of Warsaw (COP 19). Study Requested by the EU Directorate General for Internal Policies. Policy Department A: Economic and Scientific Policy'.

HLM-ENV/09-SD/2. Apendix B. High-Level Meeting on International Aviation and Climate Change, Montréal, 7–9 October 2009. Summary of Discussions.

Hovi, Jon, Stokke, Olav and Ulfstein, Geir (2005). *Implementing the Climate Regime: International Compliance*, London; Sterling, VA, Earthscan.

IATA (2004). 'A35-WP/85. Working Paper: Aviation and Climate Change. Presented by the International Air Transport Association (IATA)'.

ICAO. Environment Branch of ICAO (2010). *ICAO Environmental Report 2010: Aviation and Climate Change*, Montreal, ICAO.

ILC (2006). *Fragmentation of International Law: Difficulties Arising from the Diversification and Expansion of International Law: Report of the Study Group of the International Law Commission.* UN Doc. A/CN.4/L.682.

IMO (2014). Update on IMO's Work to Address Emissions from Fuel Used for International Shipping. Note by the IMO to the 40th Session of the Subsidiary Body for Scientific and Technological Advice, Bonn, Germany, 4–15 June 2014. Agenda Item 11(c) Emissions from Fuel Used for International Aviation and Maritime Transport.

Kahn Ribeiro, S., Kobayashi, S., Beuthe, M., Gasca, J., Greene, D., Lee, D.S., Muromachi, Y., Newton, P.J., Plotkin, S., Sperling, D., Wit, R. and Zhou, P.J. (2007). *Transport and Its Infrastructure: In Climate Change 2007: Mitigation: Contribution of Working Group III to the Fourth Assessment Report of the Intergovernmental Panel on Climate Change*, O.R. Davidson, B. Metz, P.R. Bosch, R. Dave, L.A. Meyer (eds.), Cambridge, UK; New York, Cambridge University Press.

Klabbers, Jan (2011). 'Contending Approaches to International Organization: Between Functionalism and Constitutionalism', in, Jan Klabbers and Åsa Wallendahl (eds.), *Research Handbook on the Law of International Organizations: Research Handbooks in International Law*, Cheltenham; Northampton, MA, Edward Elgar.

Kulovesi, Kati (2011). '"Make Your Own Special Song, Even If Nobody Else Sings Along": International Aviation Emissions and the EU Emissions Trading Scheme', Climate Law, 2(4) 535–558.

Lindstad, Haakon, Asbjørnslett, Bjørn E. and Strømman, Anders H. (2011). 'Reductions in Greenhouse Gas Emissions and Cost by Shipping at Lower Speeds', *Energy Policy*, 39(6), 3456–3464.

Liu, Miaojia and Kronbak, Jacob (2010). 'The Potential Economic Viability of Using the Northern Sea Route (NSR) as an Alternative Route between Asia and Europe', *Journal of Transport Geography*, 18(3), 434–444.

MARPOL Resolution 8 (1997) on 'CO$_2$ Emissions from Ships'.

Martinez Romera, Beatriz and Asselt, Harro van (2015). 'The International Regulation of Aviation Emissions: Putting Differential Treatment into Practice', *Journal of Environmental Law*, 27(2) 259–283.

Mayer, Benoit (2012). 'Case C-366/10, Air Transport Association of America and Others v. Secretary of State for Energy and Climate Change, with Annotation by B. Mayer', *Common Market Law Review*, 49(3), 1113–1140.

MEPC 59/24. Report of the Marine Environment Protection Committee on its 59th Session.

MEPC.203(62) on Amendments to the Annex of the Protocol of 1997 to Amend the International Convention for the Prevention of Pollution from Ships, 1973, as Modified by the Protocol of 1978 Relating Thereto (Inclusion of Regulations on Energy Efficiency for Ships in MARPOL Annex VI) adopted 15 July 2011.

MEPC.229(65) On Promotion of Technical Co-Operation and Transfer of Technology Relating to the Improvement of Energy Efficiency of Ships.

Montini, Massimiliano (2011). 'Reshaping Climate Governance for Post-2012', *European Journal of Legal Studies*, 4(1), 7–24.

Morgera, Elisa (2012). 'Introduction to European Environmental Law from an International Environmental Law Perspective', *Edinburgh Europa Paper Series*.

Oberthür, Sebastian (2003). 'Institutional Interaction to Address Greenhouse Gas Emissions from International Transport: ICAO, IMO and the EU Burden-Sharing Agreement', *Project Deliverable No. D 3, Final Draft. Ecologic – Institute for International and European Policy.*

Oberthür, Sebastian (2003). 'Institutional Interaction to Address Greenhouse Gas Emissions from International Transport: ICAO, IMO and the Kyoto Protocol', *Climate Policy*, 3(3), 191–205.

Oberthür, Sebastian (2006). 'The Climate Change Regime: Interactions of the Climate Change Regime with ICAO, IMO and the EU Burden-Sharing Agreement', in, Sebastian Oberthür and Thomas Gehring (eds.), *Institutional Interaction in Global Environmental Governance: Synergy and Conflict among International and EU Policies: Global Environmental Accord: Strategies for Sustainability and Institutional Innovation*, Cambridge, MA, MIT Press.

Oberthür, Sebastian and Gehring, Thomas (2006). 'Conceptual Foundations of Institutional Interaction', in, Sebastian Oberthür and Thomas Gehring (eds.), *Institutional Interaction in Global Environmental Governance: Synergy and Conflict among International and EU Policies: Global Environmental Accord: Strategies for Sustainability and Institutional Innovation*, Cambridge, MA, MIT Press.

Oberthür, Sebastian and Ott, Hermann (1999). *The Kyoto Protocol: International Climate Policy for the 21st Century*, New York, Springer.

Onidi, Olivier (2008). 'A Critical Perspective on ICAO', *A Critical Perspective on ICAO, Air & Space Law*, 33(1), 38.

Penner, Joyce E., Intergovernmental Panel on Climate Change. Working Group I. and Intergovernmental Panel on Climate Change. Working Group III. (1999). *Aviation and the Global Atmosphere: A Special Report of IPCC Working Groups I and III in Collaboration with the Scientific Assessment Panel to the Montreal Protocol on Substances That Deplete the Ozone Layer*, Cambridge, Cambridge University Press.

Petersen, Malte (2008). 'The Legality of the EU's Stand-Alone Approach to the Climate Impact of Aviation: The Express Role Given to the ICAO by the Kyoto Protocol', *Review of European Community & International Environmental Law*, 17(2), 196–204.

Pickering, J., Jotzo, F. and Wood, P.J. (2013). 'Splitting the Difference in Global Climate Finance: Are Fragmentation and Legitimacy Mutually Exclusive?', CCEP Working Paper 1308, November 2013. Crawford School of Public Policy, Australian National University.

Pümpel, Herbert (2016). 'Aviation and the Impacts of Climate Change · Maintaining Aviation Safety: Regulatory Responses to Intensifying Weather Events', *Carbon & Climate Law Review*, 10(2) 113–117.

Rossouw, Marius and Theron, Andre (2012). 'Investigation of Potential Climate Change Impacts on Ports adn Maritime Operations around the Souther African Coast', in, R. Asariotis and Hassiba Benamara (eds.), *Maritime Transport and the Climate Change Challenge*, 1st ed., New York, Earthscan.

Rothengatter, Werner (2010). 'Climate Change and the Contribution of Transport: Basic Facts and the Role of Aviation', *Transportation Research Part D: Transport and Environment*, 15(1), 5–13.

Sbolci, Luigi (2011). 'Supplementary Means of Interpretation', in, Enzo Cannizzaro, Mahnoush H. Arsanjani and Giorgio Gaja (eds.), *The Law of Treaties beyond the Vienna Convention*, Oxford; New York, Oxford University Press.

Schermers, Henry G. and Blokker, Niels (2011). *International Institutional Law: Unity within Diversity*, 5th rev. ed., Boston, Martinus Nijhoff Publishers.

Shi, Yubing (2014). 'Greenhouse Gas Emissions from International Shipping: The Response from China's Shipping Industry to the Regulatory Initiatives of the International Maritime Organization', *International Journal of Marine and Coastal Law*, 29(1), 85–123.

Statement from the International Civil Aviation Organization (ICAO) to the Sixth Session of the Ad Hoc Working Group on Long-Term Cooperative Action under the Convention (AWG-LCA6) (Bonn, Germany, 1–12 June 2009).

Statement on GHG Issues by the observers of IUCN. IMO MEPC 59, Closing Plenary, 17 July 2009 (Response to J10 paper & GHG debate; reproduced in the session report MEPC 59/24/Add.1).

Stern, N.H. (2007). *The Economics of Climate Change: The Stern Review*, Cambridge, England, Cambridge University Press.

Truxal, Steven (2011). 'The ICAO Assembly Resolutions on International Aviation and Climate Change: Historic Agreement, Breakthrough Deal and the Cancun Effect', *Air & Space Law*, 36(3), 217–242.

Tunteng, Verki Michael (2012). *Legal Analysis on the Inclusion of Civil Aviation in the European Union Emissions Trading System*, Montreal; Canada, Faculty of Law. McGill University.

UN Doc. FCCC/SBSTA/1996/13, Paragraph 61.

United Nations Convention on the Law of the Sea, Montego Bay, adopted 10 December 1982, in force 16 November 1994, 21 International Legal Materials (1982), 1261. 1833 UNTS 3.

Vienna Convention on the Law of Treaties. Vienna, adopted 23 May 1969, in force 27 January 1980. 8 ILM 679.

Villiger, Mark E. (2011). 'The Rules on Interpretation: Misgivings, Misunderstandings, Miscarriage? The 'Crucible' Intended by the International Law Commission', in, Enzo Cannizzaro, Mahnoush H. Arsanjani and Giorgio Gaja (eds.), *The Law of Treaties beyond the Vienna Convention*, Oxford; New York, Oxford University Press.

Vooren, Bart Van and Wessel, Ramses A. (2013). *EU External Relations Law: Text, Cases and Materials*. Cambridge, UK, Cambridge University Press.

Yamin, Farhana and Depledge, Joanna (2004). *The International Climate Change Regime: A Guide to Rules, Institutions and Procedures*, Cambridge, UK; New York, Cambridge University Press.

Young, Margaret A. (2011). *Trading Fish, Saving Fish: The Interaction between Regimes in International Law*, Cambridge, UK; New York, Cambridge University Press.

Young, Margaret A. (2012). 'Regime Interaction in Creating, Implementing and Enforcing International Law', in, Margaret A. Young (ed.), *Regime Interaction in International Law: Facing Fragmentation*, Cambridge; New York, Cambridge University Press.

5   The consequences of regime interaction

Chapter 4 detailed the types of interaction relevant to the research topic, where the presence of tensions and the existence of opportunities for synergy between regimes were identified. This chapter explores the consequences, or outcomes, of these interactions, framed by the regulatory, operational and conceptual interactions set out in the previous chapter. This entails the conflicts and synergies resulting from the overlapping regimes, mainly focused on the significance of interaction from a law-making perspective. The consequences analyzed here are not exhaustive or fixed, since regimes are in constant evolution and can develop new interactions, and thus consequences. However, the consequences discussed in this chapter are the most relevant ones, as identified by participants to the regimes and/or in the academic literature. Although the chapter divides consequences into conflicts and synergies, this division is not clear cut since there may be synergistic aspects to conflicts and vice versa.

Conflicts

As defined in Chapter 2, the book is concerned with interactions between hard-law treaty-based regimes (i.e. the climate, ICAO and IMO regimes). However, not all the elements and objects interacting within the regimes are hard law; in fact the majority of them in the case of IBF are soft law at most, such as body decisions. This fact affects the analysis of the consequences of interaction by defying the traditional definition of normative conflicts. Therefore, this section identifies the various forms of tension, including what the literature refers to as 'political conflicts'.[1] Regarding legal conflicts, Chapter 2 adopted the following definition: '*a situation where two rules or principles suggest different ways of dealing with a problem*'.[2] It has been argued that this definition is well suited to climate change-related tensions.[3] This section deals with the three main conflicts derived from the interaction between regimes, which '*suggest different ways*' to address three main problems:

1   Conflicting objectives and purposes in the regimes which question the stringency of present and future regulation;

2   Conflicting principles of equal and differential treatment, which challenge how the burdens of mitigation can be distributed; and
3   Conflicts in preferences for economic versus technical regulation challenge the choice of regulatory instruments, which is linked to the essence of the regimes.

For each of these conflicts, a dual analysis is provided for climate and aviation and climate and maritime transport; however, the conflicts depend upon the particularities of the ICAO and IMO regimes, so the consequences of interaction are not necessarily symmetrical.

The stabilization of GHG emissions and the growth of international transport: conflicting aims and objectives?

The first discernible tension between the climate and ICAO regimes and the climate and the IMO regimes refers to the divergence in the objectives and purposes of the regimes.[4] The fact that the three regimes gravitate towards different aims can be seen to deny, *a priori*, the existence of a common ground for values, principles and concepts to '*pursue limitation or reduction*' of GHG emissions.[5] However, this difference does not necessarily mean that the regimes' objectives are in conflict *per se*,[6] rather that it shows that the *raison d'être* of the treaties, upon which the regimes built their existence, were poles apart. Here, the issue of historical context[7] plays an essential role in understanding these differences, especially with regards to the objectives of ICAO and IMO and whether or not the promotion of transport, which is an aim embedded in the regimes, comes at the detriment of environmental goals.

Chapter 3 introduced the objectives of the regimes and Chapter 4 elaborated on issues of mandates and competences, which are further explored here. Although there is an apparent contradiction between the mandates and competences of the regimes (i.e. economic/commercial versus environmental objectives),[8] both the ICAO and IMO regimes have incorporated, one way or another, environmental aims in their work, and have developed regulations tackling an array of environmental problems. Moreover, ICAO and the IMO have included goals to reduce the climate impact of their sectors.

First, it is necessary to clarify the extent to which the climate regime's objectives are binding upon parties. As stated in Chapter 3, the overarching objective, which applies to the climate regime as a whole (i.e. to the Convention and any related legal instruments),[9] is set out in Article 2 of the UNFCCC:

The ultimate objective of this Convention and any related legal instruments that the Conference of the Parties may adopt is to achieve, in accordance with the relevant provisions of the Convention, stabilization of greenhouse gas concentrations in the atmosphere at a level that would prevent dangerous anthropogenic interference with the climate system. Such a level should be achieved within a time-frame sufficient to allow ecosystems to adapt naturally to climate change, to ensure that food production is not threatened and to enable economic development to proceed in a sustainable manner.

This long-term goal that the convention established for the regime is, to sum up: to stabilize GHG concentrations in the atmosphere '*at a level that would prevent dangerous anthropogenic interference with the climate system*', which is to be achieved within a vaguely defined time frame. As such, the Convention does not propose an absolute ban on the emissions of greenhouse gases or on the activities causing such emissions, but to stabilize them. In this way the UNFCCC establishes an environmental threshold in order to prevent dangerous interference with the climate system or, in other words, it sets an environmental quality standard similar to those used in different environmental areas by other multilateral environmental agreements.[10] However, the variables offered as a benchmark for the threshold or standard in the article are subject to interpretation.[11]

In terms of articulating a legal obligation, the provision can be regarded as '*an ill-defined obligation*'.[12] However, some authors have argued that the Cancun Agreements[13] to keep global temperatures within 2°C over pre-industrialized levels is tantamount to the 'quantification' of the convention's objective.[14] A logical next step in the climate negotiations would have been to translate this 2°C target into an emissions limit consistent with the temperature target. A global emissions limit is arguably necessary in order to allocate reductions and limitations to countries and/or sectors, or at least be used as a benchmark to measure bottom-up country approaches.[15] Here, the role of state actors and non-state actors, especially epistemic communities, has been acknowledged in the understanding and interpretation of the legal definition of Article 2.[16] Crucially, in Paris a long-term goal to hold '*the increase in the global average temperature to well below 2°C above pre-industrial levels and pursuing efforts to limit the temperature increase to 1.5°C above pre-industrial levels*' was agreed.[17] Despite the '*exercise of linguistic gymnastics: how to craft "creative language" that mentions 1.5 degrees without making it the official operational goal*',[18] the 1.5°C goal stands as an important development in the regime.[19]

While the legal relevance of Article 2 in determining the purpose of the climate regime is uncontested, the character of the article as a '*real, legally binding commitment of the Parties is partially denied*',[20] given the difficulties in interpreting unequivocally the wording of the article and the lack of concrete obligations.[21] This means that the article is binding for the parties in the sense that it imposes an obligation to meet the overall objective of the treaty but that it lacks a '*real, legally binding force for itself*' since it '*does not define further obligations for action of the Parties which would put the objective in concrete terms*'.[22] These obligations would need to be developed in the future. Nonetheless, the article has, according to international law, a role in interpreting the regime. Indeed, it functions '*as a rule for interpretation*' of the obligations established in the UNFCCC, KP, PA and subsequent outcomes.[23] This objective implicitly refers to IBF emissions, since the UNFCCC calls for action from all sectors of the economy.

While the climate regime was established to achieve the global goal of stabilizing GHG emissions in the atmosphere, and has been narrowed down to be consistent with a 2°C target, the ICAO and IMO regimes were set up to promote and manage the development of air and maritime international transport. This relates to some particularities of the regimes: first, while ICAO's regime was born out of a need for airspace regulation in a new and expansive sector, the regulation of maritime transport, whether customary or not, was centuries old, and so the need for the IMO's regime was primarily one of coordination. Second, while the Chicago Convention not only establishes ICAO but also regulates the basis for international aviation, the IMO Convention focused solely on establishing the organization. Third, while there is no mandate for environmental action in the Chicago Convention, but rather objectives set by the organization's soft-law instruments, the IMO's mandate in environmental matters comes from the IMO Convention, which was amended so as to include them, but also from other hard-law instruments such as the LOS or MARPOL. Finally, and as a consequence of the previous point, there is an ongoing debate within IMO, since its inception, over the scope of its regulatory role and the regime has achieved far wider competences not only in technological aspects, but also in political and economic aspects. Conversely there has traditionally been no such debate in ICAO regarding the clear division between the technological and economic reach of its regulations. Despite their differences, ICAO and the IMO, which were based upon the economic, social and trade values of promoting international air and sea transport, now regulate significant areas of the environmental field, where climate-related issues constitute a present-day Gordian knot.

Regarding ICAO, Article 44 of the Chicago Convention defines its objectives as follows:

> The aims and objectives of the Organization are to develop the principles and techniques of international air navigation and to foster the planning and development of international air transport so as to:
>
> (a) Ensure the safe and orderly growth of international civil aviation throughout the world;
> (b) Encourage the arts of aircraft design and operation for peaceful purposes;
> (c) Encourage the development of airways, airports, and air navigation facilities for international civil aviation;
> (d) Meet the needs of the peoples of the world for safe, regular, efficient and economical air transport;
> (e) Prevent economic waste caused by unreasonable competition;
> (f) Ensure that the rights of contracting States are fully respected and that every contracting State has a fair opportunity to operate international airlines;
> (g) Avoid discrimination between contracting States;
> (h) Promote safety of flight in international air navigation;
> (i) Promote generally the development of all aspects of international civil aeronautics.[24]

The double objective of the Chicago Convention, to be carried out through ICAO, is, on the one hand, to '*develop the principles and techniques of international air navigation*' and on the other, '*to foster the planning and development of international air transport*'. Regarding the first objective, ICAO can develop principles and techniques of air transport through the adoption of Annexes to the Chicago Convention. Regarding the second objective, ICAO can only promote the development of air transport through guidelines and policy recommendations. The first one relates to the technical work, the second one to what can be considered air transport economics. This finds a parallel in contracting parties to the commitments of the Chicago Convention, since they are to conform with measures adopted in ICAO, to the greatest possible extent with regards to SARPs and attempt to conform to other recommendations. '*In effect, this bifurcation implicitly reflects the agreement of the international community of States which signed the Chicago Convention that ICAO could adopt Standards in the technical fields of air navigation and could only offer guidelines in the economic field.*'[25] According to Ruwantissa Abeyratne, ICAO has so far '*successfully avoided underlying political contentions brought to bear by the issues it addressed, the question has been asked as to whether ICAO could continue to divorce aeronautical or technical issues from underlying political nuances*'. In his opinion, '*The answer would seem to lie in the environment within which ICAO functions and the principles upon which, under the Chicago Convention, ICAO could work.*'[26]

The Preamble to the Chicago Convention also contains some guidelines on the aims and objective of the convention. It states that international civil aviation intends to promote '*friendship and understanding*' and '*cooperation,*' and that it '*may be developed in a safe and orderly manner*' in which '*international air transport services may be established on the basis of equality of opportunity and operated soundly and economically*'.[27] Indeed, such economic aims appear in Article 44, specifically in '(*a*) *Ensure the safe and orderly growth of international civil aviation throughout the world*', '*d*) *Meet the needs of the peoples of the world for safe, regular, efficient and economical air transport*' and '(*e*) *Prevent economic waste caused by unreasonable competition*'. Furthermore, Article 4 states that '*[e]ach contracting State agrees not to use civil aviation for any purpose inconsistent with the aims of this Convention.*'

Although no environmental objectives were included in ICAO constituent instruments back in the 1940s, increasing awareness about the impact of aviation on the environment has connected the regime with environmental areas, first noise and later emissions. However, the Chicago Convention hasn't been amended so as to include the environment among the organization's objectives; rather the environmental aims have been introduced in the regime via Assembly Resolutions.[28] In 2010, the 37th ICAO Assembly officially recognized the purpose of '*environmental protection and sustainability of air transport*' as one of the three '*strategic objectives*' of the organization. Two years later, the Council[29] interpreted and extended the reach of Article 44 from the objective of fostering the development of air transport to fostering the development of '*a sound and economically-viable civil aviation system*', a concept that, as Ruwantissa Abeyratne states, is not defined in any known air law document.[30] At the same time, ICAO has set its *'strategic objectives'* for 2014–2016,[31] to include the economic development of air transport and environmental protection, that is, to *'achieve the sustainable growth of the global civil aviation system'*.[32]

The legal status of this environmental objective is certainly beneath the ones established in the Chicago Convention, since those are, at most, soft law while the Chicago Convention is hard law. However, parties to ICAO have accepted that the environmental functions and aims of the organization are not without meaning. However, the degree of commitment of the parties and the organization's shift towards environmental objectives find its rationale only through the concept of sustainable development. This implies that the regulation of environmental matters, such as climate change, doesn't conflict with the ICAO regime's objective set out in Chicago, as they have evolved, especially through practice. However, how much of 'sustainable' and of 'development' there is, and what is the reach of the principle[33] can be seen only in the specific regulations. In this connection, ICAO has established an aspirational global goal for the sector to achieve carbon-neutral growth from 2020 onwards,[34] which would imply a stabilization of CO_2 emissions of between 682 and 755 megatons.[35] Nonetheless, the goals are deemed as insufficient *'to ensure the sector does its fair share to achieve a 2 degree goal'*[36] since the *'unconstrained growth in aviation emissions will not be compatible with 2050 climate stabilization goals'*.[37]

Climate-related Assembly Resolutions tend to include in their preambles introductory formulas on the climate regime's objective such as: *'Whereas the ultimate objective of the United Nations Framework Convention on Climate Change (UNFCCC) is to achieve stabilization of greenhouse gas (GHG) concentrations in the atmosphere at a level that would prevent dangerous anthropogenic interference with the climate system'*[38] or *'Noting the scientific view that the increase in global average temperature above pre-industrial levels ought not to exceed 2°C.'*[39] However, when it comes to the text of the recommendations, the same resolution states that *'emphasis should be on those policy options that will reduce aircraft engine emissions without negatively impacting the growth of air transport'*[40]; in other words, the climate reduction objectives are subordinated to fostering aviation growth. In this connection, among the potential options on the table,[41] CORSIA succeeded because it fit the idea of achieving *'carbon neutral growth from 2020'*[42] exclusively through the reduction of emissions outside the sector. This, allegedly, destroys incentives for companies to actually reduce their emissions through, for example, investments in technology.[43] The mechanism has been criticized for its lack of ambition[44] in terms of the chosen baseline year, the exceptions provided and, very importantly, the fact that it would only be mandatory from 2027.[45] No surprise, CORSIA was the preferred option by the industry. Critically, it can be argued that ICAO has set its own target for the sector, which is not aligned with the 2°C (1.5°C) guiding goals of the climate regime. Now ICAO has to decide which credits will be eligible under CORSIA; the quality of these credits will be, again, a test of the weight that sustainable development and environmental objectives have in the ICAO regime.[46]

Conversely, the IMO's constituent document includes environmental objectives as part of its mandate, which has been further developed in various regulations affecting maritime transport. As explained in Chapter 3, the mandate of the IMO is set out in various instruments, including the IMO convention as well as the LOS or MARPOL to which the IMO is a custodian.[47] The purposes of the IMO, as stated in the Convention, are:

(a) To provide machinery for co-operation among Governments in the field of governmental regulation and practices relating to technical matters of all kinds affecting shipping engaged in international trade; to encourage and facilitate the general adoption of the highest practicable standards in matters concerning the maritime safety, efficiency of navigation and prevention and control of marine pollution from ships; and to deal with administrative and legal matters related to the purposes set out in this Article;

(b) To encourage the removal of discriminatory action and unnecessary restrictions by Governments affecting shipping engaged in international trade so as to promote the availability of shipping services to the commerce of the world without discrimination; assistance and encouragement given by a Government for the development of its national shipping and for purposes of security does not in itself constitute discrimination, provided that such assistance and encouragement is not based on measures designed to restrict the freedom of shipping of all flags to take part in international trade;

(c) To provide for the consideration by the Organization of matters concerning unfair restrictive practices by shipping concerns in accordance with Part II;

(d) To provide for the consideration by the Organization of any matters concerning shipping and the effect of shipping on the marine environment that may be referred to it by any organ or specialized agency of the United Nations;

(e) To provide for the exchange of information among Governments on matters under consideration by the Organization.[48]

Article 1(a) and (d) refers to environmental protection as a specific aim, both the pursuit of high standards in the '*prevention and control of marine pollution from ships*' and any matters related to '*the effect of shipping on the marine environment*'. Notwithstanding, the promotion '*of the availability of shipping services to the commerce of the world without discrimination*' is set in Article 1(b). At the same time in the IMO's most recent Strategic Plan, where acting on climate change is included, states that the mission of IMO is '*to promote safe, secure, environmentally sound, efficient and sustainable shipping through cooperation*'.[49]

The IMO Assembly Resolution 963(23), which mandates the MEPC to act upon GHG emissions, mentions in its preamble, under the formula '*being aware*' the UNFCCC's ultimate objective,[50] which entails an interpretative value. The 61st session of the MEPC included in its agenda the debate about the establishment of a reduction target or cap for the sector;[51] however, the issue has been subsequently postponed.[52] The debate was framed by two submissions with diametrical views: from Norway, who argued for a target in line with the climate regime[53] and from the WSC, who found that setting a target for the sector was *'inappropriate in the absence of a broader approach to regulating transportation emissions at the national and global level'*.[54] In 2015, in the context of the run-up to Paris, discussions over a CO_2 emissions target for the sector retuned via the Marshall Islands proposal to set up a *fair share* at the 68th session of the MEPC. Although there was no progress on it, the adoption of an IMO a Roadmap for a *'comprehensive IMO Strategy on reduction of GHG emissions from ships'*[55] at the 70th MEPC includes a dialogue on the 'levels of ambition' for the maritime sector.

Environmental NGOs have claimed that *'the shipping industry is by any measure a mature and well-developed industry, and as such, its targets must reflect those of developed countries.'*[56] At the same time, prompted by the Rio+20 Summit, the IMO has approached the principle of sustainable development by presenting the concept of a Sustainable Maritime Transportation System.[57]

Summary of issues

Reflecting upon the above discussion, it can be concluded that the promotion of international transport and the management of their associated environmental impacts, including climate change, are objectives solidly nested in the ICAO and IMO regimes, either through soft-law or hard-law instruments. Moreover, both regimes have incorporated the aims of sustainable development in their work. However, climate change transcends other environmental issues, because of the intrinsic difficulties linked to the nature of the problem, but also because limiting and reducing GHG emissions is perceived as a fundamental constraint to business growth and development, as well as challenging the original objectives of the regimes and its entrenched values. As such, stringent limits to emissions are highly unlikely to emerge under these conditions.

Here the key question is the degree of influence exerted by the climate change regime in pushing its climate objectives upon the ICAO and IMO. If we take the 2°C target as a benchmark of the UNFCCC Article 2, no document in ICAO or IMO has embraced the target or sought to quantify their reductions in relation to it. Rather, the Assembly Resolutions refer to the small contribution of their sectors to the problem, and in the case of the IMO, they boast of being the most energy and cost-efficient mode of transport, despite the recent and forecasted increase in activity and therefore emissions.[58] However, some regime participants, both State and non-state, have acted as a vehicle for interaction, challenging this perception. Although both regimes have made statements on the aims and steps they plan to take towards tackling the climate impact of their sectors, they have yet to formally embrace the 2-degree target. In this connection, at the 38th ICAO Assembly ICSA posited that

> [t]he primary objective shared by environmental NGOs is to see that greenhouse gas emissions from international aviation are reduced to a level that,

in the context of limiting temperature rises to no more than 2 degrees, represents a fair and equitable contribution by the sector.[59]

Therefore ICSA invited the ICAO Assembly to recognize '*that national and regional MBMs are essential tools in the interim if the sector is to make its fair contribution to ensure global warming remains below 2 degrees*'.[60] In a similar fashion, CAN has expressed the need to link ICAO's measures to the 2-degree target:

> measures under ICAO must be designed to meet ambitious targets, in line with staying well below 2 degrees of warming. The specific target for the global aviation sector may be set by ICAO, but failing that it must be set by the UNFCCC, and in any case the adequacy of any target for the sector should be reviewed regularly by the UNFCCC.[61]

Similarly, with regard to a quantification of the measures in IMO, a joint statement of NGOs to the MEPC in 2009 called for GHG emissions from international shipping to be reduced '*to at least 40% below 1990 levels by 2020 and at least 80% below 1990 levels by 2050. These figures are consistent with the latest estimates of reductions required to limit global warming to below 2°C.*'[62] Furthermore, it affirmed that in case the IMO fails to set a sufficient target, '*NGOs will call for the targets to be set by the UNFCCC.*'[63] Also, epistemic communities play a very important role[64] and NGOs have provided a platform for experts to stimulate and shape the debate.[65] This study finds that, in this connection, epistemic communities are a very relevant component of interaction between regimes.

The question that needs to be clarified here, for the sake of continuity in next chapter, is whether there exists a legal conflict in the sense provided in the book, that is, '*a situation where two rules or principles suggest different ways of dealing with a problem*'. The answer is dependent on the way we consider the objectives of the regimes, only as they are set in hard-law instruments[66] or in a more holistic way.

With regards to climate and ICAO, there is an apparent conflict between the regimes' objectives set out in Article 2 of the UNFCCC and Article 44 of the Chicago Convention. However, some remarks can be made with regards to the UNFCCC objective: first, the article lacks concreteness, although parties to the regime have agreed *a posteriori*, through a COP decision to stabilize temperature increases at 2°C, and recently the PA has definitively secured the 2°C goal in the regime; and second the climate regime embraces issues such as not compromising the development of nations.[67] With regards to ICAO, there are other nuances in Chicago, since the air regime was set up to provide for the world, not just some States or interests.[68]

Also, developments through soft law and other instruments in the ICAO and IMO regimes reveal an entrenchment of environmental aims in general, and climate change in particular, in the work of these organizations. Additionally, dealing with the environmental impacts of international transport in the climate arena also serves the purpose of maintaining their forum hegemony. However, the conflict seems to arise from the fact that the economic and commercial objectives (i.e. the promotion and development of air and maritime transport) have been the main rationale of the ICAO and IMO regimes, since their inception. Here, the principle of sustainable development, which has been embraced by the regimes, has a role to play in the narrative of reconciling objectives.[69] Nonetheless, the idiosyncrasies, values and underlying power of industry in both regimes suggest that these diverging objectives will be difficult to reconcile on a practical level. This has expressed itself in the low levels of speed and stringency of the measures pursued in ICAO and IMO.

Therefore, rather than a legal conflict, the diverging objectives of the regimes, as explained above, can be seen as a political conflict, demonstrating, at most, legal ridges. However, this objective dichotomy, between stabilizing GHG emissions and promoting the growth of international transport, has been deemed to be a major condition to developing meaningful regulation.[70] While this seems to be the case, the question is whether the conflict can be overcome and/or turned into synergy. It is worth reflecting upon the fact that the understanding and development of the regimes' objectives in ICAO and IMO are based on values and norms which also respond to exchanges and overlaps with other regimes; for example, certain values and norms of the trade regime are very present in ICAO and IMO, as are environmental concerns in IMO.

Fitting differential treatment into non-discriminatory regimes and the quest for allocating the burden of IBF emissions

The most sensitive and complex issue in the overlaps of the climate, ICAO and IMO regimes is the clash between treaty principles of differential and equal treatment, which inform the regulation of international aviation and shipping GHG emissions.[71] This conflict has become more acute with the pressing need to reduce GHG emissions, posited by the scientific community and with some participants of the regimes, namely the EU, adopting unilateral measures. Given the relevance of this issue in the negotiations, a considerable part of this chapter is devoted to discussing it.

The equal application of international law comes from the principle of 'sovereignty equality' of States, which maintains that: '*All States enjoy sovereign equality. They have equal rights and duties and are equal members of the international community, notwithstanding differences of an economic, social, political or other nature.*'[72] However, equality has been strongly questioned as the ideal basis of international life given the wide economic differences in the international community.[73]

The use of differential and contextual norms[74] in the environmental field has increased since the Stockholm conference, with a preference for basing the differentiation on the resources and capabilities of countries.[75] In the climate change arena, a trend has been observed whereby provisions of contextual treatment are increasingly taking over from the differential ones,[76] and there is also a trend towards more differentiation.[77] However, in some other areas of international law, differentiation is becoming less and less acceptable, such as the trade regime.[78] In any case, differential treatment does not aim to create permanent exceptions but '*a temporary legal inequality to wipe out an inequality in fact*',[79] while establishing '*new forms of cooperation at the international level*'.[80] This is done through the differentiated allocation of rights and entitlements and the redistribution of resources.[81] Since being formulated in the Rio Declaration,[82] the principle of CBDR has manifested in different environmental regimes though an array of provisions.[83] The principle comprises various categories of differential treatment in multilateral environmental agreements.[84] Implementation of the principle, as well as other equity principles to lessen frictions between developed and developing countries, covers both substantive and procedural aspects. Substantive aspects include both differentiation of duties and compensatory preferential treatment with respect to building capacity, the transfer of technologies and financing.[85] Procedural aspects include membership in committees and bodies and qualified voting, where the involvement of a certain number of developing countries is required.[86] Although '*equitable differentiation probably has become the price to be paid to ensure universal participation in environmental agreements concerned with global problems*',[87] factors of and for differentiation can be considered in various fashions.[88] In international law, some other concepts have been used to address situations where equal treatment is the rule,[89] such as the case of '*the special interests and needs of developing countries*' contained in UNCLOS[90] or in the '*special and differential treatment*' recognized in the trade regime.[91] These different categories of favourable treatment for developing countries allow for differentiation to occur in ways that can '*preserve formal equality within the instrument's four corners and leave the discriminating to the margins*'.[92]

The fundamental role that the CBDRRC principle plays in climate regime has been widely acknowledged,[93] where the UNFCCC has incorporated differential treatment between countries as a guiding principle.[94] Such differentiation in favour of developing countries reflects the idea that while there is a common responsibility for the climate problem, the biggest share of the burden in mitigating and adapting to climate change is to be borne by the developed countries.[95] However, developed countries have argued that their level of economic development and capacity to address the climate problem gives them a moral responsibility, rather than a liability, to aid developing countries.[96] The principle is articulated in the climate regime through differentiated obligations and implementation,[97] including assistance to developing countries in a variety of forms.[98] The climate regime has made use of both methods of differentiation (i.e. obligations and implementation).[99] Here, the PA has changed the landscape with an agreement for all parties that '*provides an historical 'U-turn' in international climate governance on the vexed question of differentiation*'[100] with a new nuanced form of differentiation between developed and developing countries,[101] which is relevant for the regulation of IBF.[102]

Despite the ongoing contestations over the correct interpretation of the principle[103] and its future,[104] the principle of CBDRRC guides the further normative development of the climate regime[105] and should arguably also be applied in connection to emissions from international aviation and maritime transport. With global climate governance increasingly shifting towards venues outside of the UNFCCC,[106] questions arise as to what role the CBDRRC principle plays in other regimes. This includes its potential role within the ICAO and IMO regimes with regards to the regulation of GHG emissions.

Arguably, the principle should play a part, given that parties to the UNFCCC, which include nearly all countries of the world, are bound by it.[107] In general, it can be observed that developing countries are keen to extend the principle to other arenas. However, developed countries on the whole oppose such an extension, arguing that it should remain limited to the climate regime and that it could jeopardize the effectiveness of any regulations developed on that basis.[108] In particular, developed countries have become opposed to developing countries' interpretation of CBDRRC as a juxtaposition of a group of developed countries, which are included in Annex I of the UNFCCC/Annex B of the KP, and a group of developing countries. To developed countries, this binary distinction no longer reflects reality, with a group of emerging economies drifting away from their old peers.[109] In line with this view, a trend in the UN climate regime can be observed, in which differential treatment for developing countries as a group has increasingly shifted towards a more tailored approach to differentiation, taking into account factors such as the vulnerability and capacity of countries.[110]

The KP calls for a differentiation in commitments, where only countries listed in Annex B of the KP hold limitation and reduction commitments.[111] It seems from the wording of Article 2.2 that differential treatment with regard to the regulation of IBF is the favoured option, since the article states that '*Annex I shall pursue*'. However, this opinion is highly contested, since the article points towards ICAO and the IMO as the preferred fora for advancing negotiations and these regimes work on equal basis premises. This contradiction allows for opinions for and against differential treatment among actors.[112] The question becomes especially relevant because the principles supporting equal treatment and non-discrimination are given in their respective constitutive instruments and have been secured through the regimes' practices. However, changes brought with the PA – as compared to the rigid differentiation of the KP – are likely to ease the issue.

Allusions to the CBDRRC principle in the negotiations under the ICAO and the IMO are not infrequent,[113] both from a legal and a political point of view. In such battles, a counter argument is normally based on the global nature of these sectors and that therefore any solutions should assume an equal treatment of aircraft and vessels.[114] However, the resolutions adopted by the ICAO Assembly[115] and the MEPC at the IMO[116] have included, under soft formulas, terms such as '*acknowledging*' and '*being cognizant*', respectively, an approximation of both specialized agencies to the principles enshrined in the UNFCCC, KP and the PA, including the CBDRRC principle. This doesn't mean that CBDRRC has been subscribed by the regimes and the question of if, and to what extent, the principle will apply to future regulation remains open,[117] in particular at the IMO.

Differential and equal treatment in ICAO

The CBDRRC principle clashes with some of the core principles underlying the international regulation of aviation, which is based upon equal treatment. The

Chicago Convention preamble states that '*international civil aviation may be developed in a safe and orderly manner and that international air transport services may be established on the basis of equality of opportunity and operated soundly and economically*'. Furthermore, Article 44 (f) and (g) states among the ICAO objectives, that the organization shall '*[e]nsure that the rights of contracting States are fully respected and that every contracting State has a fair opportunity to operate international airlines*' and '*[a]void discrimination between contracting States*'. These are the so-called principles of non-discrimination and equal opportunities. Furthermore, the Convention also establishes that air regulations shall apply '*to the aircraft of all contracting States without distinction as to nationality*'.[118] The primacy of equal treatment provided in the ICAO regime is very much connected to the global nature of the aviation sector, which suggests that any regulation should treat all aircraft equally. However, the regime has allowed for certain differentiation such as special treatment for developing countries in the context of air transport and trade.[119]

The fact that CBDRRC has partially entered ICAO has been acknowledged by the ILC, since the ICAO's 36th Assembly.[120] The ICAO Assembly Resolution 38–18 on developing an MBM states in its recital that ICAO members '*[a]cknowledg[e] the principles and provisions on common but differentiated responsibilities and respective capabilities, with developed countries taking the lead under the UNFCCC and the Kyoto Protocol*'.[121] However, the resolution immediately proceeds in the following paragraph to '*[a]cknowledg[e] the principles of non-discrimination and equal and fair opportunities to develop international aviation set forth in the Chicago Convention*'. It is clear that the soft language of acknowledgement is not a full embracement of the CBDRRC principle.[122] Therefore, the question of whether the principle will apply to future regulation remains open.[123] However, arguably, the principle has recently been given a boost by the ICAO's 38th Assembly which has been asked to develop an MBM that '*should take into account the principle of common but differentiated responsibilities and respective capabilities, the special circumstances and respective capabilities, and the principle of non-discrimination and equal and fair opportunities*'.[124] Nonetheless, the inclusion of the CBDRRC principle into the ICAO resolution is likely to result in conflict at the formal negotiations due to take place in 2016.[125] A total of 48 countries – namely the United States, Australia, New Zealand, Canada, Japan, the Republic of Korea and member States from the EU and the European Civil Aviation Conference[126] – have placed reservations against the Annex of AR 38–18 on CBDRRC as a guiding principle for MBMs,[127] and have warned about the consequences of differential norms for international aviation. An explanation for this partial embodiment of the principle and the resistance of developed countries to the extension in the application of CBDRRC to the regulation of aviation is given in French and Rajamani: '*It has alerted these countries, arguably, to the extent of their folly, as they perceive it, in agreeing to the breadth and depth of differential treatment in the climate regime, and the precedential value it appears to have generated.*'[128] However, other explanations for the negotiating behaviour of countries in climate issues can be found in the consequences of the institutionalized country grouping provided by the split between Annex I and non-Annex I, which amplified the divide between developing and industrialized countries, obstructing the convention's objective.[129]

From the measures taken in ICAO so far, discussions on differential treatment have taken place mostly in the context of MBMs. The aircraft CO_2 emissions standard as a SARP is, in essence, an equal treatment norm, which will, therefore, apply to all new airplanes. Conversely, in the establishment of a CORSIA there is more scope for controversy regarding if and how to apply CBDRRC, where differentiation has been included.

It is worth noting what the ICAO regime has done in 'receiving' the principle of CBDRRC, aside from acknowledging its existence in the climate regime: first, the separation between establishing a regulation for the sector, or for member States, has been highlighted so as to insinuate that the CBDRRC is not applicable;[130] second, Assembly Resolution 37–19 introduced a '*de minimis*' clause, so as to exempt from MBMs all aircraft operators from States that make up less than 1% of global air traffic.[131] The '*de minimis*' clause is also contained in the Assembly Resolution 38–18,[132] which was a source of conflict in the last ICAO Assembly that ended up with a request for revision to the Council.[133] Third, ICAO '*has sought to reframe the language to decouple it from the UNFCCC*'[134] by using the term Special Circumstances and Respective Capabilities of Developing Countries (SCRCDC), something that ICAO is more familiar with, but also that removes the issue of historical responsibility. Fourth, ICAO has pointed towards the use of revenues with regards to differentiation.[135] And finally, ICAO has launched assistance projects for developing countries in the context of State Action Plans both, with the GEF and the EU. Based on the above it can be inferred that the focus of differentiation in ICAO was drifting from equal treatment and non-discrimination, on the basis of nationality, towards the inclusion of some differentiation, mainly through implementation and assistance rather than main obligations.

Efforts with regards to CBDRRC and international aviation already exist at the regional level, which have highlighted the conflict between the climate and aviation regimes. Specifically, the inclusion of aviation in the EU ETS has posed the question of whether a party to both ICAO and the climate regimes shall in regulating international aviation apply equality or embrace differentiation.[136] By regulating international aviation, the EU allocated emissions under criteria of its own and the CDBRRC principle was hardly embodied in the design.[137] However, some exceptions are granted on certain types of flight, including military flights[138] and on commercial flights on a *de minimis* basis,[139] as well as for third countries taking equivalent measures.[140] Aside from these exceptions, the only deference to developing countries relates to the discretionary use of revenues obtained by EU member States. While the directive encourages using these revenues to finance climate mitigation and adaptation, '*especially to developing countries*',[141] the demarcation of revenues was not established as compulsory. The EU has differentiated between developed and developing countries and also made distinctions between developing countries[142] with regards to other climate change norms, but the inclusion of aviation in the EU ETS was not one of them.[143] However, although the Aviation Directive Impact Assessment refers to CBDRRC and maintains that the Aviation Directive conforms with the principle,[144] the EU dismissed CBDRRC as applicable to the directive, simply stating that the only basis for the directive is the principle of equal treatment.[145]

As Scott and Rajamani argue, differentiation between countries in the Directive would have increased the legitimacy of a measure with international aspirations. In their view, CBDRRC is still relevant, even if, as argued by the EU, the Directive applies to business and not to countries per se. Neither should a sectoral approach undermine differential treatment.[146] Furthermore, they argue that it is possible '*to take the principle of CBDRRC into account, while treating all airlines and passengers flying on the same route in the same way*'. In spite of the contentiousness of the EU Aviation Directive, the EU position on CBDR was not challenged by the claimants in the ATAA Case, and neither the Court's Advocate General[147] nor the final ruling[148] focused on this as an issue. Nonetheless, some arguments on the accordance of the Aviation Directive with the principle of equal treatment of the Chicago Convention and the Open Skies Agreement can be found in the Advocate's Opinion.[149] The wave of criticism received by the EU[150] triggered a change in the Union's policy with regards to differentiation. Even if the EU does not explicitly refer to CBDRRC as such in its aviation regulation, differentiation has gained ground with regards to equality. This can be observed in the spirit of the Commission's proposal to amend the aviation directive,[151] where differentiation is granted by way of an exemption to flights to and from developing countries with less than a 1% share of total revenue/tonne kilometres of international aviation. The proposal defines these countries through the criteria of countries benefiting from preferential access to the EU market,[152] namely, those which are not classified in 2013 by the World Bank as high-income or upper-middle income countries.[153]

While the aviation directive proposal displays a renewed will to accommodate the special circumstances of developing countries, it preserves equal treatment for all operators on the same route; that is, exceptions are for routes from these countries, regardless of the nationality of aircraft and exceptions are not offered to all operators from these countries flying other routes. Although the future of the inclusion of international aviation in the EU ETS, and with it the issue of differential treatment, is, at the time of writing uncertain, the developments at the EU level have shaped the debate at the international level[154] by spurring a wave of reactions. At the 38th ICAO assembly, objections were raised, via reservations to the Resolution A38–18, to the use of differential treatment for aviation, citing market distortions and discrimination that would contravene the Chicago Convention and ICAO's working principles that oppose the application of CBDR in regional schemes.[155] Jos Delbeke, director general of the European Commission's directorate general for Climate Action, stated that

> whether market-based measures involve taxes, levies or emissions trading, the system adopted by ICAO or applied by States must be non-discriminatory

for all airlines. Non-discrimination is one of the most important principles of international aviation law, and should be fully respected.

However, in the same speech he supported CBDRRC pointing towards the redistribution of revenues as a way forward: '*we are open to considering how this could be reflected in the use of revenues coming from further market-based action agreed in ICAO.*'[156] The conflict comes from the fact that '*ICAO has to ensure adherence by States to the principles of aviation as adopted within the ICAO regulatory umbrella.*'[157]

Nonetheless, CORSIA embraced some differentiation; the second phase of the mechanism (from 2027) is mandatory for all States that have an individual share of international aviation activities in year 2018 RTKs higher than 0.5% of total RTKs or whose cumulative share in the list of States from the highest to the lowest amount of RTKs reaches 90% of total RTKs are required to participate. Significantly, least developed countries, small island developing states and landlocked developing countries are exempted from this core obligation, unless they volunteer. This differentiation is far from the Annex I and non-Annex I divide, from which the climate change regime has moved away with the PA. It can be argued that this U-turn in CBDRRC has also facilitated the negotiations in ICAO.[158]

Differential and equal treatment in the IMO

The situation in the IMO regime has many similarities with the one described for ICAO, due to the existence of a '*principle of non-discriminatory regulation of all ships in international trade irrespective of flag or ownership and the principle of no more favourable treatment* [NMFT] *of ships flying the flag of a non-party to any mandatory IMO treaty instrument*'.[159] These principles positing the equal treatment of ships are found in Article 1(b) of the IMO Convention and the IMO treaties. They are supported by the regime's longstanding practice whereby there is no precedent for differential treatment of vessels based on nationality in any of the IMO conventions and instruments.[160] The *rationale* is to be found in the very nature of the sector and the system of ship registries, where the recourse to foreign-flagging is swelling.[161] Among other objectives, Article 1(b) aims for the organization

> [t]o encourage the removal of discriminatory action and unnecessary restrictions by Governments affecting shipping engaged in international trade so as to promote the availability of shipping services to the commerce of the world without discrimination; assistance and encouragement given by a Government for the development of its national shipping and for purposes of security does not in itself constitute discrimination, provided that such assistance and encouragement is not based on measures designed to restrict the freedom of shipping of all flags to take part in international trade.

These principles of equal treatment, that aim to ensure a level playing field, conflict with the principle of CBDRRC, to which parties hold different views on the exact content and role that it could play in the regulation of emissions from international maritime transport, in a future IMO instrument.[162] In 2008, the 57th session of the MEPC agreed on a number of principles as a basis for future regulation, coherent with the IMO framework,[163] which were proposed by Denmark, Marshall Islands, BIMCO, ICS, INTERCARGO, INTERTANKO and OCIMF.[164] Principle number two in the list states that any regulation developed with regards to GHG emissions shall be '*binding and equally applicable to all flag States in order to avoid evasion*'.[165] To elucidate the issue around CBDRRC, the Sub-Division for Legal Affairs of the IMO presented a study on the reach or Article 2.2 KP with regards to the application of differential treatment in the IMO. The analysis concluded that the article should not be interpreted restrictively, and that '*any measures that are adopted by IMO in this context shall be applicable across the board in the same way as are other regulations adopted by the Organization.*'[166] Furthermore, the study concluded that concepts such as the CBDRRC '*have limited, if any, application in IMO-based conventions*'[167]

The IMO negotiations are highly polarized between developing and developed countries' members regarding the issue of equal and differential treatment; however, a new perspective on reconciliation of the principles has emerged. Non-state actors, particularly environmental NGOs, have informed the debate and contributed to the reconceptualization of CDBRRC and its reconciliation with equal treatment.[168] For example, CSC and the WWF contributed to the work of the GHG-WG 3 with a submission on the ways in which differentiated application could be achieved, and even suggested that '*the UNFCCC allows for a global shipping measure, provided that developing countries do not incur net incremental costs, and that a rebate mechanism could achieve this.*'[169] However, some countries, led by China and India,[170] were not satisfied with combining equal and differential treatment through financial compensation to developing countries, which they have expressed repeatedly.[171]

Issues around CBDRRC also arose when the EEDI and SEEMP were adopted. These are equal treatment norms and, as such, apply to all ships regardless of nationality. However, China, Saudi Arabia and South Africa were not in favour of a regulation on GHG that embodied the CBDRRC principle and so the measure was adopted by resorting to a vote. In their submission, they stated that introducing the same responsibilities to ships flying the flag of developing countries is a clear deviation from the UN Framework Convention on Climate Change and its KP, '*breaching the principle of CBDR by developed and developing countries*'.[172]

However, most of the debate about CBDRRC has taken place around MBMs, where the talks are at a stalemate,[173] and an array of options for an MBM have been submitted by regime participants and considered by the organization. One way or another, all of the options envision some kind of differentiation. In the words of Per Kågeson:

> One can thus identify two possible ways of making equal treatment, regardless of flag and ownership, go hand-in-hand with CBRD: 1. Global application with economic compensation to non-Annex I Parties; 2. Application

limited to journeys to Annex I countries with or without compensation to third Parties.[174]

These are in conflict in the sense that the principles of CBDRRC and non-discrimination and NMFT point towards different ways to deal with the issue, namely, the burden of reducing emissions can be borne by all states or just by developed countries. However, the IMO regime seems to have already started exploring options on how to deal with the reconciliation of both principles, since a legal solution in the VCLT cannot be applied here.[175] Indeed, a reconciliation of the principle of CBDRRC and the principle of non-discrimination as stated in the IMO Regime and the NMFT incorporated in all IMO treaties can be only be achieved through '*compromise interpretation*'.[176] In this compromise, the IMO regime is exploring concepts and ways of accommodating differences, which in return may be of use for other issues in the future, both within the IMO regime,[177] but also as a model for other regimes. Given this conflictive dilemma it becomes crucial for participants to exchange knowledge and experience with the climate regime.

In this connection, even in the context of MARPOL Annex VI, the issue of CBDRRC has featured as the main reason for recourse to voting. The same debate has paralyzed progress on MBMs. However, a compromise solution on differential treatment was reached at the 65th session of the MEPC. Among other issues discussed at the MEPC 65, the importance of a MRV system to provide data for further regulation was acknowledged, especially by developed countries; however, the discussions resulted in a stalemate. Most developing countries refuse to negotiate until a resolution on technical cooperation and technology transfer was agreed. Therefore, a resolution on the Promotion of Technical Co-Operation and Transfer of Technology Relating to the Improvement of Energy Efficiency of Ships[178] was adopted, indicating a willingness to accommodate both the universal application of measures with differentiation, through implementation assistance and finance. Arguably, '*with the Resolution now adopted, this barrier to discussions on further measures has been lifted*'.[179] However, the lack of progress since then proves that the conciliation of differential and equal treatment in the IMO is still a hard nut to crack.[180]

Introducing market-based measures into standard-setting regimes: conflicts around the choice of instruments

Market-based instruments for international bunker fuels

The climate change regime has embraced the use of flexible and economically efficient instruments, including the use of MBMs, to reduce GHG emissions. The UNFCCC states among the guiding principles that '*taking into account that policies and measures to deal with climate change should be cost-effective so as to ensure global benefits at the lowest possible cost*'.[181] The basis of cost efficiency – that is, reducing emissions how, when and where it is most economically rational to do so – is appropriate since it is irrelevant for the climate where in the world the emissions are reduced. Therefore, the KP laid the groundwork for various flexibility mechanisms, including an emissions trading system.[182] This system has been accompanied by the establishment of national and regional tradable emission allowances schemes, such as the EU ETS, which puts a price on emissions.[183] Under Article 6 of the PA,[184] two market-based instruments have been established, although this implementation needs to be further detailed. First, a framework for the international trade of emissions units, so-called Internationally Transferable Mitigation Outcomes (ITMO);[185] and second a mechanism to mitigate GHG and support sustainable development, the so-called Sustainable Development Mechanism (SDM) or Mitigation Mechanism.[186]

Although emissions from international aviation and maritime transport fall outside KP and therefore they are not included in existing instruments, the adoption of MBMs have been the subject of extensive study and discussion in the ICAO and IMO regimes. In particular, the debate around regulating the emissions from these sectors has been advanced by the inclusion of aviation into the EU ETS.[187] ICAO and the IMO have systematically reinforced the idea of being the appropriate fora for developing the framework to tackle GHG emissions from their respective sectors, over the climate forum. After years of prevarication over the potential for operational, technological and alternative fuels measures, ICAO and the IMO have acknowledged the role of MBMs as a means to bridge the gap in emissions reductions. In this connection, they have emphasized the need for action at the international level despite delays in adopting measures, and their opposition to others who enact such measures.[188]

To accomplish environmental objectives such as GHG emissions reduction, towards a desired reduction target, the regimes can choose various instruments. They are grouped in two basic categories: command-and-control regulation and economic instruments. The first group of measures set requirements for compliance with specific technology or performance standards or outright bans that aim to provide signals and behaviour change for firms and individuals. The second group establishes a price incentive to achieve environmental objectives. There is also room for hybrid instruments, such as those setting a floor price or ceiling price for emissions. These measures can be also applied at the international level.

Economic instruments, otherwise called MBMs, can be price based (such as the use of taxes, charges, subsidies and liability rules) or quantity based (such as cap and trade or tradable allowances systems, where the price is determined by the scarcity of allowances).[189] It is widely held that MBMs are the most efficient way to price carbon.[190] Within this category, price instruments are less able to guarantee that a target will be achieved[191] and the establishment of a market for permits or allowances offers more flexibility than a taxation option, since it is claimed that externalities can be reduced in a more cost-efficient way.[192] Conversely, a tax on emissions would be more efficient than an emissions trading system because it can provide '*greater flexibility over time*'.[193] Ultimately, how emissions trading compares to taxation is contingent upon the specific method used for allocating emission allowances, where auctioning will be closer to taxation than grandfathering.[194] The choice of one instrument and design over another is usually based upon multiple parameters, related to the specific sector to which it is applied. However, in choosing an instrument to respond to climate change, political factors may be stronger than the *'basic insights of economic theory'*.[195] An important issue here is the question of revenues raised by MBMs; taxes for example tend to generate more public revenue than most quantity instruments, so they are likely to be more attractive to governments.[196] However, industry usually favours instruments in this order: subsidies, grandfathered allowances, auction allowances and, finally, taxes.[197]

MBMs can be adopted by countries and regions or globally.[198] Global taxes can be defined as taxes adopted by a group of countries on a coordinated basis, and whose revenue could also be used as a source of international finance.[199] It is also worth noting that the establishment of an MBM for international aviation and maritime transport raises issues regarding the use of the potential revenues.[200] Specifically, there is scope for global taxes imposed on both sectors that can generate additional finance to invest in climate change adaptation[201] and mitigation measures in developing countries.[202]

One of the main reasons to support a revenue raising measure is found in the polluter pays principle (PPP), which in the case of the climate regime is considered to build on and complement the CBDRDR principle.[203] In this connection, MBMs including a large degree of 'grandfathering' of allowances are considered to be regressive, since they are effectively allocating allowances of an economic value to the polluters free of charge, whereas they should be paying, according to the PPP, for the environmental cost of their activities. The inclusion of offsetting in an emissions trading system has a number of benefits, including improving cost-effectiveness, allowing for potential co-benefits and, subject to location, profits for developing countries. However, emissions offsetting has some drawbacks such as concerns over integrity (verification) and disincentives for long-term technological change.[204]

Here the situation between ICAO and the IMO differs widely. While the air transport regime contains specific provisions on exemptions for taxing aviation and the prohibition of taxing fuel, there is no such prohibition in the maritime transport regime. Nonetheless, progress towards the development of an MBM is further advanced in the ICAO forum.[205]

With regards to establishing a market-based measure for international transport, conceptualizations and interpretations over the content of differential treatment play an essential role in advancing negotiations. Some other ideas towards resolving the conundrum have come from non-state actors, such as the safeguards in regards of CBDR for global schemes in aviation and shipping proposed by NGOs.[206] For example, in the global aviation sector, differential treatment of routes and the channelling of revenues were two of the options for applying the principle of differentiation which were the outcome of a stakeholder workshop organized by WWF in 2012.[207] Within the shipping arena, the International Maritime Emission Reduction Scheme (IMERS), one of the proposals for maritime transport emissions reduction at the IMO, includes a number of recommendations/suggestions to deal with the CBDRRC versus equal treatment problems in IMO, which can be potentially transferred to the ICAO regime.[208]

ICAO and the thin line between taxes, charges and emissions trading

ICAO has acknowledged the role of MBMs as a means to bridge the gap in emissions reductions.[209] Emphasis has been put on the need for action at the international level; however, until 2016, ICAO delayed adopting policies, and opposed other agencies that have enacting such measures.[210] Here, a main challenge comes from the tax-exempted status of international aviation. The Chicago Convention contains specific provisions on exemptions for levying aviation and the prohibition of taxing fuel used in international aviation, and subsequent resolutions have followed the same principles.[211]

The ICAO regime distinguishes between two categories within the concept of levies, namely, charges and taxes. While the function of a charge is to finance the costs of providing facilities and services for civil aviation, the purpose of taxes is, in principle, to raise general national and local government revenues that are usually applied for non-aviation purposes. As argued in Chapter 4, through regulatory and conceptual interaction with the climate regime, a third model has entered the regime, namely emissions trading, which has forced the ICAO regime to redefine taxes and the role of economic instruments to deal with environmental problems.[212]

Regarding charges, under the Chicago Convention, each contracting State commits to provide in its territory the necessary safe infrastructure to facilitate air navigation (i.e. airports, radio and meteorological services).[213] These are regularly improved through SARPs and joint financing schemes.[214] These facilities are open to use by foreign aircraft under the same conditions of national aircraft, and in connection with that use, '*charges that may be imposed or permitted to be imposed by a contracting State for the use of such airports*' with certain limits[215] and requirements.[216] However, Article 15 contains a prohibition of charges:

> No fees, dues or other charges shall be imposed by any contracting State in respect solely of the right of transit over or entry into or exit from its territory of any aircraft of a contracting State or persons or property thereon.

As Bin Cheng points out, concerns around charges have been at the centre of ICAO's attention since its inception. The main reason for that worry was the increasing need for airlines to contribute, along with contracting States, to the financing of aviation ground facilities.[217] While some progress and agreement was reached in connection with charges for the use of airports,[218] the question of '*collecting and equitably distributing the proceeds of charges for en route air navigation services*' proved to be complex and was ruled out of ICAO's negotiation processes for a period of time.[219] Eventually, the question of desirability for charges *en route* was left to the discretion of ICAO member States. However, '*in imposing charges States should follow a reasonable policy with careful attention to their impact on the economic position of international air transport.*'[220] The main difference with airport charges is that the emphasis is placed on the effect that charges have on the cost of operators.[221] Additionally, with regard to taxation, Article 24 (a) contains a prohibition of taxes based on customs duties on the fuel used by aircraft, among other operational costs. The article states that:

> Fuel, lubricating oils, spare parts, regular equipment and aircraft stores on board an aircraft of a contracting State, on arrival in the territory of another contracting State and retained on board on leaving the territory of that State shall be exempt from customs duty, inspection fees or similar national or local duties and charges. This exemption shall not apply to any quantities or articles unloaded, except in accordance with the customs regulations of the State, which may require that they shall be kept under customs supervision.

Taxation on international aviation could levy the fuel, the ticket or the trip. While taxing tickets or trip receives minimal legal challenges,[222] fuel taxation is more controversial, given the exemption of international aviation fuel taxation contained in Article 24 of the Chicago Convention.[223] Furthermore, 'over 2500 *bilateral air transport agreements*'[224] contain the exemption on taxing international fuel on reciprocal bases, something that has been encouraged by ICAO's policy. However, the taxation of fuel purchased for international flights within state jurisdictions or domestic flights, even if the fuel was purchased abroad, is not prohibited.[225]

Although there are sound arguments to tax international aviation, including the cross-border environmental damage and the rather low level of current taxation,[226] international aviation is not taxed, neither is it subject to VAT, reflecting the objective of excluding exports from international transport.[227] Legal impediments to fuel charges and taxation came at a particular historical moment in aviation, where it was used as a means to kick-start a global aviation industry.[228] However, the situation has evolved after decades of rapid growth, and now the environmental impacts of aviation, including climate change, are at the centre of aviation policy-making. In this new landscape, the use of charges and taxes for climate purposes is to be considered.[229] Some observers support the idea of '*a corrective tax on aviation to address greenhouse effects*'[230] or another type of levy to put a price on carbon emissions, whether an indirect tax[231] or for example a levy for adaptation purposes,[232] which can be considered a type of '*tax on resource use*'.[233]

Carbon taxes are not exactly the same as fuel taxes since they target more precisely the cause of pollution (i.e. the carbon content of the fuel). The status of this type of charge is debated with regards to the prohibition of Article 24.[234] Some dissonant voices say that ICAO's opposition to taxation as a political barrier rather than a legal one and that the restrictions in the use of taxes and charges come from the rejection of using aviation to raise local revenues. However, this argument overlooks the main purpose of an environmental charge or tax, which is to tackle emissions.[235]

Interaction with the climate regime has given arguably a boost to MBMs in general, including the specific reconsideration of the prohibitions and limitations on taxes and charges for international aviation for climate-related purposes. Also, the concept of emissions trading has been introduced into the ICAO regime through interaction with the climate regime,[236] resulting in a conceptual jump from a technical command-and-control regulation regime to one that is considering the use of politically charged economic instruments. These conceptual incursions, however, are not free from controversy or a divergence of opinion among regime participants. Here, a particular cause of conflict is the definition of emissions trading under the ICAO regime, since no instrument has been issued to date to clarify the relation between climate charges, taxes and emissions trading. The status of emissions trading in the ICAO regime is also the subject of debate, although this very much depends on the specific choice and design of the measure. Some observers argue that it will be effectively a levy related to the fuel consumed in aviation activities.[237] Therefore, policy debates centre on the question of whether applying a levy on those emissions constitutes a tax or a charge and thus contravene the Chicago convention and other instruments adopted by the ICAO Assembly and Council. Many countries have also called emissions trading a charge or a tax, contravening the Chicago convention. In this connection, the ATAA case evidenced that there is no unanimous agreement on what emissions trading is, legally speaking, since it was alleged to contravene the Chicago Convention's tax and charge prohibitions.[238] Here the ATAA ruling can help to clarify and add to the legal canvas on MBMs for aviation, further shaping the concept.[239]

With regards to emissions trading, two more tensions arise. First, since it is a quantity instrument, a cap or target is intrinsic in the definition and needs to be set. Here, ICAO meets again with the issue of establishing a target, which may not be in line with the climate objective. Second, the revenues raised by emissions schemes are typically, if not totally, partially, directed to mitigation or adaptation to climate change. Within ICAO there is a preference for the idea of revenues being redirected to the sector, which may clash with other ideas expressed in the climate regime on using the potential revenues from aviation (and also shipping) to help finance the Green Climate Fund.[240] The 39th ICAO Assembly commended ICAO and its member States to

> express a clear concern, through the UNFCCC process, on the use of international aviation as a potential source for the mobilization of revenue for climate finance to the other sectors, in order to ensure that international aviation would not be targeted as a source of such revenue in a disproportionate manner.[241]

In this connection, future regulations must be designed so as to avoid conflict.

However, in the end, ICAO has opted for offsetting MBM, CORSIA, which is less problematic with regards to the tax debate. CORSIA envisions the allocation of responsibility to be achieved on an airline basis system with some route-based exemptions. CORSIA covers flights between countries (take-off and landing) covered by the scheme.[242] Airlines are due to report emissions yearly to their country authorities, which in turn report back to ICAO. Airlines are required to purchase offsets for the excess of emissions from the baseline.[243] IATA, '*the industry body representing the vast majority of mainly legacy carriers has for years resisted all attempts to price aviation carbon*'[244] but finally supported this option[245] and pushed for an emissions allocation given to airlines as the fairest way of doing so. That said, the stake that countries have with regards of their airlines and routes made the agreement mixed.

IMO and command-and-control measures

No similar legal conflicts (i.e. a prohibition norm versus a permissive norm) are found in the IMO regime, although the introduction of an MBM has been met with political resistance in the maritime sector. Leaving aside differential treatment issues, the use of economic instruments is new to the IMO regime and the introduction of such concepts has proved controversial.[246] Introducing MBMs presents three sets of challenges: the first group refers to the tradition in using command and control to deal (internationally agreed and implemented nationally) with environmental problems.[247] The second challenge refers to the inherent risk and complexity of economic instruments since they leave the freedom of how to abate emissions mainly to the shipowners, meaning they can suffer from design problems if they are not levied universally. Third, command and control is the generally favoured approach to regulation at the IMO.[248] The reasons for this can be attributed to two facts: first, command-and-control measures and standards are easier to apply universally and equally than are the implications of an MBM.[249] Second, IMO delegations usually include representatives from the shipping industry in major maritime countries, and if not then they tend to work in close cooperation and consultation with industry, ensuring that their opinion is sufficiently represented. In this way the shipping industry is able to lobby for regulations that '*favour existing companies and constitute some sort of barrier for newcomers*'.[250] As Shuo Ma explains, with the potential adoption of an MBM, control over technological development and uptake is given to the market, which stands to undermine the lobbying power and influence of industry in influencing specific standards and hence technologies.

A discussion over MBMs was opened at the 53rd Session of the MEPC in 2005, although no significant debate took place at that session. The first submissions by parties on the issue of MBMs were made at the 54th MEPC by Norway and the United Kingdom[251] and, during the following four sessions of the MEPC other submissions were made,[252] so that by the 59th MEPC there was already a number of proposals for an MBM, driving the debate over whether and how an MBM should be applied in the global shipping sector. Following the IMO Study,[253] a number of measures were put forward for consideration. The MEPC 59 agreed by majority on the need for MBMs as part of a package designed to achieve emissions reductions. However, parties remain divided over the question of MBMs, with the United States, Australia, Japan and the EU countries supporting the adoption of an MBM, while developing countries, especially the BRIC nations, are against it. Developing countries have opposed MBMs on a number of grounds, including incompatibilities with climate measures and the WTO, a lack of capacity or competence of the IMO to develop an MBM, and issues of differentiation.

In fact, after the lack of agreement on international maritime emissions at COP 15 in Copenhagen, the MEPC started to consider mandatory measures for all ships, regardless their flag and ownership through MARPOL Annex VI.[254] While the organization has been successful in establishing technological and operational measures,[255] consideration of MBMs for the sector has fallen out of the agenda. However, the IMO created, at MEPC 60, an expert group on MBMs. Although the group evaluated different proposals and there was some deliberation on the legal implications of the measures in the MEPC, it has proved impossible, thus far, to find a way forward. Nonetheless, under the decarbonization Roadmap agreed at the 70th session, the debate on MBMs is likely to be back to the discussions.

Synergies

To date, overlaps between the regimes have not led to many synergistic outcomes (i.e. an aggregate positive effect or positive outcome of the interactions).[256] However, some have occurred, and, crucially, there are possibilities for some more to occur if the regimes find a will to advance in the negotiations. Most of the potential for synergies relates to the issue of finance and the establishment of an MBM to reduce emissions.

In this connection, the GEF-UNDP-ICAO Project[257] and the GEF-UNDP-IMO Project,[258] addressed extensively in Chapter 4, can be seen as a synergistic outcome of the overlap between regimes, while at the same time providing a space for interaction where further synergistic outcomes can emerge. These are relevant at the implementation level but could also help advance discussions on CBDRRC, since these partnerships provide for differentiation through assistance. This is very clearly illustrated with the case of CORSIA. The capacity building and financial assistance for voluntary action plans on emissions reductions[259] through this venture with the GEF and UN programme built the support from developing countries needed for the adoption of the CORSIA mechanism.[260] In this connection, similar synergistic effects might come from GloMEEP.

A second group of synergies refers to the establishment of MBMs; in particular, the adoption of CORSIA can be seen as a synergistic outcome of the interaction between the ICAO and climate regimes; that is, a success in introducing an MBM (economic measure) in a standard-setting (technical) regime. However, at the time of writing, it is unclear how CORSIA would be finally defined since the framework agreed upon at the ICAO 39th Assembly needs to develop the essential 'building blocks' of the mechanism. For example, the deadline for the implementation of MRV is 2019, and the accounting system[261] and the eligibility criteria for the offsets need to be agreed still. Here, it remains to be seen how CORSIA will interact with the climate regime, in particular with the use of CDM, and the mechanisms outlined in Article 6 of the PA from 2020. In this connection, the development of the rule book for the PA in the forthcoming years is crucial, since it will establish the future of the carbon market and the standards to be applied to credits.[262] The parallel discussions about offsets at the ICAO and the PA negotiations need to be integrated for the synergies to emerge. As suggested by the literature, '*it is imperative to closely link the further development of CORSIA under ICAO with Article 6 evolution under the UNFCCC*'.[263]

Undoubtedly, there is an enormous potential for synergies, in particular from the use of offsets, but also the use of revenues raised by the MBMs for climate mitigation and adaptation.[264] There is also room for synergies between the ICAO and IMO regimes, such as in terms of setting targets or caps that are consistent and consider trans-sector leakage, and the establishment of MBMs, where both sectors could share a market for the trading of allowances, thus benefiting from cross-sector flexibility.

Conclusions

This chapter has examined the consequences of interactions between the climate and ICAO and IMO regimes, aiming to answer the question: *What are the consequences, in terms of conflicts and synergies, of the interaction for the allocation and regulation of international aviation and international maritime transport?* In answering that question, this chapter has also addressed the following sub-questions: *How do diverging objectives and purposes of the regimes affect the pursuance of meaningful regulation? How can the burden of mitigation be distributed given the existence of divergent principles between regimes? What are the implications of the CBDRRC principle entering systems based on equal and non-discriminatory treatment? And, how do conflicts and synergies between the climate, ICAO and IMO regimes affect the choice of regulatory instrument?*

Overall, this chapter has identified the presence of conflicts, under the definition adopted, at the level of objectives, principles and norms. While these conflicts have an inherently political dimension, they are not insurmountable and in fact they contain significant potential for synergistic outcomes.

While dealing with climate change is currently part of the work carried out in the ICAO and the IMO regimes, there are elements at the normative and institutional level of both systems that slows regulatory progress.[265] As with other sectors, the main constraint to progress is the powerful conflict between the desire to promote growth in these sectors while reducing emissions. At the same time the interactions with the climate regime, a sphere with its own norms and characteristics, creates additional challenges.

From all the conflicts, fitting differential treatment in non-discriminatory regimes has been highlighted as the most relevant challenge. Although the CBDRRC principle underpins the whole climate regime, including emissions from international transport, its role in the allocation and regulation of emissions from IBF outside the climate regime is contested. The regimes of ICAO and the IMO work, as a rule, on an equal and non-discriminatory basis,[266] so the introduction of a principle that embodies differentiated treatment faces a number of challenges. From the struggles of reconciling differential and equal treatment, a number of options for adapting the content of CBDRRC to these traditionally non-discriminatory regimes have been put forward. There is also potential for the creation of new concepts that incorporate both principles. The interaction of the climate regime with ICAO and IMO in the light of its principles has been acknowledged by the International Law Association,[267] but not as having a conflictual character: rather that the principle is increasingly invoked in ICAO and IMO where it is due to play a role.[268] As Jutta Brunne puts it:

> [T]he regime objective is a yardstick for the credibility of global climate action, while the CBDR principle provides a yardstick for the fairness of the associated burden sharing. Together, the objective and CBDR help define what it takes to build a legitimate climate regime.[269]

Regarding the synergistic outcomes of interaction, the chapter has highlighted the potential for the issue of finance and the establishment of an MBM to reduce emissions. In particular the chapter has pointed out towards the prospective synergies between CORSIA and the MBMs under the UNFCCC.

Notes

1 See Chapter 2 on the work of Harro van Asselt, *The Fragmentation of Global Climate Governance: Consequences and Management of Regime Interactions* (Edward Elgar Publishing Limited, 2014).
2 See Chapter 2 on the definition proposed by the ILC. See, ILC, *Fragmentation of International Law: Difficulties Arising from the Diversification and Expansion of International Law. Report of the Study Group of the International Law Commission.* UN Doc. A/CN.4/L.682. (2006).
3 H.v. Asselt, *The Fragmentation of Global Climate Governance: Consequences and Management of Regime Interactions.* (2014).
4 It was singled out as highly important for determining the tone of the interaction between the climate regime with ICAO and the IMO. Sebastian Oberthür, 'The Climate Change Regime: Interactions of the Climate Change Regime with ICAO, IMO and the EU Burden-Sharing Agreement', in *Institutional Interaction in Global Environmental Governance: Synergy and Conflict among International and EU Policies: Global Environmental Accord: Strategies for Sustainability and Institutional Innovation* (Sebastian Oberthür and Thomas Gehring eds., 2006).
5 Kyoto Protocol to the United Nations Framework Convention on Climate Change, Kyoto, 10 December 1997, in force 16 February 2005, 37 International Legal Materials (1998). 2303 UNTS 148. (1997). Article 2.2. See chapter four.
6 The same idea is applied in the Climate and the WTO regimes. See, H.v. Asselt, *The Fragmentation of Global Climate Governance: Consequences and Management of Regime Interactions.* (2014).
7 See, Margaret A. Young, 'Introduction: The Productive Friction between Regimes', in *Regime Interaction in International Law: Facing Fragmentation* (Margaret A. Young ed., 2012).
8 This dialectic between the protection of the environment and the need for economic development is a key question underpinning the evolution of international environmental law, see, Malcolm N. Shaw, *International Law* (Cambridge University Press 6th ed., 2008). 849.

9   Including the Paris Agreement, which reads in its Article 2.1: '*The Agreement, in enhancing the implementation of the Convention, including its objective, aims to strengthen the global response to the threat of climate change.*'

10 See Farhana Yamin and Joanna Depledge, *The International Climate Change Regime: A Guide to Rules, Institutions and Procedures* (Cambridge University Press, 2004). 60–65; Patricia W. Birnie et al., *International Law and the Environment* (Oxford University Press 3rd ed., 2009). 358.

11 See and account on the issues around the interpretation of Article 2.2 in Konrad Ott and Gernot Klepper, 'Reasoning Goals of Climate Protection: Specification of Article 2 UNFCCC', *Federal Environmental Agency*, (2004); Michael Oppenheimer and Annie Petsonk, 'Article 2 of the UNFCCC: Historical Origins, Recent Interpretations', *Climatic Change*, 73(3), (2005). 195–226.

12 Alexander Zahar, 'The Climate Change Regime', in *Routledge Handbook of International Environmental Law* (Shawkat Alam ed., 2013). 352.

13 The goal of keeping global warming below 2°C above pre-industrial levels was agreed upon in COP15 and assimilated to the UNFCCC process in COP16. In the light of the IPCC Fifth Assessment Report in 2014, the goal could be tightened to 1.5°C.

14 Jutta Brunnée, 'An Agreement in Principle? The Copenhagen Accord and the Post-2012 Climate Regime', in *Law of the Sea in Dialogue* (Holger Hestermeyer et al. eds., 2011). 51–53. As stated: '*With this central concept quantified, the Article 1 objective provides not just general direction to states' efforts, but sets a bar against which the credibility of emissions reduction commitments can be measured.*'

15 See, Oliver Geden and Silke Beck, 'Renegotiating the Global Climate Stabilization Target', *Nature Climate Change*, 4(9), (2014). 747–748.

16 Olivia Gippner, 'The 2°C target: A European Norm Enters the International Stage – Following the Process to Adoption in China', *International Environmental Agreements: Politics, Law and Economics*, 6(1), (2014). 49–65. On influence of the European Union and the role of epistemic communities as a vehicle of influence. See also, M. Oppenheimer and A. Petsonk, (2005).

17 UNFCCC, Paris Agreement (Paris, 12 December 2015, in force 4 November 2016) FCCC/CP/2015/L.9. (2015). Art. 2.1(a).

18 Radoslav S. Dimitrov, 'The Paris Agreement on Climate Change: Behind Closed Doors', *Global Environmental Politics*, 16(3), (2016). 4.

19 See, Carl-Friedrich Schleussner et al., 'Science and Policy Characteristics of the Paris Agreement Temperature Goal', *Nature Climate Change*, 6(9), (2016). 827–835.

20 K. Ott and G. Klepper, (2004).

21 For example: '*dangerous anthropogenic interference with the climate system*' or '*that food production is not threatened*', etc. See, Joyeeta Gupta and Harro van Asselt, 'Helping Operationalise Article 2: A Transdisciplinary Methodological Tool for Evaluating When Climate Change Is Dangerous', *Global Environmental Change*, 16(1), (2006). 83–94.

22 K. Ott and G. Klepper, (2004). 39.

23 Ibid. at. 39.

24 Convention on International Civil Aviation, adopted 7 December 1944, entered into force 4 April 1947. 15 UNTS 295, as amended, ICAO Doc. 7300/9 (2006) (hereinafter Chicago Convention), (1944). Article 44.

25 Ruwantissa Abeyratne, *Convention on International Civil Aviation: A Commentary* (Springer, 2014). 233.

26 Ibid. at. 87.

27 Chicago Convention, Preamble.

28 R. Abeyratne, *Convention on International Civil Aviation: A Commentary.* (2014). 515–524.

29 8th meeting of its 196th Session in June 2012.

30 Ruwantissa Abeyratne, *Aviation and Climate Change: In Search of a Global Market Based Measure* (Springer, 2014).

31 See ICAO Council Strategic Objectives at ICAO's website: http://icao.int/about-icao/Pages/Strategic-Objectives.aspx (last accessed December 2016).
32 See ICAO's vision Statement at http://icao.int/about-icao/Pages/vision-and-mission.aspx (last accessed December 2016).
33 Christina Voigt, *Sustainable Development as a Principle of International Law: Resolving Conflicts between Climate Measures and WTO Law* (Martinus Nijhoff Publishers, 2009). She argues for a role of the principle of sustainable development principle for interpretation is conflictive situations between regimes. See further Chapter 6.
34 ICAO, Assembly Resolution A37–19: Consolidated Statement of Continuing ICAO Policies and Practices Related to Environmental Protection. Climate Change (2010).
35 ICAO. Environment Branch of ICAO, *ICAO Environmental Report 2013: Aviation and Climate Change* (ICAO, 2013). 23–25.
36 http://carbonmarketwatch.org/category/aviation-shipping./ See on the same vein, Transport and Environment, Grounded. How ICAO failed to tackle aviation and climate change and what should happen now (2010).
37 Mark Lutes and Shaun Vorster, 'Bridging the Political Barriers in Negotiating a Global Market-Based Measure for Controlling International Aviation Emissions', *Elements of a New Climate Agreement by 2015. Perspectives Series 2013. UNEP Risø*, (2013). 23.
38 ICAO, Assembly Resolution A37–19, (2010). Preamble.
39 Ibid. at. Preamble.
40 Ibid. at. Paragraph 3(b).
41 Annie Petsonk and Pedro Piris-Cabezas, 'Design of a Global Market Based Measure Bridging the Allocation Gap in the ICAO MBM: A New Proposal', *Carbon & Climate Law Review*, 10(2), (2016). 127–133; Parth Vaishnav, 'Design of a Global Market Based Measure · ICAO's Market Based Mechanism: Keep It Simple', *Carbon & Climate Law Review*, 10(2), (2016). 120–126.
42 ICAO, Assembly Resolution A38–18: Consolidated Statement of Continuing ICAO Policies and Practices Related to Environmental Protection. Climate Change (2013). Paragraph 7.
43 In all the other sectors of the economy, the buying of credits outside through projects is only supplementary.
44 Andrew Murphy, 'A False Dawn for Action on Aviation Emissions. (Published online on October 12, 2016)', *Transport and Environment*, (2016).
45 ICAO, Assembly Resolution A39–3: Consolidated Statement of Continuing ICAO Policies and Practices Related to Environmental Protection: Global Market-Based Measure (MBM) scheme (2016). Paragraph 9.
46 See further chapter 6.
47 IMO is a custodian also to a number of environmental conventions. See Chapters 3 and 4.
48 Convention on the Inter-Governmental Maritime Consultative Organization, adopted on 6 March 1948, entered into force 17 March 1958. 289 UNTS 48, amended and renamed as Convention on the International Maritime Organization, 14 November 1975, 9 UTS 61, (1948). Article 1. The convention text of 1948 made no mention of marine pollution and the environment, which was included in the 1975 and 1997 amendments and entered into force in 1984.
49 Resolution A.1060(28). Adopted on 29 November 2013. Strategic Plan for the Organization (for the six-year period 2014–2019), (2014). Currently, the IMO is in the process of developing a new strategic framework, which will be covering the period from 2018–2023.
50 IMO, Assembly Resolution A.963(23) on IMO Policies and Practices Related to the Reduction of Greenhouse Gas Emissions from Ships (2004). Preamble.
51 MEPC 61/24. Report of the Marine Environment Protection Committee on Its Sixty-First Session, (2010). 43–44. In fact, the concern came from the previous

exchanges which occurred at the AWG-LCA. The questions for debate were: '*should a reduction target be set for emissions from international shipping, and if so, what should the target be, how should it be articulated, and should it be set by UNFCCC or IMO?*'

52 MEPC 62/24. Report of the Marine Environment Protection Committee on its Sixty-second Session, (2011); MEPC 63/23. Report of the Marine Environment Protection Committee on its Sixty-third Session, (2012); MEPC 64/23. Report of the Marine Environment Protection Committee on its Sixty-fourth Session, (2012). In the 64th MEPC was indefinitely postponed.

53 MEPC 60/40/23. Alternative Emission Caps for Shipping in 2020 and 2030. Submitted by Norway, (2010).

54 MEPC 60/4/28. Emission 'Caps' and Reduction Targets. Submitted by the World Shipping Council, (2010).

55 MEPC 70/WP.7.

56 IMO, MEPC 59/4/8. IMO Must Act Decisively to Reduce GHG Emissions from Shipping If It Is to Retain Its Competence in Technical and Political Matters Related to Shipping and GHGs. Submitted by Friends of the Earth International, WWF & Greenpeace International (2009).

57 IMO, 'World Maritime Day: A Concept of Sustainable Maritime Transportation System', in *Sustainable Development: IMO's Contribution Beyond Rio+20*, (International Maritime Organization, 2013). The concept is '*at an embryonic stage*'. It intends to establish an internal mechanism to work with the industry. However, the original intention was to have a formal consultation process in conjunction with the mechanism established under the UNGA, although it was considered as '*not appropriate*'.

58 Tristan W. Smith et al., *Third IMO Greenhouse Gas Study 2014: Executive Summary and Final Report* (IMO, 2014).

59 A38-WP/288. Effective MBM to Address GHG Emissions from International Aviation. Presented by the International Coalition for Sustainable Aviation (ICSA), (2013).

60 Ibid.

61 Climate Action Network, 'Position on Market Based Measures for International Aviation', (Climate Action Network, 2013).

62 MEPC 59/4/8. 3.

63 Ibid. at. 3.

64 See for example the involvement of IPCC in ICAO, and other scientific groups in IMO. David S. Lee et al., 'Shipping and Aviation Emissions in the Context of a 2°C Emission Pathway' (Manchester Metropolitan University, 2013).

65 See for instance, MEPC 57/4/10. Immediate action and adoption of vessel speed reductions and carbon tax needed to reduce greenhouse gas emissions from shipping. Submitted by the Friends of the Earth International (FOEI), (2008). Representing other groups also: Friends of the Earth-US, Clean Air Task Force, North Sea Foundation, Bellona Foundation, European Federation for Transport and Environment, and Swedish NGO Secretariat on Acid Rain. They introduce the IPCC findings, but also the Stern Report and even Al Gore's work to raise awareness on the need to embrace the climate change objective.

66 See comparison in, S. Oberthür, (2006). 61.

67 Climate Convention, the preamble recital 21 affirms that responses to climate change should be coordinated with social and economic development. Also Articles 3.4 on sustainable development and 3.5 with regards to trade See also, International Law Association. International Law Association. Committee on the Legal Principles Relating to Climate Change, 'The Legal Principles Relating to Climate Change, Second Report (Sofia Conference 2012)', (2012). 18–19.

68 As stated in R. Abeyratne, *Convention on International Civil Aviation: A Commentary*; R. Abeyratne, *Convention on International Civil Aviation: A Commentary*. (2014).

Foreword. The ICAO regime is due to serve '*the needs of the people of the world and not exclusively those of individual businesses and States*'.

69 See chapter four and six.

70 S. Oberthür, (2006). Oberthür picked up on the ability of ICAO and IMO to embrace the climate objective as not hindering their main aims to be a determinant to action.

71 See for example, M. Lutes and S. Vorster, (2013). 25–26; Aydin Okur, 'The Challenge of Regulating Greenhouse Gas Emissions from International Shipping and the Complicated Principle of "Common But Differentiated Responsibilities"', (2012).

72 1970 Declaration on Principles of International Law.

73 All states are equal, but some states are more equal than others. An adaptation to the international dimension of the infamous phrase of George Orwell's *Animal Farm*.

74 Daniel Barstow Magraw, 'Legal Treatment of Developing Countries: Differential, Contextual and Absolute Norms', *Colorado Journal of International Environmental Law and Policy*, 1 (1990). 69. Magraw distinguishes three types of norms in international law, namely: absolute equal treatment norms, which set the same standards for all countries; differential treatment norms, which grant favourable treatment to developing States; and contextual treatment norms, which '*without specifically mentioning developing countries, require or [allow] consideration of characteristics that typically vary according to the economic developmental situation in a country*'. Provisions of contextual treatment provide, outwardly, identical treatment to all States but their application either requires or permits differentiation by considering factors that vary between countries. The indeterminacy inherent to contextual norms allows for the advantages of flexibility but also implies that the specific application of the norm can be contested. Contextual norms make use of formulas such as 'as far as possible', 'reasonably', 'justice and equity', 'appropriate for each country', 'countries abilities', 'cooperation and assistance'.

75 Ibid.

76 See Joost Pauwelyn, 'The End of Differential Treatment for Developing Countries? Lessons from the Trade and Climate Change Regimes', *Review of European, Comparative & International Environmental Law*, 22(1), (2013). 29–41.

77 See below next section. Harro van Asselt et al., 'The Changing Architecture of International Climate Change Law', in *Research Handbook on Climate Change Mitigation Law* (G. van Calster et al. eds., 2014).

78 See, Peter Lichtenbaum, 'Special Treatment vs. Equal Participation: Striking a Balance in the Doha Negotiations', American. University International Law Review, 17. (2002). 1. Lichtenbaum argues that the combination of special treatment with equal participation since the Uruguay Round, 'has not provided satisfactory results for developing countries' and that the Doha Declaration approach to special treatment, reflects tensions between the two approaches, where '*while the concept of special treatment will always be a component of the WTO negotiations, its use to avoid market liberalization is problematic and should be reserved for cases where it is truly essential.*'

79 Philippe Cullet, 'Differential Treatment in International Law: Towards a New Paradigm of Inter-State Relations', *European Journal of International Law*, 10(3), (1999). 557. On this point, he refers to the work of Emmanuel Decaux, *La Réciprocité en droit international* (Librairie générale de droit et de jurisprudence, 1980).

80 P. Cullet, 'Differential Treatment in International Law: Towards a New Paradigm of Inter-State Relations'. (1999). 582.

81 Philippe Cullet, *Differential Treatment in International Environmental Law* (Ashgate, 2003). 32–33.

82 Rio Declaration on Environment and Development, UN Doc. A/CONF.151/26 (vol. I) reprinted in (1992) 31 ILM 874 (1992). Adopted at the United Nations Conference on Environment and Development in Rio de Janeiro, Brazil from 3–14 June 1992, (1992). Principle 7: '*States shall cooperate in a spirit of global partnership to conserve, protect and restore the health and integrity of the Earth's ecosystem. In view of the*

different contributions to global environmental degradation, States have common but differentiated responsibilities. The developed countries acknowledge the responsibility that they bear in the international pursuit to sustainable development in view of the pressures their societies place on the global environment and of the technologies and financial resources they command.' Note that the principle, unlike Article 3(1) of the UNFCCC, does not include the '*and respective capabilities*' phrasing. See also Chapter 3.

83 Ulrich Beyerlin, 'Policies, Principles, and Rules', in *The Oxford Handbook of International Environmental Law: Oxford Handbooks* (Daniel Bodansky et al. eds., 2007). 441–442. In analyzing the reach of Principle 7, he posits that differentiated responsibility is not a rule but rather a 'source from which subsequent rules may emerge'.

84 For a comprehensive description of categories in environmental treaties, see Lavanya Rajamani, *Differential Treatment in International Environmental Law* (Oxford University Press, 2006). 87–128. Also, Tuula Honkonen, *The Common but Differentiated Responsibility Principle in Multilateral Environmental Agreements: Regulatory and Policy Aspects* (Wolters Kluwer Law & Business; Kluwer Law International, 2009).

85 Dinah Shelton, 'Equity', in *The Oxford Handbook of International Environmental Law: Oxford Handbooks* (Daniel Bodansky et al. eds., 2007). 639–662 and 656–658.

86 P. Cullet, *Differential Treatment in International Environmental Law*. (2003). 72–76.

87 D. Shelton, (2007). 662.

88 For an overview on the notion of the principle and its multiple possibilities, see Pieter Pauw et al., 'Different Perspectives on Differentiated Responsibilities a State-of-the-Art Review of the Notion of Common but Differentiated Responsibilities in International Negotiations', *Discussion Paper 6/2014. Deutsches Institut für Entwicklungspolitik*, (2014).

89 Christopher D. Stone, 'Common but Differentiated Responsibilities in International Law', *The American Journal of International Law*, 98(2), (2004). 299.

90 See, Preamble of the United Nations Convention on the Law of the Sea, Montego Bay, adopted 10 December 1982, in force 16 November 1994, 21 International Legal Materials (1982), 1261. 1833 UNTS 3, (1982).

91 WTO agreements GATT, GATS and TRIPS contain provisions on differential treatment for developing countries in three fronts, namely market protection, market access and implementation. On the relation of special and differential treatment with the most favoured nation principle see, M. J. Trebilcock and Robert Howse, *The Regulation of International Trade* (Routledge 3rd ed., 2005). 49–82.

92 C.D. Stone, (2004). 300.

93 See, for example Jutta Brunnée and Stephen J. Toope, *Legitimacy and Legality in International Law: An Interactional Account* (Cambridge University Press, 2010). 151–170.

94 UNFCCC, Article 3.1. For an overview on the principle see also Chapter 3.

95 For a summary of underpinning philosophical questions related to CDBR, especially in relation to the polluter pays principle see, James Nickel and Daniel Magraw, 'Philosophical Issues in International Environmental Law', in *The Philosophy of International Law* (Samantha Besson and John Tasioulas eds., 2010). 453–471.

96 L. Rajamani, *Differential Treatment in International Environmental Law*. (2006). 86.

97 The requirements in terms of content and timetable for national communications are different for Annex I and non-Annex I Parties. And they are dependent on assistance. UNFCCC, Article 4.7 links the obligation of reporting emissions for developing countries conditional to financing by developed partners.

98 UNFCCC, Article 4.3, 4.4 and 4.5. Including financial assistance in implementing the Convention through financial mechanisms (Art 11. UNFCCC) and the promotion, finance and transfer of technology (Art.4.5 UNFCCC and 10.c KP).

99 See, Rowena Maguire, 'The Role of Common but Differentiated Responsibility in the 2020 Climate Regime: Evolving a New Understanding of Differential Commitments', *Climate Change Law Review*, 4, (2013). 1–10.

100 A. Savaresi, 'The Paris Agreement: A New Beginning?', *Journal of Energy and Natural Resources Law*, 34(1), (2016), 16, at 22.

101 D. Bodansky, 'The Paris Climate Change Agreement: A New Hope?', *American Journal of International Law*, 110, (2016) 288–319; and Lavanya Rajamani, 'Ambition and Differentiation in the 2015 Paris Agreement: Interpretative Possibilities and Underlying Politics', *International and Comparative Law Quarterly*, 65(2), (2016), 493.

102 Beatriz Martinez Romera, 'The Paris Agreement and the Regulation of International Bunker Fuels', *Review of European Comparative & International Environmental Law*, 25(2), (2016). 215–227.

103 For example the division of countries of Annex I and non-Annex I based on the OECD criteria has been deemed as a lapse in the regime. See, Joanna Depledge and Yamin Farhana, 'The Global Climate Change Regime: A Defense', in *The Economics and Politics of Climate Change* (Dieter Helm and Cameron Hepburn eds., 2009). 443–446; Joyeeta Gupta, 'A History of International Climate Change Policy', *Wiley Interdisciplinary Reviews: Climate Change*, 1(5), (2010). 160–161.

104 See for example, Tuula Honkonen, 'The Principle of Common but Differentiated Responsibility in Post-2012 Climate Negotiations', *Review of European Community & International Environmental Law*, 18(3), (2009). 257–267. A proposed interpretation on the CBDRRC principle for the 2015 agreement is given in, Lavanya Rajamani et al., 'International Law Association – Washington Conference (2014): Legal Principles Relating to Climate Change (July 2, 2014). Report of the International Law Association's Committee on Legal Principles Relating to Climate Change (Washington, 2014)', (2014). 17–28.

105 T. Honkonen, 'The Principle of Common but Differentiated Responsibility in Post-2012 Climate Negotiations'. (2009).

106 See, Harro van Asselt, 'Alongside the UNFCCC: Complementary Venues for Climate Action', (Centre for Climate and Energy Solutions, May 2014); Daniel Bodansky, 'Multilateral Climate Efforts beyond the UNFCCC' (Centre for Climate and Energy Solutions, 2011). Also, Biermann et al. 2009; Keohane and Victor 2010; Moncel and Van Asselt 2012; Van Asselt and Zelli 2014.

107 I.L.A. International Law Association. Committee on the Legal Principles Relating to Climate Change, (2012). 13.

108 ICAO and the IMO are examples of regimes working under equal premises where developed countries have objected to differential treatment with arguments such as market distortion and the imperilment of the legal and political working practices. For example, the opposition to CBDR as a guiding principle for a market-based mechanism in ICAO AR 38–18 Annex. Written Statement of Reservation by Lithuania on behalf of the member States of the European Union and 14 other member States of the European Civil Aviation Conference (ECAC) with regard to ICAO Assembly Resolution A38–18, (2013). 3 Also, the argument that leaving emerging economies without reduction commitments would endanger the achievement of the climate regime's objective has been put forward by countries such as the United States. See also the reservations by countries such as Australia, Canada, New Zealand and the United States at www.icao.int/Meetings/a38/Pages/resolutions.aspx

109 In 2006 China surpassed the United States as the world largest GHG emitter of CO_2. Data available at the UN Statistics Division, in http://mdgs.un.org/unsd/mdg/SeriesDetail.aspx?srid=749

110 Bali can be considered as the inflection point of this trend. See also, J. Pauwelyn, (2013). Pauwelyn argues that the end of differential treatment for developing countries does not necessarily mean the end of differentiation, but rather the beginning of an era of more effective and equitable differentiation based on specific criteria, needs and development. In the same vein see, H.v. Asselt et al., 'The Changing

Architecture of International Climate Change Law'. (2014). However, other scholars are more sceptical about the outcomes of the increasing symmetry in commitments in the climate regime. See, Duncan French and Lavanya Rajamani, 'Climate Change and International Environmental Law: Musings on a Journey to Somewhere', *Journal of Environmental Law*, 25(3), (2013). 437–461. They are of the view that this phenomenon of *'greater deference to national circumstances and, hence towards differentiation for all (rather than just for developing countries)'* includes only *'token references'* to the special needs of least developed countries or small island developing states.

111 Annex B was modified in Doha with new commitments for the second period of Kyoto (2013–2020).

112 Christiana Figueres, UNFCCC executive secretary, highlighted the difference between domestic and international emissions in this connection. She stated at the Aviation and Environment Summit in Geneva, September 2010 that *'Emissions from domestic activities form part of Parties' total national emissions, and are addressed under the UNFCCC according to the CBDR principle. On the other hand, goals and targets set by ICAO refer to international aviation emissions and would be managed according to ICAO's principle of equal treatment for airlines.'* Available at: www.greenaironline.com/news.php?viewStory=921 (last accessed December 2016).

113 This author has conducted research visits to both the ICAO and the IMO, attending sessions as an observer to the Colloquium on Aviation and Climate Change previous to the 37th ICAO Assembly, in May 2010, and the MEPC 61 and MEPC 62, in 2011.

114 This lack of progress is due mainly to the lack of agreement in the use of differential treatment in the allocation of those international emissions to countries. While domestic emissions have fallen within the scope of national commitments, international emissions remain undefined.

115 ICAO, Assembly Resolution A36–22: Consolidated Statement of Continuing ICAO Policies and Practices Related to Environmental Protection (2007). Appendix J, K and L. ICAO, Assembly Resolution A37–19, (2010). Recital and.

116 IMO, MEPC. 229(65) Promotion of Technical Co-Operation and Transfer of Technology Relating to the Improvement of Energy Efficiency of Ships, (2013).

117 I.L.A. International Law Association. Committee on the Legal Principles Relating to Climate Change, (2012). 13.

118 Chicago Convention. Article 11.

119 General Agreement on Trade in Services (GATS). Adopted 15 April 1994. 1869 UNTS 183. Annex on Air Transport, (1994).

120 I.L.A. International Law Association. Committee on the Legal Principles Relating to Climate Change, (2012). 13.

121 Assembly 38th Session, Report of the Executive Committee on Agenda Item 17, Annex. A38-WP/430.

122 Ibid.

123 I.L.A. International Law Association. Committee on the Legal Principles Relating to Climate Change, (2012). 13.

124 Assembly 38th Session, Report of the Executive Committee on Agenda Item 17, Annex. A38-WP/430.

125 During the 39th ICAO Assembly.

126 The ECAC includes members outside the EU.

127 Annex on the guiding principles for the design and implementation of market-based measures for international aviation. Guiding Principle P.

128 See, D. French and L. Rajamani, (2013). 5–7. Furthermore, the authors argue that such developments have pushed the *'developed states to swing the pendulum in the other direction in more recently negotiated areas of international environmental law'*. They use as an example the draft text of the Minamata Convention on Mercury.

129 Paula Castro et al., 'Constructed Peer Groups and Path Dependence in International Organizations: The Case of the International Climate Change Negotiations', *Global Environmental Change*, 25(0), (2014). 109–120. This study contrasts institutionalized country groupings with voluntary country coalitions. Empirical research weighted the effects of differential treatment in future climate negotiations, finding that the generation of new incentives that favour group cohesion and enhanced socialization among delegates result in deeper group divisions and institutional path dependence, on top of the original gap.

130 This follows the same logic as the EU has applied by not embracing CBDRRC when it included aviation in the EU ETS, whereby it regulates aircraft operators and not countries, therefore CDDRRC doesn't apply. See discussion in, Joanne Scott and Lavanya Rajamani, 'EU Climate Change Unilateralism', *European Journal of International Law*, 23(2), (2012). 469–494. In that connection, the EU has been accused of not assuring that '*the implications of its Directive for developing and developed countries airlines are equal.*' see, Henri J. Nkuepo, 'EU ETS Aviation Discriminates against Developing Countries', *Africa's Trade Law Newsletter*, 7, (2012). 6.

131 Reservations were based on the fact that the threshold left only 26 states above the line and that the threshold exempted come developed countries, which is not in line with CDBRRC, as well as the potential for distortion in terms of carriers operating the same route. According to Lutes and Vorster, for all that, '*large parts of the ICAO council no longer support this exemption*' M. Lutes and S. Vorster, (2013). 26.

132 AR 38–18 Paragraph 16.b '*exemptions for the application of MBMs on routes to and from developing States whose share of international civil aviation activities is below the threshold of 1% of total revenue ton kilometres of international civil aviation activities, until the global scheme is implemented*'. This also connects with Paragraph 21 that states: '*special circumstances and respective capabilities of developing States could be accommodated through de minimis exemptions from, or phased implementation for, the application of an MBM to particular routes or markets with low levels of international aviation activity, particularly those serving developing States.*'

133 Paragraph 17 In connection with *de minimis* exemption, the EU has attempted to redefine the concept by exempting flights to and from developing countries with less than a 1% share of total revenue of international aviation. The EU Commission proposal defines these countries through the criteria of countries benefiting from preferential access to the EU market, namely, those which are not classified in 2013 by the World Bank as high-income or upper-middle income countries.

134 M. Lutes and S. Vorster, (2013). 26.

135 Paragraph 24 and Annex n) '*where revenues are generated from MBMs, it is strongly recommended that they should be applied in the first instance to mitigating the environmental impact of aircraft engine emissions, including mitigation and adaptation, as well as assistance to and support for developing States*'.

136 Coraline Goron, 'The EU Aviation ETS Caught between Kyoto and Chicago: Unilateral Legal Entrepreneurship in the Multilateral Governance System', Green-Gem Doctoral Working Papers Series, (2012). 10.

137 See, Joanne Scott and Lavanya Rajamani, 'EU Climate Change Unilateralism', *SSRN eLibrary*, (2012); Benito Müller, 'From Confrontation to Collaboration? CBDR and the EU ETS Aviation Dispute with Developing Countries', *Oxford Energy and Environmental Brief*, (2012); J. Pauwelyn, (2013).

138 See the full list of exclusions in the Annex I of the Directive 2008/101/EC of 19 November 2008 Amending Directive 2003/87/EC so as to Include Aviation Activities in the Scheme for Greenhouse Gas Emission Allowance Trading within the Community, [2009] L8/3. OJ L 8. 13.1.2009.

139 Commercial flights under 243 flights per period for three consecutive four-month periods or those with total annual emissions lower than 10 000 tonnes.

140 Directive 2008/101/EC.Article 25a.
141 Ibid.; ibid. at. Article 3.d (4).
142 J. Pauwelyn, (2013). 38. Pauwelyn points out that the EU Directive distinguishes the group of '*economically more advanced developing countries*'.
143 See, ibid. at. 38.
144 COM(2006) 818 SEC(2006) 1685. Impact Assessment of the Inclusion of Aviation Activities in the Scheme for Greenhouse Gas Emission Allowance Trading within the Community. 51–54. The assessment of the measure for developing countries concerns the additional demand for JI and CDM credits and states that '*the measure would be fully in line with the principle of "common but differentiated responsibilities" under the UNFCCC. Incorporation of aviation emissions from routes to/from EU airports into the EU ETS would first of all be a measure taken by the Community as an Annex I Party to the UNFCCC. In terms of the economic impacts, a larger proportion of compliance costs would naturally be borne by Annex I carriers as they generally have a higher market share on the routes covered. However, carriers from developing countries that are able to operate in competition with Annex I carriers on such routes would of course need to be covered in order to avoid a) distortions of competition and b) discrimination as to nationality in line with the Chicago Convention.*'
145 See discussion in, J. Scott and L. Rajamani, (2012). In that connection, the EU has been accused of not assuring that '*the implications of its Directive for developing and developed countries airlines are equal,*' see, H.J. Nkuepo, (2012). 6.
146 J. Scott and L. Rajamani, (2012). 479–487.
147 Case-366/10. Opinion of Advocate General Kokott delivered on 6 October 2011.
148 AATA Case C-366/10, (Court of Justice of the European Union).
149 Case-366/10. Opinion of Advocate General Kokott delivered on 6 October 2011.
150 India, for example, raised a number of objections to the inclusion of international aviation in the EU ETS with regards to CBDR. See also the Joint Declaration of Moscow.
151 Commission Proposal COM(2013) 722. Proposal for a Directive of the European Parliament and of the Council amending Directive 2003/87/EC establishing a scheme for greenhouse gas emission allowance trading within the Community, in view of the implementation by 2020 of an international agreement applying a single global market-based measure to international aviation emissions.
152 Regulation (EU) No 978/2012 of 25 October 2012 applying a Scheme of Generalised Tariff Preferences and Repealing Council Regulation (EC) No 732/2008, OJ L 303, 31.10.2012. And, Commission Delegated Regulation (EU) No 154/2013 of 18 December 2012 amending Annex II to Regulation (EU) No 978/2012 of the European Parliament and of the Council applying a Scheme of Generalised Tariff Preferences. OJ L 48, 21.2.2013.
153 Such exemption would translate into an exclusion of around 80 countries '*in a non-discriminatory basis*'. See COM(2013) 722. Proposal for a Directive of the European Parliament and of the Council Amending Directive 2003/87/EC Establishing a Scheme for Greenhouse Gas Emission Allowance Trading Within the Community. 3. See the list of countries at the EU Commission's Climate Action website. Provisional list of countries referred to in recital 10 and the Annex to Commission proposal COM(2013)722 to amend Directive 2003/87/EC, to/from which it is proposed that routes be exempted from the EU ETS for the period from 2014 to 2020. Available at: http://ec.europa.eu/clima/policies/transport/aviation/docs/country_list_en.pdf
154 D. French and L. Rajamani, (2013).
155 Written Statement of Reservation by Lithuania on Behalf of the Member States of the European Union and 14 other Member States of the European Civil Aviation Conference (ECAC) with Regard to ICAO Assembly Resolution A38-18.
156 Jos Delbeke, Speech at the Conference: A New Flightplan – Getting Global Aviation Climate Measures Off the Ground, (7 February 2012), (2012).

157 R. Abeyratne, *Aviation and Climate Change: In Search of a Global Market Based Measure*. (2014). 2014.
158 B. Martinez Romera, (2016).
159 Andreas Chrysostomou and Eivind S. Vagslid, 'Climate Change: A Challenge for IMO Too', in *Maritime Transport and the Climate Change Challenge* (R. Asariotis and Hassiba Benamara eds. 1st ed., 2012). 81.
160 However, Article 207 of UNCLOS recognizes differential treatment for land-based pollution of the marine environment. It is also worth noting that the IMO has not taken a differential approach neither with regards to the Montréal Protocol on substances that deplete the ozone layer, nor to the Basel convention on the trans boundary movement of waste.
161 '*In January 2013, a new historical record share of 73 per cent of the world fleet was "flagged out", that is, the nationality of the vessel's owner was different from the flag under which the vessel was registered. In other words, for almost three out of every four, shipowners chose a flag different from their own nationality. The remaining 27 per cent are kept under the national flag because either the owner considered the national flag competitive in terms of costs and services provided, or he may not have had a choice, as is often the case for government cargo and cabotage traffic.*', UNCTAD Review of Maritime Transport 2013, (2013). 55.
162 For an account on the *problématique* of CBDRRC with regards to MBMs in IMO see, Per Kågeson, 'Applying the Principle of Common but Differentiated Responsibility to the Mitigation of Greenhouse Gases from International Shipping', Working Papers in Transport Economics from the Centre for Transport Studies Stockholm No. 2011:5, (2011).
163 MEPC 57/21. Report of the Marine Environment Protection Committee on Its Fifty-Seven Session, (2008).
164 MEPC 57/4/2. Future IMO Regulation Regarding Green House Gas Emissions from International Shipping. Submitted by Denmark, Marshall Islands, BIMCO, ICS, INTERCARGO, INTERTANKO and OCIMF, (2008).
165 MEPC 57/21. Report of the Marine Environment Protection Committee on Its Fifty-Seven Session, (2008).
166 MEPC 58/4/20. Legal Aspects of the Organization's Work on Greenhouse Gas Emissions in the Context of the Kyoto Protocol, (2008).
167 Ibid.
168 For an overview on options see, Saiful Karim and Shawkat Alam, 'Climate Change and Reduction of Emissions of Greenhouse Gases from Ships: An Appraisal', *Asian Journal of International Law*, 1 (2011). 131.
169 GHG-WG 3/3/3. Review of Proposed MBMs. The IMO, Global MBMs That Reduce Emissions and the Question of Principles. Submitted by Clean Shipping Coalition (CSC) and World Wide Fund for Nature (WWF), (2011).
170 Yubing Shi, 'Greenhouse Gas Emissions from International Shipping: The Response from China's Shipping Industry to the Regulatory Initiatives of the International Maritime Organization', *International Journal of Marine and Coastal Law*, 29(1), (2014). 85–123.
171 MEPC/58/4/32. Application of the Principle of "Common but Differentiated Responsibilities" to the Reduction of Greenhouse Gas Emissions from International Shipping. Submitted by China and India, (2008); MEPC 61/5/24. Reduction of GHG Emissions from Ships. Uncertainties and Problems in Market-Based Measures. Submitted by China and India, (2010); MEPC 61/5/19. Reduction of GHG Emissions from Ships. Market-Based Measures: Inequitable Burden on Developing Countries. Submitted by India, (2010). 47.
172 See, Saiful Karim, 'IMO Mandatory Energy Efficiency Measures for International Shipping: The First Mandatory Global Greenhouse Gas Reduction Instrument for

an International Industry', *Macquarie Journal of International and Comparative Environmental Law*, 7, (2011). 111.

173 For more detail see next section.

174 P. Kågeson, (2011). 38 He also states that if there is no agreement (i.e. political negotiation) among Annex I countries *'that clearly honours the CBDR principle the current deadlock will continue'*.

175 The study of the Legal Division pointed in that direction, arguing that no legal conflicts in this sense can emerge from the conflicting principles.

176 James Harrison, 'Recent Developments and Continuing Challenges in the Regulation of Greenhouse Gas Emissions from International Shipping', *University of Edinburgh School of Law Research Paper* Series No. *2012/12*, (University of Edinburgh, 2012).

177 The IMO was confronted with other international problems which were framed under differential treatment, such as the Montréal Protocol or the Basel Convention.

178 IMO, Promotion of Technical Co-Operation and Transfer of Technology Relating to the Improvement of Energy Efficiency of Ships, MEPC Res. 229(65). MEPC 65/22, Annex 4.

179 For a legal overview see, Sophia Kopela, *Climate Change and the International Maritime Organization: Another Breakthrough at the Marine Environment Protection Committee?* (2013). Available at: www.asil.org/insights/volume/17/issue/24/climate-change-and-international-maritime-organization-another

180 This is also highlighted in Daniel Bodanski, 'Regulating Greenhouse Gas Emissions from Ships: The Role of the International Maritime Organization', in *Ocean Law Debates: The 50-Year Legacy and Emerging Issues for the Years Ahead* (H. Scheiber, N. Oral and M. Kwon eds., forthcoming 2017).

181 UNFCCC article 3(3).

182 Fanny Missfeldt, 'Flexibility Mechanisms: Which Path to Take after Kyoto?', *Review of European Community & International Environmental Law*, 7(2), (1998). 128–139.

183 For an overview see, Rutger de Witt Wijnen and Sander Simonetti, 'Internaional Emissions Trading and Green Investment Schemens', in *Legal Aspects of Carbon Trading: Kyoto, Copenhagen and Beyond* (David Freestone and Charlotte Streck eds., 2009). 157–175.

184 A study of Article 6 is offered in Andrei Marcu, 'Carbon Market Provisions in the Paris Agreement (Article 6). CEPS Special Report No. 128 / January 2016, Brussels, *Centre for European Policy Studies*, (2016).

185 Paris Agreement. Article 6.2 and 6.3.

186 Ibid. at. Article 6.4–6.7.

187 See, C. Goron, (2012). 10–12.

188 See, in regards of the inclusion of aviation in the EU ETS, the mutual agreement clause included in Assembly Resolution A36–22. Similarly, the IMO reaction to the proposal to include maritime transport in the EU ETS from 2023. IMO, 'IMO Secretary-General Speaks out against Regional Emission Trading System. Briefing: 03 (9 January 2017)', (2017). Available at: www.imo.org/en/MediaCentre/PressBriefings/Pages/3-SG-emissions.aspx

189 For a summary on the main characteristics of command-and-control and economic instruments, and price and quantity instruments, see Cameron Hepburn, 'Carbon Taxes, Emissions Trading and Hybrid Schemes', in *The Economics and Politics of Climate Change* (Dieter Helm and Cameron Hepburn eds., 2009). 365–384; Daniel Bodansky, *The Art and Craft of International Environmental Law* (Harvard University Press, 2010). 80–84. Also, P.W. Birnie et al., *International Law and the Environment*. (2009). 786–800.

190 Nicholas Stern, *The Economics of Climate Change: The Stern Review: Executive Summary* (Cambridge, 2007). 18–19.

191 C. Hepburn, 'Carbon Taxes, Emissions Trading and Hybrid Schemes'. (2009). 369.

192 See Barry C. Field and Martha K. Field, *Environmental Economics: An Introduction* (McGraw-Hill/Irwin 3rd ed., 2002). Chapter 4, 12 and 13. However there are some

sceptical voices, F. FitzRoy and E. Papyrakis, *An Introduction to Climate Change Economics and Policy* (Earthscan, 2010). 121–127.

193 C. Hepburn, 'Carbon Taxes, Emissions Trading and Hybrid Schemes'. (2009). 372. See, advantages of tax over trading systems for climate purposes in, Reuven S. Avi-Yonah and David M. Uhlmann, 'Combating Global Climate Change: Why a Carbon Tax Is a Better Response to Global Warming than Cap and Trade', *Standford Environmental Law Journal* 28(1), (2009). 3–50; European Environment Agency, 'Resource-Efficient Green Economy and EU Policies', *EEA Report. No 2/2014*, (2014).

194 Harro van Asselt, 'Emissions Trading: The Enthusiastic Adoption of an Alien Instrument', in *Climate Change Policy in the European Union: Confronting the Dilemmas of Mitigation and Adaptation?* (Andrew Jordan et al. eds., 2010). 126.

195 See the argument in, C. Hepburn, 'Carbon Taxes, Emissions Trading and Hybrid Schemes'. (2009). 365–384.

196 Peter R. Orszag, 'Implications of a Cap-and-Trade Program for Carbon Dioxide Emissions', in *Carbon Dioxide Emissions* (James P. Mulligan ed., 2010). 135–138.

197 As D. Ellerman has stated, the adoption of emissions trading by the European Union was the product of two failures: the Commission's failed initiative for an EU-wide carbon energy tax in 1992 and the failure of the fight against it in the Kyoto negotiations in 1997. The first failure was due to member States opposing it because of their autonomy in taxation, also EU fiscal measures require unanimity and are subject to industry lobbying. '*Six months after opposing emissions trading, the commission embraced it.*' See, A. Denny Ellerman and Barbara K. Buchner, 'The European Union Emissions Trading Scheme: Origins, Allocation, and Early Results', *Review of Environmental Economics and Policy*, 1(1), (2007). 9–31 For an example of strong opposition of the industry to green taxation of aviation see, 'IATA comments on the proposal to introduce a "green" tax on passenger air transport (Anteprojeto de Reforma da Fiscalidade Verde) 4 August 2014', (2014).

198 Steven Truxal and Rupert Dunbar, 'Evaluating Three Levels of Environmental Taxation in Aviation: Global Limitation, EU Determination and UK Self-interest', in *Market Instruments and Sustainable Economy* (A.Y. Sterling and D.A.A. de Assis eds., 2012).

199 Michael Keen and Jon Strand, 'Indirect Taxes on International Aviation', International Monetary Fund Working Paper, WP/06/124 (2006). 4. However, if environmental taxes are not established internationally, they can entail 'loss of competitiveness for domestic industry and regressive impacts that disadvantage the poor' in, E.E. Agency, (2014). 75.

200 Michael Keen, Ian Parry and Jon Strand, 'Market-Based Instruments for International Aviation and Shipping as a Source of Climate Finance', Policy Research Working Paper 5950, The World Bank & International Monetary Fund, (2012).

201 Cameron Hepburn and Benito Muller, *International Air Travel and Greenhouse Gas Emissions: A Proposal for an Adaptation Levy* (The World Economy, 2010).

202 An overview is offered in Amparo Grau, 'Critical Legal Review of Tax-Related Financial Mechanisms for Climate Protection in Developing Countries', in *Critical Issues in Environmental Taxation: Volume VIII* (C.D. Soares et al. eds., 2010). 157–162.

203 See further, I.L.A. International Law Association. Committee on the Legal Principles Relating to Climate Change, (2012). 15–16.

204 Jonathan L. Ramseur, 'The Role of Offsets in a Greenhouse Gas Emissions Cap-and-Trade Programme: Potential Benefits and Concerns', in *Carbon dioxide emissions* (James P. Mulligan ed., 2010). 1–41.

205 In 2013, the 64th meeting of the MEPC at the IMO decided to hold discussions on market-based measures, which hasn't come back to the Agenda item 5 on GHGs, to date. Conversely, ICAO agreed on CORSIA in October 2016.

206 Transport and Environment, *FAQ: Bunker Emissions at Copenhagen December 2009*, (2009).

207 M. Lutes and S. Vorster, (2013). 26–32 Also, for an overview on the current situation with CBDR in the ICAO negotiations see ibid.

Markus W. Gehring and Cairo A. R. Robb, 'Addressing the Aviation and Climate Change Challenge. A Review of Options', *ICTSD Programme on Trade and Environment: Trade and Sustainable Energy Series*, (2013). 18.

208 M.W. Gehring and C.A.R. Robb, (2013). 18.

209 ICAO, Assembly Resolution A37–19, (2010). See also, Annie Petsonk and Guy Turner, 'Market-Based Measures: Achieving Carbon Neutral Growth from 2020', in *ICAO Environmental Report 2013: Aviation and Climate Change* (Environment Branch of ICAO ed., 2013).

210 See, with regards of the inclusion of aviation in the EU ETS, the mutual agreement clause included in Assembly Resolution A36–22.

211 See, ICAO Council, ICAO's Policies on Taxation in the Field of International Air Transport. Doc. 8632-C/968 (2000). the third edition of a resolution of the council from 1996.

212 It is unsurprising that the Chicago Convention contains no mention of emissions trading, since the concept was developed only decades after the convention was agreed upon.

213 Chicago Convention, articles 28 and 69.

214 Bin Cheng, *The Law of International Air Transport* (Stevens; Oceana Publications, 1962). 157.

215 Chicago Convention, Article 15 on Airport and similar charges. Charges '*shall not be higher, (a) As to aircraft not engaged in scheduled international air services, than those that would be paid by its national aircraft of the same class engaged in similar operations, and (b) As to aircraft engaged in scheduled international air services, than those that would be paid by its national aircraft engaged in similar international air services*'.

216 Chicago Convention, Article 15 on Airport and similar charges. Such charges shall be published and communicated to the ICAO and are subject to review by the Council.

217 B. Cheng, *The Law of International Air Transport*. (1962). 158.

218 Ibid. at. 158–160. He points out that as early as 1946, the Interim Assembly of the PICAO requested the Interim Council to study the issue, which was commissioned again to the ICAO Council in Resolution A1–66 and Resolution A2–.14. In 1954 a report on International Airport Charges was prepared by the Air Transport Committee and a conference was convened for the purpose of discussing the topic.

219 Ibid. at. 161–164. Similarly, a conference focused on charges for navigation facilities was convened in 1958, named the Route Facilities Charges conference.

220 ICAO, Proceedings of the Route Facilities Charges Conference, 2 vols., Doc 7874 (1958), (1958). 9.

221 B. Cheng, *The Law of International Air Transport*. (1962). 163.

222 With more or less success, taxes on aviation have been introduced in the United Kingdom, the Netherlands, Sweden, Denmark, Malta, Ireland, France, Germany and Belgium. See, Hugo Gordijn, 'The Dutch Aviation Tax; Lessons for Germany?', *Paper to be Presented at Infraday-2010*, Berlin (8–9 October 2010), (2010).

223 See, ICAO's Policies on Taxation in the Field of International Air Transport, the third edition of a resolution of the council from 1996.

224 D. Brack, *International Trade and Climate Change Policies* (Taylor & Francis, 2013). 104.

225 However, bilateral agreements on air services usually include this prohibition to tax.

226 M. Keen and J. Strand, (2006). As they explained, airlines pay corporate tax on earnings under standard rules of international taxation, typically under reciprocal agreements they are taxed in the country of residence. Also, domestic aviation fuel is subject to VAT, although it can be credited. Additionally, aviation is subject to a number of fees and charges for services such as airport landing charges, passenger security charges, route facility charges.

227 See, ibid. at. 4–8.
228 On the tax exonerations, '*the rationale for these legal undertakings is by no means clear*'. It may reflect an attitude common in the early days of the industry, where international air travel was conceived as having only positive externalities and was due to be promoted, see, ibid. at. 28.
229 Not only are they being forced to change behaviour and invest in technology development, but they are also attractive for the purpose of raising considerable revenues. See M. Keen and J. Strand, *Fiscal Affairs Department, International Monetary Fund*, (2006). 48. See also, A. Grau, 'Critical Legal Review of Tax-Related Financial Mechanisms for Climate Protection in Developing Countries'. (2010).
230 See for example, Eckhard Pache, The Possibility of Introducing a Kerosene Tax on Domestic Flights in Germany. Legal opinion commissioned by the Federal Environmental Agency. Germany, Umweltbundesamt (2005).
231 M. Keen and J. Strand, (2006). A tax proposal for jet fuel was discussed in the European Union in 2005. See, A.D. Ellerman and B.K. Buchner, (2007). 264–266.
232 See, C. Hepburn and B. Muller, *International Air Travel and Greenhouse Gas Emissions: A Proposal for an Adaptation Levy*. (2010).
233 P.W. Birnie et al., *International Law and the Environment*. (2009). 799–801.
234 See in that connection the argumentation of Advocate Kokott. Case-366/10. Opinion of Advocate General Kokott delivered on 6 October 2011. paragraph 233.
235 Jin Liu, *Legal Regulation of Aircraft Engine Emissions in the Age of Climate Change* (University College London, 2011). 151–176. The author argues the Article 24 does not prohibit environmental taxes, it is ICAO that insists on that. She bases her opinion on the interpretation of the court in two rulings on ticket taxes applied by the Netherlands and the United Kingdom, where '*the purpose of the tax rather than the form of it*' approach was followed by the courts to support the legality of the levies. See, Ruling of the Dutch Supreme Court, in the case Board of Airline Representatives in the Netherlands v. The State of The Netherlands (Ministry of Finance) and the English High Court on R (on the application of the Federation of Tour Operators and others) v. Her Majesty's Treasury.
236 In the same vein see, C. Goron, (2012).
237 Although a charge on fuel is not the same as a charge on emissions. See the argumentation of Advocate Kokott in the ATAA Case and Eckhard Pache, On the Compatibility with Legal Provisions of Including Greenhouse Gas Emissions from International Aviation in the EU Emission allowance Trading Scheme as a Result of the Proposed Changes to the EU Emission Allowance Trading Directive (2008).
238 Case C-366/10.
239 See, Glen Plant, 'Air Transport Association of America v. Secretary of State for Energy and Climate Change', *The American Journal of International Law*, 107(1), (2013). 183.
240 UN, Report of the Secretary-General's High-level Advisory Group on Climate Change Financing. Work Stream 2: Paper on Potential Revenues from International Maritime and Aviation Sector Policy Measures, (2010).
241 ICAO, Assembly Resolution A39–2: Consolidated Statement of Continuing ICAO Policies and Practices Related to Environmental Protection. Climate Change (2016). Paragraph 16.
242 States that have an individual share of international aviation activities in year 2018 RTKs higher than 0.5% of total RTKs or whose cumulative share in the list of States from the highest to the lowest amount of RTKs reaches 90% of total RTKs are required to participate, except least developed countries (LDCs), small island developing states (SIDS) and landlocked developing countries (LLDCs) unless they volunteer. ICAO, 'Submission by the International Civil Aviation Organization to the Forty-fifth Session of the UNFCCC Subsidiary Body for Scientific and

Technological Advice (SBSTA45). Agenda Item 10 (b): Emissions from fuel used for international aviation and maritime transport', (2016).

243 The offsetting requirement for airlines is calculated differently for the pilot phase and the first phase. And from phase two, the offsets will be determined on a more airline individual basis.

244 Transport and Environment, 'Global Deal or No Deal? Your Free Guide to ICAO's 38th Triennial Assembly', (2013). 7. In the same document the think tank stated that *'To some extent Europe's decision to stop the clock called IATA's bluff. Having focussed on building opposition to the EU ETS, IATA suddenly realised that getting some progress going in ICAO was now critical to its whole anti-ETS strategy.'*

245 IATA endorsed, by majority, in 2013 the idea of developing a global market-based measure. However, the industry argues that 'MBMs are only a gap filler and that sometime around 2030 technological and operational innovations, along with biofuels, will render them unnecessary See, ibid. at. 7.

246 Shuo Ma, 'Using Economic Measures for Global Control of Air Pollution from Ships', in *The Handbook of Maritime Economics and Business* (C. Grammenos ed., 2013). 494–496.

247 Either through setting pollution standards such as the NOx code, through technical norms such as rules for double hull or through procedural requirements such as ballast water management.

248 S. Ma, (2013). 494–496.

249 Even if applied universally, MBMs would discriminate because of the gap between shipping industries in different countries, so discrimination of the ship operator is based solely on cost efficiency. Also, in the case of emission trading, a permit system would likely favour the big shipping companies.

250 S. Ma, (2013). 495.

251 MEPC 54/4/7. Input on Further Work on the IMO GHG Policy. Submitted by Norway, (2006).

252 By the EC countries and Norway in 2006, 2007 Sweden, Norway, Denmark, 2008 IMarest, WWF, Denmark including countries but also OCIMF, ICS, CLIA.

253 Ø. Buhaug et al., *Second IMO Greenhouse Gas Study 2009: Executive Summary* (IMO, 2009).

254 See, A. Chrysostomou and E.S. Vagslid, 'Climate Change: A Challenge for IMO Too'. (2012). 75–111.

255 See section 4.1.2.2 on the EEDI.

256 See Chapter Two.

257 GEF Project Concept number 5054 runs under the rubric *"Transforming The Global Aviation Sector: Emissions Reductions From International Aviation"*.

258 GEF. Project Identification Form. Transforming the Global Maritime Transport Industry towards a Low Carbon Future through Improved Energy Efficiency. GEF Project ID:1 5508.

259 See further information on ICAO Climate Change Action Plan on ICAO's website: www.icao.int/environmental-protection/Pages/action-plan.aspx

260 ICAO, Assembly Resolution A39–3: Consolidated Statement of Continuing ICAO Policies and Practices Related to Environmental Protection: Global Market-Based Measure (MBM) Scheme.

261 This opens questions on the issue of double counting, which is addressed in the climate regime for NDCs but it is uncertain how it would work with CORSIA.

262 The ICAO, Assembly Resolution A39–2 refers to the developments in the climate regime to be considered.

263 Andreas Arvanitakis and Bjørn Dransfeld, 'Offsets under ICAO's GMBM: A Robust Design Approach for Ensuring Environmental Integrity of Offsets under a Global MBM Scheme for International Aviation in the light of the Paris Agreement', Umweltbundesamt, Project No. 74138 (Berlin, Herausgeber Deutsche Emissionshandelsstelle

im Umweltbundesamt, 2016). 4. See Chapter 6 in this book on the management of interactions between regimes.

264 See, A. Petsonk and G. Turner, 'Market-Based Measures: Achieving Carbon Neutral Growth from 2020'. (2013).

265 See chapter three.

266 See chapter three.

267 See the work of the I.L.A. International Law Association. Committee on the Legal Principles Relating to Climate Change, (2012). And the previous report stating the scope of the Committees report: International Law Association Committee on the Legal Principles Relating to Climate Change, 'The Legal Principles Relating to Climate Change, First Report (La Hague Conference 2010)', (2010).

268 I.L.A. International Law Association. Committee on the Legal Principles Relating to Climate Change. (2012). 13.

269 J. Brunnée, 'An Agreement in Principle? The Copenhagen Accord and the Post-2012 Climate Regime'. (2011). 70.

Bibliography

A38-WP/288. Effective MBM to Address GHG Emissions from International Aviation. Presented by the International Coalition for Sustainable Aviation (ICSA).

Abeyratne, Ruwantissa. *Convention on International Civil Aviation: A Commentary*, Switzerland, Springer International Publishing.

Abeyratne, Ruwantissa (2014). *Aviation and Climate Change: In Search of a Global Market Based Measure*, New York, Springer.

Abeyratne, Ruwantissa (2014). *Convention on International Civil Aviation: A Commentary*, New York, Springer.

Arvanitakis, Andreas and Dransfeld, Bjørn (2016). 'Offsets under ICAO's GMBM: A Robust Design Approach for Ensuring Environmental Integrity of Offsets under a Global MBM Scheme for International Aviation in the Light of the Paris Agreement', *Umweltbundesamt, Project no: 74138*.

Asselt, Harro van (2010). 'Emissions Trading: The Enthusiastic Adoption of an Alien Instrument', in, Andrew Jordan, Dave Huitema, Harro van Asselt, Tim Rayner and Frans Berkhout (eds.), *Climate Change Policy in the European Union: Confronting the Dilemmas of Mitigation and Adaptation?*, Cambridge, Cambridge University Press.

Asselt, Harro van (2014). 'Alongside the UNFCCC: Complementary Venues for Climate Action', Centre for Climate and Energy Solutions.

Asselt, Harro van (2014). *The Fragmentation of Global Climate Governance: Consequences and Management of Regime Interactions*, Cheltenham, UK, Edward Elgar Publishing Limited.

Asselt, Harro van, Mehling, Michael A. and Kehler Siebert, Clarisse (2014). 'The Changing Architecture of International Climate Change Law', in, G. van Calster, W. Vandenberghe and L. Reins (eds.), *Research Handbook on Climate Change Mitigation Law*, Cheltenham, Edward Elgar.

Assembly Resolution A36–22: Consolidated Statement of Continuing ICAO Policies and Practices Related to Environmental Protection.

Assembly Resolution A37–19: Consolidated Statement of Continuing ICAO Policies and Practices Related to Environmental Protection: Climate Change.

Assembly Resolution A38–18: Consolidated Statement of Continuing ICAO Policies and Practices Related to Environmental Protection: Climate Change.

Assembly Resolution A39–2: Consolidated Statement of Continuing ICAO Policies and Practices Related to Environmental Protection: Climate Change.

Assembly Resolution A39–3: Consolidated Statement of Continuing ICAO Policies and Practices Related to Environmental Protection: Global Market-Based Measure (MBM) Scheme.

Assembly Resolution A.963(23) on IMO Policies and Practices Related to the Reduction of Greenhouse Gas Emissions from Ships.

Avi-Yonah, Reuven S. and Uhlmann, David M. (2009). 'Combating Global Climate Change: Why a Carbon Tax Is a Better Response to Global Warming than Cap and Trade', *Stanford Environmental Law Journal*, 28(1), 3–50.

Barton, Jane (2008). 'Including Aviation in the EU Emissions Trading Scheme: Prepare for Take-Off', *Journal for European Environmental & Planning Law*, 5(2), 183–198.

Beyerlin, Ulrich (2007). 'Policies, Principles, and Rules', in, Daniel Bodansky, Jutta Brunnée and Ellen Hey (eds.), *The Oxford Handbook of International Environmental Law: Oxford Handbooks*, Oxford; New York, Oxford University Press.

Birnie, Patricia W., Boyle, Alan E. and Redgwell, Catherine (2009). *International Law and the Environment*, 3rd ed., Oxford; New York, Oxford University Press.

Bodansky, Daniel (2010). *The Art and Craft of International Environmental Law*, Cambridge, MA, Harvard University Press.

Bodansky, Daniel (2011). 'Multilateral Climate Efforts beyond the UNFCCC', Centre for Climate and Energy Solutions.

Bodanski, Daniel (forthcoming 2017). 'Regulating Greenhouse Gas Emissions from Ships: The Role of the International Maritime Organization', in, N. Oral, M. Kwo and H. Scheiber (eds.), *Ocean Law Debates: The 50-Year Legacy and Emerging Issues for the Years Ahead*. Leiden, Brill

Brack, D. (2013). *International Trade and Climate Change Policies*, London, Taylor & Francis.

Brunnée, Jutta (2011). 'An Agreement in Principle? The Copenhagen Accord and the Post-2012 Climate Regime', in, Holger Hestermeyer, Nele Matz-Lück, Anja Seibert-Fohr and Silja Vöneky (eds.), *Law of the Sea in Dialogue*, Berlin; Heidelberg, Max-Planck-Gesellschaft zur Förderung der Wissenschaften e.V., Springer.

Brunnée, Jutta and Toope, Stephen J. (2010). *Legitimacy and Legality in International Law: An Interactional Account*, Cambridge; New York, Cambridge University Press.

Buhaug, Øyvind, Corbett, James J., Eyring, Veronika Endresen, Øyvind, Faber, Jasper, Hanayama, Shinichi, Lee, David S., Lee, Donchool, Lindstad, Håkon, Markowska, Agnieszka Z. Mjelde, Alvar, Nelissen, Dagmar, Nilsen, Jørgen, Pålsson, Christopher, Wanquing, Wu, Winebrake, James J., Yoshida, Koichi (2009). *Second IMO Greenhouse Gas Study 2009: Executive Summary*, London, UK, IMO.

Castro, Paula, Hörnlein, Lena and Michaelowa, Katharina (2014). 'Constructed Peer Groups and Path Dependence in International Organizations: The Case of the International Climate Change Negotiations', *Global Environmental Change*, 25, 109–120.

Cheng, Bin (1962). *The Law of International Air Transport*, London; New York, Stevens; Oceana Publications.

Chrysostomou, Andreas and Vagslid, Eivind S. (2012). 'Climate Change: A Challenge for IMO Too', in, R. Asariotis and Hassiba Benamara (eds.), *Maritime Transport and the Climate Change Challenge*, 1st ed., New York, Earthscan.

Climate Action Network (CAN), (2013). 'Position on Market Based Measures for International Aviation'. Climate Action Network.

COM(2013) 722. Proposal for a Directive of the European Parliament and of the Council Amending Directive 2003/87/EC Establishing a Scheme for Greenhouse Gas Emission Allowance Trading within the Community.

Convention on the Inter-Governmental Maritime Consultative Organization, adopted on 6 March 1948, entered into force 17 March 1958. 289 UNTS 48, Amended and Renamed as Convention on the International Maritime Organization, 14 November 1975, 9 UTS 61.

Convention on International Civil Aviation, adopted 7 December 1944, entered into force 4 April 1947. 15 UNTS 295, as amended, ICAO Doc. 7300/9 (2006), (hereinafter Chicago Convention).

Cullet, Philippe (1999). 'Differential Treatment in International Law: Towards a New Paradigm of Inter-State Relations', *European Journal of International Law*, 10(3), 549.

Cullet, Philippe (2003). *Differential Treatment in International Environmental Law*, Aldershot, Hants, England; Burlington, VT, Ashgate.

Decaux, Emmanuel (1980). *La Réciprocité en droit international*, Paris, Librairie générale de droit et de jurisprudence.

Depledge, Joanna and Yamin, Farhana (2009). 'The Global Climate Change Regime: A Defense', in, Dieter Helm and Cameron Hepburn (eds.), *The Economics and Politics of Climate Change*, Oxford; New York, Oxford University Press.

Dimitrov, Radoslav S. (2016). 'The Paris Agreement on Climate Change: Behind Closed Doors', *Global Environmental Politics*, 16(3). 1–11.

Directive 2008/101/EC of 19 November 2008 Amending Directive 2003/87/EC so as to Include Aviation Activities in the Scheme for Greenhouse Gas Emission Allowance Trading within the Community, [2009] L8/3. OJ L 8 (13 January 2009).

Ellerman, A. Denny and Buchner, Barbara K. (2007). 'The European Union Emissions Trading Scheme: Origins, Allocation, and Early Results', *Review of Environmental Economics and Policy*, 1(1), 66–87.

European Environment Agency (2014). 'Resource-Efficient Green Economy and EU Policies', *EEA Report. No 2/2014*.

Field, Barry C. and Field, Martha K. (2002). *Environmental Economics: An Introduction*, 3rd ed., New York, McGraw-Hill; Irwin.

FitzRoy, F. and Papyrakis, E. (2010). *An Introduction to Climate Change Economics and Policy*, London, Earthscan.

French, Duncan and Rajamani, Lavanya (2013). 'Climate Change and International Environmental Law: Musings on a Journey to Somewhere', *Journal of Environmental Law*. 25(3), 437–461.

Geden, Oliver and Beck, Silke (2014). 'Renegotiating the Global Climate Stabilization Target', *Nature Climate Change*, 4(9), 747–748.

Gehring, Markus W. and Robb, Cairo A.R. (2013). 'Addressing the Aviation and Climate Change Challenge: A Review of Options', *ICTSD Programme on Trade and Environment. Trade and Sustainable Energy Series*.

General Agreement on Trade in Services (GATS) Adopted 15 April 1994. 1869 UNTS 183. Annex on Air Transport.

GHG-WG 3/3/3. Review of Proposed MBMs: The IMO, Global MBMs That Reduce Emissions and the Question of Principles. Submitted by Clean Shipping Coalition (CSC) and World Wide Fund for Nature (WWF).

Gippner, Olivia (2014). 'The 2°C Target: A European Norm Enters the International Stage: Following the Process to Adoption in China', *International Environmental Agreements: Politics, Law and Economics*, 6(1). 49–65.

Gordijn, Hugo (2010). 'The Dutch Aviation Tax; lessons for Germany?', *Paper to be Presented at Infraday-2010*, Berlin (8–9 October 2010).

Goron, Coraline (2012). 'The EU Aviation ETS Caught Between Kyoto and Chicago: Unilateral Legal Entrepreneurship in the Multilateral Governance System', Green-Gem Doctoral Working Papers Series.

Grau, Amparo (2010). 'Critical Legal Review of Tax-Related Financial Mechanisms for Climate Protection in Developing Countries', in, C.D. Soares, J. Milne, H. Ashiabor and K. Deketelaere (eds.), *Critical Issues in Environmental Taxation: Volume VIII*, Oxford, Oxford University Press.

Gupta, Joyeeta (2010). 'A History of International Climate Change Policy', *Wiley Interdisciplinary Reviews: Climate Change*, 1(5), 636–653.

Gupta, Joyeeta and Asselt, Harro van (2006). 'Helping Operationalise Article 2: A Transdisciplinary Methodological Tool for Evaluating When Climate Change Is Dangerous', *Global Environmental Change*, 16(1), 83–94.

Harrison, James (2012). 'Recent Developments and Continuing Challenges in the Regulation of Greenhouse Gas Emissions from International Shipping', *University of Edinburgh School of Law Research Paper 2012/12*.

Hepburn, Cameron (2009). 'Carbon Taxes, Emissions Trading and Hybrid Schemes', in, Dieter Helm and Cameron Hepburn (eds.), *The Economics and Politics of Climate Change*, Oxford; New York, Oxford University Press.

Honkonen, Tuula (2009). *The Common but Differentiated Responsibility Principle in Multilateral Environmental Agreements: Regulatory and Policy Aspects*, Alphen aan den Rijn, The Netherlands, Wolters Kluwer Law & Business; Kluwer Law International.

Honkonen, Tuula (2009). 'The Principle of Common but Differentiated Responsibility in Post-2012 Climate Negotiations', *Review of European Community & International Environmental Law*, 18(3), 257–267.

'IATA, (2014). Comments on the Proposal to Introduce a "Green" Tax on Passenger Air Transport (Anteprojeto de Reforma da Fiscalidade Verde), 4 August 2014.

ICAO (2016). 'Submission by the International Civil Aviation Organization to the Forty-Fifth Session of the UNFCCC Subsidiary Body for Scientific and Technological Advice (SBSTA45). Agenda Item 10 (b): Emissions from Fuel Used for International Aviation and Maritime Transport'.

ICAO. Environment Branch of ICAO (2013). *ICAO Environmental Report 2013: Aviation and Climate Change*, Montreal, ICAO.

ICAO's Policies on Taxation in the Field of International Air Transport. Doc. 8632-C/968.

ICAO, Proceedings of the Route Facilities Charges Conference, 2 vols., Doc. 7874 (1958).

ILC (2006). *Fragmentation of International Law: Difficulties Arising from the Diversification and Expansion of International Law: Report of the Study Group of the International Law Commission*. UN Doc. A/CN.4/L.682.

IMO (2013). 'World Maritime Day: A Concept of Sustainable Maritime Transportation System', *Sustainable Development: IMO's Contribution beyond Rio+20*.

IMO (2017). 'IMO Secretary-General Speaks out against Regional Emission Trading System. Briefing: 03 (9 January 2017).

International Law Association, Committee on the Legal Principles Relating to Climate Change, (2010). 'The Legal Principles Relating to Climate Change, First Report (La Hague Conference 2010)'.

International Law Association. Committee on the Legal Principles Relating to Climate Change, (2012). 'The Legal Principles Relating to Climate Change, Second Report (Sofia Conference 2012)'.

Kågeson, Per (2011). 'Applying the Principle of Common but Differentiated Responsibility to the Mitigation of Greenhouse Gases from International Shipping', Working

Papers in Transport Economics from the Centre for Transport Studies Stockholm. No 2011:5.

Karim, Saiful (2011). 'IMO Mandatory Energy Efficiency Measures for International Shipping: The First Mandatory Global Greenhouse Gas Reduction Instrument for an International Industry', *Macquarie Journal of International and Comparative Environmental Law*, 7, 111.

Karim, Saiful and Alam, Shawkat (2011). 'Climate Change and Reduction of Emissions of Greenhouse Gases from Ships: An Appraisal', *Asian Journal of International Law*, 1, 131.

Keen, Michael, Parry, Ian and Strand, Jon (2012). 'Market-Based Instruments for International Aviation and Shipping as a Source of Climate Finance', Policy Research Working Paper 5950, The World Bank & International Monetary Fund.

Keen, Michael and Strand, Jon (2006). 'Indirect Taxes on International Aviation', Fiscal Affairs Department, International Monetary Fund. International Monetary Fund Working Paper, WP/06/124.

Lee, David S., Lim, Ling and Owen, Bethan (2013). 'Shipping and Aviation Emissions in the Context of a 2°C Emission Pathway', Manchester Metropolitan University.

Lichtenbaum, Peter (2002). 'Special Treatment vs. Equal Participation: Striking a Balance in the Doha Negotiations', *American University International Law Review*, 17, 1–41.

Lutes, Mark and Vorster, Shaun (2013). 'Bridging the Political Barriers in Negotiating a Global Market-Based Measure for Controlling International Aviation Emissions', *Elements of a New Climate Agreement by 2015. Perspectives Series 2013. UNEP Risø*, 21.

Ma, Shuo (2013). 'Using Economic Measures for Global Control of Air Pollution from Ships', in, C. Grammenos (ed.), *The Handbook of Maritime Economics and Business*, London, Taylor & Francis.

Magraw, Daniel Barstow (1990). 'Legal Treatment of Developing Countries: Differential, Contextual and Absolute Norms', *Colorado Journal of International Environmental Law and Policy*, 1, 69.

Maguire, Rowena (2013). 'The Role of Common but Differentiated Responsibility in the 2020 Climate Regime: Evolving a New Understanding of Differential Commitments', *Climate Change Law Review*, 4, 1–10.

Marcu, Andrei (2016). 'Carbon Market Provisions in the Paris Agreement (Article 6): CEPS Special Report No. 128/January 2016', *Centre for European Policy Studies*.

Martinez Romera, Beatriz (2016). 'The Paris Agreement and the Regulation of International Bunker Fuels', *Review of European Comparative & International Environmental Law*, 25(2), 215–227.

MEPC 54/4/7. Input on Further Work on the IMO GHG Policy. Submitted by Norway.

MEPC 57/21. Report of the Marine Environment Protection Committee on Its Fifty-Seven Session.

MEPC 57/4/2. Future IMO Regulation Regarding Green House Gas Emissions from International Shipping. Submitted by Denmark, Marshall Islands, BIMCO, ICS, INTERCARGO, INTERTANKO and OCIMF.

MEPC 57/4/10. Immediate Action and Adoption of Vessel Speed Reductions and Carbon Tax Needed to Reduce Greenhouse Gas Emissions from Shipping. Submitted by the Friends of the Earth International (FOEI).

MEPC 58/4/20. Legal Aspects of the Organization's Work on Greenhouse Gas Emissions in the Context of the Kyoto Protocol.

MEPC 58/4/32. Application of the Principle of "Common but Differentiated Responsibilities" to the Reduction of Greenhouse Gas Emissions from International Shipping. Submitted by China and India.

MEPC 59/4/8. IMO Must Act Decisively to Reduce GHG Emissions from Shipping If It Is to Retain Its Competence in Technical and Political Matters Related to Shipping and GHGs. Submitted by Friends of the Earth International, WWF & Greenpeace International.

MEPC 60/4/28. Emission 'Caps' and Reduction Targets. Submitted by the World Shipping Council.

MEPC 60/40/23. Alternative Emission Caps for Shipping in 2020 and 2030. Submitted by Norway.

MEPC 61/5/19. Reduction of GHG Emissions from Ships. Market-Based Measures: Inequitable Burden on Developing Countries. Submitted by India.

MEPC 61/5/24. Reduction of GHG Emissions from Ships: Uncertainties and Problems in Market-Based Measures. Submitted by China and India.

MEPC 61/24. Report of the Marine Environment Protection Committee on Its Sixty-First Session.

MEPC 62/24. Report of the Marine Environment Protection Committee on Its Sixty-Second Session.

MEPC 63/23. Report of the Marine Environment Protection Committee on Its Sixty-Third Session.

MEPC 64/23. Report of the Marine Environment Protection Committee on Its Sixty-Fourth Session.

MEPC 229(65) Promotion of Technical Co-Operation and Transfer of Technology Relating to the Improvement of Energy Efficiency of Ships.

Missfeldt, Fanny (1998). 'Flexibility Mechanisms: Which Path to Take after Kyoto?', *Review of European Community & International Environmental Law*, 7(2), 128–139.

Müller, Benito (2012). 'From Confrontation to Collaboration? CBDR adn the EU ETS Aviation Dispute with Developing Countries', *Oxford Energy and Environmental Brief*.

Müller, Benito and Hepburn, Cameron (2010). 'International Air Travel and Greenhouse Gas Emissions: A Proposal for an Adaptation Levy', *The World Economy*, Blackwell Publishing. 33(6), 830–849.

Murphy, Andrew (2016). 'A False Dawn for Action on Aviation Emissions. (Published online on October 12, 2016)', *Transport and Environment*.

Nickel, James and Magraw, Daniel (2010). 'Philosophical Issues in International Environmental Law', in, Samantha Besson and John Tasioulas (eds.), *The Philosophy of International Law*, Oxford; New York, Oxford University Press.

Nkuepo, Henri J. (2012). 'EU ETS Aviation Discriminates against Developing Countries', *Africa's Trade Law Newsletter*, 7, 1–6.

Oberthür, Sebastian (2006). 'The Climate Change Regime: Interactions of the Climate Change Regime with ICAO, IMO and the EU Burden-Sharing Agreement', in, Sebastian Oberthür and Thomas Gehring (eds.), *Institutional Interaction in Global Environmental Governance: Synergy and Conflict among International and EU Policies: Global Environmental Accord: Strategies for Sustainability and Institutional Innovation*, Cambridge, MA, MIT Press.

Okur, Aydin (2012). 'The Challenge of Regulating Greenhouse Gas Emissions from Internaional Shipping and the Complicated Principle of "Common but Differentiated Responsibilities"', *Dokuz Eylül Üniversitesi Hukuk Fakültesi Dergisi*, 13(1), 27–49.

Oppenheimer, Michael and Petsonk, Annie (2005). 'Article 2 of the UNFCCC: Historical Origins, Recent Interpretations', *Climatic Change*, 73(3), 195–226.

Orszag, Peter R. (2010). 'Implications of a Cap-and-Trade Program for Carbon Dioxide Emissions', in, James P. Mulligan (ed.), *Carbon Dioxide Emissions*, New York, Nova Science Publishers.

Ott, Konrad and Klepper, Gernot (2004). 'Reasoning Goals of Climate Protection: Specification of Article 2 UNFCCC', *Federal Environmental Agency*.

Pauw, Pieter, Bauer, Steffen, Richerzhagen, Carmen, Brandi, Clara and Schmole, Hanna (2014). 'Different Perspectives on Differentiated Responsibilities a State-of-the-Art Review of the Notion of Common but Differentiated Responsibilities in International Negotiations', *Discussion Paper 6/2014. Deutsches Institut für Entwicklungspolitik*.

Pauwelyn, Joost (2013). 'The End of Differential Treatment for Developing Countries? Lessons from the Trade and Climate Change Regimes', *Review of European, Comparative & International Environmental Law*, 22(1), 29–41.

Paris Agreement (Paris, 12 December 2015, in force 4 November 2016) FCCC/CP/2015/L.9.

Petsonk, Annie and Piris-Cabezas, Pedro (2016). 'Design of a Global Market Based Measure · Bridging the Allocation Gap in the ICAO MBM: A New Proposal', *Carbon & Climate Law Review*, 10(2). 127–133.

Petsonk, Annie and Turner, Guy (2013). 'Market-Based Measures: Achieving Carbon Neutral Growth From 2020', in, Environment Branch of ICAO (ed.), *ICAO Environmental Report 2013: Aviation and Climate Change*. Montreal, Environmental Branch of the International Civil Aviation Organization.

Plant, Glen (2013). 'Air Transport Association of America v. Secretary of State for Energy and Climate Change', *The American Journal of International Law*, 107(1), 183.

Rajamani, Lavanya, Peel, Jacqueline, Hohmann, Harald, Schwarte, Christophe, Shibata, Akiho, Brunnee, Jutta, Halvorssen, Anita Margrethe, Murase, Shinya, Maljean-Dubois, Sandrine, Osofsky, Hari M., Takamura, Yukari, Gavouneli, Maria, Brus, Marcel M.T.A., French, Duncan, Rønne, Anita, Strydom, Hennie and Bodansky, Daniel (2014). 'International Law Association – Washington Conference (2014): Legal Principles Relating to Climate Change (July 2, 2014). Report of the International Law Association's Committee on Legal Principles Relating to Climate Change (Washington, 2014)'.

Ramseur, Jonathan L. (2010). 'The Role of Offsets in a Greenhouse Gas Emissions Cap-and-Trade Programm: Potential Benefits and Concerns', in, James P. Mulligan (ed.), *Carbon Dioxide Emissions*, New York, Nova Science Publishers.

Resolution A.1060(28). Adopted on 29 November 2013. Strategic Plan for the Organization (for the six-year period 2014–2019).

Schleussner, Carl-Friedrich, Rogelj, Joeri, Schaeffer, Michiel, Lissner, Tabea, Licker, Rachel, Fischer, Erich M., Knutti, Reto, Levermann, Anders, Frieler, Katja and Hare, William (2016). 'Science and Policy Characteristics of the Paris Agreement Temperature Goal', *Nature Climate Change*, 6(9), 827–835.

Scott, Joanne and Rajamani, Lavanya (2012). 'EU Climate Change Unilateralism', *European Journal of International Law*, 23(2), 469–494.

Shaw, Malcolm N. (2008). *International Law*, 6th ed., Cambridge, UK; New York, Cambridge University Press.

Shelton, Dinah (2007). 'Equity', in, Daniel Bodansky, Jutta Brunnée and Ellen Hey (eds.), *The Oxford Handbook of International Environmental Law: Oxford Handbooks*, Oxford; New York, Oxford University Press.

Shi, Yubing (2014). 'Greenhouse Gas Emissions from International Shipping: The Response from China's Shipping Industry to the Regulatory Initiatives of the International Maritime Organization', *International Journal of Marine and Coastal Law*, 29(1), 85–123.

Smith, T.W.P., Jalkanen, J. P., Anderson, B. A., Corbett, J. J., Faber, J., Hanayama, S., O'Keeffe, E., Parker, S., Johansson, L., Aldous, L., Raucci, C., Traut, M., Ettinger, S., Nelissen, D., Lee, D. S., Ng, S., Agrawal, A., Winebrake, J. J., Hoen, M., Chesworth,

S., Pandey, A. (2014). *Third IMO Greenhouse Gas Study 2014: Executive Summary and Final Report*, London, UK, IMO.

Stern, Nicholas (2007). *The Economics of Climate Change: The Stern Review: Executive Summary*, Cambridge, Cambridge University Press.

Stone, Christopher D. (2004). 'Common but Differentiated Responsibilities in International Law', *The American Journal of International Law*, 98(2), 276–301.

Transport and Environment (2013). 'Global Deal or No Deal? Your Free Guide to ICAO's 38th Triennial Assembly'. Transport and Environment. Available at: http://www.transport environment.org/what-we-do/aviation.

Trebilcock, M.J. and Howse, Robert (2005). *The Regulation of International Trade*, 3rd ed., London; New York, Routledge.

Truxal, Steven and Dunbar, Rupert (2012). 'Evaluating Three Levels of Environmental Taxation in Aviation: Global Limitation, EU Determination and UK Self-Interest', in, A.Y. Sterling and D.A.A. de Assis (eds.), *Market Instruments and Sustainable Economy*, Madrid, Spain, Instituto de Estudios Fiscales.

UN (2010). Report of the Secretary-General's High-level Advisory Group on Climate Change Financing. Work Stream 2: Paper on Potential Revenues from International Maritime and Aviation Sector Policy Measures, New York, United Nations.

UNCTAD (2013). Review of Maritime Transport 2013. UNCTAD/RMT/2013, Geneva, United Nations Publication.

United Nations Convention on the Law of the Sea, Montego Bay, adopted 10 December 1982, in force 16 November 1994, 21 International Legal Materials (1982), 1261. 1833 UNTS 3.

Vaishnav, Parth (2016). 'Design of a Global Market Based Measure – ICAO's Market Based Mechanism: Keep It Simple', *Carbon & Climate Law Review*, 10(2). 120–126.

Voigt, Christina (2009). *Sustainable Development as a Principle of International Law: Resolving Conflicts between Climate Measures and WTO Law*, Leiden; Boston, Martinus Nijhoff Publishers.

Wijnen, Rutger de Witt and Simonetti, Sander (2009). 'Internaional Emissions Trading and Green Investment Schemens', in, David Freestone and Charlotte Streck (eds.), *Legal Aspects of Carbon Trading: Kyoto, Copenhagen and Beyond*, Oxford; New York, Oxford University Press.

Written Statement of Reservation by Lithuania on Behalf of the Member States of the European Union and 14 other Member States of the European Civil Aviation Conference (ECAC) with Regard to ICAO Assembly Resolution A38–18.

Yamin, Farhana and Depledge, Joanna (2004). *The International Climate Change Regime: A Guide to Rules, Institutions and Procedures*, Cambridge, UK; New York, Cambridge University Press.

Young, Margaret A. (2012). 'Introduction: The Productive Friction between Regimes', in, Margaret A. Young (ed.), *Regime Interaction in International Law: Facing Fragmentation*, Cambridge; New York, Cambridge University Press.

Zahar, Alexander (2013). 'The Climate Change Regime', in, Shawkat Alam (ed.), *Routledge Handbook of International Environmental Law*, New York, Routledge.

6 Managing interaction

This chapter aims to apply a suitable framework for the management of the outcomes of the interactions between the climate, ICAO and IMO regimes in regulating GHG emissions. In doing so, the chapter explores two related options that can be of help in managing interaction, namely: legal techniques and institutional cooperation.[1] The chapter also delves into the benefits and requirements to promoting regime interaction. The chapter concludes by suggesting some ways forward for policy-making.

Approaches in the ILC study

As introduced in Chapter 2, the approaches contemplated in international law for dealing with the specifics of interaction, deriving from the fragmentation of international law, have been reviewed in the ILC Study.[2] The VCLT helps to shed light over the interpretation of international agreements[3] and the ILC have helped to further clarify the techniques contained in the VCLT for the avoidance and resolution of legal conflicts.[4] These concern treaty drafting and amendment, conflict clauses and rules on interpretation of the VCLT, particularly regarding the principle of systemic integration and priority rules,[5] which suitability and reach for the management of conflicts has been widely covered in the literature.[6]

This chapter assesses if and how the traditional legal approaches to managing the conflictive consequences of interaction can be applied to the cases discussed in the previous chapter. Although legal approaches are the primary ways of addressing the relationship between treaties, their role in the specifics of the topic addressed in this study is limited. Such limitation is due to two reasons: first that 'in order for the international rules on conflicts between treaties to apply, an actual conflict must exist.'[7] In this connection the book has adopted a broad concept of conflict where the interactions between the climate, ICAO and IMO regimes can fit. Second, the application of the VCLT is limited to treaty instruments although conflicts can also come from treaty body outcomes, which is the case of much of the material studied here. Third, the very nature of the legal approaches focuses on avoiding and resolving conflicts; therefore the management of synergies, so as to enhance them, is beyond their scope and capabilities.[8] As such, these techniques 'call upon a dispute-settlement body or a lawyer seeking to find out what the law is'.[9]

Treaty amendment and the drafting of new treaties

The first and probably most effective method to avoid conflicts between the climate, ICAO and IMO regimes would be to draft a new treaty clarifying the objective, principles and measures to regulate IBF emissions, or amend[10] the existing problematic norms, so as to avoid frictions between regimes. However, the chances of political agreement on the terms are restricted, though amendments could target just a few norms in the three regimes. First, article 2.2 of the KP could be redefined to clarify the terms of the relationship. Amendment of the UNFCCC, and the adoption of annexes or their amendments, would require a consensus or a three-fourths majority vote, in the absence of consensus.[11] The KP follows the same rules.[12] Although difficult and lengthy, amendments are possible if there is sufficient political will; a relevant example is the Doha Amendment of the KP, which was adopted in 2012. However parties to the KP, Chicago and the IMO Convention are not the same, so there would still be controversy with regards to the third parties. Crucially, there was an opportunity, in the context of the Paris Agreement, to clarify the relationship between regimes and/or establishing who, how and when IBF emissions can be regulated. This could have been done in by including IBF in the commitments of the parties, if an agreement of allocating these emissions to countries were possible, or by incorporating a conflict clause.[13]

Regarding the ICAO regime, amendments to the Chicago Convention so as to include environmental objectives and to allow for differential treatment or to remove prohibitions on taxes for climate purposes, while clarifying the status of emissions trading, are also theoretically possible. Once the Assembly's quorum requirement is fulfilled (i.e. the majority of the contracting States shall be present), adopting amendments to the Convention would require a two-thirds majority vote.[14] However, the assembly usually adopts its recommendations by consensus, so the majority vote would be the second preferred option. However, as stated in Chapter 3, the Chicago Convention hasn't been amended significantly since its inception[15] and it is unlikely that it would occur for the sake of addressing climate change. Nonetheless, it is a possibility. However, as pointed out in Chapter 4, the existence of thousands of bilateral agreements based on the Convention make it very difficult to (for example) remove the prohibition of fuel taxation. Indeed all the subsequent bilateral agreements would require individual amendment. As such, the easiest way to introduce some kind of regulation would be through Annexes to the Convention. However, these do not have the same legal force, and so conflicts would still exist.

More promising options to avoid conflicts are offered by the adoption of an international agreement for GHG emissions, under ICAO's auspices, although it would be the first time that an environmental treaty is adopted with ICAO as a venue, since, thus far, environmental concerns have been dealt with through Annex 16 of the Chicago Convention.[16] However, the agreement on the GMBM CORSIA in ICAO has been done through an Assembly Resolution,[17] where further work in defining the details and implementing the scheme needs to be accomplished in the forthcoming years. Here, and although this would be the adequate avenue to deal with conflicts, careful attention needs to be paid to the interaction with the climate regime so as to avoid conflicts and enhance synergies, in particular with the market mechanisms envisioned in the Paris Agreement.[18]

In connection with the IMO regime, amendments to the IMO Convention, in order to accommodate differential treatment for the case of climate change, would require the support of a two-thirds majority vote of the Assembly, whose quorum is the majority of members,[19] entering into force 12 months after the acceptance by two-thirds of IMO members.[20] As with ICAO and the climate regime, the IMO Assembly aims for its decisions to be adopted by consensus, as the preferred option. The IMO Convention has been amended on a number of occasions, involving essential issues such as the incorporation of environmental objectives into the work of the organization. However, as with ICAO, the easier and faster option to avoid conflicts remains in the drafting of a new instrument, so as to create an MBM for reducing GHG emissions from shipping. With regards to potential conflicts with MARPOL Annex VI, regarding CBDRRC, an amendment would be much easier to achieve given the 'tacit acceptance procedure' used by the MEPC.[21]

However, if the treaty changes or amendments or new treaty drafting are not adopted unanimously, the problem of reservations would come into play, creating conflicts with the parties opposed to change. Rules regarding reservations are found in Article 19 of the VCLT, which grants the freedom to formulate reservations, except if the reservations are expressly prohibited, or a certain type of reservations is allowed only if a reservation is incompatible with the object and purpose of the treaty. This, however, is '*a matter of appreciation*'.[22]

Amendments could also occur in any of the three regimes in the form of a new separate agreement by parties to modify their respective treaty, as far as the possibility of such a modification is provided for or is not prohibited by the treaty and '*does not affect the enjoyment by the other parties of their rights under the treaty or the performance of their obligations*' or '*does not relate to a provision, derogation from which is incompatible with the effective execution of the object and purpose of the treaty as a whole*'.[23] However, the ILC made a distinction between amendments of treaties referring to changes in the provisions of a treaty with effects on all of the parties and modification of treaties refereeing to *inter se agreements* (i.e. agreements only between some of the parties and warned about the potential for conflicts).[24]

Treaty interpretation and systemic integration

Treaty interpretation is the second method of avoiding conflicts and is relevant not only in the context of being used by courts and tribunals at international and domestic level, but also it can serve governments and diplomats when establishing preferences at the law-making and implementation level, both internationally and when establishing regulation at the national sphere.[25]

Articles 31 and 32 of the VCLT set forth the basic rules of treaty interpretation. While Article 31 contains the general rule of interpretation, Article 32 is supplementary to it. However, the ILC study maintains that there is no division between the articles and that both operate in conjunction. Nonetheless, it has been pointed out[26] that a distinction exists and reflects the will of parties in the techniques detailed in article 31 and the lack of them in 32 (i.e. it is supplementary because it is not what the parties finally adopted).

The most fundamental rule is that a treaty shall be interpreted '*in good faith in accordance with the ordinary meaning to be given to the terms of the treaty in their context and in the light of its object and purpose*'.[27] This textual rule[28] of interpretation is complemented with a contextual rule that comprises '*its preamble and annexes*' including '*any agreement relating to the treaty which was made between all the parties in connection with the conclusion of the treaty*' and '*any instrument which was made by one or more parties in connection with the conclusion of the treaty and accepted by the other parties as an instrument related to the treaty.*'[29]

Furthermore, together with text and context, interpretation must take into account, '*any subsequent agreement between the parties regarding the interpretation of the treaty or the application of its provisions*',[30] '*any subsequent practice in the application of the treaty which establishes the agreement of the parties regarding its interpretation*'[31] and '*any relevant rules of international law applicable in the relations between the parties*'.[32] With regards to supplementary means of interpretation, Article 32[33] includes recourse to the preparatory work of the treaty and the circumstances of its conclusion: to confirm the meaning resulting from the general rule or to determine the meaning when Article 31 '*leaves the meaning ambiguous or obscure*'[34] or '*leads to a result which is manifestly absurd or unreasonable*'.[35]

The emphasis on one or the other aspect of these rules of interpretation reflects different approaches to interpretation; textualism, intentionalism and the teleological approach. The latter focuses on the object and aims of the treaty, which is particularly useful in framework conventions and institutions, since the organs and bodies created obey the purpose of resolving a particular international concern.[36] Although teleological interpretation is best suited for dealing with the climate, ICAO and IMO treaties, an analysis of Article 2.2 has been offered by many scholars, including in this study,[37] and hasn't helped to resolve the encountered country positions around issues such as CBDRRC in the three regimes.

The ILC study pointed towards Article 31.3(c) of VCLT (the use of '*any relevant rules of international law applicable in the relations between the parties*') as a way to address conflicts, which has given expression to the principle of systemic integration. This principle posits to take the perspective of the conflicting norms as a '*contribution to some generally shared – "systemic" – objective*'.[38] Systemic integration can be defined as the process where '*international obligations are interpreted in reference to their normative environment ("system")*',[39] which includes interpretation against the background of general international law and '*to take into account the normative environment more widely*', which in the age of framework and implementation treaties is translated into '*mutually supportiveness*'.[40] This technique differs widely from other rules, since it aims to '*harmonize the apparently conflicting norms by interpreting them so as to render them compatible*'.[41] Despite the value of the principle of systemic integration in avoiding '*clinical isolation*' of regimes from public international law,[42] its status is not universally recognized under general international law.[43] Therefore, the literature has posited that it is only safe to regard the principle as '*an aspiration or objective rather than a principle*'.[44]

Here, the principle of systemic integration could be of help to ease some tensions between regimes in relation to the principle of sustainable development.[45] This is relevant, for example, for the interpretation of the objective of the regimes and the design of MBMs in ICAO and the IMO. Importantly, the UN Sustainable Development Goals (SDGs) were adopted in 2015[46] and include a specific goal (and associated targets) on climate change. The SDGs came into effect on January 2016 and will guide actions at the international level over the next 15 years.

From the treaty interpretation techniques provided above, the possibility of parties subscribing to an interpretation agreement could solve the conflict over, for example, the principle of CBDRRC by either excluding or forcing its application. Subsequent practice is more difficult to apply given that the legal nature of treaty bodies is difficult to prove and establish, especially given the uncertainty in the status of treaty body decisions.[47]

Conflict clauses

Conflict clauses[48] are another means to deal with conflict between treaties by establishing which treaty prevails in case of collision. This technique for conflict resolution requires that States avow in the treaties '*what to do with subsequent or prior conflicting treaties*',[49] by giving priority, claiming priority or determining priority through a given indicator. However, conflict clauses suffer from three main characteristics: conflict clauses do not apply to third parties, they are often unclear and they are not often used in practice.[50]

The first question to ask is whether the climate, ICAO and IMO contain such conflict clauses. The answer is a simple negative, for the three of them. Although it can be argued that Article 2.2 of the KP is a conflict clause, it was not design so as to provide priority between treaties, as explained previously in this book.[51] Furthermore, Article 2.2 of the KP has been the cause of multiple controversies, particularly with regards to challenges to CBDRRC. In the words of the chairman of the MEPC and the head of IMO's Air Pollution and Climate Change Section of the Marine Environment Division: '*it can be safely claimed that the wording of article 2.2 has been the main reason why the IMO has not yet been able to enact a GHG regime for international shipping in a timely and comprehensive manner.*'[52]

Conflict clauses, which could be introduced in any of the conflicting treaties, are a straightforward method to resolve conflicts by indicating the order of priority, with regards to other treaties and therefore shedding light over the obligations of involved parties. The inclusion of a conflict clause could also be directed towards a specific principle of a treaty (whether the choice of parties is differential or equal treatment), which the parties agree to preserve from forthcoming instruments. This is the case of the conflict clause contained in Article 311.6 of the UNCLOS,[53] where parties '*agree that there shall be no amendments to the basic principle relating to the common heritage of mankind set forth in article 136 and that they shall not be party to any agreement in derogation thereof.*' If one of the treaties were providing such a clause, the conflict would be resolved at least over the question of principles.

With regards to the introduction of a conflict clause in any of the new instruments developed in the climate, ICAO and IMO regimes, some recommendations are to be borne in mind for the legislator. Some authors have advocated for the introduction of a procedure when drafting new norms, including listing all the legal instruments that a treaty may have an impact on, followed by a consultation and assessment of those impacts with relevant States and organizations.[54]

As explained in Chapter 4, in the context of the PA, a clause devoted to IBF was drafted for the negotiating text. However, the challenging task of reaching a global climate agreement in Paris, and to avoid a Copenhagen-like anticlimax,[55] requires a change in diplomacy and atmosphere[56] which led to the exclusion of the clause in the final text. In carrying out the difficult task of bridging countries' positions and finding a compromise, highly conflictive matters that were considered not essential for the agreement were, reasonably, called upon to be removed. This politics of omission[57] led to the exclusion of thorny issues from the negotiating table. The case for excluding IBFs was arguably particularly clear: first, international aviation and shipping are not equally crucial economic sectors for all countries; second, those countries with a strong interest in the sector/s have been, historically, very unwilling to compromise positions, specifically around the issue of differential and equal treatment;[58] and finally, discussions on the inclusion of IBFs had the potential to imperil an agreement because they evoke the rigid division between developed and developing countries, as suggested by Article 2.2 of the Kyoto Protocol.

However, given the potential of IBFs to bridge the gap towards overall climate objectives,[59] and the lack of progress in the negotiations in ICAO and the IMO over the last decades, much of which is based on article 2.2 KP,[60] the Paris outcome is a missed opportunity to clarify fundamental aspects encumbering IBF regulation.

Fundamentally, the relationship between the climate, ICAO and IMO regimes is unclear and the interactions among these regimes have caused a number of conflicts, which have inhibited progress.[61] Notwithstanding other sensitive issues, there are four main areas of friction. First, there is disagreement over the competent forum to regulate IBFs. Second, there is disagreement over the principles applying to IBF regulation. In particular, there are diverging views on whether differential treatment in favour of developing countries should apply to the aviation and shipping sectors, which, otherwise, would work under equal treatment premises. Third, there is disagreement over the emissions reduction target to be achieved by IBFs, which is dependent on the objectives set up in the constitutive instruments of the ICAO and the IMO regimes. And fourth, there is disagreement over the way to achieve these reductions, specifically, the use and design of market-based mechanisms.

Parties could have specified in the PA the relationship between the climate, ICAO and IMO regimes, shedding light on the obligations of involved parties, in the form of a conflict clause. This was advocated in the literature.[62] Oberthür and colleagues, for instance, suggested that the following text could have straightened out the most important aspects in need of clarification:

> Parties shall work through and with other relevant international organizations and agreements, inter alia the International Civil Aviation Organization, the International Maritime Organization, and the Montreal Protocol on Substances that Deplete the Ozone Layer, in accordance with their internal rules and procedures, so as to ensure that these organizations and agreements contribute fully and increasingly to achieving the long-term mitigation and adaptation goals of this Agreement, including through the mobilization of technical and financial support and capacity building, as appropriate.[63]

First, regarding the competent forum, the clause could have departed from the delegation of *negotiations* to ICAO and IMO established in Article 2.2 of the KP, to a delegation of *regulation*. The KP does not clarify the relationship between instruments, since Article 2.2 is merely '*a provision delimiting the scope of the climate treaties by delegating the negotiation of rules*' on IBF.[64] Second, in line with a delegation of regulation, the provision could have acknowledged that ICAO and the IMO shall work in conformity with their internal rules and procedures. Unlike Article 2.2 of the KP, this would have avoided conflicts related to CBDRRC as a guiding principle entering regimes which traditionally work under equal treatment. Third, however, a strong signal on the contribution of the sectors to the climate target would have been desirable, so as to avoid unambitious regulations in ICAO and the IMO. Additionally, indications regarding the measures to achieve emission reductions and contributions to financing climate adaptation and mitigation would have been useful too. However, the inclusion of such a clause could have also exacerbated the troubles in ICAO and the IMO related to accepting external mandates from the climate regime, and have undermined regulatory competition with the climate regime.[65]

Priority rules

Another technique of conflict resolution is the application of treaty priority rules, which aim to establish which international treaties should prevail, taking into account their status, temporality and specificity.[66]

First, *lex superior derogat lex inferiori*, which establishes a hierarchy of norms, although as posited in the ILC Study, aside from Article 103 of the UN Charter and peremptory norms (*jus cogens*), there is no such hierarchy between international treaties. Following this logic, this rule does not apply to conflicts between the climate, ICAO and IMO treaties since there is no hierarchy between them as they operate, so to speak, at the same level.

Second, *lex posterior derogate legi priori* (i.e. where new norms prevail over old norms), which aims to deal with '*the application of successive treaties relating to the same subject matter*'.[67] However, since the climate treaties, and the Chicago

Convention or the IMO Convention, vary extensively in their context and scope of the matter they regulate, this rule cannot be applied to addressing conflicts between them.[68] Furthermore, since the three regimes are constantly updated to address their aims and objectives through treaty bodies and organs, it is very difficult to establish temporality. Although it is contested,[69] the opinion of the ILC Study[70] is that priority rules on subsequent treaties could be extended from strictly '*treaties relating to same subject matters*'. According to the ILC, the criterion of the same subject matter '*seems already fulfilled if two different rules or sets of rules are invoked in regards of the same matter*'.[71] In this connection it would be possible to establish priority among treaties, and it could be argued that Article 2.2 of the KP with regards of CBDRRC prevails over the equal treatment provisions in ICAO and IMO, with regards to the regulation of GHG emissions.

Third, *lex specialis derogate legi generali* (i.e. where special norms prevail over general ones).[72] This rule is difficult to apply since the '*specialis*' depends on the angle at which the subject matter is approached. For example it could be argued that the KP is more specific than the Chicago Convention or the IMO Conventions, or the other way around, depending on the point of view. Indeed, it is a highly subjective undertaking to determine which rules are more specific, if we cannot determine first whether to take a climate or international aviation or international maritime transport standpoint. A common-sense approach would be to assume they are of equal *lex specialis*. Also, some norms within a treaty can be more specialized while the whole treaty cannot be, such as Annex VI with regards to MARPOL.

Approaches beyond the ILC study

Given that for the conflictive outcomes found in the interaction legal avenues offer limited solutions, this study has pursued a wider methodological scope, allowing for other techniques to complement and offer solutions to conflicts that enable synergies. While the ILC Study recognized that the solutions proposed in its study face limitations,[73] legal scholars have posited the suitability of considering options beyond the ones proposed in the ILC Study, especially with regards to the climate change regime.[74]

As introduced in Chapter 2, the pursuit of approaches beyond international law, or, to be precise, beyond the traditional set of tools detailed in the ILC study, refers mainly to institutional cooperation and coordination. A further step out of the law domain involves autonomous action by State and non-state actors, which also offers possibilities for managing interaction. Here, the fundamental question is if and how these approaches can help, first, to avoid and resolve conflicts impeding progress in the law-making and second to enhance or scale up synergies.

Institutional cooperation and coordination

The obligation to cooperate is deeply rooted in international law,[75] and the principle of international cooperation in environmental matters can be traced to the Stockholm Declaration, which stipulated that '*international matters concerning the protection and improvement of the environment should be handled in a co-operative spirit*.[76] The Rio Declaration introduced the concept of '*global partnership*',[77] which upgraded the obligation to cooperate in environmental matters; it has been argued that although principles 7 and 13 of the Rio Declaration are directed to States, the concept of global partnership may also be extended to non-state entities, such as IGOs, corporations, NGOs and civil society.[78]

Institutional cooperation, otherwise known as 'interplay management' in the international relations literature,[79] can be close to legal approaches. For example, in the case of COP decisions, they can be considered for treaty interpretation or as treaty changes, but they can also be regarded in the light of the process leading to their adoption in terms of institutional coordination.[80] Institutional cooperation and coordination between regimes' treaty bodies and organs can take a variety of shapes. First, they can be unilateral or joint, depending on whether they come from unilateral decisions in the regimes or decisions involving communication between regimes. Second, they can be *ad hoc* or structural, depending on whether they entail isolated acts or permanent structures. Third, they can have legal basis or simply use informal channels. Finally, they can involve the regimes' decision-making bodies or bureaucracies.[81] The following sections explore the existing cooperation between regimes to further identify new cooperation opportunities.

Existing cooperation

Existing coordination between the climate, ICAO and IMO regimes has been introduced in Chapter 4, in the context of regulatory and administrative interaction.[82] Oberthür's study identified three conditions under which the interaction of ICAO and IMO with the climate regime would move from the 'disruptive'[83] stage to a more constructive one. He argued that this would occur, first, by enhancing the threat of regulation of GHG emissions from international transport under the climate change regime. Second, by undertaking unilateral domestic action by various countries, in particular the EU; and third, by furthering a learning process within ICAO and IMO, that is, a closer coordination of efforts under ICAO, IMO and the climate change regime that could facilitate and accelerate progress and enhance synergies.

The decision-making bodies as well as the secretariats of the climate, ICAO and IMO regimes have received mandates and invitations to engage in cooperation.[84] In Chapter 4, it was argued that the regimes have pursued a route down this third avenue by experimenting with coordination and cooperation, beyond the mandates established in their legal instruments.[85] However some examples of the willingness towards cooperation can be traced back to 1997. For example, in the context of the MARPOL conference, a resolution on CO_2 emissions from ships was adopted, where the IMO secretary general was invited to cooperate with the executive secretary of the UNFCCC in the exchange of information on GHG emissions.[86] With regards to the climate regime,

> institutional coordination between the climate secretariat and other bureaucracies has mainly concerned observership, mutual attendance at meetings,

scientific cooperation and information exchange, but these activities provide an important contribution to raising awareness about the existence of interactions, as well as their (potential) consequences.[87]

The only decision on institutional cooperation comes from a COP decision and is rather vague in its terms.[88] In this way, the interactions between regimes can extend to 'normative influence'.

Enhancing institutional cooperation

There are a few ways to enhance institutional cooperation between the climate, ICAO and IMO regimes, the main one being the promotion of cooperation between bureaucracies. Interaction between secretariats has the advantage of occurring out of the realm of the political tangles inherent to the negotiation and decision-making processes taking place in the climate, ICAO and IMO bodies. In theory this should make easier to exchange information and focus on the content and substance of dialogues. However, issues of mandates of the secretariats, transparency and legitimacy also need to be considered[89] since the legal capacity of bureaucracies is limited by their constituent instruments. As such, not all parties may be equally happy if, for example, the ICAO and IMO secretariat engage in cooperation with the climate regime, bypassing state consent. Also parties may be scared of entering into some kind of concession through the back door.[90] In this connection there are other risks in institutional cooperation; for example, in their study on bureaucracies,[91] Biermann and Siebenhüner tested the reach and influence of a number of secretariats in environmental governance against the hypothesis that the higher the level of technical expertise, the higher the influence that bureaucracies may exert. This hypothesis was confirmed with regard to the IMO secretariat, which draws its influence from '*the ability of the staff to pool technical knowledge and the excellent contact with the industry*'.[92] Similar assumptions can be made of the ICAO Secretariat, based on their strong technical knowledge and industry contacts.[93] On the other hand, the climate secretariat is overloaded and its freedom is quite constrained.[94] This could raise concerns over whether coordination may become dominated by procedures, principles and concepts of the strongest regimes.[95]

Bureaucracies play an essential role in providing the regime participants and other regimes with information.[96] Institutional learning and information exchange are of relevance in regime interaction.[97] Cooperation through bureaucracies may take place formally, through the specific mandates and mutual agreements, but also through institutional arrangements. Informal cooperation takes place in a more flexible manner with bureaucracies acting outside the established channels. Cooperation among secretariats would be more fluent if the climate, ICAO and IMO regimes were to cooperate in an area of common interest, which may be difficult given their diverging objectives. However, their current cooperation could be enhanced with a view of resolving existing conflicts by establishing a more permanent cooperation through an agreement with specific scope, objectives and means for cooperation. This could occur, for example, through regular exchanges of information or an agreement to intensify mutual observership.

Another option is to establish a working group between the climate and the ICAO secretariat and the climate and IMO secretariat to address a specific issue. This group could also be tripartite and possibly lead to the establishment of a permanent committee for IBF emissions. Or, for example, it could cooperate to conduct a study on a potential MBM covering international aviation and maritime transport. Furthermore, cooperation could be enhanced by instituting a technical joint expert group to deliver support in the negotiations or provide a common consultative legal group, where, for example, all the queries and concerns over differential and equal treatment could be directed and dealt with. Such groups would be very useful since country delegations in the climate forum are usually environment ministries whose knowledge on IBF may be limited, and delegations to the ICAO and the IMO involve transport ministries whose expertise on general climate may also be incomplete.

It is difficult to know exactly how this enhancement of cooperation and coordination will address the conflicts at stake. However, a permanent arrangement could serve to discuss the scope of the objective and target for emissions reductions and the reach of equal treatment and CBDRRC, while presenting the possibilities for MBMs and climate finance in a more objective, scientific light. In conclusion, and as has been discussed in the literature, there are numerous advantages in the form of resolving tensions, building capacity and promoting better understanding that can result from inter-regime learning, knowledge sharing and conceptual interaction.[98]

Autonomous interaction management

Autonomous interaction is a political approach to the management of interaction defined by the choices made by individual actors, whether they are States or non-state actors. It has two main characteristics: first, action from States differs from the implementation of international instruments, since the aim is not to implement acquired obligations but to address the overlap of two regimes. Second, actions from States or non-States differ from their role as participants in the negotiation and law-making processes of the regimes.[99]

In defining autonomous interaction management the literature offers some examples.[100] Some successful unilateral action in environmental issues include the *Canadian Artic Water Prevention Pollution Act*[101] prompting the adoption of Article 234 UNCLOS, so-called the 'Arctic Exception', or the EU double-hull regulation,[102] which accelerated the introduction of double-hull requirements in MARPOL. However, in some cases, such as the regulation of ballast water discharges,[103] unilateralism can spoil advances in the negotiations because of the accompanying threats and uncertainty.

In this connection, it can be argued that the inclusion of aviation in the EU ETS and the EU proposal for a MRV for the shipping sector are a way for the EU to fulfil its climate obligations, but also to steer the interaction between regimes, by establishing an MBM that applies to international aviation.[104] This unilateral action has provoked a number of reactions in ICAO, such as the removal of a mutual consent clause, the elaboration of a list of principles that a potential MBM should conform to and the adoption of CORSIA. In a similar fashion, the potential adoption of a MRV measure in the maritime sector has steered the IMO towards adopting its own measures. However, unilateral action in international aviation and maritime transport has proved to be complex and controversial. Here the book merely points towards this way of management; however, an in-depth analysis of the reach of autonomous interaction would require a different type of research.

Promoting regime interaction

Young has proposed[105] a legal framework for regime interaction. According to Young, there are multiple legal bases for regime interaction, namely: parallel membership, mutual agreements expressing the consent of States to allow normative and institutional interplay mutual agreement, and institutional arrangements, where consent is entrenched through an agreement of the organizations.[106] The latter can emerge from '*formal or informal arrangements within and between international institutions*',[107] whose rationale reflects the need '*to learn, share and adopt information from external sources*'.[108] While the ILC Study recommended recourse to international law to coordinate inter-regime cooperation, '*the law must leave room for political processes to resolve pluralistic problems*' so that the greatest value of law is in creating accountability for those processes.[109]

However, since institutional arrangements often touch upon normative matters and can even influence the negotiation of international law norms (directly or indirectly), questions arise over legitimacy. With regards to consent and sovereignty, there is no problem in the climate, ICAO and IMO regimes enhancing their cooperation, since they already have mandates to cooperate trough their decision-making bodies and secretariat. Indeed, it is possible to go beyond these mandates as part of their capacities to collaborate over their implied powers.[110] However, it might be more difficult for the climate secretariat to engage in institutional cooperation outside the mandate, since the regime is quite sensitive to the issue of consent. On the other hand, ICAO and the IMO have more autonomy, at least with regards to representation in their councils and in their culture of tacit contentment in passing certain regulations. This issue relates to Koskenniemi's warning on 'managerialism' by biased regime experts operating without members' consent. This risk is compounded by the increasingly technocratic nature of international law and politics.[111] Given their internal expertise and high reliance upon their technical strength, coupled with accusations of a lack of transparency and participation of civil society in ICAO,[112] there is a risk that the ICAO and IMO regimes could dominate the climate regime in a process of institutional interaction. However, the law can offer solutions to the risks of 'managerialism' and, in this connection, accountable regime interaction has been posited as something to strive for.[113] Young proposes mechanisms and procedural safeguards to ensure accountable regime interaction, including openness, transparency, participation and ongoing scrutiny and review.[114] In view of those mechanisms, there is a case to be made that potential arrangements established for institutional cooperation between the climate, ICAO and IMO regimes should be subjected to processes whereby transparency and involvement of stakeholders is guaranteed, and whereby scrutiny and review are continuingly applied.

Given that there is potential for conflict avoidance and resolution, and enhancement of synergies in the *'productive friction between regimes'*,[115] the promotion of regime interaction should arguably be pursued in the case of the regulation of international aviation and maritime transport emissions. While problems such as exclusivity of forum – the denial of the role and competence of regimes, lack of transparency and openness between regimes, and the request for parallel membership – are impediments to interaction, some measures promote it. The main means of promoting interaction come from domestic policy coordination; however, national coordination with regards to climate, air and maritime transport may not be enough *'given the variety of goals and agendas'*.[116] A second way is through mutual learning and information-sharing, where the interaction between ICAO, IMO and the climate regime has the most promising prospects. Third, as Young has pointed out, the allocation of resources for the purpose of regime interaction is a decisive factor in the promotion of interaction.[117]

Conclusions

The international law-making process is not free of shortcomings or what C.W. Jenks called 'imperfections',[118]

> some of which can be eliminated by forethought and prudence, whereas others, being inherent in the nature of the process, give rise to problems for which appropriate solutions must be found on the assumption that the imperfection itself cannot be wholly eliminated.[119]

The points at which regimes overlap these imperfections translate into conflicts or tensions. This chapter has aimed to answer the question, *How can these tensions be overcome?* In doing so it has given an account of approaches to managing interaction, both to avoid and resolve tensions and to enhance synergies between the climate, ICAO and IMO regimes. These approaches range from legal techniques posited by the ILC study that takes the VCLT as the primary source of solutions to institutional cooperation or autonomous management.

From a legal perspective, the most promising solutions to conflicts arise from the drafting of new treaties. However, PA did not deal with the issue of IBF. Therefore, the potential regulation under a convention in ICAO and the IMO fora will represent a unique opportunity for addressing the conflicts, whether political or normative, with regards to the diverging objectives, principles and choice of regulation. However, this chapter has clarified that in the run-up to those agreements, inter-regime learning and knowledge sharing provided by institutional coordination and cooperation between the regimes' decision-making and administrative bodies may play a more effective role, not only in helping resolve conflicts but also in exploring areas of mutual benefit. However, in enhancing institutional cooperation, issues of legitimacy and 'managerialism' have been stressed, highlighting the need to ensure accountability of interaction. This chapter has also indicated some examples of institutional coordination the regimes could adopt, advocating a preference for permanent arrangements and structures.

Notes

1 See Chapter 2.
2 ILC, *Fragmentation of International Law: Difficulties Arising from the Diversification and Expansion of International Law. Report of the Study Group of the International Law Commission.* UN Doc. A/CN.4/L.682, (2006).
3 On the value of the VCLT see, Ian Brownlie, *Principles of Public International Law* (Oxford University Press 7th ed., 2008). 607–638.
4 Vienna Convention on the Law of Treaties. Vienna, adopted 23 May 1969, in force 27 January 1980. 8 ILM 679, (1969).
5 See chapter two.
6 See, among others, the work of Joost Pauwelyn, *Conflict of Norms in Public International Law: How WTO Law Relates to Other Rules of International Law* (Cambridge University Press, 2003); C. Wilfred Jenks, 'Conflict of Law-Making Treaties', *British Year Book of International Law*, 30, (1953). 401; R. Wolfrum et al., *Conflicts in International Environmental Law* (Springer, 2003); Erich Vranes, 'The Definition of "Norm Conflict" in International Law and Legal Theory', *European Journal of International Law*, 17(2), (2006). 395–418.
7 Harro van Asselt et al., 'Global Climate Change and the Fragmentation of International Law', *Law & Policy*, 30(4), (2008). 429.
8 See explanation in Harro van Asselt, *The Fragmentation of Global Climate Governance: Consequences and Management of Regime Interactions*, (2013). 61.
9 International Law Commission, Fragmentation of International Law: Difficulties Arising from the Diversification and Expansion of International Law. Report of the Study Group of the International Law Commission. UN. Doc. A/CN.4/L.682 (2006). Paragraph 475.
10 Vienna Convention on the Law of Treaties. (1969). Part IV on amendment and modification of treaties. Article 39–41.
11 United Nations Framework Convention on Climate Change. New York, 9 May 1992, in force 21 March 1994, 31 International Legal Materials (1992), 849 (1992). article 15 and 16.
12 See, full explanation on Sebastian Oberthür and Hermann Ott, *The Kyoto Protocol: International Climate Policy for the 21st Century* (Springer, 1999). 257–259.
13 See further in this chapter, section on conflict clauses.
14 Chicago Convention, Article.
15 See Chapter 3 at 'Conclusions'.
16 See Chapter 3.
17 ICAO, Assembly Resolution A39–3: Consolidated Statement of Continuing ICAO Policies and Practices Related to Environmental Protection – Global Market-Based Measure (MBM) scheme, (2016).
18 See Chapters 5 and 7.
29 IMO Convention, Article 14.
20 IMO Convention, Article 66–68.
21 See Chapter 3.
22 I. Brownlie, (2008). 614.

23 VCLT, Article 41.
24 ILC Report, (2006). Paragraph 295–323. See also, especially on the residual character of inter se agreements in VCLT, Malgosia Fitzmaurice and Panos Merkouris, 'Uniformity versus Specialization: The Quest for a Uniform Law of Inter-State Treaties', *University of Groningen Faculty of Law Research Paper Series No. 05/2014*, (2014).
25 Riccardo Pavoni, 'Mutual Supportiveness as a Principle of Interpretation and Law-Making: A Watershed for the "WTO-and-Competing-Regimes" Debate?', *European Journal of International Law*, 21(3), (2010). 649–679.
26 I. Brownlie, (2008). 631–633.
27 VCLT, Article 31.1. However, Article 31.4 provides for consideration of any special meaning given to a term '*if it is established that the parties so intended*'.
28 With regards to the text, Article 33 allows for the use of interpretation of treaties authenticated in two or more languages.
   VCLT, Article 33.
29 VCLT, Article 31.2.
30 VCLT, Article 31.3(a).
31 VCLT, Article 31.3(b).
32 VCLT, Article 31.3(c).
33 Article 32, included other inputs to interpretation not referenced in Article 31, such as the *travaix preparatoires* of a treaty. These are called '*supplementary means of interpretation*'.
34 VCLT, Article 32(a).
35 VCLT, Article 32(b).
36 However, the literature has posited concerns about the reach of it. See, G.G. Fitzmaurice, 'Law and Procedure of the International Court of Justice: Treaty Interpretation and Certain Other Treaty Points', *British Yearbook of International Law*, 28(1), (1951); Edward Gordon, 'The World Court and the Interpretation of Constitutive Treaties: Some Observations on the Development of an International Constitutional Law', *American Journal of International Law*, 59(4), (1965). 794–833.
37 See Chapter Four.
38 ILC Report, (2006). Paragraph 412.
39 Ibid. at. Paragraph 413.
40 Ibid. at. Paragraph 414–417.
41 Ibid. at. Paragraph 441.
42 International Law Association. International Law Association. Committee on the Legal Principles Relating to Climate Change, 'The Legal Principles relating to Climate Change, Second Report (Sofia Conference 2012)', (2012). 36.
43 G.O. Zabalza, *The Principle of Systemic Integration: Towards a Coherent International Legal Order*. Berlin, Lit Verlag (2012). Chapter six. See also, Campbell McLachlan, 'The Principle of Systemic Integration and Article 31(3)(C) of the Vienna Convention', *International and Comparative Law Quarterly*, 54(2), (2005), 279–320.
44 H.v. Asselt et al., (2008).
45 Christina Voigt, *Sustainable Development as a Principle of International Law: Resolving Conflicts between Climate Measures and WTO Law* (Martinus Nijhoff Publishers, 2009). See chapter five.
46 UN General Assembly, Transforming Our World: The 2030 Agenda for Sustainable Development, 21 October 2015, A/RES/70/1 (2015).
47 H.v. Asselt, *The Fragmentation of Global Climate Governance: Consequences and Management of Regime Interactions*. (2013). 83.
48 The concept and main characteristics of conflict clauses was introduced in Chapter 4 in the context of questioning the nature of Article 2.2 of the KP as a conflict clause.
49 ILC Report, (2006). Paragraph 267.
50 H.v. Asselt, *The Fragmentation of Global Climate Governance: Consequences and Management of Regime Interactions*. (2013). 85–86.

51 See Chapter 4.
52 Andreas Chrysostomou and Eivind S. Vagslid, 'Climate Change: A Challenge for IMO Too', in *Maritime Transport and the Climate Change Challenge* (R. Asariotis and Hassiba Benamara eds., 2012). p. 81. See similar arguments in Saiful Karim and Shawkat Alam, 'Climate Change and Reduction of Emissions of Greenhouse Gases from Ships: An Appraisal', *Asian Journal of International Law*, 1, (2011). 131.
53 United Nations Convention on the Law of the Sea, Montego Bay, adopted 10 December 1982, in force 16 November 1994, 21 International Legal Materials (1982), 1261. 1833 UNTS 3, (1982).
54 C.W. Jenks, (1953); R. Wolfrum et al., (2003). Referred to in, Harro Van Asselt, 'Managing the Fragmentation of International Climate Law', in *Climate Change and the Law, Ius Gentium: Comparative Perspectives on Law and Justice 21* (Erkki J. Hollo et al. eds., 2013).
55 Meinhard Doelle, 'The Legacy of the Climate Talks in Copenhagen: Hopenhagen or Brokenhagen?', *Carbon and Climate Law Review*, 4(1), (2010). 86.
56 Unlike previous COPs, the heads of State and government joined the conference at the beginning rather than the end. Compared to COP15, the text presented to the delegates in Paris was much more developed and condensed.
57 Stephen Holmes, 'Gag Rules or the Politics of Omission', in *Constitutionalism and Democracy* (Jon Elster and Rune Slagstad eds., 1988). 19.
58 Sophia Kopela, 'Climate Change, Regime Interaction, and the Principle of Common but Differentiated Responsibility: The Experience of the International Maritime Organization', 24 *Yearbook of International Environmental Law*, (2013). 70–101; Beatriz Martinez Romera and Harro van Asselt, 'The International Regulation of Aviation Emissions: Putting Differential Treatment into Practice', *Journal of Environmental Law*, (2015). 259; Per Kågeson, 'Applying the Principle of Common but Differentiated Responsibility to the Mitigation of Greenhouse Gases from International Shipping', Working Papers in Transport Economics from the Centre for Transport Studies Stockholm No. 2011:5, (2011).
59 David S. Lee et al., 'Shipping and Aviation Emissions in the Context of a 2°C Emission Pathway' (Manchester Metropolitan University, 2013). On the potential of sectoral agreements to tackle climate change, see Daniel Bodansky, 'Multilateral Climate Efforts beyond the UNFCCC', (Centre for Climate and Energy Solutions, Arlington, November 2011); Daniel Bodansky, 'International Sectoral Agreements in a Post-2012 Climate Framework', Working Paper Prepared for the Pew Center on Global Climate Change, (2007).
60 See chapter four.
61 Sebastian Oberthür, 'Institutional Interaction to Address Greenhouse Gas Emissions from International Transport: ICAO, IMO and the Kyoto Protocol', *Climate Policy*, 3(3), (2003). 191.
62 Sebastian Oberthür et al., 'Getting Specific on the 2015 Climate Change Agreement: Suggestions for the Legal Text with an Explanatory Memorandum', Working Paper. Washington, DC: Agreement for Climate Transformation 2015 (ACT 2015), (2015); I. Gençsü and M. Hino, 'Raising Ambition to Reduce International Aviation and Maritime Emissions', Working Paper, *New Climate Economy*, The Global Commission on the Economy and Climate (2015).
63 S. Oberthür et al., (2015). 17.
64 Sebastian Oberthür, 'The Climate Change Regime: Interactions of the Climate Change Regime with ICAO, IMO and the EU Burden-Sharing Agreement', in *Institutional Interaction in Global Environmental Governance: Synergy and Conflict among International and EU Policies: Global Environmental Accord: Strategies for Sustainability and Institutional Innovation* (Sebastian Oberthür and Thomas Gehring eds., 2006). 53.
65 See S. Oberthür, (2003).
66 ILC Report, (2006).
67 VCLT, Article 30.3.

68 See reasoning in, Yubing Shi, 'Greenhouse Gas Emissions from International Shipping: The Response from China's Shipping Industry to the Regulatory Initiatives of the International Maritime Organization', *International Journal of Marine and Coastal Law*, 29(1), (2014). 85–123.

69 R. Wolfrum et al., (2003). 151.

70 ILC Report, (2006). Paragraph 253–256.

71 Ibid. at. Paragraph 23.

72 Ibid. at. Paragraph 59–61.

73 International Law Association. Committee on the Legal Principles Relating to Climate Change, (2012).

74 Margaret A. Young, 'Climate Change Law and Regime Interaction', *Climate Change Law Review*, (2011). 147–157; Harro van Asselt, (2013); Harro van Asselt, 'Legal and Political Approaches in Interplay Management: Dealing with the Fragmentation of Global Climate Governance', in *Managing Institutional Complexity: Regime Interplay and Global Environmental Change: Institutional Dimensions of Global Environmental Change* (Sebastian Oberthür and Olav Schram Stokke eds., 2011); Harro van Asselt and Fariborz Zelli, 'Connect the Dots: Managing the Fragmentation of Global Climate Governance Earth System', Governance Working Paper No. 25. Lund and Amsterdam: Earth System Governance Project, (2012); Kati Kulovesi, 'Climate Change and Trade: At the Intersection of Two International Legal Regimes', in *Climate Change and the Law* (Erkki J. Hollo et al. eds., 2013).

75 'United Nations, Charter of the United Nations, 24 October 1945, 1 UNTS XVI'. Articles 55 and 56.

76 Stockholm Declaration on the Human Environment. 11 ILM 1416, (1972). Principle 24.

77 Rio Declaration on Environment and Development, U.N. Doc. A/CONF.151/26 (vol. I) reprinted in (1992) 31 ILM 874 (1992). Adopted at the United Nations Conference on Environment and Development in Rio de Janeiro, Brazil from 3–14 June 1992, (1992). Preamble states: '*With the goal of establishing a new and equitable global partnership through the creation of new levels of co-operation among States, key sectors of societies and people*'.

78 L. Kurukulasuriya and N.A. Robinson, *Training Manual on International Environmental Law* (United Nations Environment Programme. Division of Environmental Policy Development Law ed., Division of Policy Development and Law, United Nations Environment Programme, 2006). 29–30.

79 Sebastian Oberthür, 'Interplay Management: Enhancing Environmental Policy Integration among International Institutions', *International Environmental Agreements: Politics, Law and Economics*, 9(4), (2009). 374–376.

80 H.v. Asselt, *The Fragmentation of Global Climate Governance: Consequences and Management of Regime Interactions* (2013). 91.

81 The division is taken from, ibid. at. 91–104.

82 See chapter four.

83 See, Sebastian Oberthür, 'Institutional Interaction to Address Greenhouse Gas Emissions from International Transport: ICAO, IMO and the EU Burden-Sharing Agreement', *Project Deliverable No. D 3, Final Draft. Ecologic: Institute for International and European Policy*, (2003). 3–6.

84 See Chapter 4, where coordination in the context of regulatory interaction has been already discussed.

85 See Chapter 4.

86 MARPOL, Resolution MP/CONF.3/35, 1997.

87 H.v. Asselt, *The Fragmentation of Global Climate Governance: Consequences and Management of Regime Interactions* (2013). 305.

87 Decision 13/CP.8. Cooperation with other Conventions. UN Doc. FCCC/CP/2002/7/Add.1, (2002).

89 Margaret A. Young, 'Toward a Legal Framework for Regime Interaction: Lessons from Fisheries, Trade, and Environmental Regimes', *Proceedings of the Annual Meeting (American Society of International Law)*, 105 (2011). 107–110.

90 H.v. Asselt, *The Fragmentation of Global Climate Governance: Consequences and Management of Regime Interactions* (2013).

91 Frank Biermann and Bernd Siebenhüner, *Managers of Global Change: The Influence of International Environmental Bureaucracies* (MIT Press, 2009).

92 Sabine Campe, 'The Secretariat of the International Maritime Organization: A Tanker for Tankers', in *Managers of Global Change: The Influence of International Environmental Bureaucracies* (Frank Biermann and Bernd Siebenhüner eds., 2009). 160. See also chapter 3.

93 See, chapter three.

94 Per-Olof Busch, 'The Climate Secretariat: Making a Living in a Straitjacket', in *Managers of Global Change: The Influence of International Environmental Bureaucracies* (Frank Biermann and Bernd Siebenhüner eds., 2009). See also chapter 3.

95 Joanne Scott, 'The Multi-Level Governance of Climate Change', *Carbon & Climate Law Review*, 5(1), (2011). 213 as cited in H.v. Asselt, *The Fragmentation of Global Climate Governance: Consequences and Management of Regime Interactions* (2013).

96 S. Oberthür, (2009). 296–310.

97 Margaret A. Young, *Trading Fish, Saving Fish: The Interaction between Regimes in International Law* (Cambridge University Press, 2011). 253–254. See an example in the case of fisheries.

98 See, Margaret A. Young, 'Introduction: The Productive Friction between Regimes', in *Regime Interaction in International Law: Facing Fragmentation* (Margaret A. Young ed., 2012).

99 S. Oberthür, (2009). 370; H.v. Asselt, *The Fragmentation of Global Climate Governance: Consequences and Management of Regime Interactions* (2013). 99–102.

100 Sebastian Oberthür and Thomas Gehring, 'Institutional Interaction: Ten Years of Scholarly Development', in *Managing Institutional Complexity: Regime Interplay and Global Environmental Change* (Sebastian Oberthür and Olav Schram Stokke eds., 2011).

101 R.B. Bilder, 'The Canadian Arctic Waters Pollution Prevention Act: New Stresses on the Law of the Sea', *Michigan Law Review*, 69(1), (1970). 1.

102 Regulation 1726/2003/EC of the European Parliament and of the Council of 22 July 2003 Amending Regulation (EC) No 417/2002 on the Accelerated Phasing-in of Double-hull or Equivalent Design Requirements for Single-hull Oil Tankers, [2003] OJ L249/1.

103 The International Convention for the Control and Management of Ships' Ballast Water and Sediments was adopted in 2004 but is not yet in force. Unilateral action in the United States and the EU has followed. See, Matej David and Stephan Gollasch, 'EU Shipping in the Dawn of Managing the Ballast Water Issue', *Marine Pollution Bulletin*, 56(12), (2008). 1966.

104 Emilie Alberola and Boris Solier, 'Including International Aviation in the EU ETS: A First Step towards a Global Scheme', in *CDC Climate*, Climate Study n°34 (2012).

105 M.A. Young, *Trading Fish, Saving Fish: The Interaction between Regimes in International Law.* (2011); ibid.; See also, M.A. Young, 'Regime Interaction in Creating, Implementing and Enforcing International Law'. (2012). 85–110.

106 M.A. Young, *Trading Fish, Saving Fish: The Interaction between Regimes in International Law.* (2011); ibid.; ibid. at. 267; See also, M.A. Young, 'Regime Interaction in Creating, Implementing and Enforcing International Law'. (2012). 85–110.

107 M.A. Young, *Trading Fish, Saving Fish: The Interaction between Regimes in International Law.* (2011); ibid.; ibid. at. 270–271.

108 Ibid. at. 270–271.

109 Ibid. at. 298–299.

110 On the theory of implied powers and 'functional necessity' see Chapters 2 and 3.
111 See, Martti Koskenniemi, 'Hegemonic Regimes', in *Regime Interaction in International Law: Facing Fragmentation* (Margaret A. Young ed., 2012); Martti Koskenniemi, 'The Fate of Public International Law: Between Technique and Politics', *The Modern Law Review*, 70(1), (2007). 1–30. See also chapter two.
112 From a presentation on MBMs given by Annie Petsonk from ICSA in the Symposium of aviation and Climate change at ICAO, May 2013, where she stated: '*ICSA's ability has been hampered by inadequate access to ICAO's processes and document*'. Furthermore, she requested ICAO to meet its obligations under international law and '*provide more transparency and participation from civil society*'.
113 M.A. Young, *Trading Fish, Saving Fish: The Interaction between Regimes in International Law*. (2011).
114 Ibid. at. 288–306.
115 Term borrowed from, M.A. Young, 'Introduction: The Productive Friction between Regimes'. (2012).
116 S. Oberthür, (2003). 201.
117 This general classification on impediments and the promotion of interaction is taken from M.A. Young, 'Regime Interaction in Creating, Implementing and Enforcing International Law'. (2012). 85–110.
118 C.W. Jenks, (1953). 402.
119 Ibid. at. 402.

Bibliography

Alberola, Emilie and Solier, Boris (2012). 'Including International Aviation in the EU ETS: A First Step towards a Global Scheme', Climate Report Research on the Economics of Climate Change n°34, CDC Climate Research.

A/RES/70/1 – Transforming Our World: The 2030 Agenda for Sustainable Development.

Asselt, Harro van (2011). 'Legal and Political Approaches in Interplay Management: Dealling with the Fragmentation of Global Climate Governance', in, Sebastian Oberthür and Olav Schram Stokke (eds.), *Managing Institutional Complexity: Regime Interplay and Global Environmental Change: Institutional Dimensions of Global Environmental Change*, Cambridge, MA, MIT Press.

Asselt, Harro van (2013). 'Managing the Fragmentation of International Climate Law', in, Erkki J. Hollo, Kati Kulovesi and Michael Mehling (eds.), Ius Gentium: Comparative Perspective on Law and Justice v. 21 *Climate Change and the Law*, Dordrecht; New York, Springer.

Asselt, Harro van, Sindico, Francesco and Mehling, Michael A. (2008). 'Global Climate Change and the Fragmentation of International Law', *Law & Policy*, 30(4), 423–449.

Asselt, Harro van and Zelli, Fariborz (2012). 'Connect the Dots: Managing the Fragmentation of Global Climate Governance Earth System', Governance Working Paper No. 25. Lund and Amsterdam: Earth System Governance Project.

Assembly Resolution A39–3: Consolidated Statement of Continuing ICAO Policies and Practices Related to Environmental Protection: Global Market-Based Measure (MBM) Scheme.

Biermann, Frank and Siebenhüner, Bernd (2009). *Managers of Global Change: The Influence of International Environmental Bureaucracies*, Cambridge, MA, MIT Press.

Bilder, R.B. (1970). 'The Canadian Arctic Waters Pollution Prevention Act: New Stresses on the Law of the Sea', *Michigan Law Review*, 69(1). 1–54.

Bodansky, Daniel (2007). 'International Sectoral Agreements in a Post-2012 Climate Framework', Working Paper Prepared for the Pew Center on Global Climate Change.

Bodansky, Daniel (2011). 'Multilateral Climate Efforts beyond the UNFCCC', Centre for Climate and Energy Solutions.

Brownlie, Ian (2008). *Principles of Public International Law*, 7th ed., Oxford; New York, Oxford University Press.

Busch, Per-Olof (2009). 'The Climate Secretariat: Making a Living in a Straitjacket', in, Frank Biermann and Bernd Siebenhüner (eds.), *Managers of Global Change: The Influence of International Environmental Bureaucracies*, Cambridge, MA, MIT Press.

Campe, Sabine (2009). 'The Secretariat of the International Maritime Organization: A Tanker for Tankers', in, Frank Biermann and Bernd Siebenhüner (eds.), *Managers of Global Change: The Influence of International Environmental Bureaucracies*, Cambridge, MA, MIT Press.

Chrysostomou, Andreas and Vagslid, Eivind S. (2012). 'Climate Change: A Challenge for IMO Too', in, R. Asariotis and Hassiba Benamara (eds.), *Maritime Transport and the Climate Change Challenge*, 1st ed., New York, Earthscan.

David, Matej and Gollasch, Stephan (2008). 'EU Shipping in the Dawn of Managing the Ballast Water Issue', *Marine Pollution Bulletin*, 56(12), 1966–1972.

Decision 13/CP.8. Cooperation with other conventions. UN Doc. FCCC/CP/2002/7/Add.1.

Doelle, Meinhard (2010). 'The Legacy of the Climate Talks in Copenhagen: Hopenhagen or Brokenhagen?', *Carbon and Climate Law Review*, 4(1), 86–100.

Fitzmaurice, G.G. (1951). 'Law and Procedure of the International Court of Justice: Treaty Interpretation and Certain Other Treaty Points', *British Yearbook of International Law*, 28. 1.

Fitzmaurice, Malgosia and Merkouris, Panos (2014). 'Uniformity versus Specialization: The Quest for a Uniform Law of Inter-State Treaties', *University of Groningen Faculty of Law Research Paper Series No. 05/2014*.

Gençsü, I. and Hino, M. (2015). 'Raising Ambition to Reduce International Aviation and Maritime Emissions', *New Climate Economy*.

Gordon, Edward (1965). 'The World Court and the Interpretation of Constitutive Treaties: Some Observations on the Development of an International Constitutional Law', *American Journal of International Law*, 59(4). 794–833.

Holmes, Stephen (1988). 'Gag Rules or the Politics of Omission', in, Jon Elster and Rune Slagstad (eds.), *Constitutionalism and Democracy*, Cambridge, Cambridge University Press.

ILC (2006). *Fragmentation of International Law: Difficulties Arising from the Diversification and Expansion of International Law. Report of the Study Group of the International Law Commission*. UN Doc. A/CN.4/L.682.

International Law Association. Committee on the Legal Principles relating to Climate Change, International Law Association. (2012). 'The Legal Principles Relating to Climate Change, Second Report (Sofia Conference 2012)'.

Jenks, C. Wilfred (1953). 'Conflict of Law-Making Treaties', *British Year Book of International Law*, 30, 401.

Kågeson, Per (2011). 'Applying the Principle of Common but Differentiated Responsibility to the Mitigation of Greenhouse Gases from International Shipping', Working Papers in Transport Economics from the Centre for Transport Studies Stockholm. No 2011:5.

Karim, Saiful and Alam, Shawkat (2011). 'Climate Change and Reduction of Emissions of Greenhouse Gases from Ships: An Appraisal', *Asian Journal of International Law*, 1, 131.

Kopela, Sophia (2013). 'Climate Change, Regime Interaction, and the Principle of Common but Differentiated Responsibility: The Experience of the International Maritime Organizatio', *24 Yearbook of International Environmental Law*. 70–101.

Koskenniemi, Martti (2007). 'The Fate of Public International Law: Between Technique and Politics', *The Modern Law Review*, 70(1), 1–30.

Koskenniemi, Martti (2012). 'Hegemonic Regimes', in, Margaret A. Young (ed.), *Regime Interaction in International Law: Facing Fragmentation*, Cambridge; New York, Cambridge University Press.

Kulovesi, Kati (2013). 'Climate Change and Trade: At the Intersection of Two International Legal Regimes', in, Erkki J. Hollo, Kati Kulovesi and Michael Mehling (eds.), Ius Gentium: Comparative Perspective on Law and Justice v. 21 *Climate Change and the Law*, Dordrecht; New York, Springer.

Kurukulasuriya, L. and Robinson, N.A. (2006). *Training Manual on International Environmental Law*, United Nations Environment Programme. Division of Environmental Policy Development Law ed., Division of Policy Development and Law, United Nations Environment Programme. Nairobi, UNEP.

Lee, David S., Lim, Ling and Owen, Bethan (2013). 'Shipping and Aviation Emissions in the Context of a 2°C Emission Pathway', Manchester Metropolitan University.

McLachlan, Campbell (2005). 'The Principle of Systemic Integration and Article 31(3)(C) of the Vienna Convention', *International and Comparative Law Quarterly*, 54(2), 279–320.

Martinez Romera, Beatriz and Asselt, Harro van (2015). 'The International Regulation of Aviation Emissions: Putting Differential Treatment into Practice', *Journal of Environmental Law* 27(2) 259–283.

Oberthür, Sebastian (2003). 'Institutional Interaction to Address Greenhouse Gas Emissions from International Transport: ICAO, IMO and the EU Burden-Sharing Agreement', *Project Deliverable No. D 3, Final Draft*. Ecologic: Institute for International and European Policy.

Oberthür, Sebastian (2003). 'Institutional Interaction to Address Greenhouse Gas Emissions from International Transport: ICAO, IMO and the Kyoto Protocol', *Climate Policy*, 3(3), 191–205.

Oberthür, Sebastian (2006). 'The Climate Change Regime: Interactions of the Climate Change Regime with ICAO, IMO and the EU Burden-Sharing Agreement', in, Sebastian Oberthür and Thomas Gehring (eds.), *Institutional Interaction in Global Environmental Governance: Synergy and Conflict among International and EU Policies: Global Environmental Accord: Strategies for Sustainability and Institutional Innovation*, Cambridge, MA, MIT Press.

Oberthür, Sebastian (2009). 'Interplay Management: Enhancing Environmental Policy Integration among International Institutions', *International Environmental Agreements: Politics, Law and Economics*, 9(4), 371–391.

Oberthür, Sebastian and Gehring, Thomas (2011). 'Institutional Interaction: Ten Years of Scholarly Development', in, Sebastian Oberthür and Olav Schram Stokke (eds.), *Managing Institutional Complexity: Regime Interplay and Global Environmental Change*, Cambridge, MA, MIT Press.

Oberthür, Sebastian, La Vina, Antonio G.M. and Morgan, Jennifer (2015). 'Getting Specific on the 2015 Climate Change Agreement: Suggestions for the Legal Text with an Explanatory Memorandum', Working Paper. Washington, DC: Agreement for Climate Transformation 2015 (ACT 2015).

Oberthür, Sebastian and Ott, Hermann (1999). *The Kyoto Protocol: International Climate Policy for the 21st Century*, New York, Springer.

Pauwelyn, Joost (2003). *Conflict of Norms in Public International Law: How WTO Law Relates to Other Rules of International Law*, Cambridge, UK; New York, Cambridge University Press.

Pavoni, Riccardo (2010). 'Mutual Supportiveness as a Principle of Interpretation and Law-Making: A Watershed for the "WTO-and-Competing-Regimes" Debate?', *European Journal of International Law*, 21(3), 649–679.

Scott, Joanne (2011). 'The Multi-Level Governance of Climate Change', *Carbon & Climate Law Review*, 5(1), 25–33.

Shi, Yubing (2014). 'Greenhouse Gas Emissions from International Shipping: The Response from China's Shipping Industry to the Regulatory Initiatives of the International Maritime Organization', *International Journal of Marine and Coastal Law*, 29(1), 85–123.

UN General Assembly, Declaration of the United Nations Conference on the Human Environment (Stockholm Declaration). U.N. Doc. A/Conf.48/14/Rev. 1(1973); 11 ILM 1416 (1972)

United Nations, Charter of the United Nations, 24 October 1945, 1 UNTS XVI.

United Nations Convention on the Law of the Sea, Montego Bay, adopted 10 December 1982, in force 16 November 1994, 21 International Legal Materials (1982), 1261. 1833 UNTS 3.

Vienna Convention on the Law of Treaties. Vienna, adopted 23 May 1969, in force 27 January 1980. 8 ILM 679.

Voigt, Christina (2009). *Sustainable Development as a Principle of International Law: Resolving Conflicts between Climate Measures and WTO Law*, Leiden; Boston, Martinus Nijhoff Publishers.

Vranes, Erich (2006). 'The Definition of "Norm Conflict" in International Law and Legal Theory', *European Journal of International Law*, 17(2), 395–418.

Wolfrum, R., Matz, N. and Völkerrecht, Max-Planck-Institut für Ausländisches Öffentliches Recht und (2003). *Conflicts in International Environmental Law*, Berlin; New York, Springer.

Young, Margaret A. (2011). 'Climate Change Law and Regime Interaction', *Climate Change Law Review*, 2, 147–157.

Young, Margaret A. (2011). 'Toward a Legal Framework for Regime Interaction: Lessons from Fisheries, Trade, and Environmental Regimes', *Proceedings of the Annual Meeting (American Society of International Law)*, 105, 107–110.

Young, Margaret A. (2011). *Trading Fish, Saving Fish: The Interaction between Regimes in International Law*, Cambridge, UK; New York, Cambridge University Press.

Young, Margaret A. (2012). 'Introduction: The Productive Friction Between Regimes', in, Margaret A. Young (ed.), *Regime Interaction in International Law: Facing Fragmentation*, Cambridge; New York, Cambridge University Press.

Young, Margaret A. (2012). 'Regime Interaction in Creating, Implementing and Enforcing International Law', in, Margaret A. Young (ed.), *Regime Interaction in International Law: Facing Fragmentation*, Cambridge; New York, Cambridge University Press.

Zabalza, G.O. (2012). *The Principle of Systemic Integration: Towards a Coherent International Legal Order*, Berlin, Zürich, Lit Verlag.

7   Conclusions and prospects

New rules and legal regimes emerge as responses to new preferences, and sometimes out of conscious effort to deviate from preferences as they existed under old regimes. They require a legislative, not a legal-technical response.[1]

[R]ecognising the broader potential of the legal framework for appropriate regime interaction gives international lawyers a different lens through which to view the making of law.[2]

This final chapter revisits briefly the scope of the book, synthesizing its main findings and contributions to the academic literature. It also suggests some ways forward for policy-making in the regulation of IBF, and points towards future research agendas.

Summary of the research scope, findings and contributions

This book has focused on the legal challenges faced in the allocation and regulation of GHG emissions from international aviation and international maritime transport in view of the limited progress made by the international community, thus far. In order to tackle this *problématique*, the book established, in Chapter 2, an analytical framework and research methodology. This included definitions of the basic concepts that underpin the analytical framework, such as what can be considered, in this context, as international law, what its sources are and what are the main elements of the law-making process. This led to the conclusion that the topic is best approached through the lens of fragmentation of international law, as it relates to climate change, and the interaction established among different regimes at the law-making stage. The analytical framework for understanding regime interaction has been built upon a burgeoning legal literature on fragmentation and regime interaction, in particular the work of Young, Dunoff and van Asselt on new frameworks for understanding and managing regime interaction. However, the study has also made use of international relations literature, particularly the work of Sebastian Oberthür.

Specifically, the book has addressed the overall legal question, set out in Chapter 1, of how the interaction between different regimes overlapping and competing in the regulation of international aviation and maritime transport (namely the climate, ICAO and IMO regimes) can be managed in order to avoid and solve conflicts and enhance synergies in the quest to reduce GHG emissions from these sectors. To address the first aspect of this question Chapter 3 presented a comprehensive mapping of the legal field in which IBF is, or could be, subject to regulation within the three selected regimes, providing a detailed account of the state of affairs, to date. Chapter 4 focused on identifying and analyzing the ways in which these interactions occur, in terms of normative overlaps, paying special attention to forum issues, but also in terms of regulatory and administrative interaction, operational interaction and conceptual interactions. Chapter 5 analyzed the outcomes of the interactions detailed in Chapter 4, analyzing the specific conflicts and synergies between the regimes. The final substantive chapter, Chapter 6, presented an analysis of how to manage the interaction between regimes, based upon the application of existing legal tools and other approaches, such as institutional coordination, to avoid and resolve the specific tensions and to enhance synergies in this given issue area. In managing institutional regime interaction between the climate, ICAO and the IMO regimes, legal tools can also be used to ensure accountability. The key findings and contributions of this research, both empirical and theoretical, are synthesized below.

In terms of its contribution to the literature, this book has first provided a case-study analysis on the fragmentation of climate change law, while serving as a test bed for new frameworks on regime interaction that are better able to accommodate regime interaction in the law-making stage. This has included an analysis of normative and institutional overlaps, their consequences and management through new typologies rich in nuance. Second, in setting the scene, the book has provided a detailed account of the law-making processes within the three regimes dealing with GHG emissions from IBF, using a systematic division of participants, processes and instruments, thus contributing to the academic literature in this area. Third, this study has contributed to the literature on the legal aspects of regulating GHG emissions from international aviation and maritime transport. In analyzing those, it has paid special attention to the CBDRRC principle, contributing to the debate over the role and future of the CBDRRC principle in climate change governance, as it relates to the issue of IBF.

Overall, it can be said that the regulation of international aviation and maritime emissions is following the trend towards increasing regulation of climatic issues outside of the venue of the climate regime. As such, it has become increasingly relevant and important to assess the interaction between the climate with the ICAO and IMO regimes, as they seek to regulate IBF. In this connection, in order to avoid conflicts, 'climate change needs to be understood in the light of pre-existing regimes.'[3]

Three main tensions between regimes challenging and impeding progress have been identified. First, there is the diverging objective of the regimes; that is, the aims to foster air and maritime transport in ICAO and IMO respectively and the stabilization of GHG in the atmosphere of the climate regime. Second, there are the conflicts around the principles of differential and equal treatment, which is highly linked to the wording of Article 2.2 of the KP. Although the CBDRRC principle underpins the whole climate regime, including emissions from international transport, its role in the allocation and regulation of emissions from IBF outside the climate regime is contested. The regimes of ICAO and the IMO work, as a rule, on an equal and non-discriminatory basis, so the introduction of a principle that embodies differentiated treatment faces a number of challenges. From the struggles of reconciling differential and equal treatment, a number of options for adapting the content of CBDRRC to these traditionally non-discriminatory regimes have been put forward. There is also potential for the creation of new concepts that incorporate both principles. In this connection, regulatory developments in ICAO and IMO suggest that the regimes will pursue differentiation through implementation, assistance to developing countries and the redirection of revenues in potential MBMs. Third, there are specific conflicts around the use of MBMs, such as prohibitions and limitations of taxation of international aviation in the Chicago Convention. With regards to MBMs, the book finds that there are potential for synergies also, and considers that interaction with the climate regime has helped to introduce and reconsider economic instruments in highly technical realms, which all in all is bringing new avenues for ICAO and IMO in the international environmental regulation. These conflicts have an inherently political dimension.

When it comes to answering the study's main research question on how interaction can be managed, an array of options is found in the literature. However, for the specifics of the conflicts identified, the most adequate avenues arise from the drafting of new treaties. Given that the PA has not shed light on the conflicts surrounding the regulation of IBF, the potential regulation under a convention in ICAO and the IMO fora will represent a unique opportunity for addressing the conflicts with regards to the diverging objectives, principles and choice of regulation. In the case of ICAO, the CORSIA framework is likely to be developed through SARPs. However, institutional cooperation between the regimes' decision-making and administrative bodies will play an essential role in the run-up to and detailing of those agreements. The book has also highlighted the need for greater accountability in institutional agreements and other ways of informal interaction.

Ways forward and future regulation

As discussed elsewhere,[4] the new system emerged from the PA in the climate regime and the actual omission of IBF in the PA has implications for the future regulation of the sectors and the interaction among the climate, ICAO and IMO regimes.

Even if IBF falls outside its scope,[5] the Paris Agreement modifies core aspects of the climate change regime, which, in turn, are likely to have indirect consequences in the regulation of IBF. These implications relate mainly to: the influence of a long-term climate stabilization objective and the commitment to progressively ratchet up ambition; the embedding of a bottom-up approach through country-driven pledges; the tempering of differential treatment; and the impulse of non-state action, including industry and carbon markets.

In the context of the long-term goal, allowing emissions from IBF to increase by a factor of two to three would contradict and jeopardize the aims of limiting an increase in the global average temperature, agreed upon in Paris.[6] As a result, parties could explore reductions in IBF, which 'remain areas where substantial ambition could be ratcheted up'.[7] Since the Paris Agreement has not dealt with the issue, IBFs are still anchored to the regime through Article 4.1 of the Convention and Article 2.2 of the Kyoto Protocol. In this connection, parties could decide to look into regulating IBFs under the UNFCCC, through the SBSTA or by tasking a new group. However, and despite limited progress, the suitability of ICAO and IMO to deal with international aviation and maritime transport, respectively, has by now been largely acknowledged by parties to the climate regime. Also, domestic reactions to the long-term goal agreed in Paris might change countries' positions and ambitions, specifically, emerging economies and the United States, facilitating the adoption of meaningful measures at ICAO and IMO. Nonetheless, given the diverging objectives of the climate regime on the one hand, and the IMO and ICAO on the other, leaving IBFs disconnected to long-term goals seems rather risky. Although IMO and ICAO have embraced sustainable development and historically dealt with several environmental problems, the main objective of the regimes is to foster international transport. In that regard, the Energy Efficiency Design Index adopted by the IMO in 2011 and the CO_2 standard to be adopted by ICAO in 2016 seem to lack the ambition to bring about adequate emissions reductions in line with the Paris Agreement, or even make any difference compared to a business-as-usual scenario.[8] Similar concerns apply to the market-based mechanism for international aviation currently under development in ICAO.[9] The negotiations in ICAO and the IMO will be the first test of the parties' political willingness after Paris.

Indeed, to meet the objectives agreed upon in Paris, parties are given leeway in choosing the domestic mitigation measures for their NDCs.[10] While none of the intended NDCs submitted before Paris (nor the NDCs submitted after COP21) contains measures on IBF,[11] countries could choose to include domestic aviation and shipping in their NDCs.[12] Furthermore, parties could decide to establish measures, such as an emissions trading system (ETS) or a tax, affecting the international part of aviation and maritime transport, which points towards the question of whether international emissions reductions from IBF, achieved as a result of a national measure, should be counted towards a country's NDC.

One of the most relevant transformations to IBF is the understanding of the CBDRRC principle in the PA, since strict differentiation, in the Kyoto Protocol sense, was difficult to reconcile with equal treatment in ICAO and the IMO.[13] The softening of CBDRRC in the Paris Agreement is likely to ease tensions and facilitate the negotiations on IBFs, which will facilitate ways to take on board differentiation while preserving the level playing field at ICAO and the IMO. For example, a given measure could preserve equal treatment on the core obligations of countries and differentiate on the fringes (through assistance and finance).[14]

Also, the COP decision adopting the PA explicitly recognizes the contribution of non-party stakeholders, including the private sector, in addressing and responding to climate change.[15] Parties invite non-state actors to scale up effort, and specifically to register them at the Non-State Actor Zone for Climate Action (NAZCA) platform,[16] while acknowledging the role of private actors in providing incentives for emission reduction activities.[17] The PA itself recognizes '*the importance of the engagements of all levels of government and various actors, in accordance with respective national legislations of Parties, in addressing climate change*'.[18] Also, in the context of the mechanism to transfer mitigation outcomes, Article 6 mentions the relevance of public and private participation. Among non-state participants, the private sector, including industry, has been highly relevant in the case of aviation and shipping.[19] The support that non-state action has received in Paris legitimizes and channels industry initiatives. This calls for an upturn of industry action in IBF too.

Crucially, the silence of the PA on IBF shows a missed opportunity for clarification of core aspects of IBF regulation and has consequences for the future regulation of the sectors. The first consequence relates to the forum shifting from the climate to the ICAO and IMO regimes; although IBFs are still linked to the climate regime, until parties decide to launch other options, negotiations on IBFs only seem to be able to continue in the SBSTA's process, which is limited to ICAO and the IMO reporting on their progress. As a result, even without an explicit delegation of IBF regulation to ICAO and the IMO, the omission of IBFs from the Paris Agreement can be seen as a further, if not final, step in the consolidation of ICAO and IMO as the multilateral forums for the regulation of international aviation and maritime transports emissions, respectively. Given that, the already weak regulatory competition between ICAO, the IMO and the climate regime will further diminish after Paris. Therefore, the trigger for meaningful action in ICAO and IMO is likely to come from 'threats' associated with unilateral action,[20] and these unilateral approaches might increase if significant action at the multilateral level remains out of reach.

In this connection, unilateral regional or country measures might prompt action at ICAO and the IMO, but also, in the absence of a reference to IBFs in the PA, these autonomous actions can serve the purpose of resolving conflictive situations between the climate regime, ICAO and the IMO. To minimize the legal and political risks that unilateral action entails, it is important that the action is perceived as legitimate.[21] The trend of unilateralism with regards to IBF initiated in the pre-Paris age[22] has, arguably, been powered and legitimized by the exclusion of IBFs from the PA.

Crucially, industry action has also been strengthened, meaning that sectoral regulation of IBF might be largely industry driven. The aviation and maritime industries can shape and influence future regulation, not only through lobbying but also through adopting voluntary early action. Indeed, the general weakness of the climate regime, ICAO and the IMO in establishing IBF regulation invites not only State unilateralism, but also voluntary actions to be pursued by the private sector. These initiatives can take a number of forms – from unilateral commitments and showcasing practices, to cooperative initiatives. However, industry-driven processes for IBFs are not without drawbacks, since companies can exert influence on climate regulation, bypassing governments and lowering the level of ambition. The main challenge will be to evaluate the plethora of non-state actions[23] and to align industry emissions reductions with the 2°C objective.[24]

Recommendations for policy-making

This book has argued that the consequences of regime interaction can be managed so as to transmute conflicts into synergies and has advocated for the promotion of regime interaction in the regulation of international aviation and international maritime transport. More specifically, the following list is a summary of recommendations that could be given for policy-making, within the three regimes:

1   Parties to the Climate Convention could change the venues where the IMO and ICAO report their progress on GHG regulation to the climate regime, from the technical SBSTA, for example, to the CMA to deal with IBF. This is for two reasons: first, the issue is no longer a technical one but a political one. Second, this reporting would be more visible and stimulate learning and debate, beyond the technical realms of the IMO and ICAO. This idea was suggested by the EU in the context of the run-up to the PA. However, it is equally relevant nowadays for the process of detailing and implementing the PA in the forthcoming years.

2   Particular attention needs to be paid to the implementation processes in the climate and ICAO regimes on developing MBMs. Specifically, the detailing of the mechanisms of article 6 of the PA (i.e. ITMO and SDM and the CORSIA). Here, parallel discussions about offsets at the ICAO and the PA negotiations need to be integrated for the synergies to emerge.

3   The climate, ICAO and IMO regimes could promote cooperation for knowledge exchanges and learning between regimes through their secretariats to overcome the negotiation impasse. This could be done by creating a permanent joint group, with experts from the climate and ICAO, the climate and IMO or even the three regimes tasked to study the legal questions and the regulatory options, specifically MBMs in a more holistic and non-political way. Here, the objective would be to acquire a shared understanding that could influence synergistically the normative process, so as to avoid filibustering in the negotiations, especially with regards to defining the fair contribution of the sectors and the reach of CBDRRC in the regulation of international aviation and maritime transport.

4   Parties to the regimes could promote regime interaction through domestic coordination, principally between different ministries and delegates to the respective international fora. The objective would be to accommodate the different ministerial agendas and to coordinate coherent action. This could be achieved by establishing regular meetings to exchange information or by creating a special group made up of experts from the three areas. Greater

regime interaction could also be achieved by stronger and more systematic engagement with NGOs involved in the three regimes. In this connection, funding might need to be provided.

5   Parties to the regimes could also pursue autonomous interaction management to overcome aporia. The same way that the EU action on aviation has 'managed' normative developments at the international level in ICAO, other parties could manage the overlaps and ultimately this would define the exact reach of regime interaction. However, unilateral (either State or regional) actions pursuing management of interaction entail legal and political risks. So as to minimize those, it would be essential that the action is not perceived as illegitimate.

6   Parties could facilitate knowledge exchanges, as well as fund and promote research and outreach, on the different aspects of IBF regulation through reports, workshops, networks, meetings, etc. Here, there is a role to be played by other non-state regime participants.

Potential for new research agendas

Given the breadth of the topic and the legal issues involved, the book has consciously left aside numerous strands of research that relate to the question of how GHG emissions from IBF can be regulated, and the barriers surrounding that potential regulation. This includes an analysis of the role and importance of the international trade regime (WTO), which is briefly discussed under limitation in Chapter 1. Also, although there is some literature on the issue, there is plenty of scope to study the vertical interactions of the climate, ICAO and IMO regimes with the EU and other major players, including how potential measures interact with the WTO.

In a separate vein, there is an opportunity to conduct research into the forthcoming developments in the dialectic between CBDRRC and equal treatment principles with regards to a potential MBM, in the IMO. This could also be informed by developments in the climate regime on the implementation of Paris Agreement. Related to this is the question of how decision-making practices in the ICAO and IMO regimes have changed as a result of dealing with climate change regulation. This has been touched upon in this study, but is an issue that could be further explored. Very importantly, the linkages and interactions between CORSIA (as well as a future MBM for shipping) and the market mechanisms of the PA will be an interesting area to look at, now that the process of detailing those agreement is a priority of the climate and ICAO regimes. Other potential research topics, related to this book, include the need to better understand the role and importance of voluntary practices and initiatives being pursued by the aviation and maritime industry in mitigating climate change. Specifically, future research could assess the role of voluntary measures in filling the gaps created by weak regulation and their potential for stimulating further regime interaction.

Notes

1 ILC, *Fragmentation of International Law: Difficulties Arising from the Diversification and Expansion of International Law. Report of the Study Group of the International Law Commission.* UN Doc. A/CN.4/L.682, (2006). 484.
2 Margaret A. Young, *Trading Fish, Saving Fish: The Interaction between Regimes in International Law* (Cambridge University Press, 2011). 301.
3 Harro van Asselt et al., 'Global Climate Change and the Fragmentation of International Law', *Law & Policy*, 30(4), (2008). 423–449.
4 Beatriz Martinez Romera, 'The Paris Agreement and the Regulation of International Bunker Fuels', *Review of European Comparative & International Environmental Law*, 25(2), (2016). 215–227. This section builds largely on this article.
5 While the PA does not exclude IBF from its long-term mitigation aims (Article 2.1(a) and 4.1), the mitigation tools (national pledges) chosen to achieve this goal are not thought to address IBFs.
6 Flightpath 1.5° FAQS & POLICY (2016), Available at: www.flightpath1point5.org/
7 Elizabeth Burleson, 'Paris Agreement and Consensus to Address Climate Challenge', ASIL INSIGHT, Forthcoming. Available at SSRN: http://ssrn.com/abstract=2710076 (2016).
8 Bill Hemmings, 'A Flying Fairy Tale: Why Aviation Carbon Cuts Won't Take Off', *Climate Home*, published online 23 February (2016); Jesper Faber and Maarten 't Hoen, *Historical Trends in Ship Design Efficiency* (Delft, CE Delft, 2016).
9 ICAO, *Views of the International Coalition for Sustainable Aviation on a Global Market-Based Measure for International Civil Aviation* (26 April 2016), Available at: www.icao. int/Meetings/HLM-MBM/Documents/HLM-GMBM.WP6-ICSA.pdf
10 UNFCCC, Paris Agreement (Paris, 12 December 2015, in force 4 November 2016) FCCC/CP/2015/L.9. (2015). Article 4.2.
11 See www4.unfccc.int/submissions/indc/Submission%20Pages/submissions.aspx
12 S. Gota et al., *Intended Nationally-Determined Contributions (INDCs) Offer Opportunities for Ambitious Action on Transport and Climate Change* (Partnership on Sustainable Low Carbon Transport, 2015). See the updated version by the same authors: *Nationally-Determined Contributions (NDCs) Offer Opportunities for Ambitious Action on Transport and Climate Change* (Partnership on Sustainable Low Carbon Transport, 2016)
13 See, for example, Mark Lutes and Shaun Vorster, 'Bridging the Political Barriers in Negotiating a Global Market-Based Measure for Controlling International Aviation Emissions', *Elements of a New Climate Agreement by 2015. Perspectives Series 2013. UNEP Risø*, (2013). 25–26; Aydin Okur, 'The Challenge of Regulating Greenhouse Gas Emissions from Internaional Shipping and the Complicated Principle of "Common But Differentiated Responsibilities"', (2012). 27; Daniel Bodanski, 'Regulating Greenhouse Gas Emissions from Ships: The Role of the International Maritime Organization', in *Ocean Law Debates: The 50-Year Legacy and Emerging Issues for the Years Ahead* (H. Scheiber, N. Oral and M. Kwon eds., forthcoming 2017); Sophia Kopela, 'Climate Change, Regime Interaction, and the Principle of Common but Differentiated Responsibility: The Experience of the International Maritime Organization', *Yearbook of International Environmental Law*, 24, (2013). 70–101.
14 See for example, Beatriz Martinez Romera and Harro van Asselt, 'The International Regulation of Aviation Emissions: Putting Differential Treatment into Practice', *Journal of Environmental Law*, (2015).
15 UNFCCC, Decision 1/CP.21, Adoption of the Paris Agreement (UN Doc. FCCC/CP/2015/10/Add.1, 29 January 2016), paragraphs 134–137, also paragraph 118.
16 See http://climateaction.unfccc.int
17 Joshua Busby, 'After Paris: Good Enough Climate Governance', *Current History*, January 2016, (2016). 3–9.

18 Decision 1/CP.21, Paragraphs 134–137.
19 ICAO/ATAG, 'Aviation: Action Statement' (2014), Available at: www.un.org/cli-matechange/summit/wp-content/uploads/sites/2/2014/09/TRANSPORT-Aviation-Action-Statement.pdf
20 Sebastian Oberthür, 'Institutional Interaction to Address Greenhouse Gas Emissions from International Transport: ICAO, IMO and the Kyoto Protocol', *Climate Policy*, 3(3), (2003). 191–205.
21 Daniel Bodansky, 'What's so Bad about Unilateral Action to Protect the Environment?', *European Journal of International Law*, 11(2), (2000). 339.
22 Kati Kulovesi, 'Addressing Sectoral Emissions Outside the United Nations Framework Convention on Climate Change: What Roles for Multilateralism, Minilateralism and Unilateralism?', *Review of European Community & International Environmental Law*, 21(3), (2012). 193.
23 See Oscar Widerberg and Philipp H. Pattberg, 'Harnessing Company Climate Action beyond Paris', *FORES Study 2015:6*, (2015); Sander Chan et al., 'Reinvigorating International Climate Policy: A Comprehensive Framework for Effective Nonstate Action', *Global Policy*, 6(4), (2015). 466.
24 See, for example, the work of the Science Based Targets initiative, a joint initiative by CDP (Climate Disclosure Project), the UN Global Compact, the World Resources Institute and WWF, intended to increase corporate ambition on climate action; see http://sciencebasedtargets.org

Bibliography

Asselt, Harro van, Sindico, Francesco and Mehling, Michael A. (2008). 'Global Climate Change and the Fragmentation of International Law', *Law & Policy*, 30(4), 423–449.

Bodanski, Daniel (forthcoming 2017). 'Regulating Greenhouse Gas Emissions from Ships: The Role of the International Maritime Organization', in, H. Scheiber, N. Oral and M. Kwon (eds.), *Ocean Law Debates: The 50-Year Legacy and Emerging Issues for the Years Ahead*. Leiden, Brill.

Bodansky, Daniel (2000). 'What's so Bad about Unilateral Action to Protect the Environment?', *European Journal of International Law*, 11(2). 339–347.

Burleson, Elizabeth (2016). 'Paris Agreement and Consensus to Address Climate Challenge', *ASIL INSIGHT*, Forthcoming. Available at SSRN: http://ssrn.com/abstract=2710076.

Busby, Joshua (2016). 'After Paris: Good Enough Climate Governance', *Current History*, January 2016, 3–9.

Chan, Sander, Asselt, Harro van, Hale, Thomas, Abbott, Kenneth W., Beisheim, Marianne, Hoffmann, Matthew, Guy, Brendan, Höhne, Niklas, Hsu, Angel, Pattberg, Philipp, Pauw, Pieter, Ramstein, Céline and Widerberg, Oscar (2015). 'Reinvigorating International Climate Policy: A Comprehensive Framework for Effective Nonstate Action', *Global Policy*, 6(4), 466–473.

Faber, Jesper, Hoen, Maarten't, Vergeer, Robert and Calleya, John (2016). *Historical Trends in Ship Design Efficiency*, Delft, CE Delft

Gota, S., Huizenga, C., Peet, K. and Kaar, G. (2015). 'Intended Nationally-Determined Contributions (INDCs) Offer Opportunities for Ambitious Action on Transport and Climate Change', *Partnership on Sustainable Low Carbon Transport*.

Hemmings, Bill (2016). 'A Flying Fairy Tale: Why Aviation Carbon Cuts Won't Take Off', *Climate Home*. Published on 23 February 2016. Available at: www.climatechangenews.com/2016/02/23/a-flying-fairy-tale-why-aviation-carbon-cuts-wont-take-off/

ILC (2006). *Fragmentation of International Law: Difficulties Arising from the Diversification and Expansion of International Law. Report of the Study Group of the International Law Commission*. UN Doc. A/CN.4/L.682.

Kopela, Sophia (2013). 'Climate Change, Regime Interaction, and the Principle of Common but Differentiated Responsibility: The Experience of the International Maritime Organization', *Yearbook of International Environmental Law*, 24. 70–101.

Kulovesi, Kati (2012). 'Addressing Sectoral Emissions outside the United Nations Framework Convention on Climate Change: What Roles for Multilateralism, Minilateralism and Unilateralism?', *Review of European Community & International Environmental Law*, 21(3), 193–203.

Lutes, Mark and Vorster, Shaun (2013). 'Bridging the Political Barriers in Negotiating a Global Market-Based Measure for Controlling International Aviation Emissions', *Elements of a New Climate Agreement by 2015. Perspectives Series 2013. UNEP Risø*, 21.

Martinez Romera, Beatriz (2016). 'The Paris Agreement and the Regulation of International Bunker Fuels', *Review of European Comparative & International Environmental Law*, 25(2), 215–227.

Martinez Romera, Beatriz and Asselt, Harro van (2015). 'The International Regulation of Aviation Emissions: Putting Differential Treatment into Practice', *Journal of Environmental Law*. 259–283.

Oberthür, Sebastian (2003). 'Institutional Interaction to Address Greenhouse Gas Emissions from International Transport: ICAO, IMO and the Kyoto Protocol', *Climate Policy*, 3(3), 191–205.

Okur, Aydin (2012). 'The Challenge of Regulating Greenhouse Gas Emissions from International Shipping and the Complicated Principle of "Common but Differentiated Responsibilities"', *Dokuz Eylül Üniversitesi Hukuk Fakültesi Dergisi*, 13(1), 27–49.

Paris Agreement (Paris, 12 December 2015, in force 4 November 2016) FCCC/CP/2015/L.9.

Widerberg, Oscar and Pattberg, Philipp H. (2015). 'Harnessing Company Climate Action beyond Paris', *FORES Study 2015*: 6.

Young, Margaret A. (2011). *Trading Fish, Saving Fish: The Interaction between Regimes in International Law*, Cambridge, UK; New York, Cambridge University Press.

Index

For Product Safety Concerns and Information please contact our EU
representative GPSR@taylorandfrancis.com
Taylor & Francis Verlag GmbH, Kaufingerstraße 24, 80331 München, Germany